Introduction

Most people don't have the first idea about the true power of stories. I'm sure you know this. I'm sure you do, because you're a reader – you're reading this book right now. You're bound to know a thing or two about it.

Maybe you're the woman on the train who doesn't ever let the raised eyebrows of grey-looking office workers put her off her comic books. Maybe you're the kid at high school who gets teased for always having his nose buried in a Stephen King. Maybe you're a writer, like me, who was always being told, "When are you going to grow up and do something useful with your life?"

It doesn't matter which one you are, just that you're one of us. You're clued in. You know what they don't. You know how it all works. Or at least, you will soon, if you keep reading this book.

It's a sad fact that most people can't even spot a story when they see one. Most people don't know that stories aren't confined by the covers of books or by half-hour slots on TV. The world is made of stories. The world is driven by stories. When a sunburned friend tells you about their holiday, it's not a straight list of everything that happened to them – it's a story, an anecdote with a plot, a beginning, a middle and an end. Each one of their holiday snaps is a story too. When you're making a decision, and you imagine the possible outcomes – what are you doing if not telling yourself a story? History is a story. Society is a story. Countries are stories. Your plans are stories. Your desires are stories. Your own memories are stories – narratives selected, trimmed and packaged by the hidden machinery in your mind. Human beings are story engines. We have to be – to understand stories is to understand the world.

Enter THE UNWRITTEN.

Mike Carey and Peter Gross's wonderful book manages to be both a fast, engaging adventure, a huge, ambitious labyrinth of forking paths, and a thoughtful exploration of the very nature of stories both on the page and in the wider world – as the very fabric that holds society together and drives it forward. This is a brave, bold and epic book. The sheer scale of what Carey and Gross have set out to achieve here, and the risks they are willing to take while doing it, fills me with all the admiration in the world (and a little bit of envy too). This, my story-loving friends, is the real deal.

I hope you'll be as delighted and dazzled by this latest collection as I have been, and, if someone should try to interrupt you while you're reading it, if someone should try to tell you to *get your head out of the clouds*, or to *stop filling your time with silly stories*, just remember this:

Without a story there is no meaning.
And the nature of the meaning depends on the nature of the story.
To understand this is to understand the true power of stories.
And so, to control the stories, to be the one doing the telling…
Well now, wouldn't that be quite a thing…?

For everyone's sake, let's hope that Mr. Carey and Mr. Gross continue to use their considerable powers wisely…

Steven Hall
2010

Steven Hall's first novel, The Raw Shark Texts, *won the Borders Original Voices Award, the Somerset Maugham Award, and was shortlisted for the Arthur C. Clarke Award. The book has been translated into thirty languages, and a film adaptation is currently in development.*

DRAMATIS PERSONAE

TOM TAYLOR

"They don't know me, because I'm not Tommy. It's more like I'm the test tube where my dad did his experiments."

Tom Taylor was the inspiration for his father's Tommy Taylor novels – the hit series of children's books starring the adventures of a boy wizard. But now he's framed for murder and on the run from the law – all courtesy of a mysterious cabal that manipulates the world's stories to strengthen their own power.

LIZZIE HEXAM

"I learn about how stories work for the same reason that soldiers learn how to strip a rifle."

Lizzie Hexam believes Tom *is* the character from the books made flesh. Sent by Wilson Taylor to protect Tom, how much more does she know than she lets on?

RICHIE SAVOY

"I'm a journalist, man. And you're the story."

The exclusive of a lifetime, that's what Richie Savoy is looking for – if he can stay alive long enough by Tom's side.

CALLENDAR

"So we've dedicated our lives to building this mansion, and now we're in the process of giving away the fucking key."

The leader of the mysterious cabal that's trying to destroy Tom's life, Callendar will stop at nothing to prevent Tom from fulfilling whatever it is that Wilson has planned for him.

PULLMAN

"Fear is a serviceable tool, I suppose… Close your eyes. I'll make this quick."

The cabal's mysterious enforcer, Pullman turns whatever he touches into fiction, but he's been alive a very long time and that life comes with vicious secrets of its own.

AMBROSIO

"You thought I was dead, Tommy Taylor. But you should have known Ambrosio always finds a way."

Tommy Taylor's nemesis in the novels, the immortal Ambrosio has taken control of prison warden Claude Chadron after the man's grief over his children's deaths opened a way for Ambrosio to enter the real world.

SUE MORGENSTERN

"Don't worry, Tom. We all got our turn at being abandoned."

Wilson Taylor's mistress, Sue Morgenstern has always carried the blame for Wilson's absences and remoteness during Tom's childhood.

WILSON TAYLOR

"All the worlds anyone ever dreamed up… they're right here."

Tom's mysterious father, Wilson Taylor has waged a one-man war against the shadowy cabal that seeks to manipulate stories for their own gain. Missing for years, he's now sent a copy of his latest Tommy Taylor novel to his editor Ernie Cole, and his plans are finally beginning to bear fruit…

the Unwritten

DEAD MAN'S KNOCK

Mike Carey & Peter Gross Script - Story - Art
Ryan Kelly Finishes - The Many Lives of Lizzie Hexam
Chris Chuckry Jeanne McGee Colorists
Todd Klein Letterer Yuko Shimizu Cover Artist
THE UNWRITTEN created by Gross and Carey

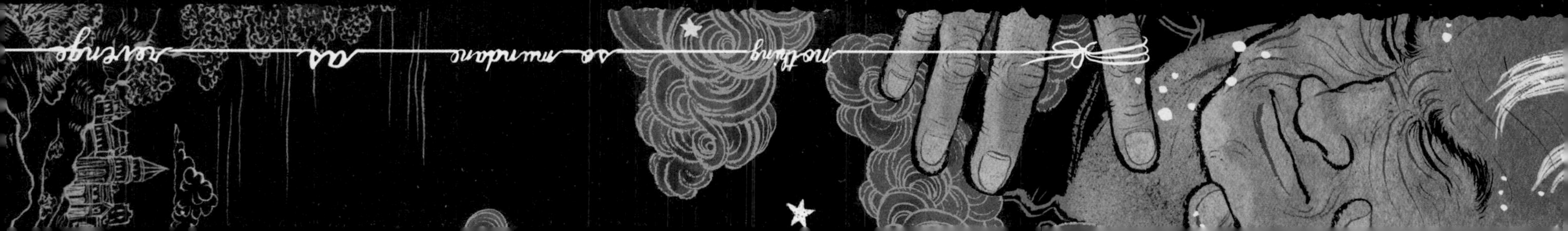
nothing so mundane as revenge

Karen Berger SVP-Executive Editor
Pornsak Pichetshote Editor-Original Series
Bob Harras Group Editor-Collected Editions
Robbin Brosterman Design Director-Books
Louis Prandi Art Director

DC COMICS

Diane Nelson President
Dan DiDio and Jim Lee Co-Publishers
Geoff Johns Chief Creative Officer
Patrick Caldon EVP-Finance and Administration
John Rood EVP-Sales, Marketing and Business Development
Amy Genkins SVP-Business and Legal Affairs
Steve Rotterdam SVP-Sales and Marketing
John Cunningham VP-Marketing
Terri Cunningham VP-Managing Editor
Alison Gill VP-Manufacturing
David Hyde VP-Publicity
Sue Pohja VP-Book Trade Sales
Alysse Soll VP-Advertising and Custom Publishing
Bob Wayne VP-Sales
Mark Chiarello Art Director

THE UNWRITTEN: DEAD MAN'S KNOCK
Published by DC Comics. Cover and compilation
Copyright © 2011 Mike Carey and Peter Gross.
All Rights Reserved. Originally published in single
magazine form as THE UNWRITTEN 13-18. Copyright
© 2011 Mike Carey and Peter Gross. All Rights
Reserved. VERTIGO and all characters, their distinctive
likenesses and related elements featured in this
publication are trademarks of DC Comics. The stories,
characters and incidents featured in this publication are
entirely fictional. DC Comics does not read or accept
unsolicited submissions of ideas, stories or artwork.
DC Comics, 1700 Broadway, New York, NY 10019
A Warner Bros. Entertainment Company.
Printed in the USA. First Printing.
ISBN: 978-1-4012-3046-3

SUSTAINABLE
FORESTRY
INITIATIVE
Certified Chain of Custody
Promoting Sustainable
Forest Management
www.sfiprogram.org
Fiber used in this product line meets the
sourcing requirements of the SFI program.
www.sfiprogram.org SGS-SFICOC-0130

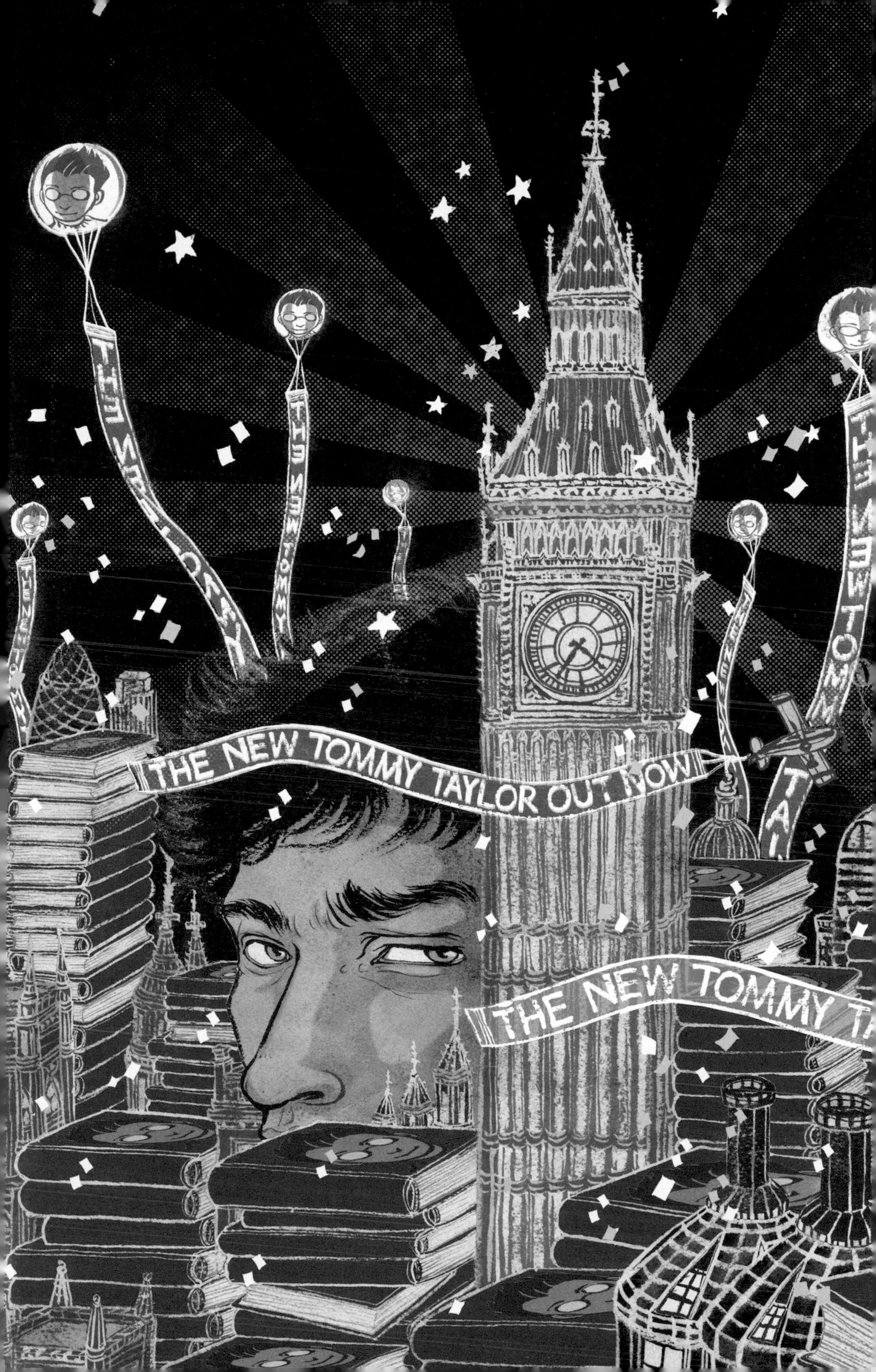
THE NEW TOMMY TAYLOR OUT NOW
THE NEW TOMMY

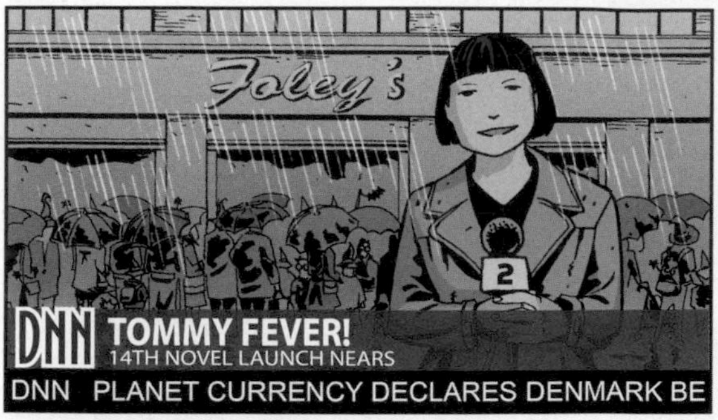
Foley's
DNN
TOMMY FEVER!
14TH NOVEL LAUNCH NEARS
DNN PLANET CURRENCY DECLARES DENMARK BE

IT'S STILL ***TWO DAYS*** TO THE OFFICIAL LAUNCH OF THE FOURTEENTH TOMMY TAYLOR NOVEL, AND DESPITE HEAVY RAINS, THE LINE AT ***FOLEY'S*** IN CHARING CROSS ROAD IS THREE-QUARTERS OF A MILE LONG... SARAH?

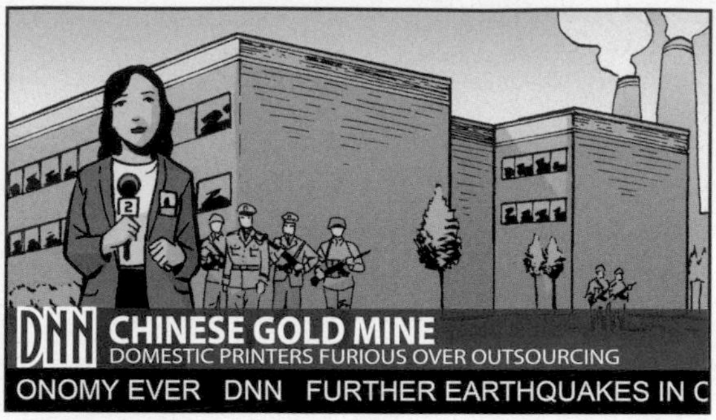
DNN
CHINESE GOLD MINE
DOMESTIC PRINTERS FURIOUS OVER OUTSOURCING
ONOMY EVER DNN FURTHER EARTHQUAKES IN C

THANKS, EILEEN. CHINESE OFFICIALS CONTINUE TO DENY THAT THE ENTIRE PRINT RUN IS BEING PRODUCED ***HERE,*** AT THIS PRINTING PLANT IN XIU-TAN.

BUT THE TIGHT SECURITY CERTAINLY ***SEEMS*** TO SUPPORT THAT THEORY.

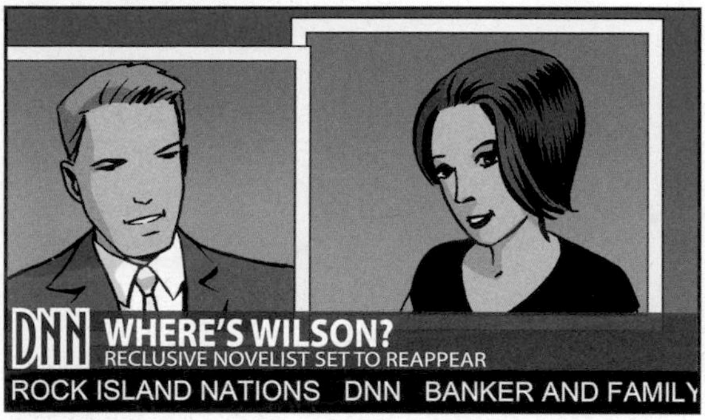
DNN
WHERE'S WILSON?
RECLUSIVE NOVELIST SET TO REAPPEAR
ROCK ISLAND NATIONS DNN BANKER AND FAMILY

AND WHAT ABOUT THOSE RUMORS THAT ***WILSON TAYLOR*** HIMSELF MIGHT BE TURNING UP FOR A SIGNING?

WELL, THAT'S ALL THEY ARE RIGHT NOW. RUMORS. BUT THEY'RE CERTAINLY ***ADDING*** TO THAT FEVER-PITCH EXCITEMENT.

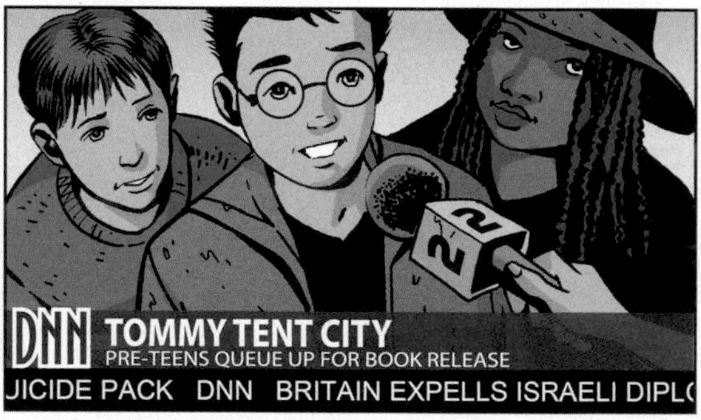
DNN
TOMMY TENT CITY
PRE-TEENS QUEUE UP FOR BOOK RELEASE
UICIDE PACK DNN BRITAIN EXPELLS ISRAELI DIPLO

WE'VE BEEN HERE SINCE, LIKE, ***TUESDAY.***

WE TAKE IT IN TURNS TO SLEEP, SO NO ONE CAN SLIP IN FRONT OF US.

IT'S SO COOL! IT'S LIKE WE'RE ALL PREGNANT WITH THE SAME BABY. AND NOW WE'RE ABOUT TO GIVE BIRTH!

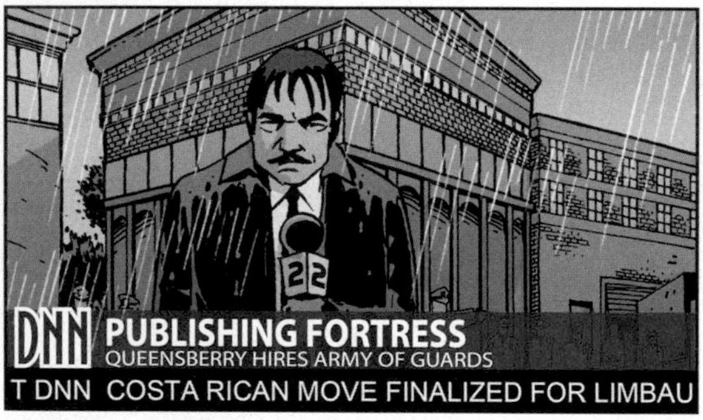
DNN
PUBLISHING FORTRESS
QUEENSBERRY HIRES ARMY OF GUARDS
T DNN COSTA RICAN MOVE FINALIZED FOR LIMBAU

PUBLISHERS QUEENSBERRY HAVE HIRED TWELVE THOUSAND SECURITY GUARDS TO SAFEGUARD AGAINST POSSIBLE PIRACY--AND ALL DELIVERIES OF THE NOVEL WILL REMAIN UNDER GUARD UNTIL ***7:00 A.M.*** ON THE MORNING OF THE ACTUAL LAUNCH.

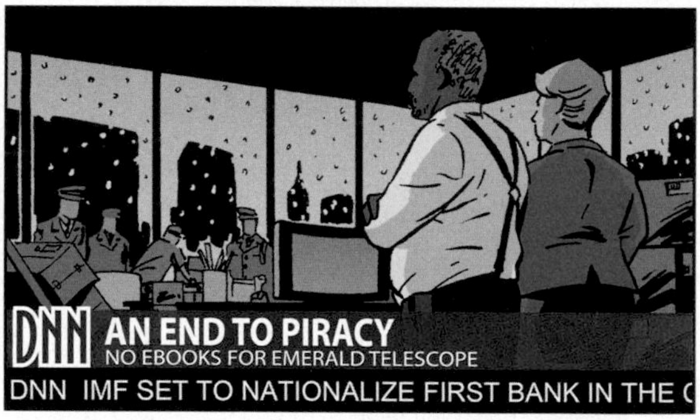
DNN
AN END TO PIRACY
NO EBOOKS FOR EMERALD TELESCOPE
DNN IMF SET TO NATIONALIZE FIRST BANK IN THE C

ERNEST COLE, THE BOOK'S EDITOR, CLAIMS THERE IS NO ELECTRONIC VERSION OF THE TEXT, SO HACKERS NEEDN'T WASTE THEIR TIME ATTACKING QUEENSBERRY'S MAIL SERVER--ALTHOUGH THAT HASN'T STOPPED THEM FROM TRYING.

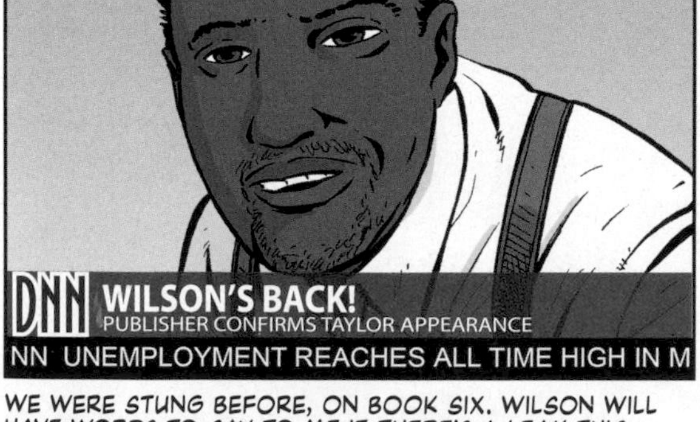
DNN
WILSON'S BACK!
PUBLISHER CONFIRMS TAYLOR APPEARANCE
NN UNEMPLOYMENT REACHES ALL TIME HIGH IN M

WE WERE STUNG BEFORE, ON BOOK SIX. WILSON WILL HAVE WORDS TO SAY TO ME IF THERE'S A LEAK THIS TIME AROUND.

UMM...I MEAN, ***IF*** HE'S SHOWING. ***I'M NOT CONFIRMING THAT.***

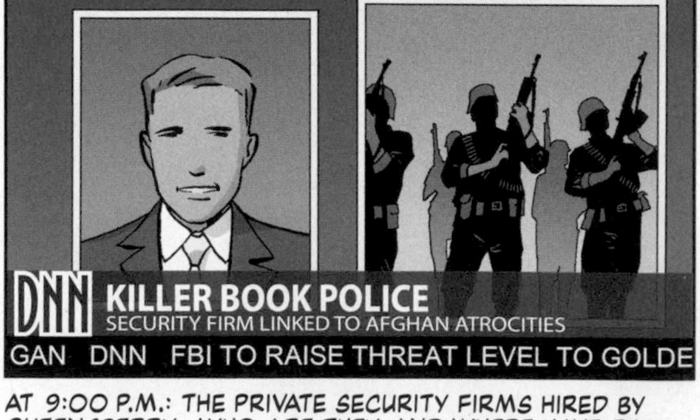
DNN
KILLER BOOK POLICE
SECURITY FIRM LINKED TO AFGHAN ATROCITIES
GAN DNN FBI TO RAISE THREAT LEVEL TO GOLDE

AT 9:00 P.M.: THE PRIVATE SECURITY FIRMS HIRED BY QUEENSBERRY--WHO ARE THEY, AND WHERE HAVE THEY WORKED BEFORE? THE ANSWERS MAY SHOCK YOU.

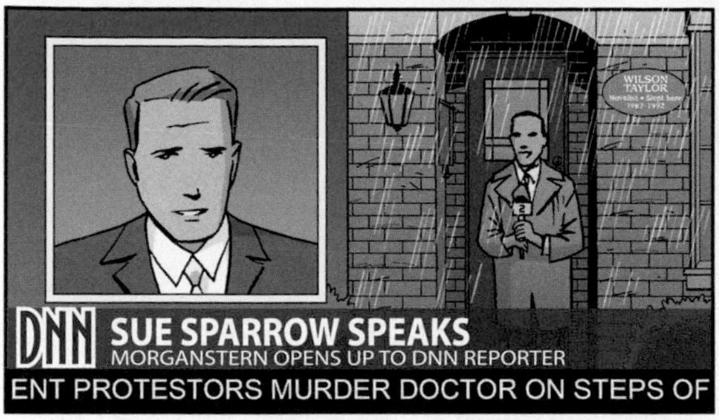
WILSON TAYLOR
Novelist • Slept here
1987-1992
DNN SUE SPARROW SPEAKS
MORGANSTERN OPENS UP TO DNN REPORTER
ENT PROTESTORS MURDER DOCTOR ON STEPS OF

NEXT UP, THOUGH, THE ***WOMAN*** IN THE CASE. MARK, YOU'VE BEEN TALKING TO ***SUE MORGANSTERN,*** WILSON TAYLOR'S FORMER MISTRESS--

THAT'S RIGHT, GARY. JUST MOMENTS AGO, I ASKED HER IF WILSON WAS COMING TO THE LAUNCH.

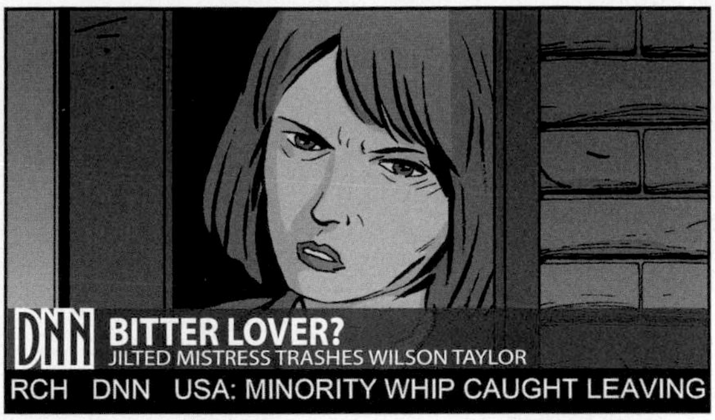
DNN BITTER LOVER?
JILTED MISTRESS TRASHES WILSON TAYLOR
RCH DNN USA: MINORITY WHIP CAUGHT LEAVING

I--WELL, I DON'T THINK THAT'S VERY ***LIKELY,*** TO BE HONEST.

HE'S SUPPOSED TO BE ***DEAD.*** DON'T YOU PEOPLE READ YOUR OWN STORIES?

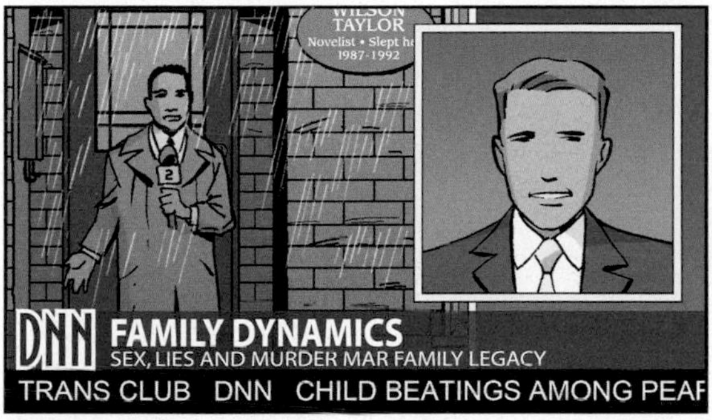
WILSON TAYLOR
Novelist • Slept he
1987-1992
DNN FAMILY DYNAMICS
SEX, LIES AND MURDER MAR FAMILY LEGACY
TRANS CLUB DNN CHILD BEATINGS AMONG PEAF

SO THAT'S FROM THE HORSE'S MOUTH. AND BEAR IN MIND, THIS WOMAN WAS CLOSER TO WILSON TAYLOR THAN ANYONE.

CERTAINLY CLOSER THAN HIS ***WIFE,*** FROM WHAT WE UNDERSTAND.

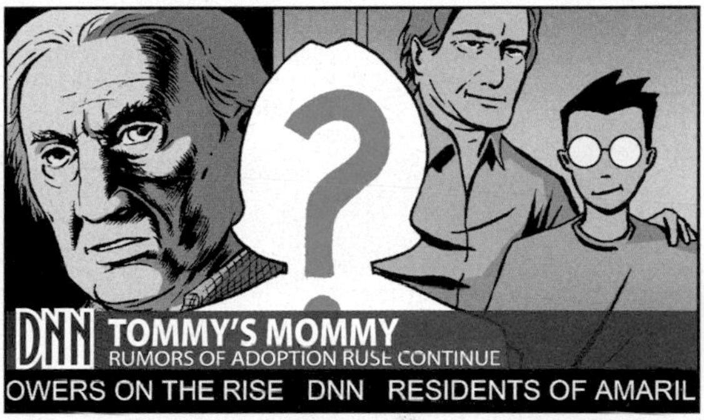
DNN TOMMY'S MOMMY
RUMORS OF ADOPTION RUSE CONTINUE
OWERS ON THE RISE DNN RESIDENTS OF AMARIL

BUT NOT MUCH IS KNOWN ABOUT ***CALLIOPE MADIGAN.*** IN LIFE, SHE WAS EVEN MORE RECLUSIVE THAN HER FAMOUS HUSBAND.

IN DEATH, SHE REMAINS AN ENIGMA.

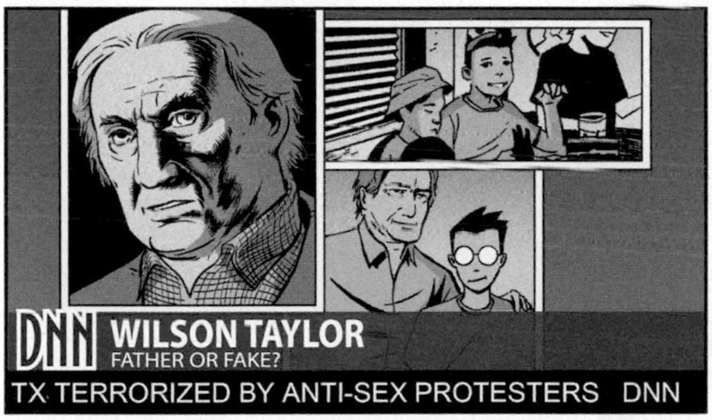
DNN WILSON TAYLOR
FATHER OR FAKE?
TX TERRORIZED BY ANTI-SEX PROTESTERS DNN

AND IF WILSON TAYLOR DOES STEP BACK INTO THE SPOTLIGHT, IT WILL BE ***TOO LATE*** FOR A FAMILY REUNION.

HIS SON, TOM, DIED THREE MONTHS AGO IN THE DONOSTIA BLAZE, WHILE STILL AWAITING TRIAL FOR MURDER.

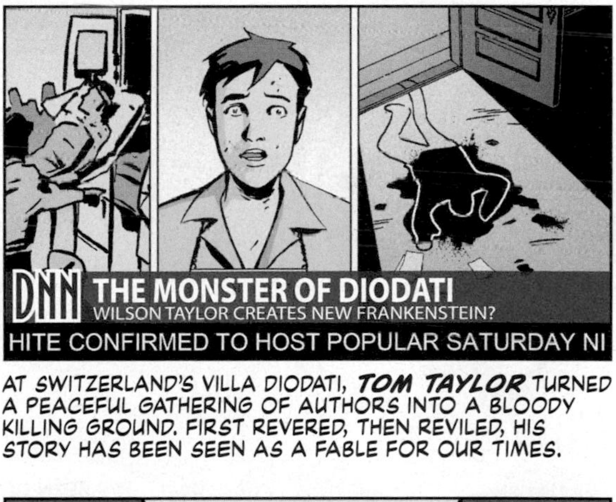
DNN THE MONSTER OF DIODATI
WILSON TAYLOR CREATES NEW FRANKENSTEIN?
HITE CONFIRMED TO HOST POPULAR SATURDAY NI

AT SWITZERLAND'S VILLA DIODATI, ***TOM TAYLOR*** TURNED A PEACEFUL GATHERING OF AUTHORS INTO A BLOODY KILLING GROUND. FIRST REVERED, THEN REVILED, HIS STORY HAS BEEN SEEN AS A FABLE FOR OUR TIMES.

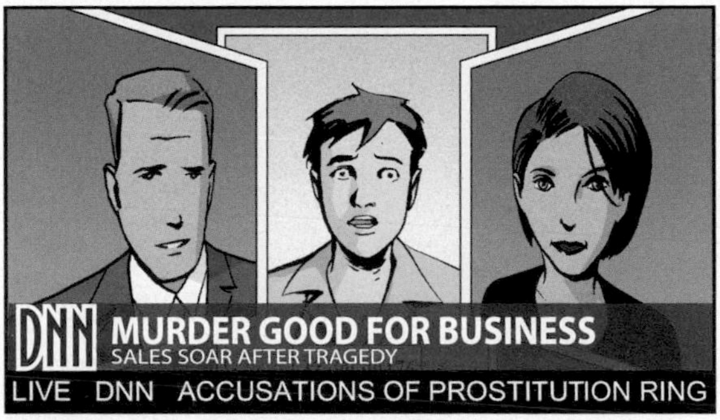
DNN MURDER GOOD FOR BUSINESS
SALES SOAR AFTER TRAGEDY
LIVE DNN ACCUSATIONS OF PROSTITUTION RING

SO THERE YOU GO. SOME JOY, SOME TRAGEDY.

A LITTLE ***MYSTERY,*** TOO, GARY.

BECAUSE I GUESS WE'LL NEVER REALLY KNOW WHAT WOULD DRIVE A MAN TO DO THE THINGS THAT TOM TAYLOR DID.

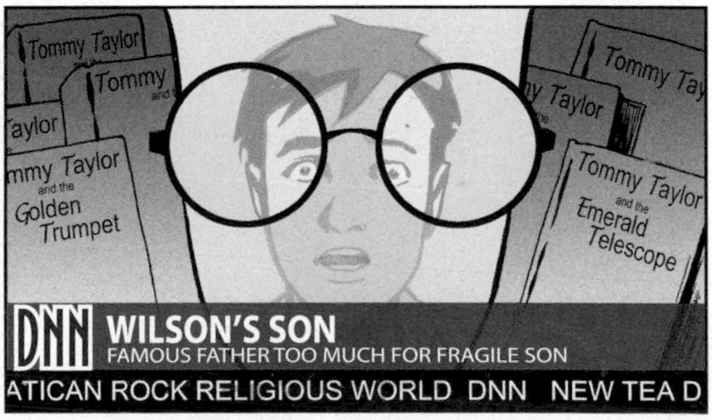
Tommy Taylor
Tommy
aylor
mmy Taylor
and the
Golden
Trumpet
Tommy Tay
y Taylor
Tommy Taylor
and the
Emerald
Telescope
DNN WILSON'S SON
FAMOUS FATHER TOO MUCH FOR FRAGILE SON
ATICAN ROCK RELIGIOUS WORLD DNN NEW TEA D

PERHAPS HE JUST COULDN'T HANDLE THE BURDEN OF FAME.

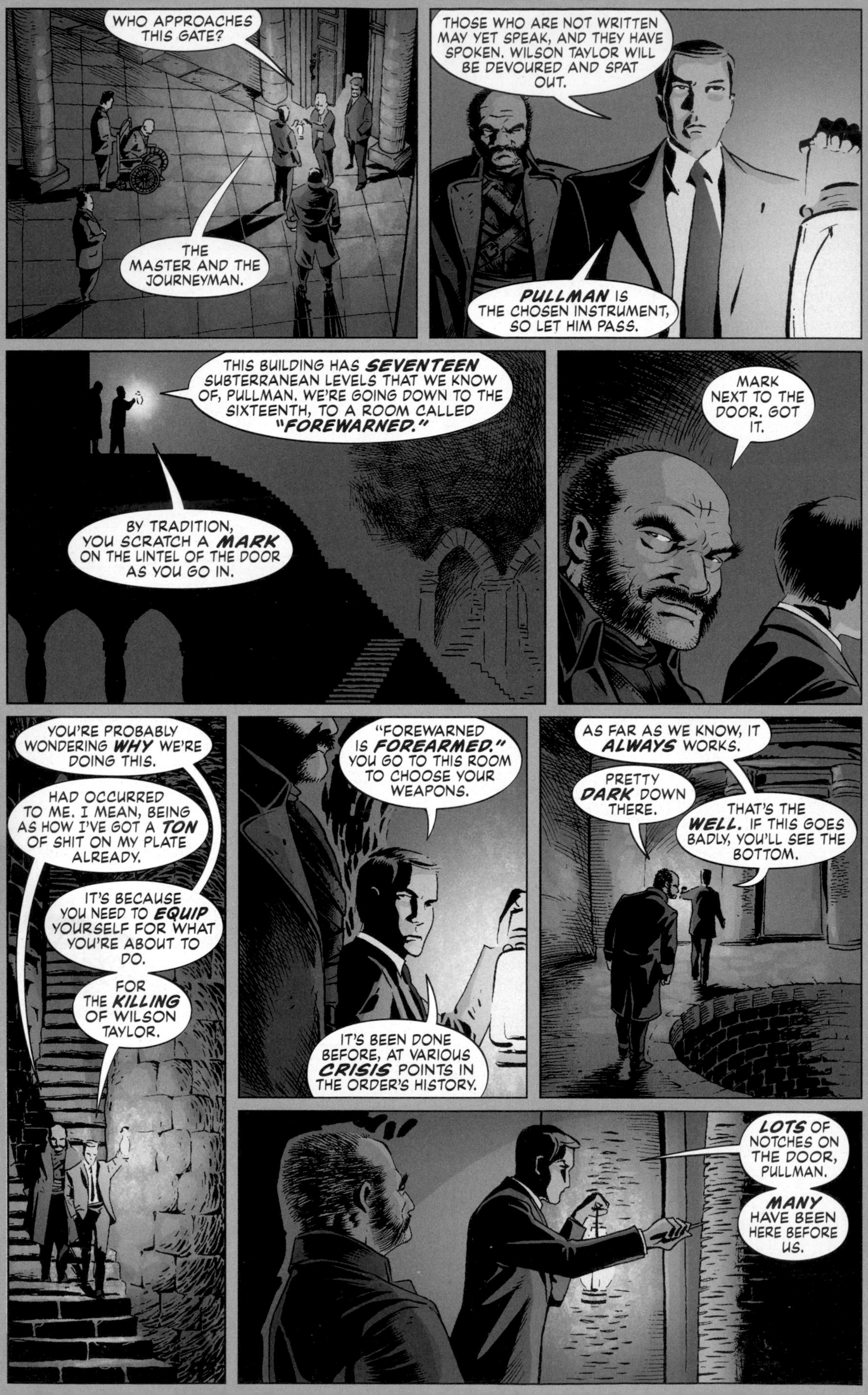
WHO APPROACHES THIS GATE?
THE MASTER AND THE JOURNEYMAN.
THOSE WHO ARE NOT WRITTEN MAY YET SPEAK, AND THEY HAVE SPOKEN. WILSON TAYLOR WILL BE DEVOURED AND SPAT OUT.
PULLMAN IS THE CHOSEN INSTRUMENT, SO LET HIM PASS.
THIS BUILDING HAS SEVENTEEN SUBTERRANEAN LEVELS THAT WE KNOW OF, PULLMAN. WE'RE GOING DOWN TO THE SIXTEENTH, TO A ROOM CALLED "FOREWARNED."
BY TRADITION, YOU SCRATCH A MARK ON THE LINTEL OF THE DOOR AS YOU GO IN.
MARK NEXT TO THE DOOR. GOT IT.
YOU'RE PROBABLY WONDERING WHY WE'RE DOING THIS.
HAD OCCURRED TO ME. I MEAN, BEING AS HOW I'VE GOT A TON OF SHIT ON MY PLATE ALREADY.
IT'S BECAUSE YOU NEED TO EQUIP YOURSELF FOR WHAT YOU'RE ABOUT TO DO.
FOR THE KILLING OF WILSON TAYLOR.
"FOREWARNED IS FOREARMED." YOU GO TO THIS ROOM TO CHOOSE YOUR WEAPONS.
IT'S BEEN DONE BEFORE, AT VARIOUS CRISIS POINTS IN THE ORDER'S HISTORY.
AS FAR AS WE KNOW, IT ALWAYS WORKS.
PRETTY DARK DOWN THERE.
THAT'S THE WELL. IF THIS GOES BADLY, YOU'LL SEE THE BOTTOM.
LOTS OF NOTCHES ON THE DOOR, PULLMAN.
MANY HAVE BEEN HERE BEFORE US.

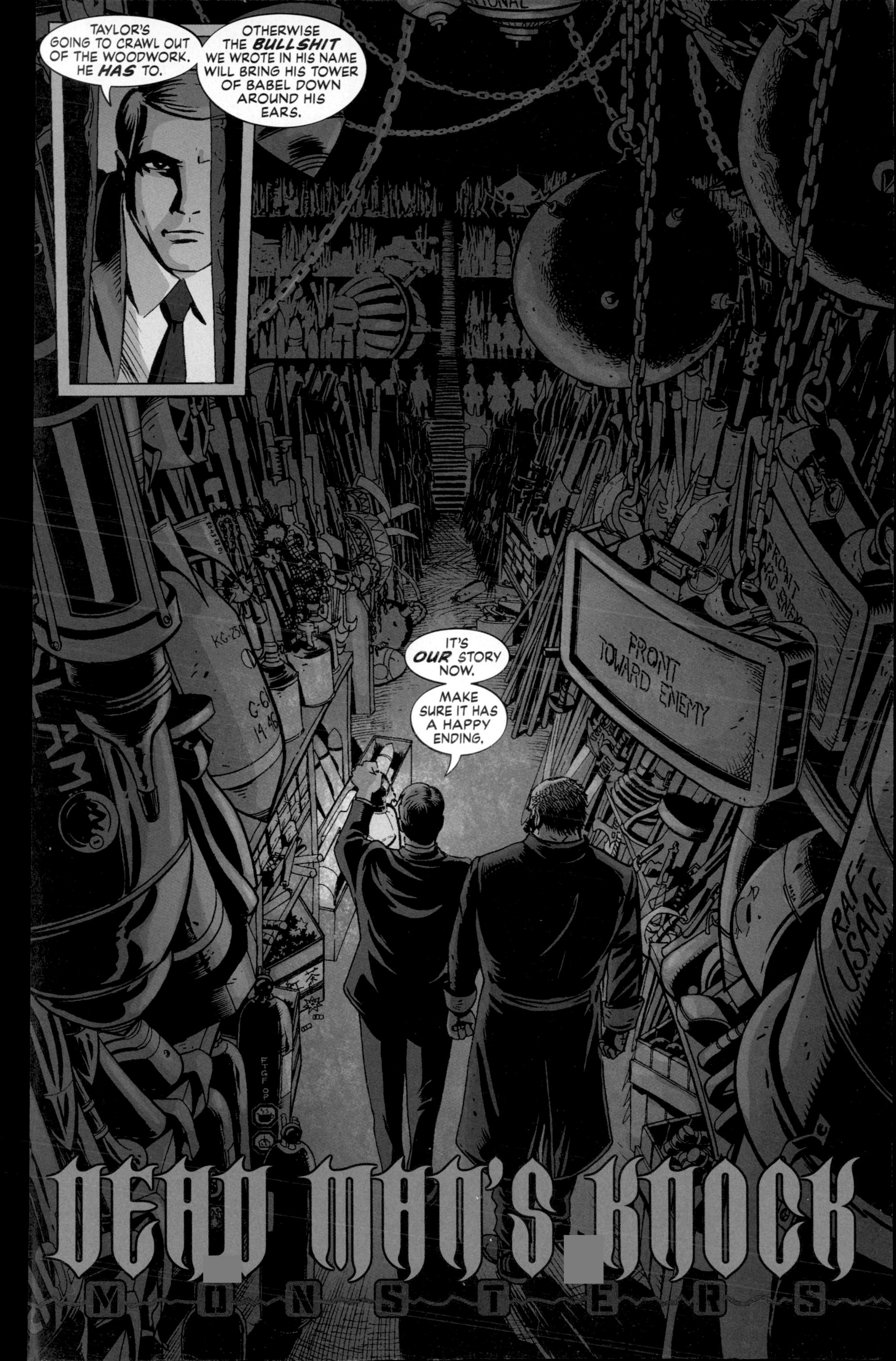
TAYLOR'S GOING TO CRAWL OUT OF THE WOODWORK. HE **HAS** TO.
OTHERWISE THE **BULLSHIT** WE WROTE IN HIS NAME WILL BRING HIS TOWER OF BABEL DOWN AROUND HIS EARS.
IT'S **OUR** STORY NOW.
MAKE SURE IT HAS A HAPPY ENDING.
FRONT TOWARD ENEMY
RAF U.S.A.A.F
DEAD MAN'S KNOCK
MONSTERS

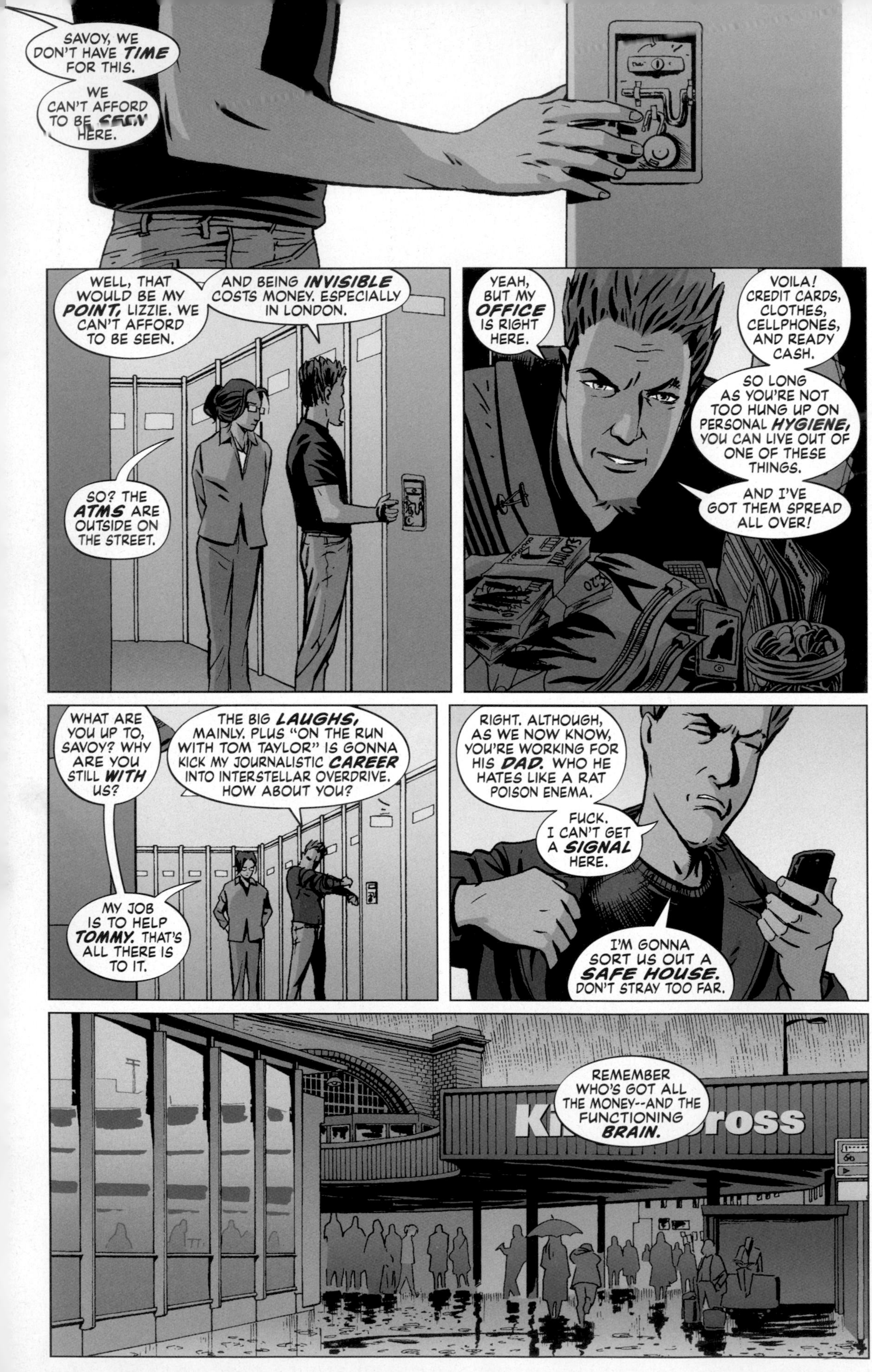
SAVOY, WE DON'T HAVE TIME FOR THIS.
WE CAN'T AFFORD TO BE SEEN HERE.
WELL, THAT WOULD BE MY POINT, LIZZIE. WE CAN'T AFFORD TO BE SEEN.
AND BEING INVISIBLE COSTS MONEY. ESPECIALLY IN LONDON.
SO? THE ATMS ARE OUTSIDE ON THE STREET.
YEAH, BUT MY OFFICE IS RIGHT HERE.
VOILA! CREDIT CARDS, CLOTHES, CELLPHONES, AND READY CASH.
SO LONG AS YOU'RE NOT TOO HUNG UP ON PERSONAL HYGIENE, YOU CAN LIVE OUT OF ONE OF THESE THINGS.
AND I'VE GOT THEM SPREAD ALL OVER!
WHAT ARE YOU UP TO, SAVOY? WHY ARE YOU STILL WITH US?
THE BIG LAUGHS, MAINLY. PLUS "ON THE RUN WITH TOM TAYLOR" IS GONNA KICK MY JOURNALISTIC CAREER INTO INTERSTELLAR OVERDRIVE. HOW ABOUT YOU?
MY JOB IS TO HELP TOMMY. THAT'S ALL THERE IS TO IT.
RIGHT. ALTHOUGH, AS WE NOW KNOW, YOU'RE WORKING FOR HIS DAD. WHO HE HATES LIKE A RAT POISON ENEMA.
FUCK. I CAN'T GET A SIGNAL HERE.
I'M GONNA SORT US OUT A SAFE HOUSE. DON'T STRAY TOO FAR.
REMEMBER WHO'S GOT ALL THE MONEY--AND THE FUNCTIONING BRAIN.

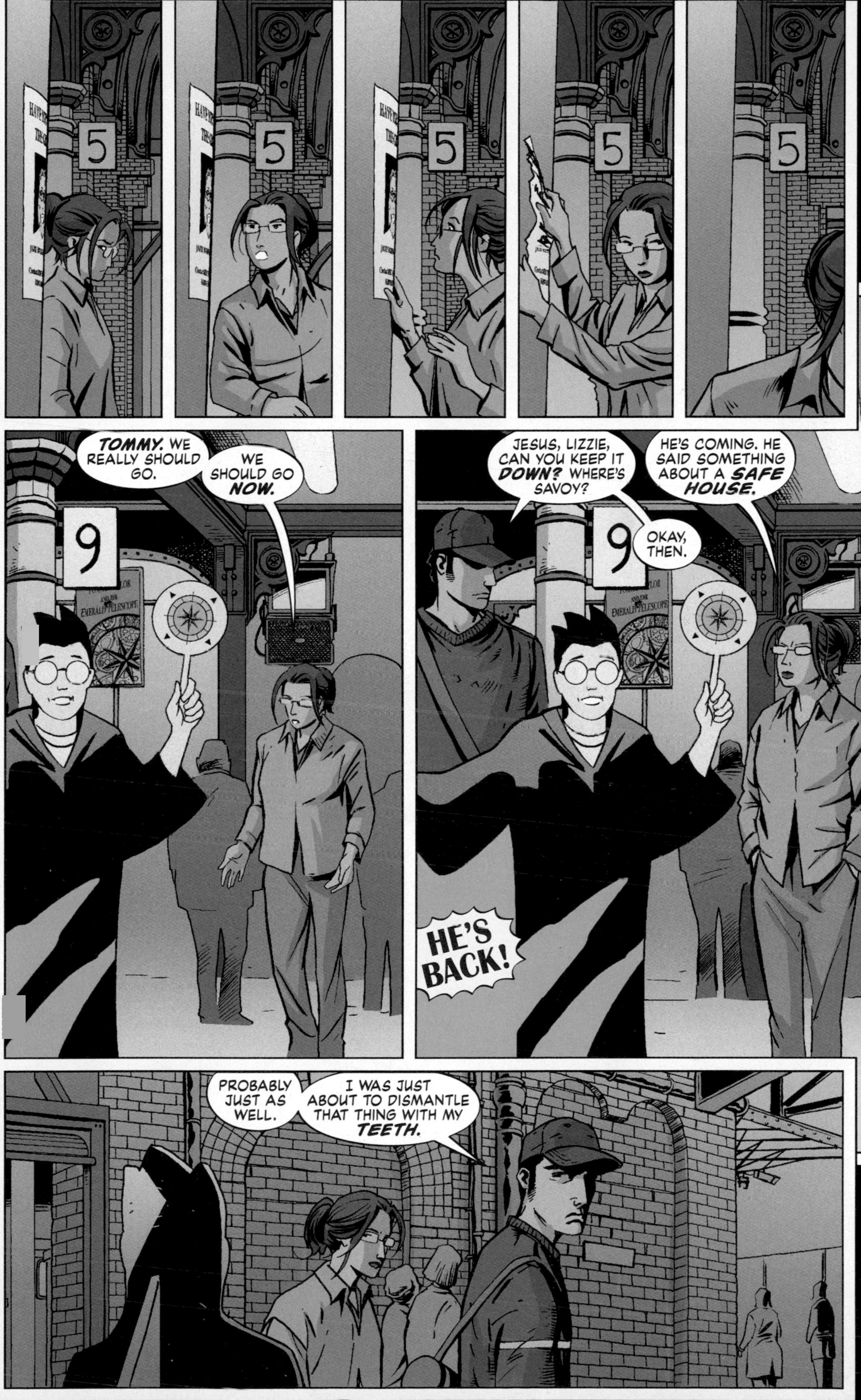
TOMMY. WE REALLY SHOULD GO.
WE SHOULD GO NOW.
JESUS, LIZZIE, CAN YOU KEEP IT DOWN? WHERE'S SAVOY?
HE'S COMING. HE SAID SOMETHING ABOUT A SAFE HOUSE.
OKAY, THEN.
HE'S BACK!
PROBABLY JUST AS WELL.
I WAS JUST ABOUT TO DISMANTLE THAT THING WITH MY TEETH.

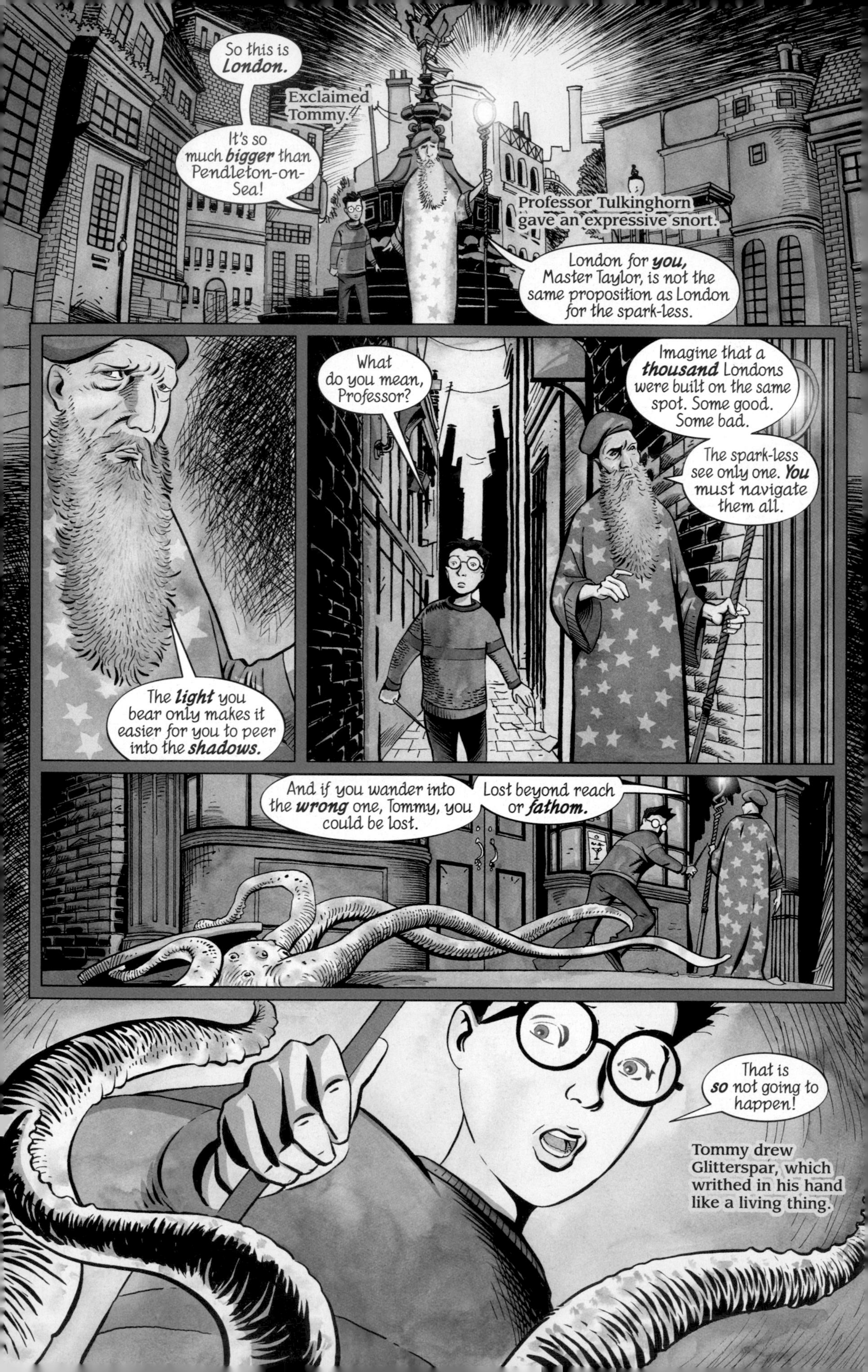
So this is **London.**
Exclaimed Tommy.
It's so much **bigger** than Pendleton-on-Sea!
Professor Tulkinghorn gave an expressive snort.
London for **you,** Master Taylor, is not the same proposition as London for the spark-less.
The **light** you bear only makes it easier for you to peer into the **shadows.**
What do you mean, Professor?
Imagine that a **thousand** Londons were built on the same spot. Some good. Some bad.
The spark-less see only one. **You** must navigate them all.
And if you wander into the **wrong** one, Tommy, you could be lost.
Lost beyond reach or **fathom.**
That is **so** not going to happen!
Tommy drew Glitterspar, which writhed in his hand like a living thing.

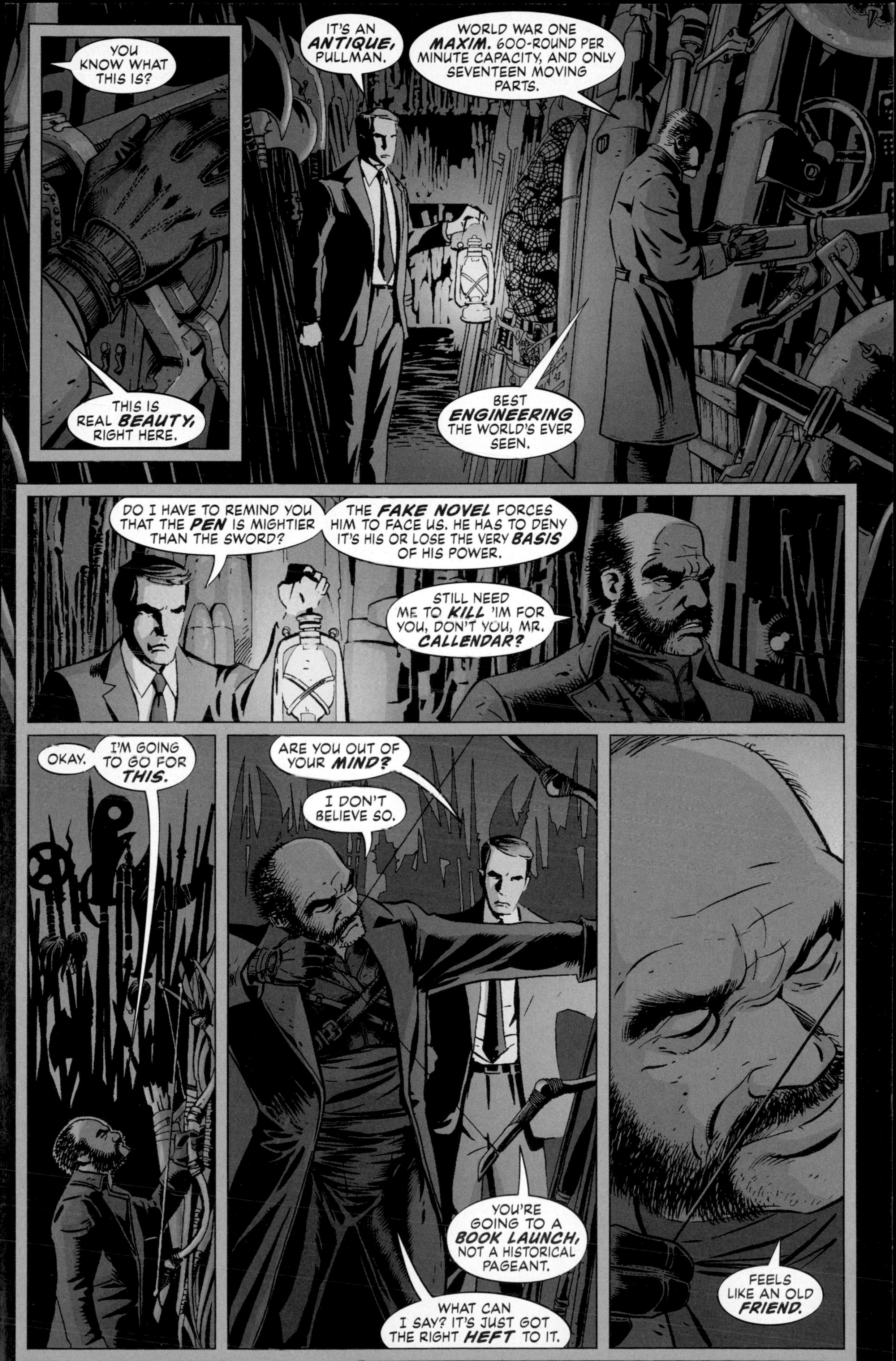

YOU KNOW WHAT THIS IS?
IT'S AN ANTIQUE, PULLMAN.
WORLD WAR ONE MAXIM. 600-ROUND PER MINUTE CAPACITY, AND ONLY SEVENTEEN MOVING PARTS.
THIS IS REAL BEAUTY, RIGHT HERE.
BEST ENGINEERING THE WORLD'S EVER SEEN.
DO I HAVE TO REMIND YOU THAT THE PEN IS MIGHTIER THAN THE SWORD?
THE FAKE NOVEL FORCES HIM TO FACE US. HE HAS TO DENY IT'S HIS OR LOSE THE VERY BASIS OF HIS POWER.
STILL NEED ME TO KILL 'IM FOR YOU, DON'T YOU, MR. CALLENDAR?
OKAY.
I'M GOING TO GO FOR THIS.
ARE YOU OUT OF YOUR MIND?
I DON'T BELIEVE SO.
YOU'RE GOING TO A BOOK LAUNCH, NOT A HISTORICAL PAGEANT.
WHAT CAN I SAY? IT'S JUST GOT THE RIGHT HEFT TO IT.
FEELS LIKE AN OLD FRIEND.

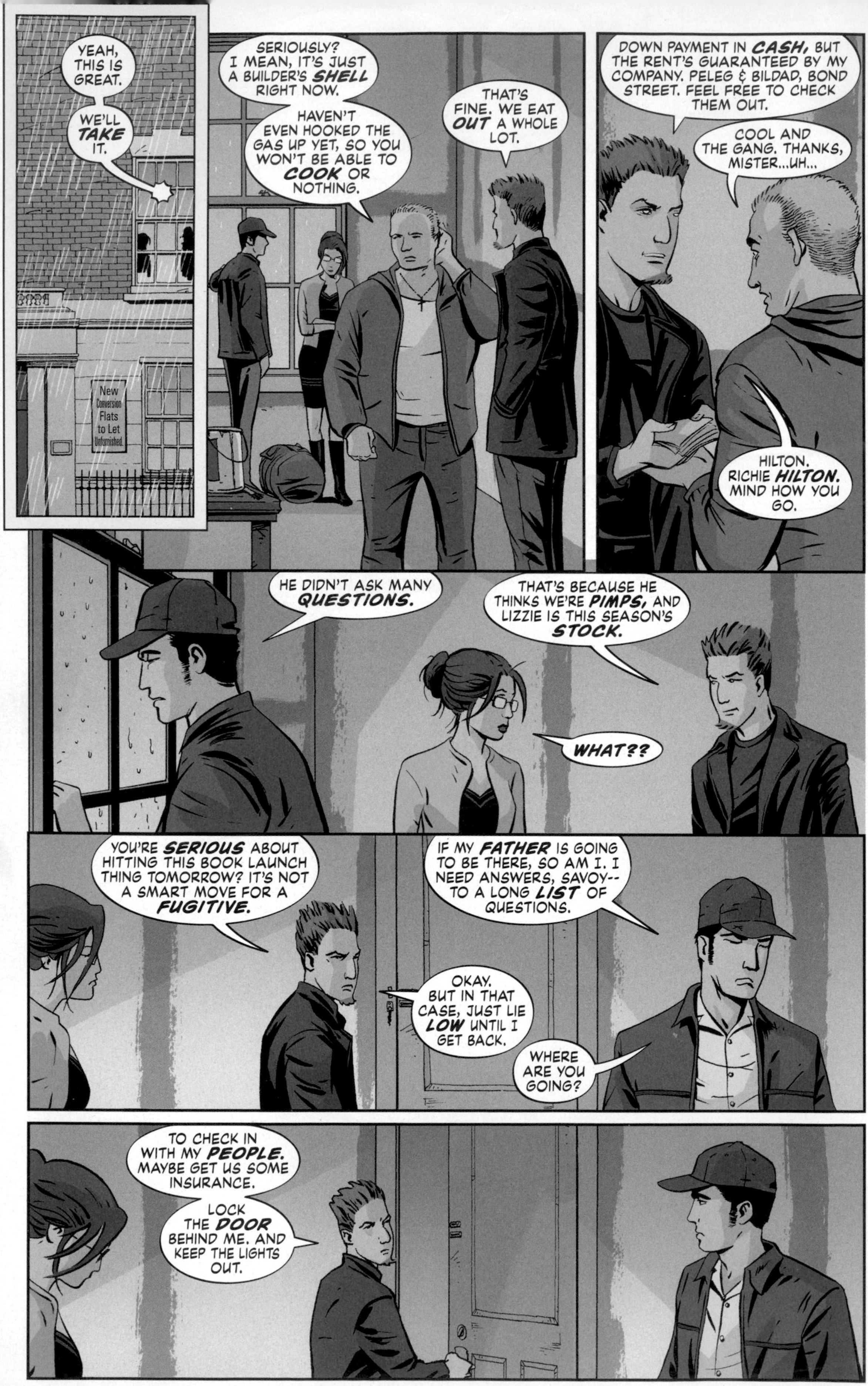

YEAH, THIS IS GREAT.
WE'LL TAKE IT.
New Conversion Flats to Let Unfurnished.
SERIOUSLY? I MEAN, IT'S JUST A BUILDER'S SHELL RIGHT NOW.
HAVEN'T EVEN HOOKED THE GAS UP YET, SO YOU WON'T BE ABLE TO COOK OR NOTHING.
THAT'S FINE. WE EAT OUT A WHOLE LOT.
DOWN PAYMENT IN CASH, BUT THE RENT'S GUARANTEED BY MY COMPANY. PELEG & BILDAD, BOND STREET. FEEL FREE TO CHECK THEM OUT.
COOL AND THE GANG. THANKS, MISTER...UH...
HILTON. RICHIE HILTON. MIND HOW YOU GO.
HE DIDN'T ASK MANY QUESTIONS.
THAT'S BECAUSE HE THINKS WE'RE PIMPS, AND LIZZIE IS THIS SEASON'S STOCK.
WHAT??
YOU'RE SERIOUS ABOUT HITTING THIS BOOK LAUNCH THING TOMORROW? IT'S NOT A SMART MOVE FOR A FUGITIVE.
IF MY FATHER IS GOING TO BE THERE, SO AM I. I NEED ANSWERS, SAVOY-- TO A LONG LIST OF QUESTIONS.
OKAY. BUT IN THAT CASE, JUST LIE LOW UNTIL I GET BACK.
WHERE ARE YOU GOING?
TO CHECK IN WITH MY PEOPLE. MAYBE GET US SOME INSURANCE.
LOCK THE DOOR BEHIND ME. AND KEEP THE LIGHTS OUT.

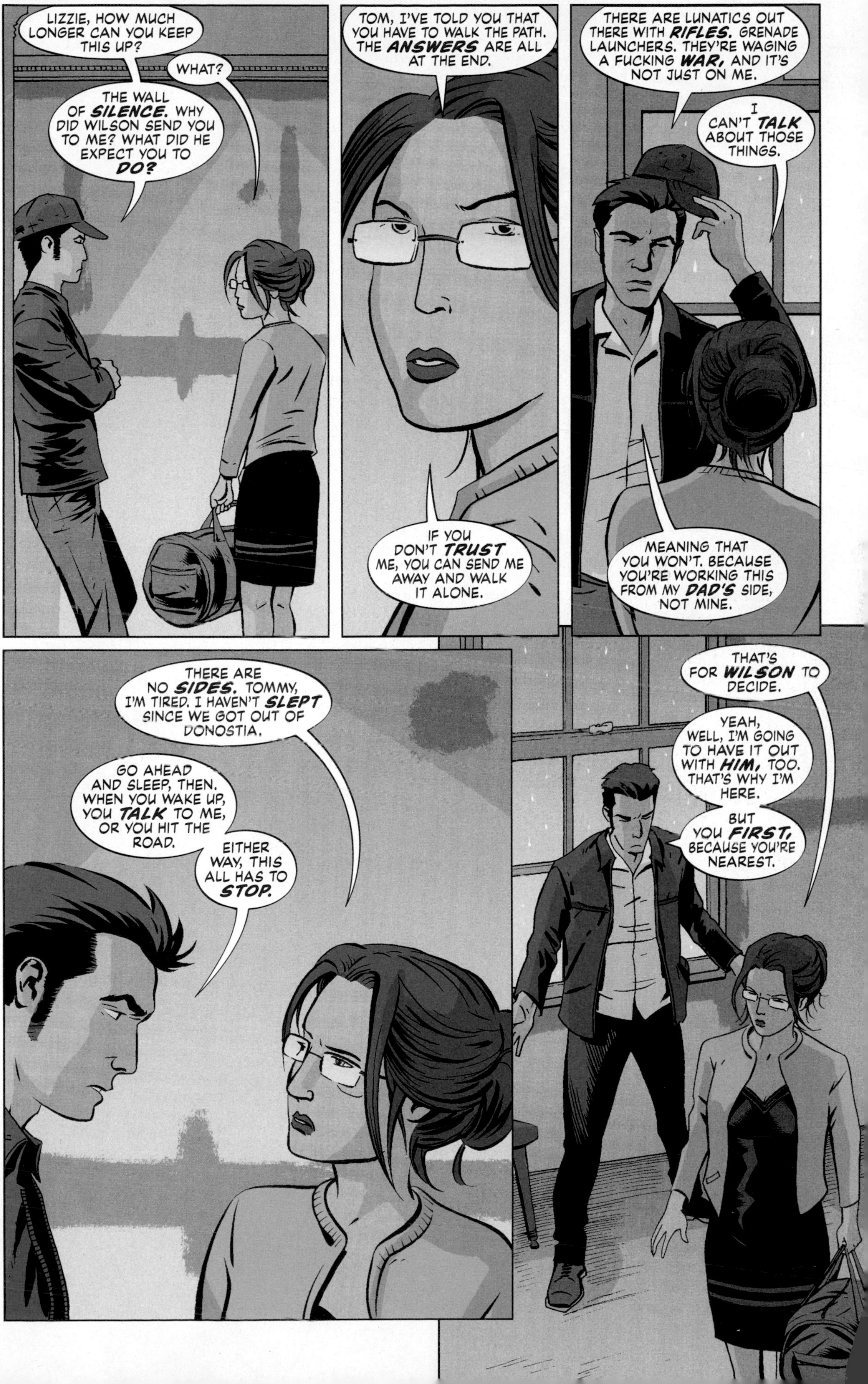
LIZZIE, HOW MUCH LONGER CAN YOU KEEP THIS UP?
WHAT?
THE WALL OF SILENCE. WHY DID WILSON SEND YOU TO ME? WHAT DID HE EXPECT YOU TO DO?
TOM, I'VE TOLD YOU THAT YOU HAVE TO WALK THE PATH. THE ANSWERS ARE ALL AT THE END.
IF YOU DON'T TRUST ME, YOU CAN SEND ME AWAY AND WALK IT ALONE.
THERE ARE LUNATICS OUT THERE WITH RIFLES. GRENADE LAUNCHERS. THEY'RE WAGING A FUCKING WAR, AND IT'S NOT JUST ON ME.
I CAN'T TALK ABOUT THOSE THINGS.
MEANING THAT YOU WON'T. BECAUSE YOU'RE WORKING THIS FROM MY DAD'S SIDE, NOT MINE.
THERE ARE NO SIDES. TOMMY, I'M TIRED. I HAVEN'T SLEPT SINCE WE GOT OUT OF DONOSTIA.
GO AHEAD AND SLEEP, THEN. WHEN YOU WAKE UP, YOU TALK TO ME, OR YOU HIT THE ROAD.
EITHER WAY, THIS ALL HAS TO STOP.
THAT'S FOR WILSON TO DECIDE.
YEAH, WELL, I'M GOING TO HAVE IT OUT WITH HIM, TOO. THAT'S WHY I'M HERE.
BUT YOU FIRST, BECAUSE YOU'RE NEAREST.

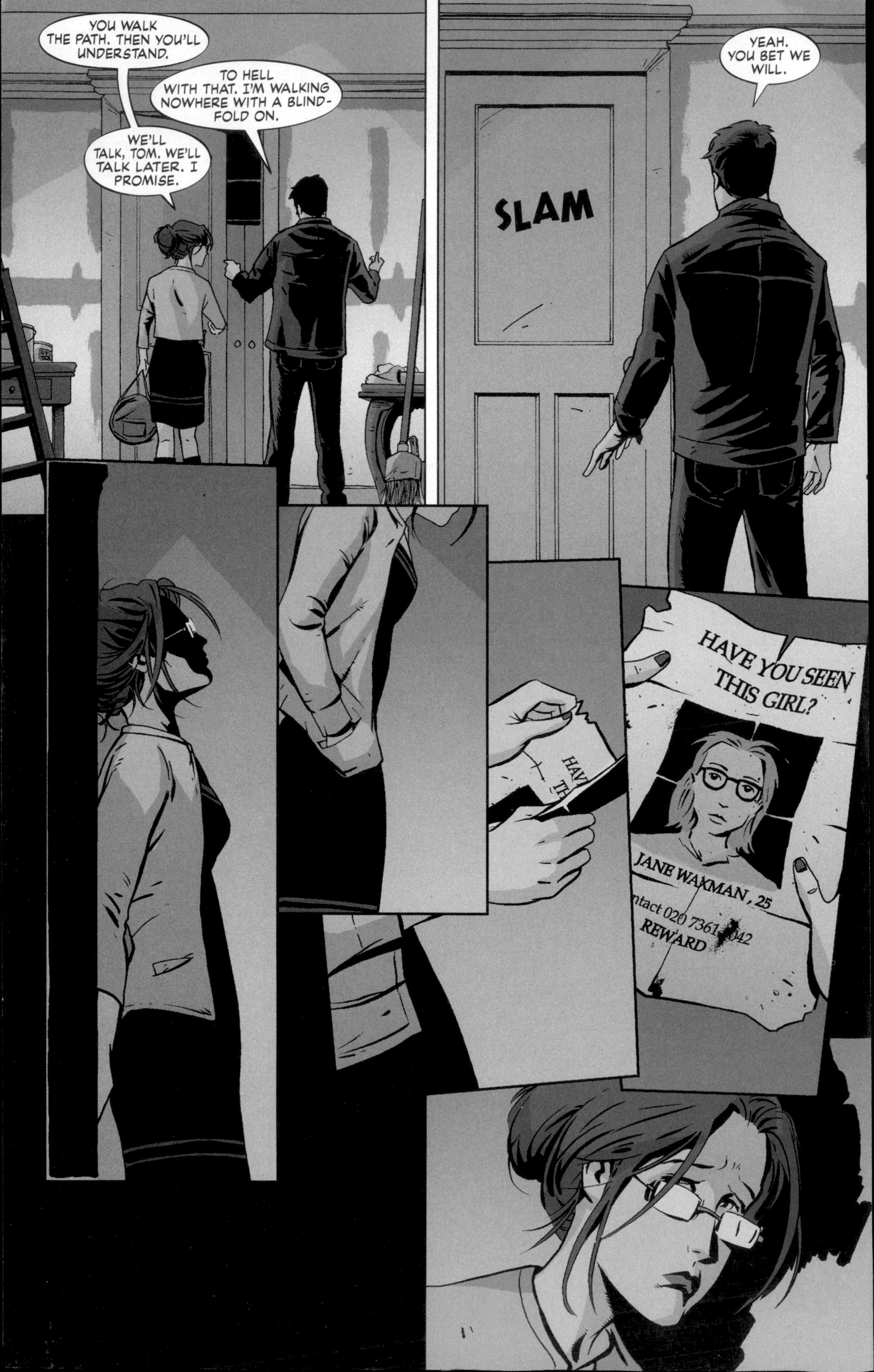
YOU WALK THE PATH. THEN YOU'LL UNDERSTAND.
TO HELL WITH THAT. I'M WALKING NOWHERE WITH A BLIND-FOLD ON.
WE'LL TALK, TOM. WE'LL TALK LATER. I PROMISE.
SLAM
YEAH. YOU BET WE WILL.
HAVE YOU SEEN THIS GIRL?
JANE WAXMAN, 25
REWARD

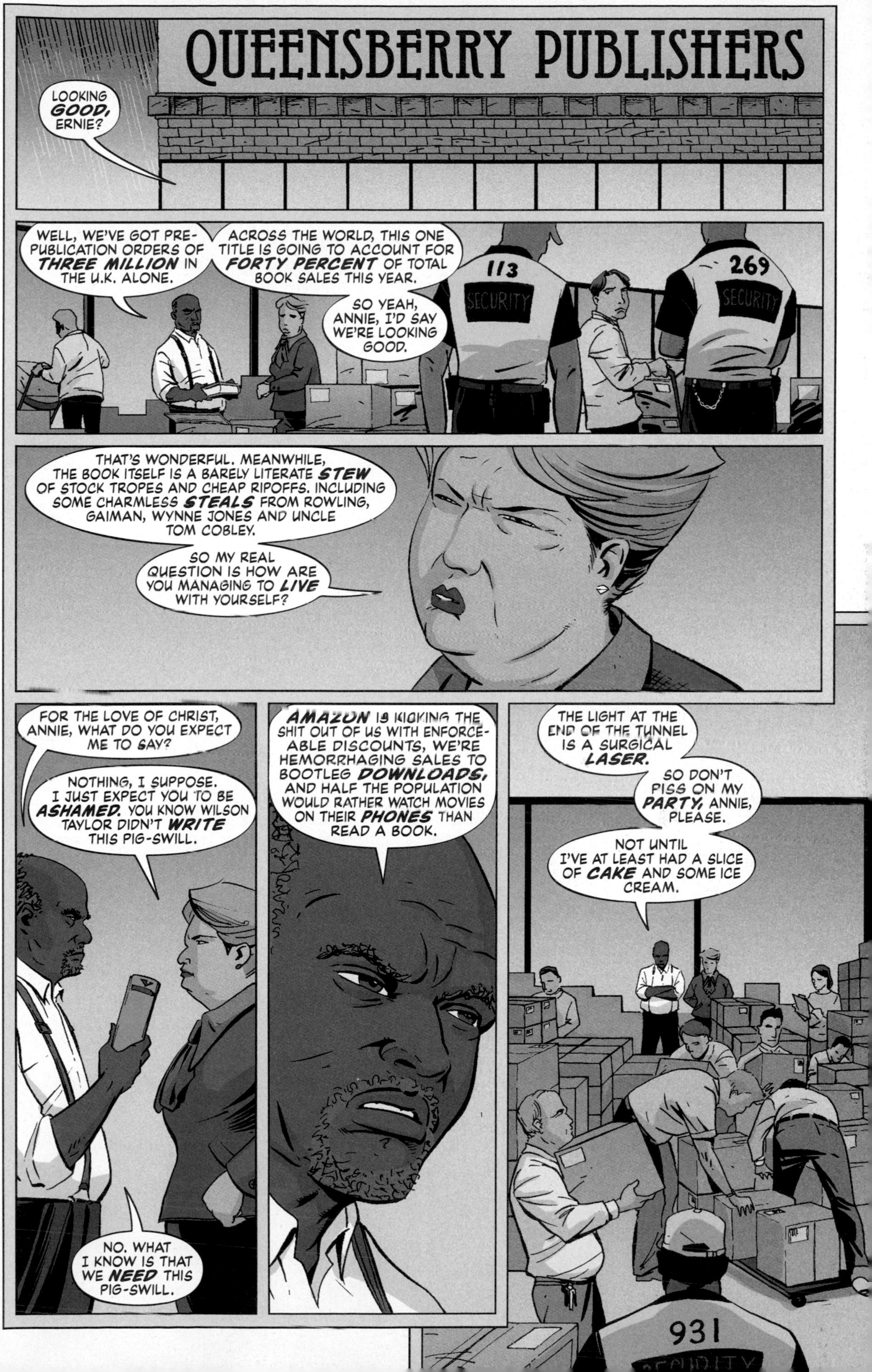
QUEENSBERRY PUBLISHERS
LOOKING GOOD, ERNIE?
WELL, WE'VE GOT PRE-PUBLICATION ORDERS OF THREE MILLION IN THE U.K. ALONE.
ACROSS THE WORLD, THIS ONE TITLE IS GOING TO ACCOUNT FOR FORTY PERCENT OF TOTAL BOOK SALES THIS YEAR.
SO YEAH, ANNIE, I'D SAY WE'RE LOOKING GOOD.
113
SECURITY
269
SECURITY
THAT'S WONDERFUL. MEANWHILE, THE BOOK ITSELF IS A BARELY LITERATE STEW OF STOCK TROPES AND CHEAP RIPOFFS. INCLUDING SOME CHARMLESS STEALS FROM ROWLING, GAIMAN, WYNNE JONES AND UNCLE TOM COBLEY.
SO MY REAL QUESTION IS HOW ARE YOU MANAGING TO LIVE WITH YOURSELF?
FOR THE LOVE OF CHRIST, ANNIE, WHAT DO YOU EXPECT ME TO SAY?
NOTHING, I SUPPOSE. I JUST EXPECT YOU TO BE ASHAMED. YOU KNOW WILSON TAYLOR DIDN'T WRITE THIS PIG-SWILL.
NO. WHAT I KNOW IS THAT WE NEED THIS PIG-SWILL.
AMAZON IS KICKING THE SHIT OUT OF US WITH ENFORCE-ABLE DISCOUNTS, WE'RE HEMORRHAGING SALES TO BOOTLEG DOWNLOADS, AND HALF THE POPULATION WOULD RATHER WATCH MOVIES ON THEIR PHONES THAN READ A BOOK.
THE LIGHT AT THE END OF THE TUNNEL IS A SURGICAL LASER.
SO DON'T PISS ON MY PARTY, ANNIE, PLEASE.
NOT UNTIL I'VE AT LEAST HAD A SLICE OF CAKE AND SOME ICE CREAM.
931

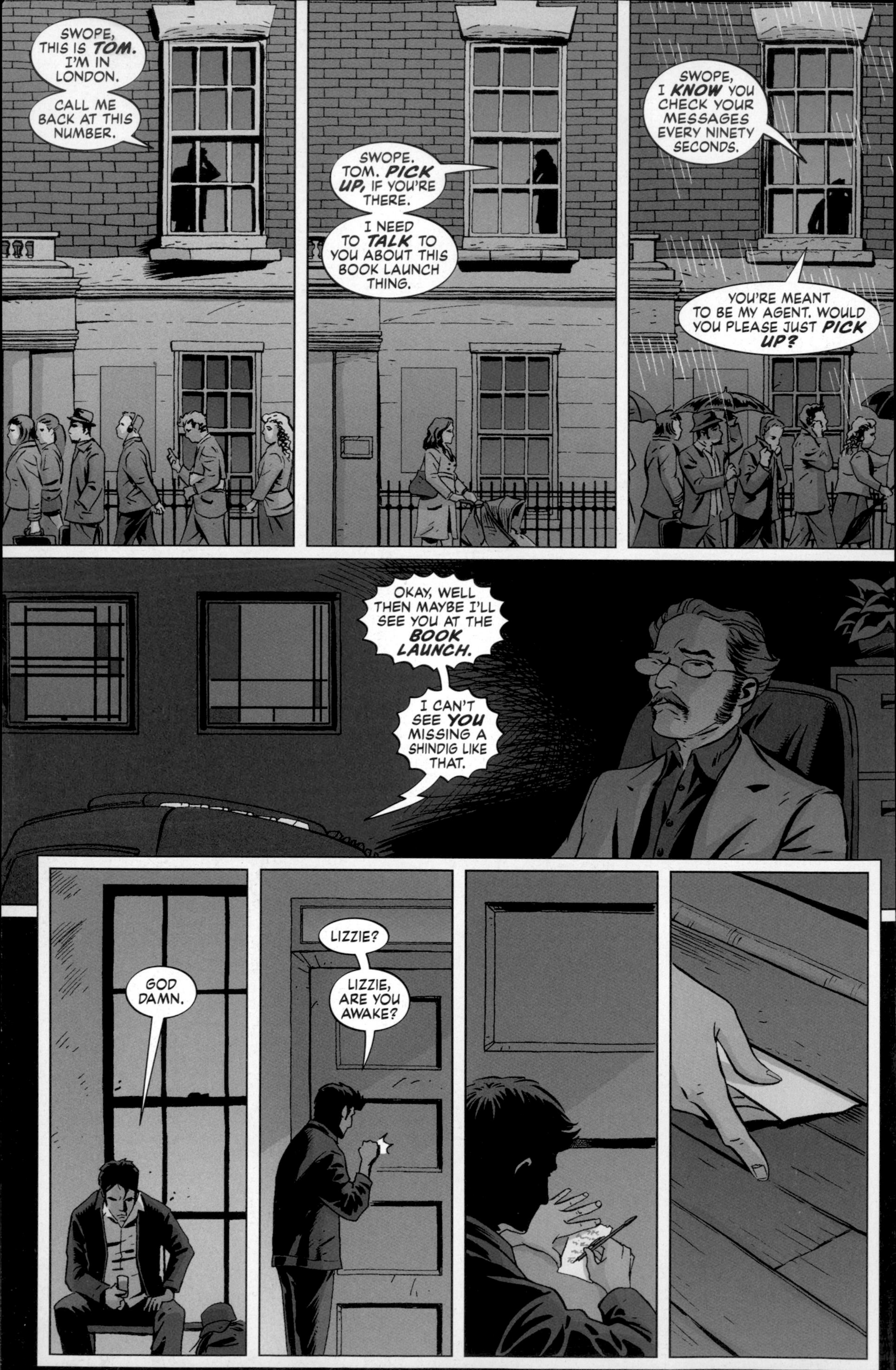
SWOPE, THIS IS TOM. I'M IN LONDON.
CALL ME BACK AT THIS NUMBER.
SWOPE. TOM. PICK UP, IF YOU'RE THERE.
I NEED TO TALK TO YOU ABOUT THIS BOOK LAUNCH THING.
SWOPE, I KNOW YOU CHECK YOUR MESSAGES EVERY NINETY SECONDS.
YOU'RE MEANT TO BE MY AGENT. WOULD YOU PLEASE JUST PICK UP?
OKAY, WELL THEN MAYBE I'LL SEE YOU AT THE BOOK LAUNCH.
I CAN'T SEE YOU MISSING A SHINDIG LIKE THAT.
GOD DAMN.
LIZZIE?
LIZZIE, ARE YOU AWAKE?

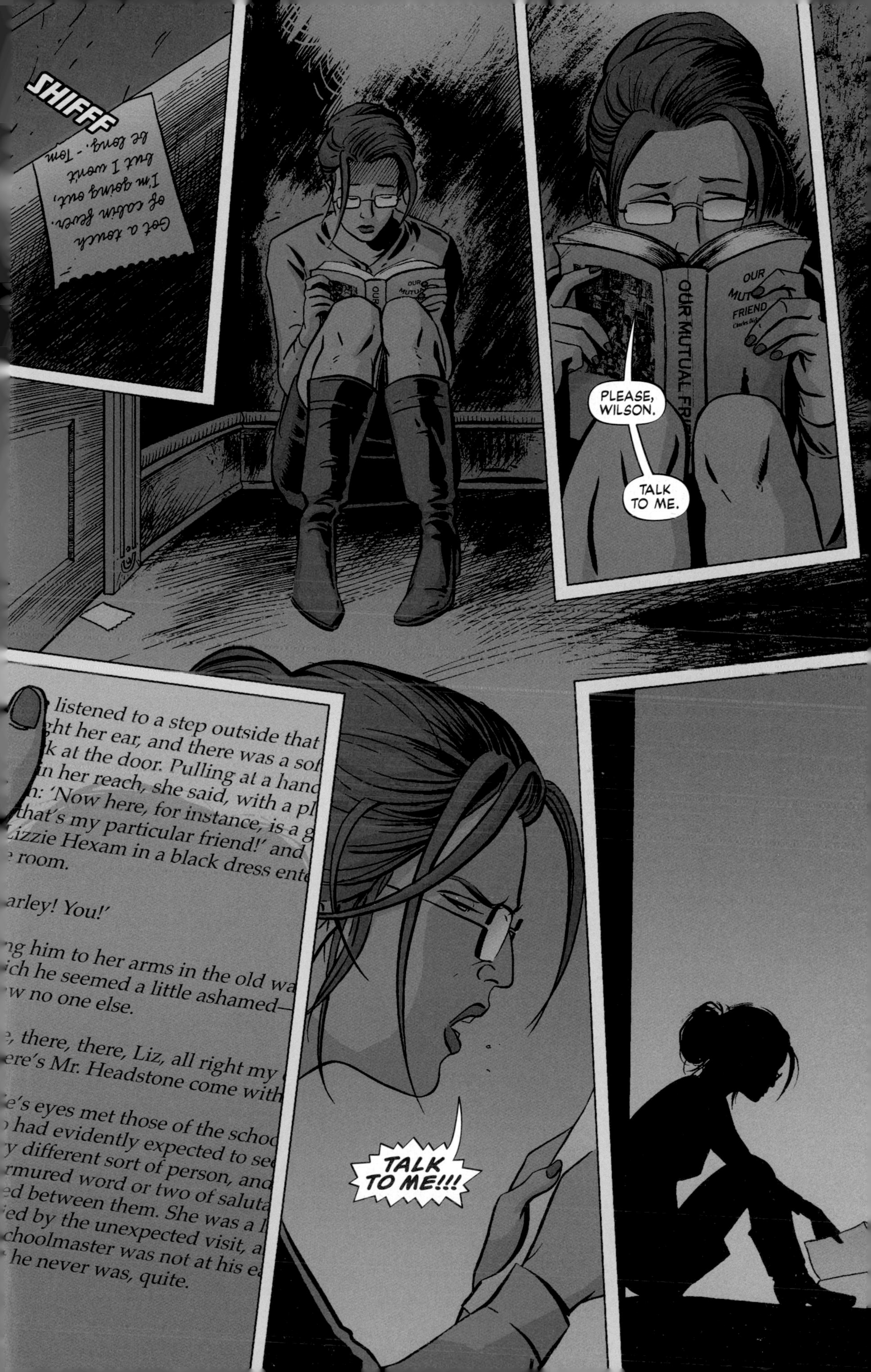
SHIFFF
Got a touch of cabin fever. I'm going out, but I won't be long. - Tom.
OUR MUTUAL FRIEND
PLEASE, WILSON.
TALK TO ME.
listened to a step outside that
ght her ear, and there was a sof
k at the door. Pulling at a hand
in her reach, she said, with a pl
n: 'Now here, for instance, is a g
that's my particular friend!' and
Lizzie Hexam in a black dress ente
e room.
arley! You!'
ng him to her arms in the old wa
ich he seemed a little ashamed—
w no one else.
, there, there, Liz, all right my
ere's Mr. Headstone come with
e's eyes met those of the schoo
had evidently expected to see
y different sort of person, and
rmured word or two of saluta
ed between them. She was a l
ed by the unexpected visit, a
choolmaster was not at his ea
he never was, quite.
TALK TO ME!!!

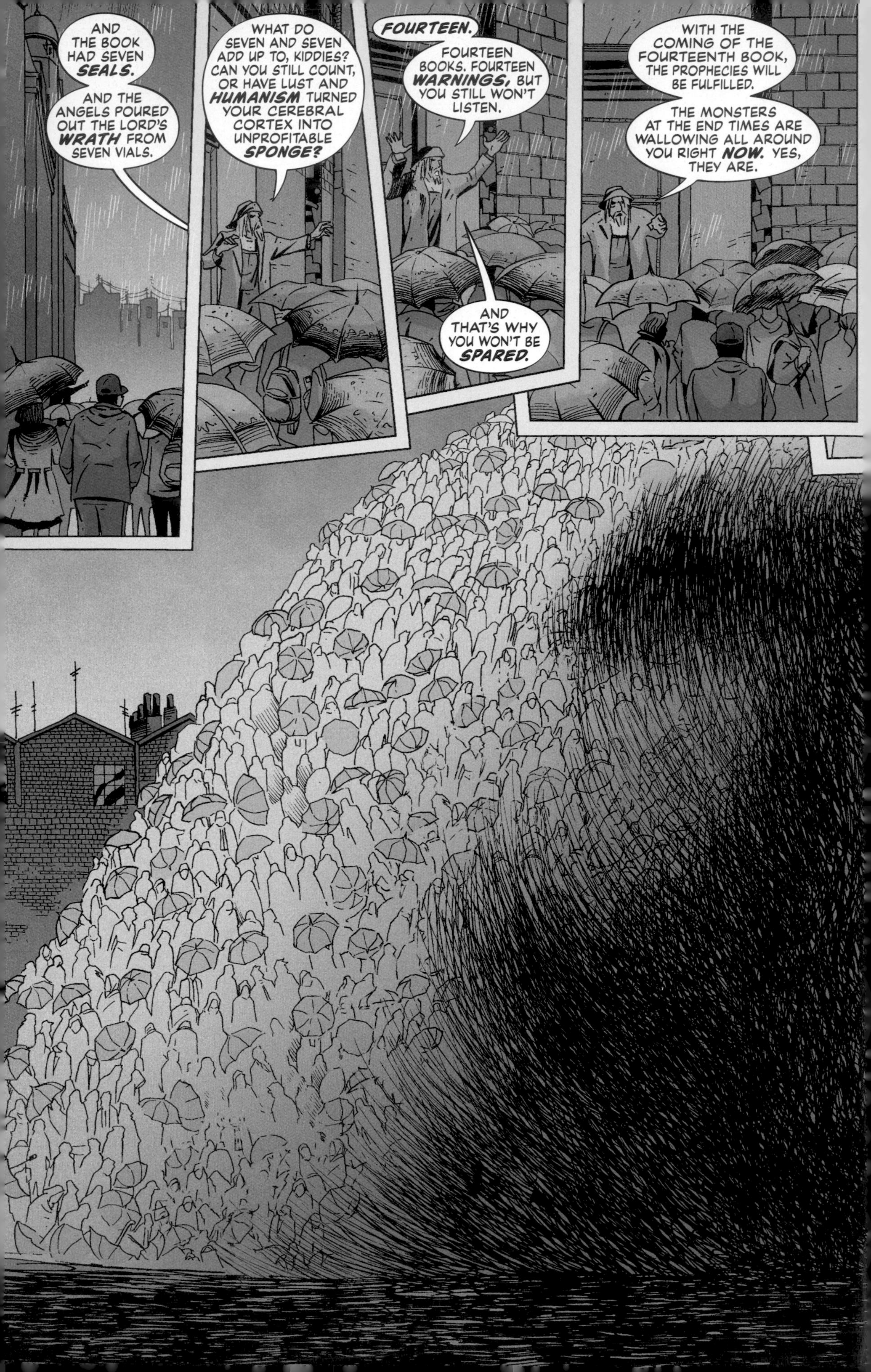
AND THE BOOK HAD SEVEN SEALS.
AND THE ANGELS POURED OUT THE LORD'S WRATH FROM SEVEN VIALS.
WHAT DO SEVEN AND SEVEN ADD UP TO, KIDDIES? CAN YOU STILL COUNT, OR HAVE LUST AND HUMANISM TURNED YOUR CEREBRAL CORTEX INTO UNPROFITABLE SPONGE?
FOURTEEN.
FOURTEEN BOOKS. FOURTEEN WARNINGS, BUT YOU STILL WON'T LISTEN.
AND THAT'S WHY YOU WON'T BE SPARED.
WITH THE COMING OF THE FOURTEENTH BOOK, THE PROPHECIES WILL BE FULFILLED.
THE MONSTERS AT THE END TIMES ARE WALLOWING ALL AROUND YOU RIGHT NOW. YES, THEY ARE.

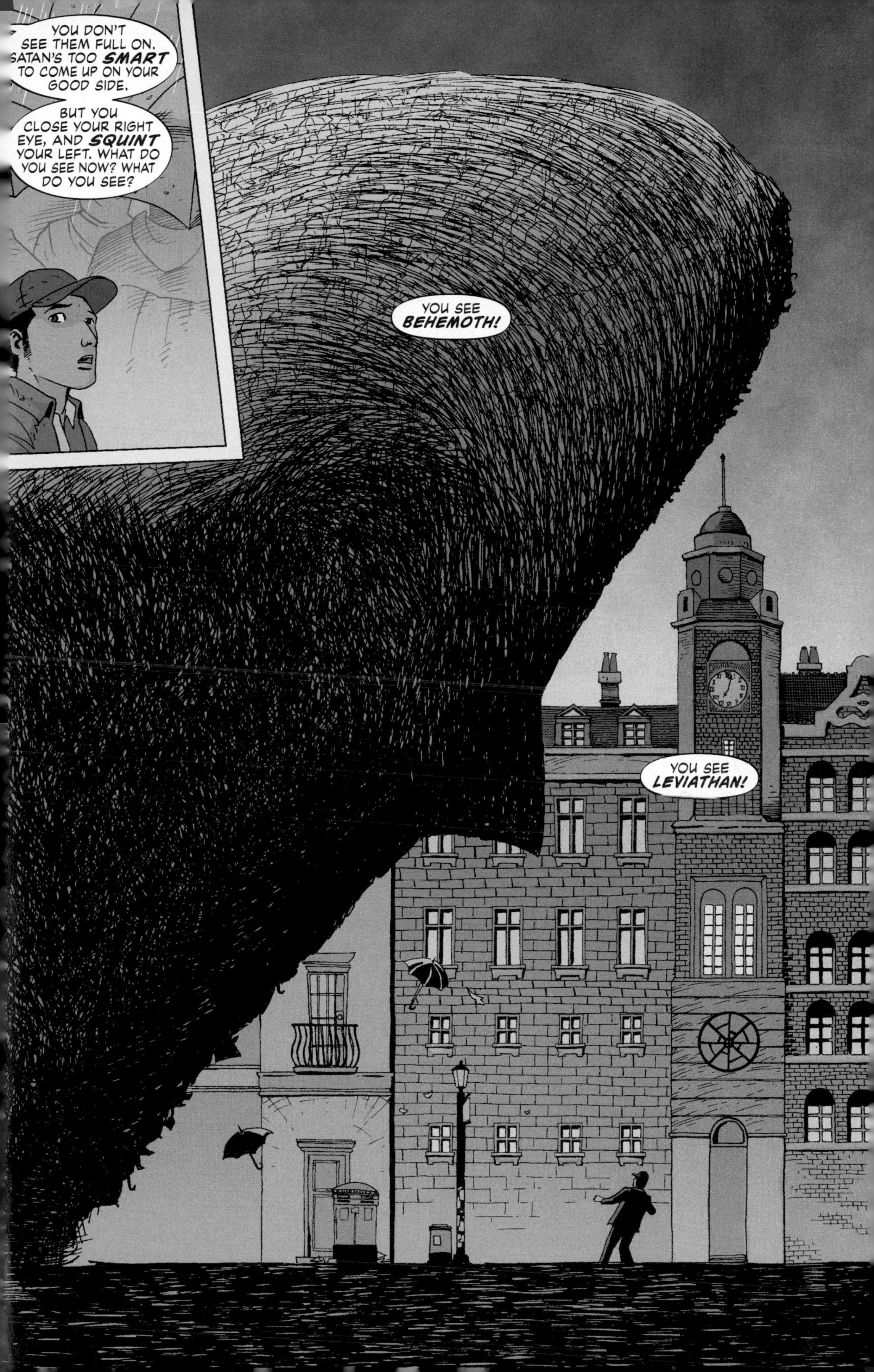
YOU DON'T SEE THEM FULL ON. SATAN'S TOO SMART TO COME UP ON YOUR GOOD SIDE.
BUT YOU CLOSE YOUR RIGHT EYE, AND SQUINT YOUR LEFT. WHAT DO YOU SEE NOW? WHAT DO YOU SEE?
YOU SEE BEHEMOTH!
YOU SEE LEVIATHAN!

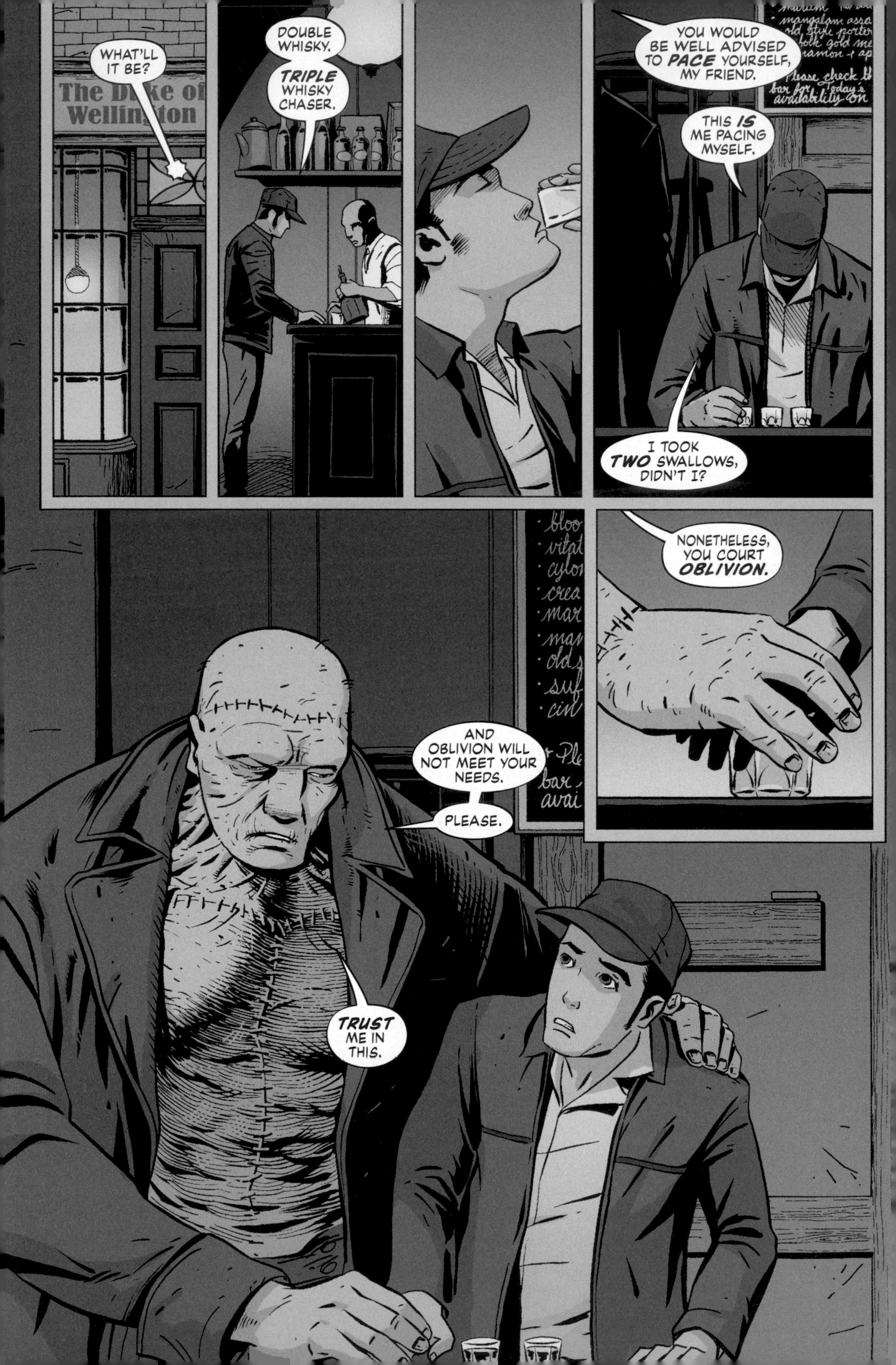

The Duke of
WHAT'LL IT BE?
DOUBLE WHISKY.
TRIPLE WHISKY CHASER.
YOU WOULD BE WELL ADVISED TO PACE YOURSELF, MY FRIEND.
THIS IS ME PACING MYSELF.
I TOOK TWO SWALLOWS, DIDN'T I?
NONETHELESS, YOU COURT OBLIVION.
AND OBLIVION WILL NOT MEET YOUR NEEDS.
PLEASE.
TRUST ME IN THIS.

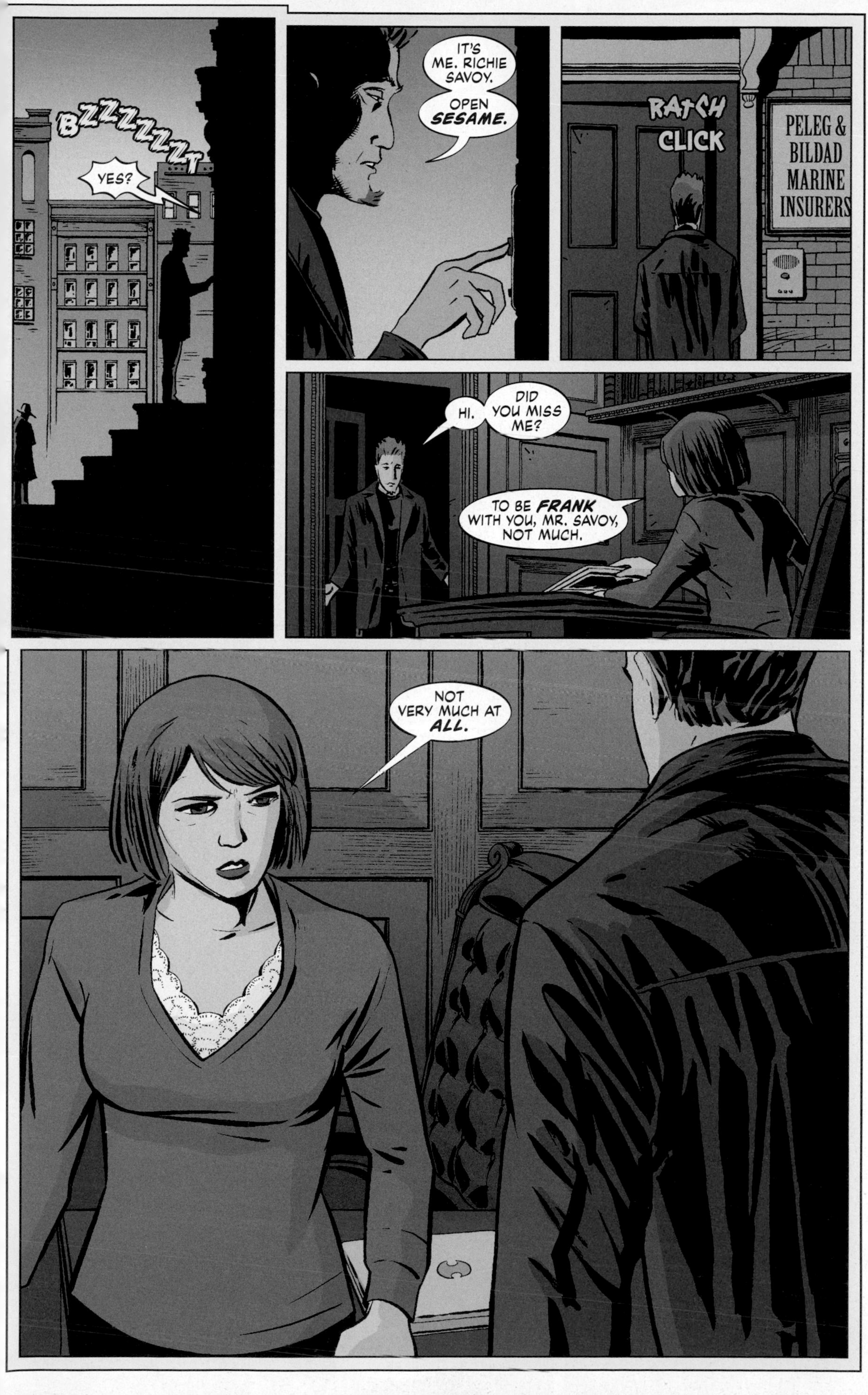
BZZZZZZZZT
YES?
IT'S ME. RICHIE SAVOY.
OPEN SESAME.
RATCH
CLICK
PELEG & BILDAD MARINE INSURERS
HI.
DID YOU MISS ME?
TO BE FRANK WITH YOU, MR. SAVOY, NOT MUCH.
NOT VERY MUCH AT ALL.

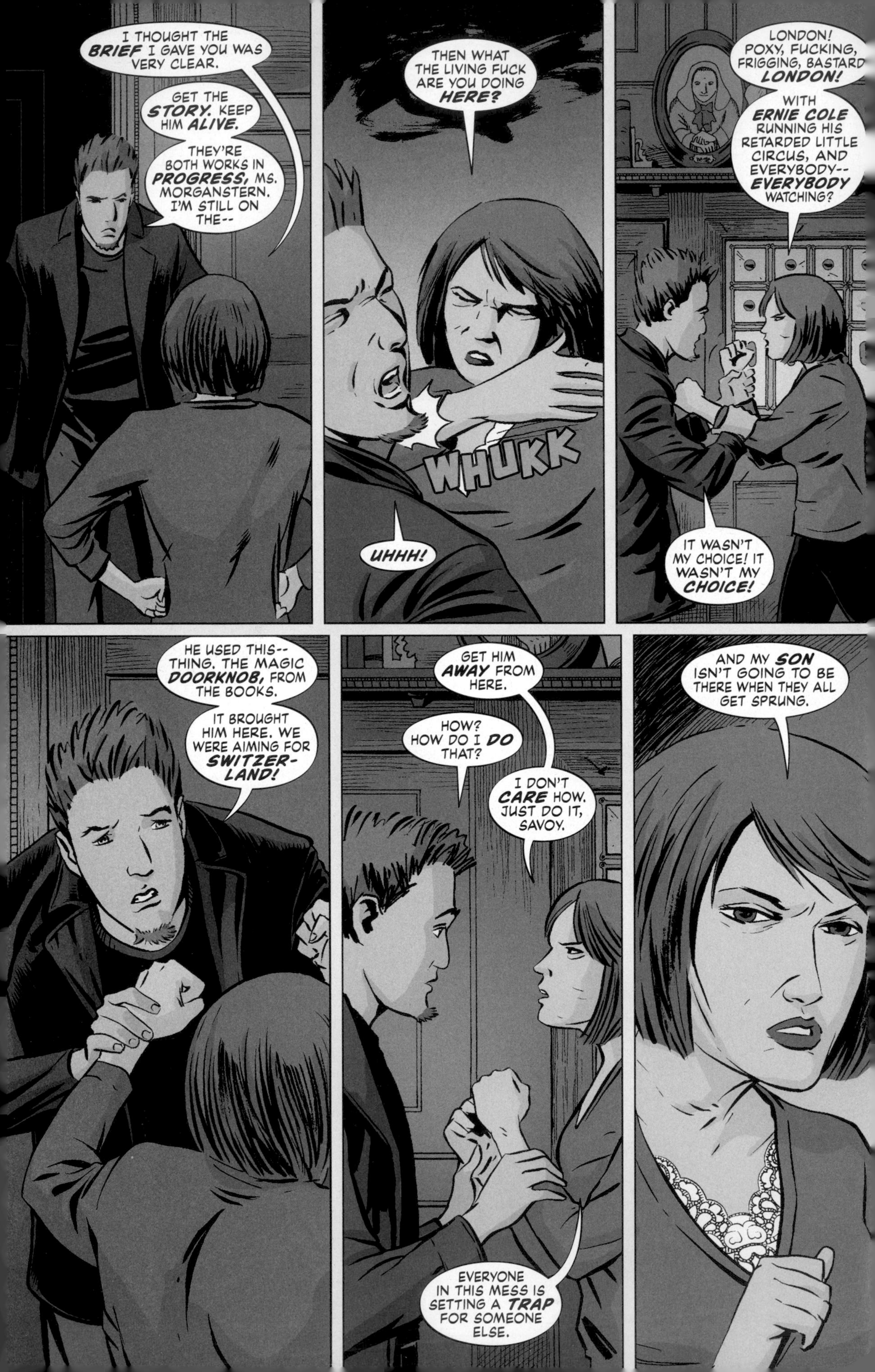
I THOUGHT THE BRIEF I GAVE YOU WAS VERY CLEAR.
GET THE STORY. KEEP HIM ALIVE.
THEY'RE BOTH WORKS IN PROGRESS, MS. MORGANSTERN. I'M STILL ON THE--
THEN WHAT THE LIVING FUCK ARE YOU DOING HERE?
WHUKK
UHHH!
LONDON! POXY, FUCKING, FRIGGING, BASTARD LONDON!
WITH ERNIE COLE RUNNING HIS RETARDED LITTLE CIRCUS, AND EVERYBODY-- EVERYBODY WATCHING?
IT WASN'T MY CHOICE! IT WASN'T MY CHOICE!
HE USED THIS-- THING. THE MAGIC DOORKNOB, FROM THE BOOKS.
IT BROUGHT HIM HERE. WE WERE AIMING FOR SWITZER-LAND!
GET HIM AWAY FROM HERE.
HOW? HOW DO I DO THAT?
I DON'T CARE HOW. JUST DO IT, SAVOY.
EVERYONE IN THIS MESS IS SETTING A TRAP FOR SOMEONE ELSE.
AND MY SON ISN'T GOING TO BE THERE WHEN THEY ALL GET SPRUNG.

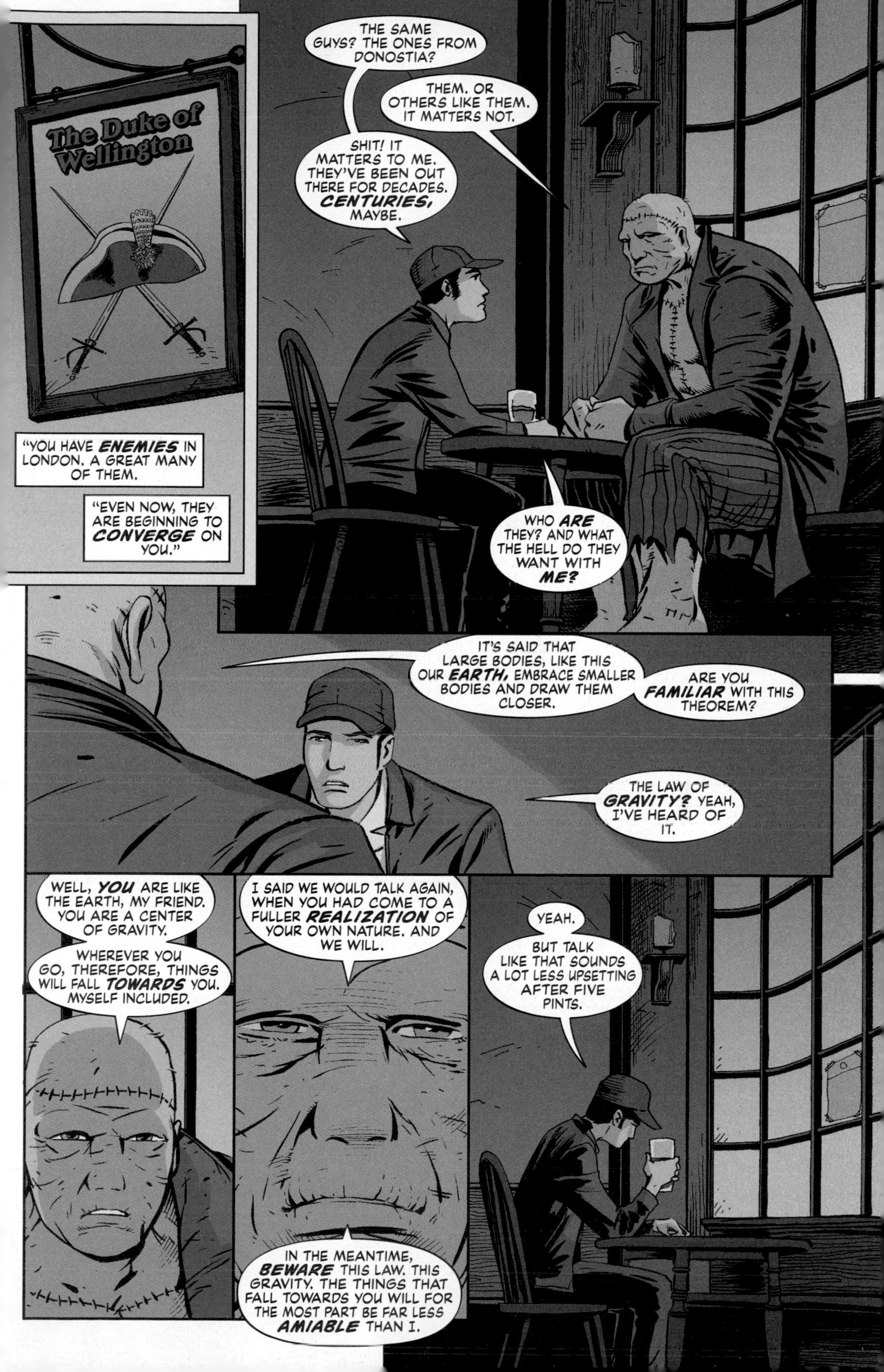
The Duke of Wellington
THE SAME GUYS? THE ONES FROM DONOSTIA?
THEM. OR OTHERS LIKE THEM. IT MATTERS NOT.
SHIT! IT MATTERS TO ME. THEY'VE BEEN OUT THERE FOR DECADES. CENTURIES, MAYBE.
"YOU HAVE ENEMIES IN LONDON. A GREAT MANY OF THEM.
"EVEN NOW, THEY ARE BEGINNING TO CONVERGE ON YOU."
WHO ARE THEY? AND WHAT THE HELL DO THEY WANT WITH ME?
IT'S SAID THAT LARGE BODIES, LIKE THIS OUR EARTH, EMBRACE SMALLER BODIES AND DRAW THEM CLOSER.
ARE YOU FAMILIAR WITH THIS THEOREM?
THE LAW OF GRAVITY? YEAH, I'VE HEARD OF IT.
WELL, YOU ARE LIKE THE EARTH, MY FRIEND. YOU ARE A CENTER OF GRAVITY.
WHEREVER YOU GO, THEREFORE, THINGS WILL FALL TOWARDS YOU. MYSELF INCLUDED.
I SAID WE WOULD TALK AGAIN, WHEN YOU HAD COME TO A FULLER REALIZATION OF YOUR OWN NATURE. AND WE WILL.
IN THE MEANTIME, BEWARE THIS LAW. THIS GRAVITY. THE THINGS THAT FALL TOWARDS YOU WILL FOR THE MOST PART BE FAR LESS AMIABLE THAN I.
YEAH.
BUT TALK LIKE THAT SOUNDS A LOT LESS UPSETTING AFTER FIVE PINTS.

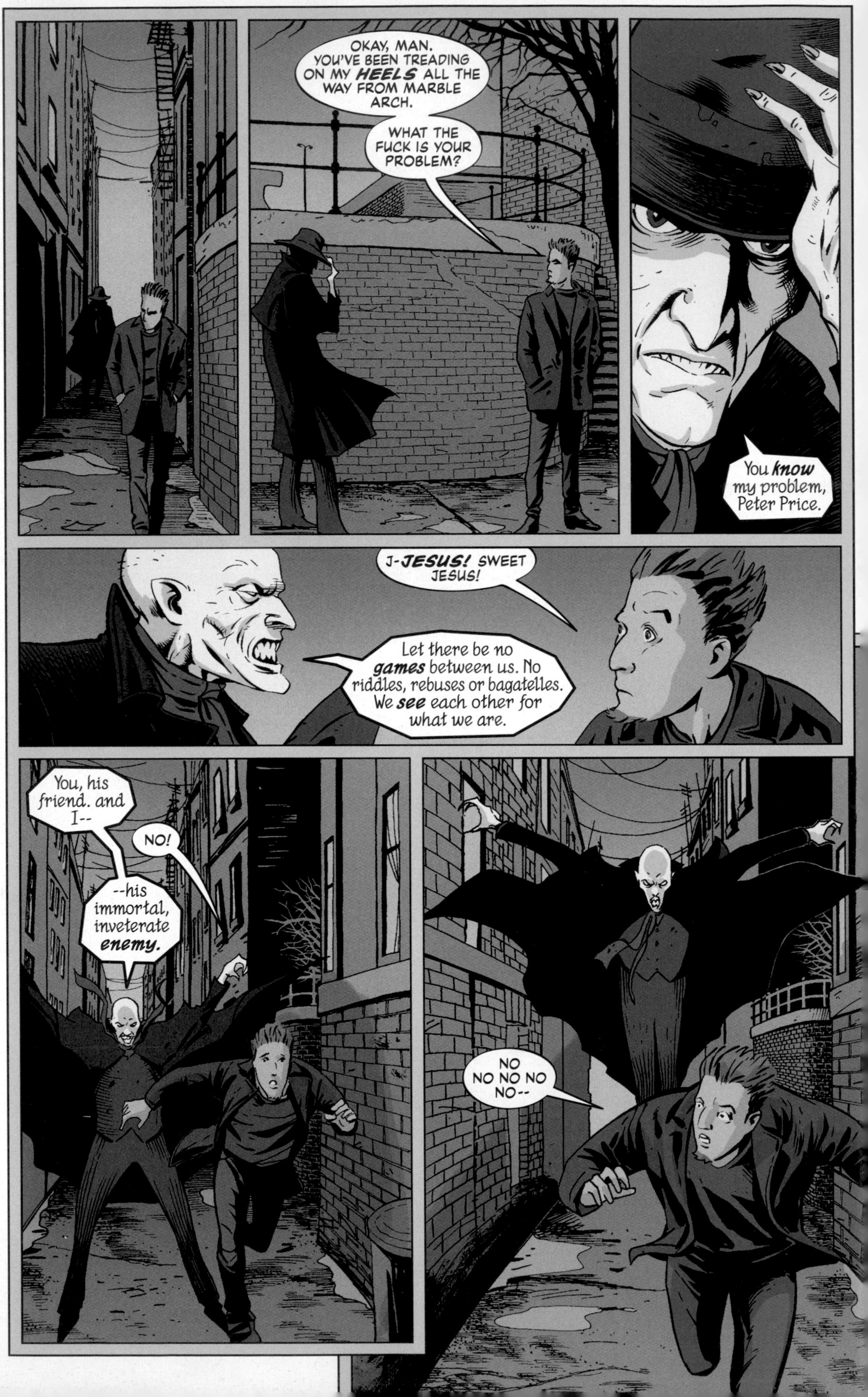
OKAY, MAN. YOU'VE BEEN TREADING ON MY HEELS ALL THE WAY FROM MARBLE ARCH.
WHAT THE FUCK IS YOUR PROBLEM?
You know my problem, Peter Price.
J-JESUS! SWEET JESUS!
Let there be no games between us. No riddles, rebuses or bagatelles. We see each other for what we are.
You, his friend. and I--
NO!
--his immortal, inveterate enemy.
NO NO NO NO NO--

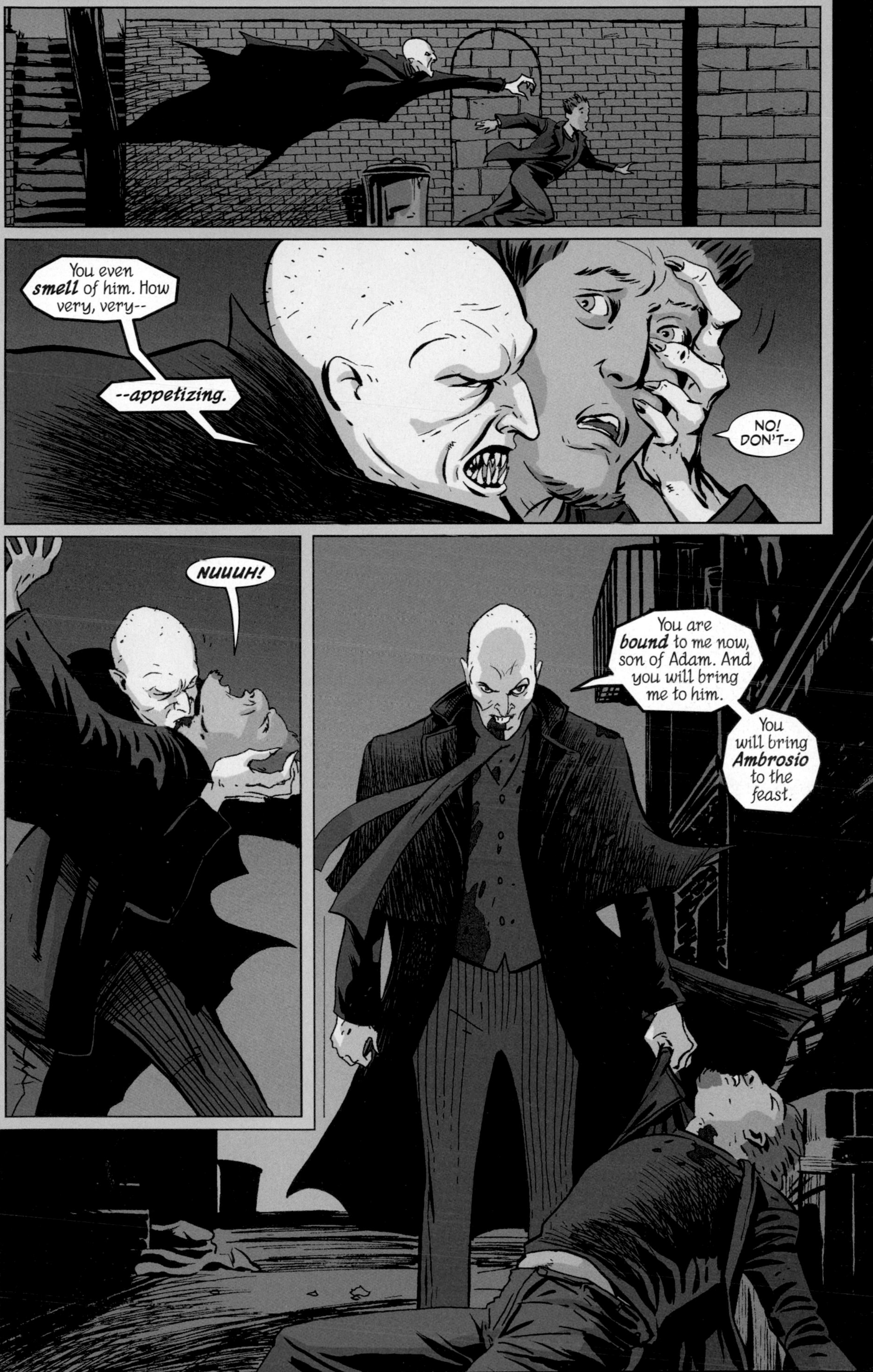
You even smell of him. How very, very--
--appetizing.
NO! DON'T--
NUUUH!
You are bound to me now, son of Adam. And you will bring me to him.
You will bring Ambrosio to the feast.

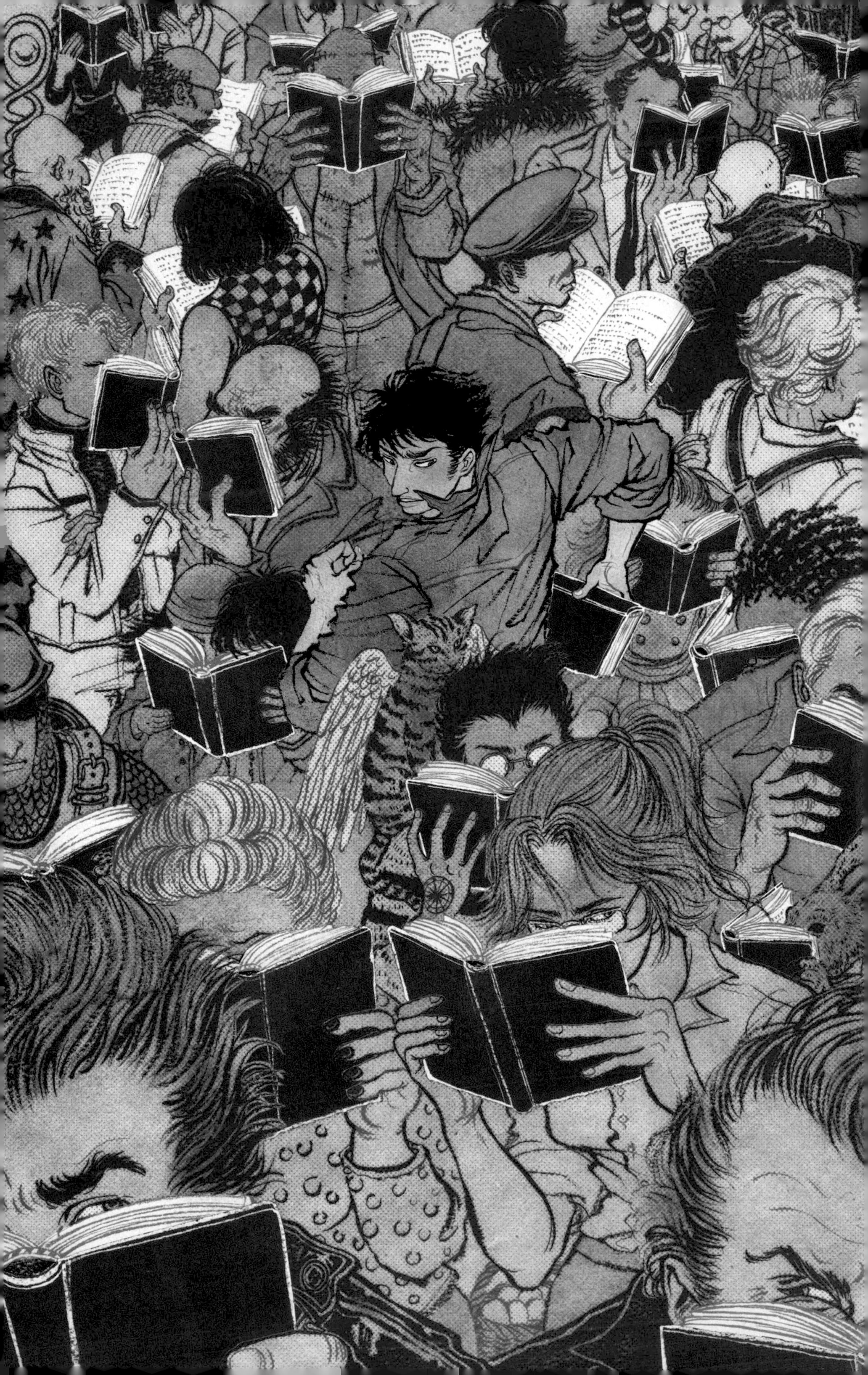

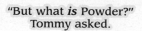
"But what *is* Powder?" Tommy asked.

The black runesword in his hand purred contentedly, its hunger for souls momentarily sated.

Lord Gabriel frowned austerely.

Powder, with a capital P, is the raw stuff of *sentience*, Master Taylor. Do they teach you *nothing* at Tulkinghorn's?

Not about *necromancy!*

Here. Look through the emerald *telescope,* if you dare.

Of all my *dark materials,* it's the one that most readily surrenders its secrets.

Aristide

You'd better not.

Wouldn't advise it.

Bad idea.

Wuff.

What did that *dog* just say?

He said "wuff." What did you *expect?*

The telescope, Tommy Taylor. There's no going *back* now. Take it and see.

Or else try your black sword against my blade of *subtlety.*

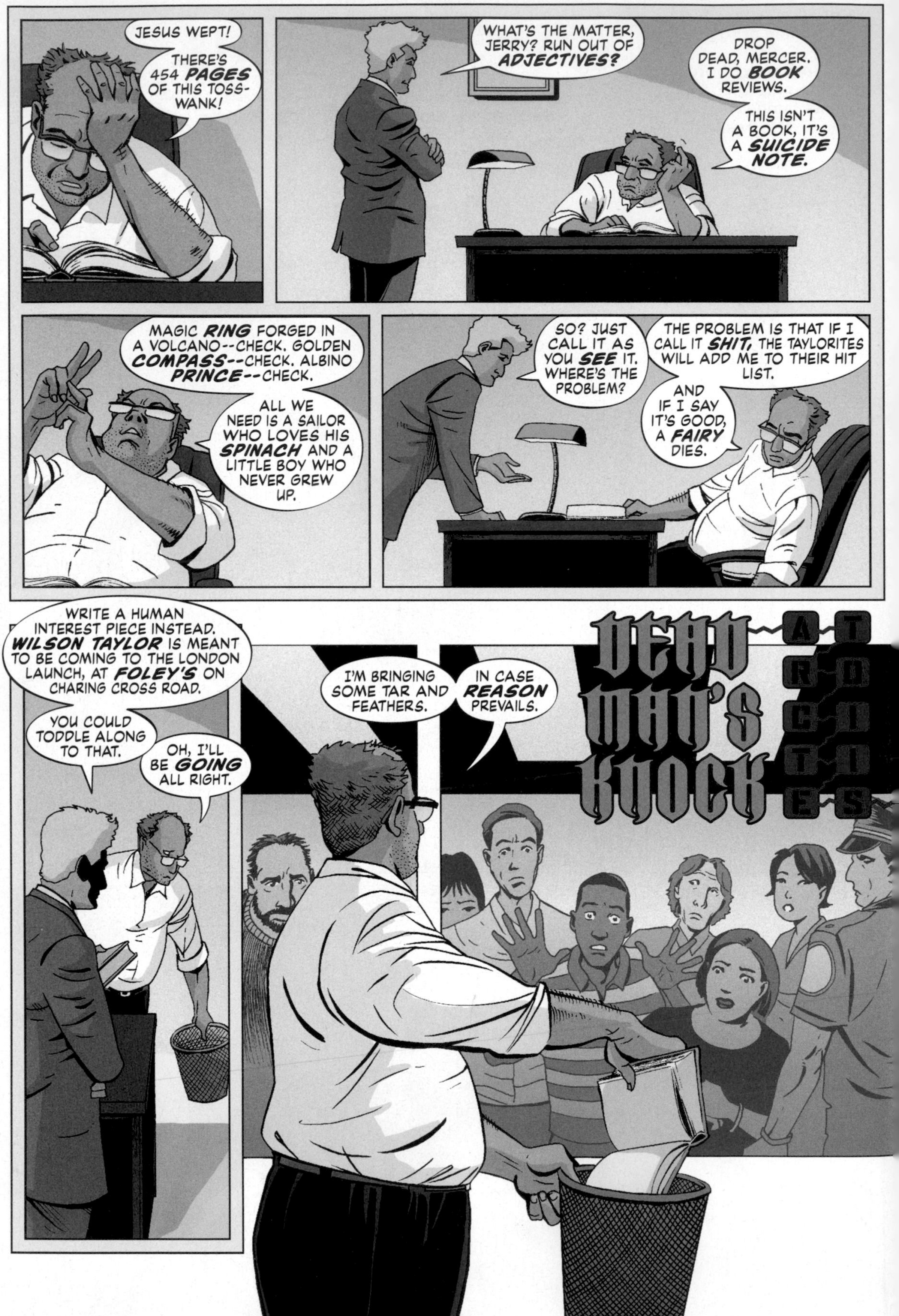
JESUS WEPT!
THERE'S 454 PAGES OF THIS TOSS-WANK!
WHAT'S THE MATTER, JERRY? RUN OUT OF ADJECTIVES?
DROP DEAD, MERCER. I DO BOOK REVIEWS.
THIS ISN'T A BOOK, IT'S A SUICIDE NOTE.
MAGIC RING FORGED IN A VOLCANO--CHECK. GOLDEN COMPASS--CHECK. ALBINO PRINCE--CHECK.
ALL WE NEED IS A SAILOR WHO LOVES HIS SPINACH AND A LITTLE BOY WHO NEVER GREW UP.
SO? JUST CALL IT AS YOU SEE IT. WHERE'S THE PROBLEM?
THE PROBLEM IS THAT IF I CALL IT SHIT, THE TAYLORITES WILL ADD ME TO THEIR HIT LIST.
AND IF I SAY IT'S GOOD, A FAIRY DIES.
WRITE A HUMAN INTEREST PIECE INSTEAD. WILSON TAYLOR IS MEANT TO BE COMING TO THE LONDON LAUNCH, AT FOLEY'S ON CHARING CROSS ROAD.
YOU COULD TODDLE ALONG TO THAT.
OH, I'LL BE GOING ALL RIGHT.
I'M BRINGING SOME TAR AND FEATHERS.
IN CASE REASON PREVAILS.
DEAD MAN'S KNOCK

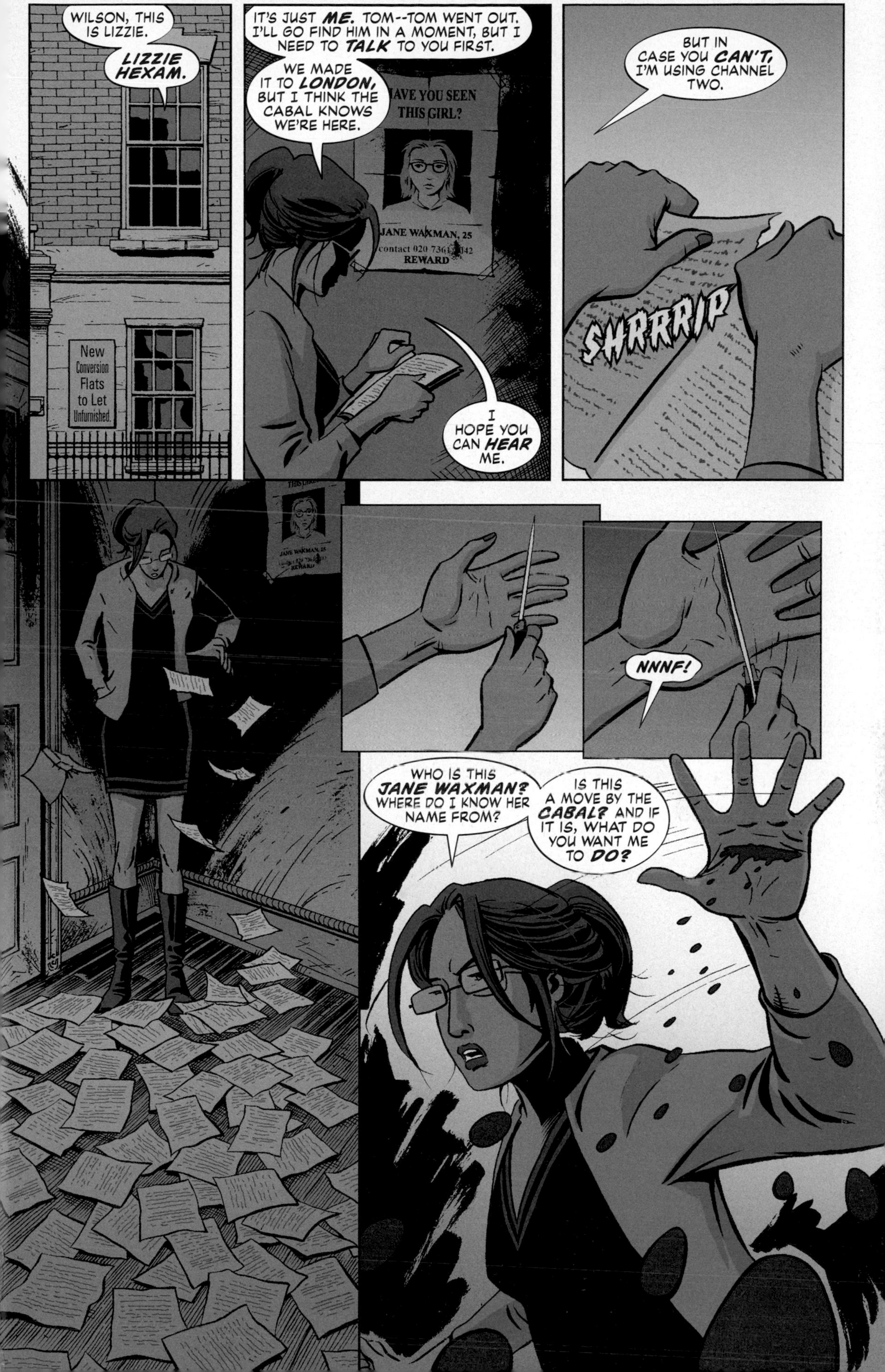
WILSON, THIS IS LIZZIE.
LIZZIE HEXAM.
New Conversion Flats to Let Unfurnished.
IT'S JUST ME. TOM--TOM WENT OUT. I'LL GO FIND HIM IN A MOMENT, BUT I NEED TO TALK TO YOU FIRST.
WE MADE IT TO LONDON, BUT I THINK THE CABAL KNOWS WE'RE HERE.
HAVE YOU SEEN THIS GIRL?
JANE WAXMAN, 25
REWARD
I HOPE YOU CAN HEAR ME.
BUT IN CASE YOU CAN'T, I'M USING CHANNEL TWO.
SHRRRIP
NNNF!
WHO IS THIS JANE WAXMAN? WHERE DO I KNOW HER NAME FROM?
IS THIS A MOVE BY THE CABAL? AND IF IT IS, WHAT DO YOU WANT ME TO DO?

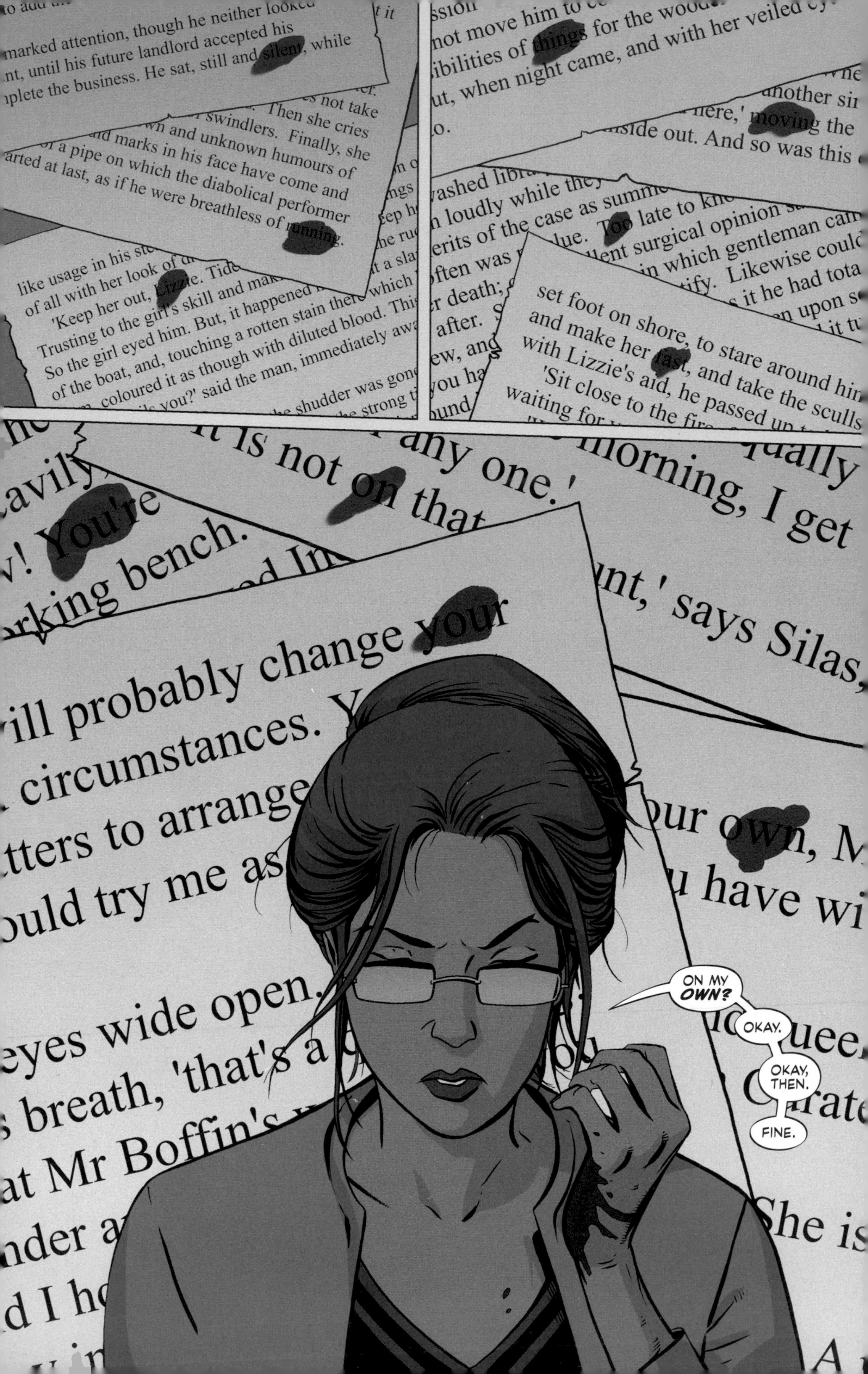
ON MY OWN?
OKAY.
OKAY, THEN.
FINE.

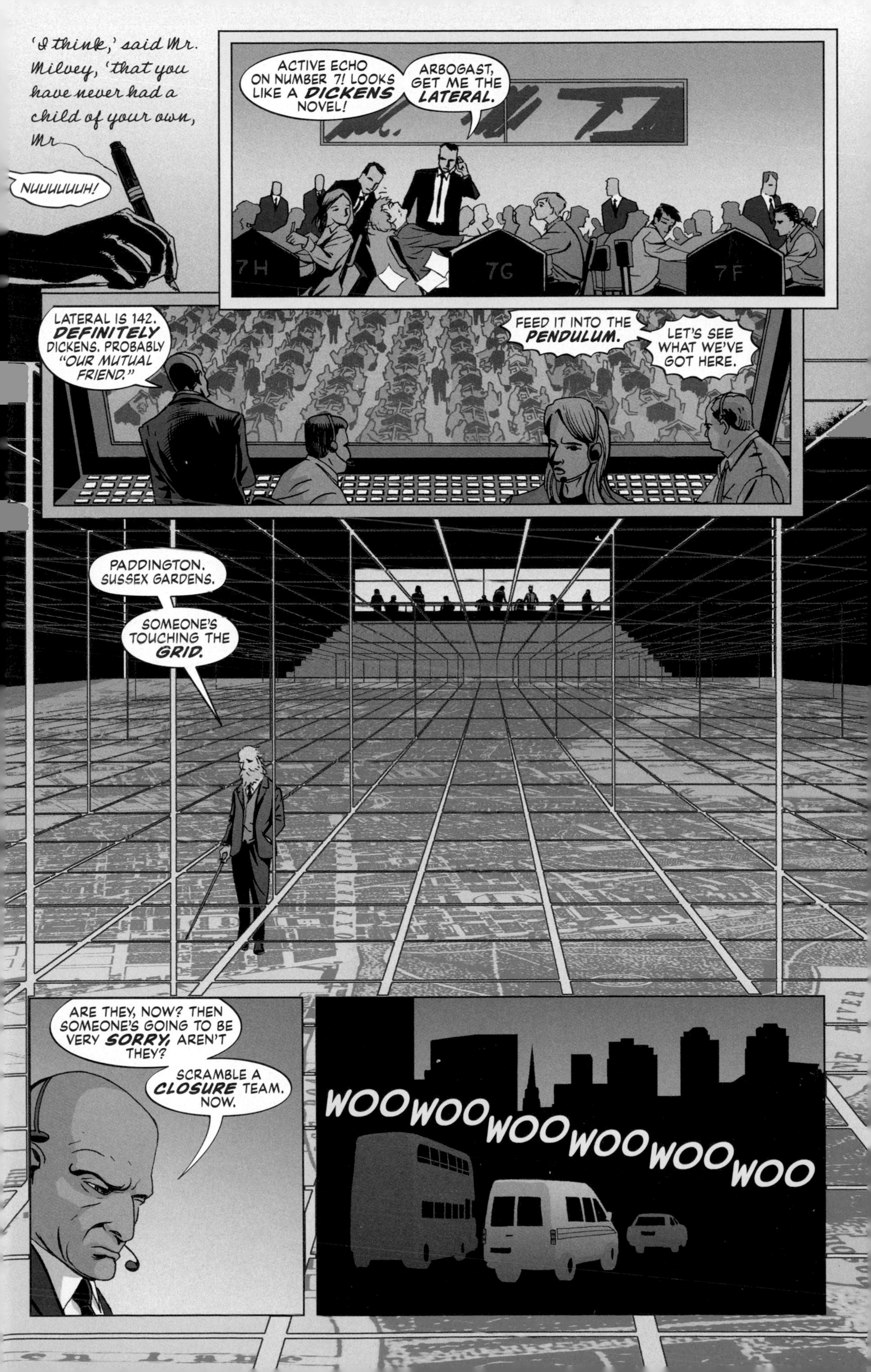
'I think,' said Mr. Milvey, 'that you have never had a child of your own, Mr
NUUUUUUH!
ACTIVE ECHO ON NUMBER 7! LOOKS LIKE A DICKENS NOVEL!
ARBOGAST, GET ME THE LATERAL.
7H
7G
7F
LATERAL IS 142. DEFINITELY DICKENS. PROBABLY "OUR MUTUAL FRIEND."
FEED IT INTO THE PENDULUM.
LET'S SEE WHAT WE'VE GOT HERE.
PADDINGTON. SUSSEX GARDENS.
SOMEONE'S TOUCHING THE GRID.
ARE THEY, NOW? THEN SOMEONE'S GOING TO BE VERY SORRY, AREN'T THEY?
SCRAMBLE A CLOSURE TEAM. NOW.
WOOWOOWOOWOOWOOWOO

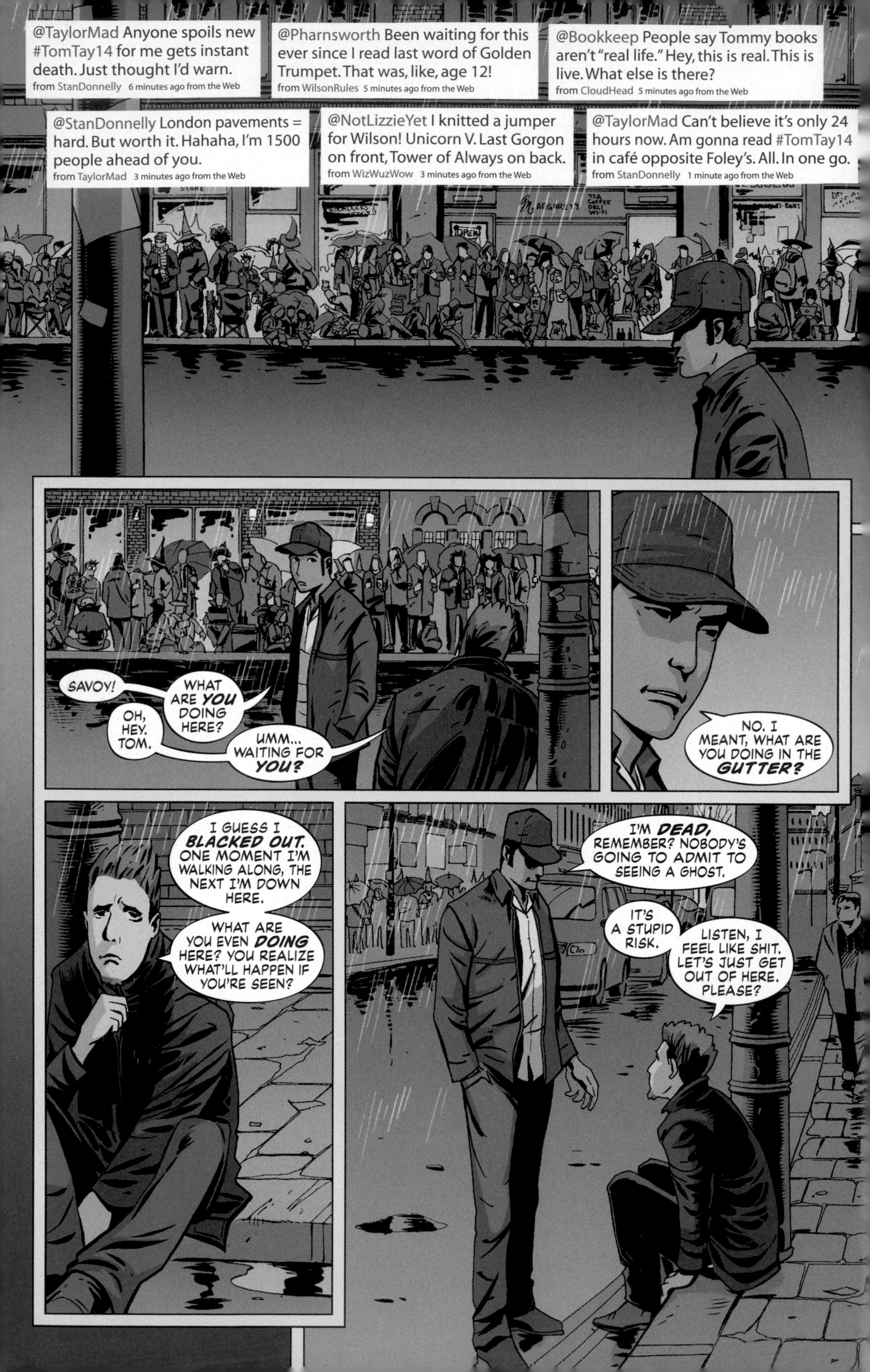

@TaylorMad Anyone spoils new #TomTay14 for me gets instant death. Just thought I'd warn.
from StanDonnelly 6 minutes ago from the Web
@Pharnsworth Been waiting for this ever since I read last word of Golden Trumpet. That was, like, age 12!
from WilsonRules 5 minutes ago from the Web
@Bookkeep People say Tommy books aren't "real life." Hey, this is real. This is live. What else is there?
from CloudHead 5 minutes ago from the Web
@StanDonnelly London pavements = hard. But worth it. Hahaha, I'm 1500 people ahead of you.
from TaylorMad 3 minutes ago from the Web
@NotLizzieYet I knitted a jumper for Wilson! Unicorn V. Last Gorgon on front, Tower of Always on back.
from WizWuzWow 3 minutes ago from the Web
@TaylorMad Can't believe it's only 24 hours now. Am gonna read #TomTay14 in café opposite Foley's. All. In one go.
from StanDonnelly 1 minute ago from the Web
SAVOY!
WHAT ARE *YOU* DOING HERE?
OH, HEY. TOM.
UMM... WAITING FOR *YOU?*
NO. I MEANT, WHAT ARE YOU DOING IN THE *GUTTER?*
I GUESS I *BLACKED OUT.* ONE MOMENT I'M WALKING ALONG, THE NEXT I'M DOWN HERE.
WHAT ARE YOU EVEN *DOING* HERE? YOU REALIZE WHAT'LL HAPPEN IF YOU'RE SEEN?
I'M *DEAD,* REMEMBER? NOBODY'S GOING TO ADMIT TO SEEING A GHOST.
IT'S A STUPID RISK.
LISTEN, I FEEL LIKE SHIT. LET'S JUST GET OUT OF HERE. PLEASE?

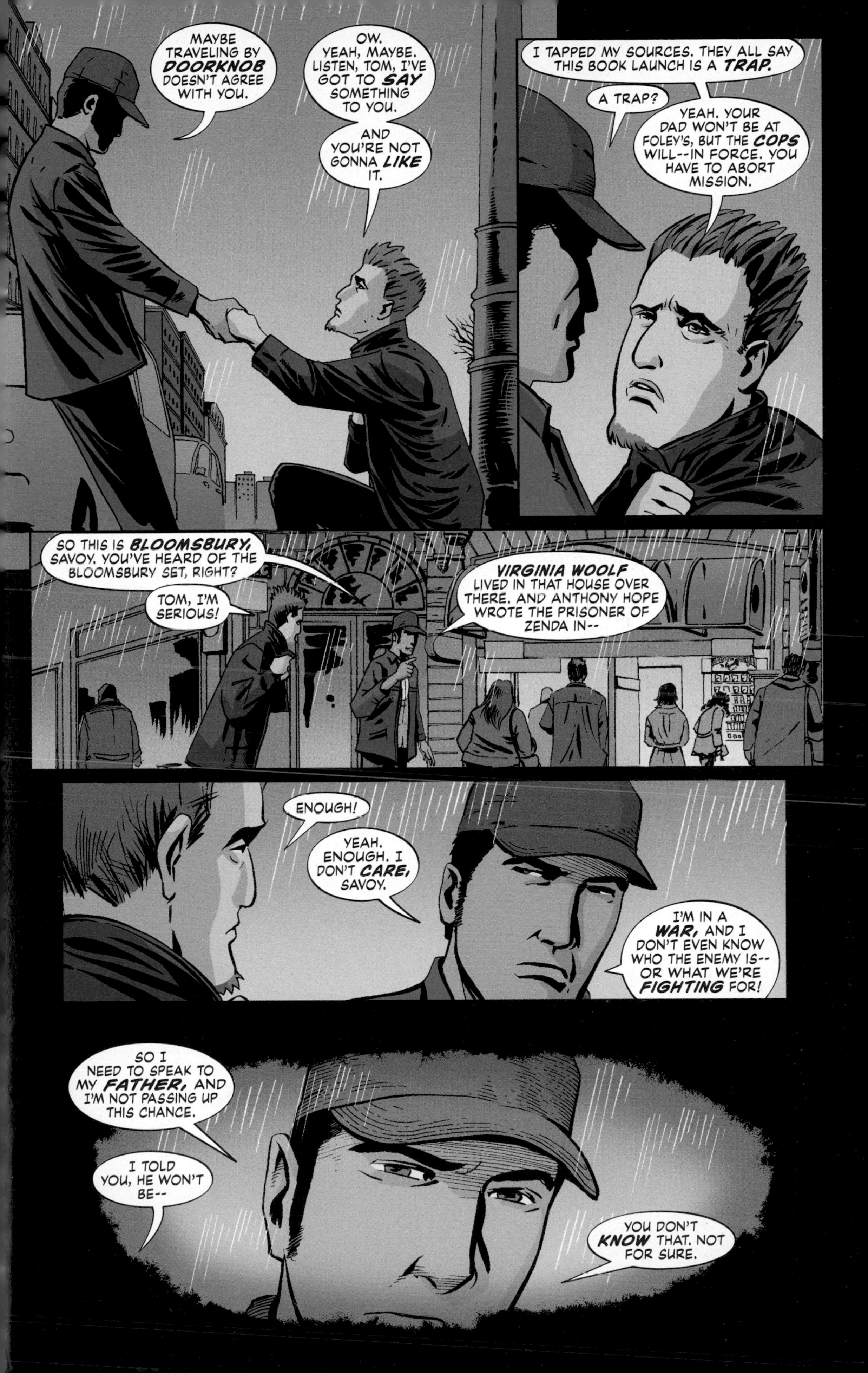
MAYBE TRAVELING BY DOORKNOB DOESN'T AGREE WITH YOU.
OW. YEAH, MAYBE. LISTEN, TOM, I'VE GOT TO SAY SOMETHING TO YOU.
AND YOU'RE NOT GONNA LIKE IT.
I TAPPED MY SOURCES. THEY ALL SAY THIS BOOK LAUNCH IS A TRAP.
A TRAP?
YEAH. YOUR DAD WON'T BE AT FOLEY'S, BUT THE COPS WILL--IN FORCE. YOU HAVE TO ABORT MISSION.
SO THIS IS BLOOMSBURY, SAVOY. YOU'VE HEARD OF THE BLOOMSBURY SET, RIGHT?
TOM, I'M SERIOUS!
VIRGINIA WOOLF LIVED IN THAT HOUSE OVER THERE. AND ANTHONY HOPE WROTE THE PRISONER OF ZENDA IN--
ENOUGH!
YEAH. ENOUGH. I DON'T CARE, SAVOY.
I'M IN A WAR, AND I DON'T EVEN KNOW WHO THE ENEMY IS--OR WHAT WE'RE FIGHTING FOR!
SO I NEED TO SPEAK TO MY FATHER, AND I'M NOT PASSING UP THIS CHANCE.
I TOLD YOU, HE WON'T BE--
YOU DON'T KNOW THAT. NOT FOR SURE.

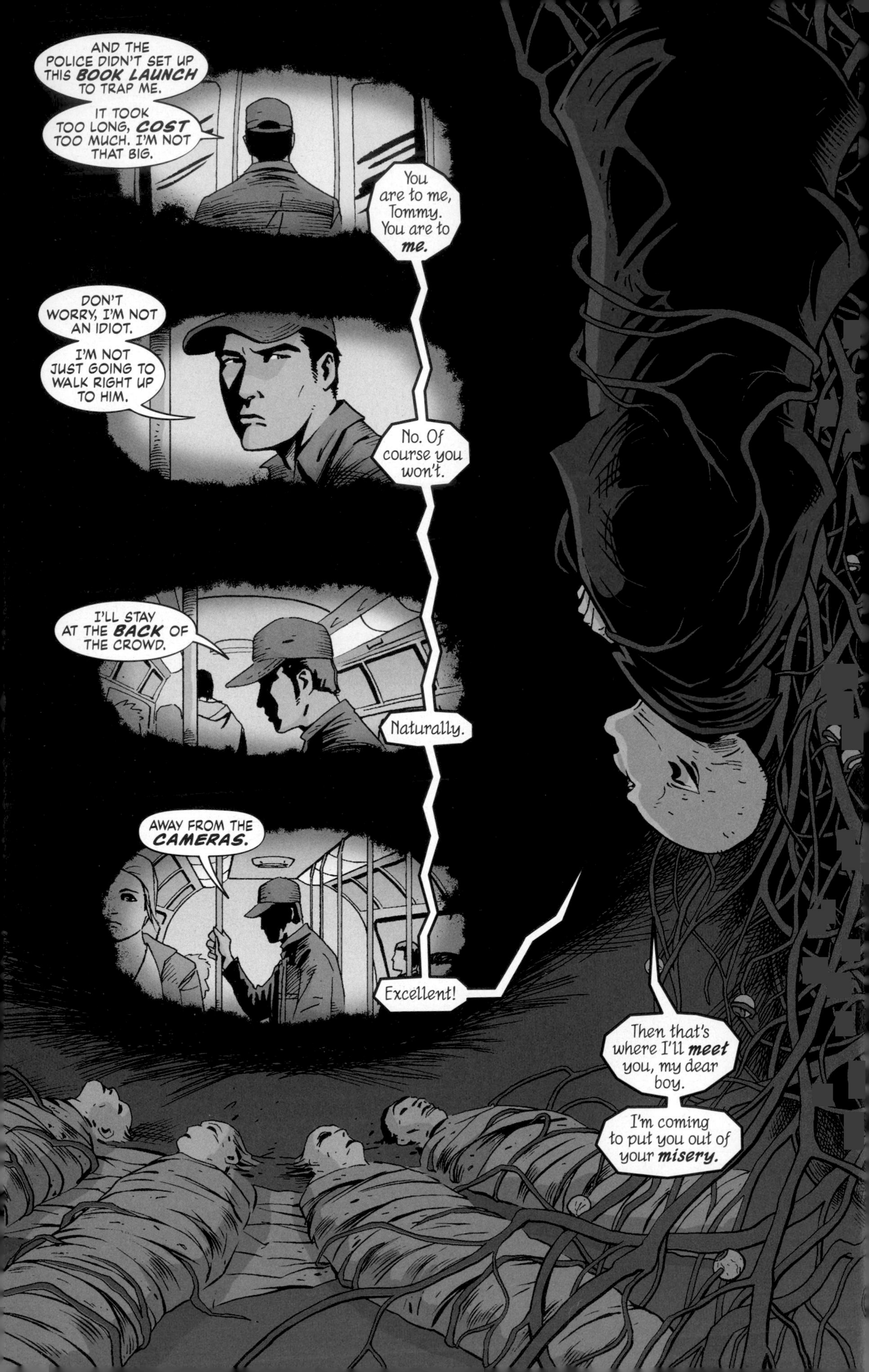
AND THE POLICE DIDN'T SET UP THIS BOOK LAUNCH TO TRAP ME.
IT TOOK TOO LONG, COST TOO MUCH. I'M NOT THAT BIG.
You are to me, Tommy. You are to me.
DON'T WORRY, I'M NOT AN IDIOT.
I'M NOT JUST GOING TO WALK RIGHT UP TO HIM.
No. Of course you won't.
I'LL STAY AT THE BACK OF THE CROWD.
Naturally.
AWAY FROM THE CAMERAS.
Excellent!
Then that's where I'll meet you, my dear boy.
I'm coming to put you out of your misery.

IF WILSON **DOES** SHOW UP, CAN YOU IMAGINE IT? IT'LL BE LIKE THE SECOND COMING OF **CHRIST.**

DNN WILSON'S BACK!
PUBLISHER CONFIRMS TAYLOR APPEARANCE
NN UNEMPLOYMENT REACHES ALL TIME HIGH IN M

SO WHAT DO YOU THINK?

I THINK YOU LOOK TEN YEARS **OLDER** UNDER A STRIP LIGHT.

CLICK

GIL, I'M SERIOUS.

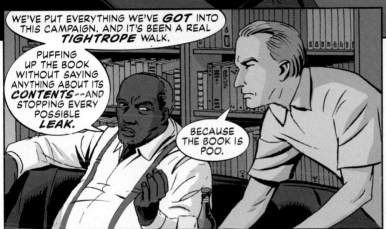

WE'VE PUT EVERYTHING WE'VE **GOT** INTO THIS CAMPAIGN. AND IT'S BEEN A REAL **TIGHTROPE** WALK.

PUFFING UP THE BOOK WITHOUT SAYING ANYTHING ABOUT ITS **CONTENTS**--AND STOPPING EVERY POSSIBLE **LEAK.**

BECAUSE THE BOOK IS POO.

OH, THAT DOESN'T **BEGIN** TO DESCRIBE IT.

AND IT'S NOT WRITTEN BY **WILSON.**

IT'S...NOT IN HIS **USUAL** STYLE.

IT'S FUNNY. I NEVER **THOUGHT** YOU WERE ABOUT THE BOTTOM LINE, ERNIE.

AFTER EIGHT YEARS, YOU CAN STILL **SURPRISE** ME.

IT'S NOT JUST ABOUT THE **MONEY,** GIL. THERE ARE OTHER FACTORS INVOLVED.

OF COURSE.

AND THE WHOLE **BOARD** GOT TO VOTE ON--

I HAVE TO GO WALK KUB. YOU **FORGOT** YESTERDAY.

CHRIST.

I'LL BE SO **GLAD** WHEN THIS IS OVER.

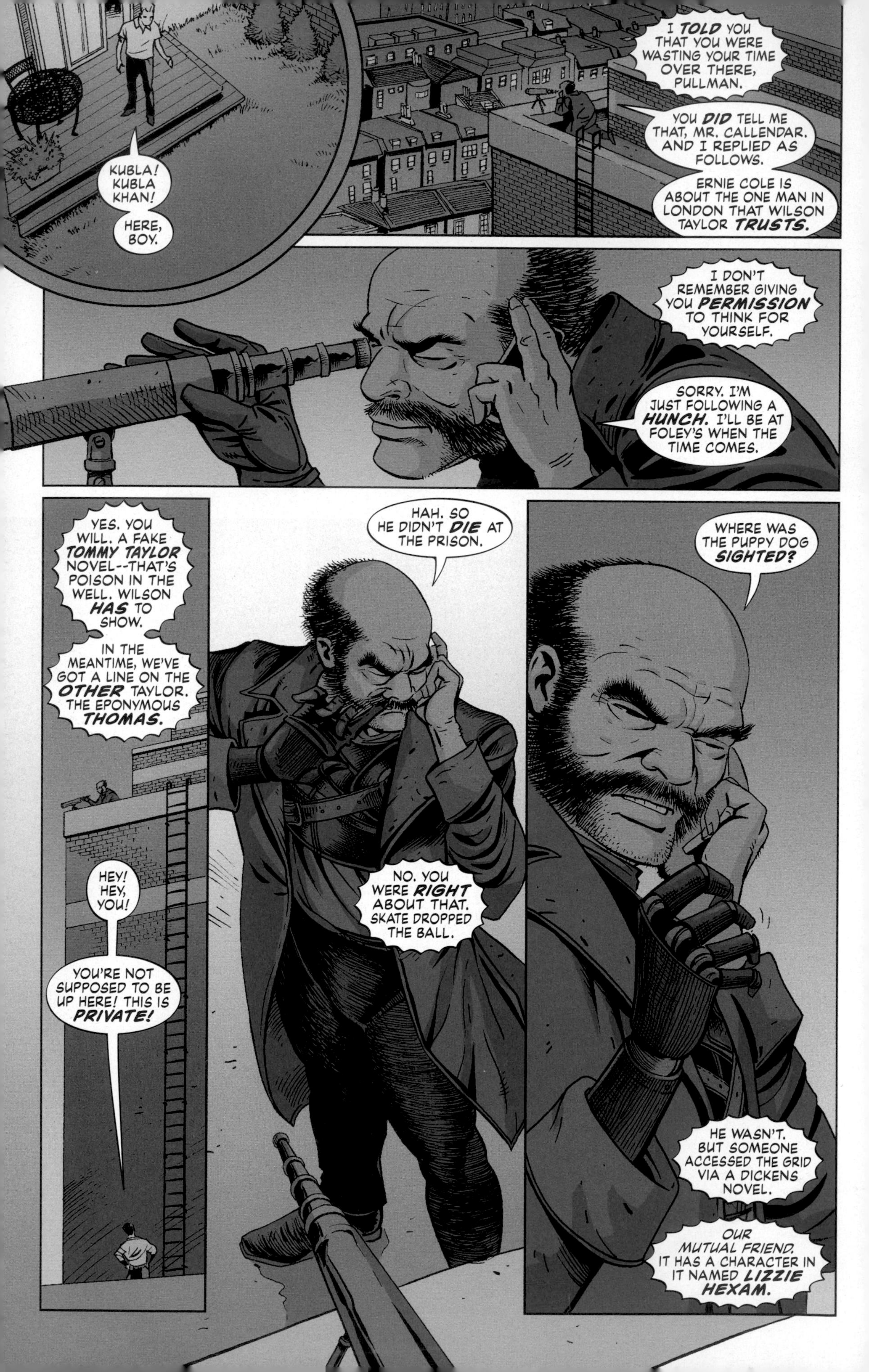
KUBLA! KUBLA KHAN!
HERE, BOY.
I TOLD YOU THAT YOU WERE WASTING YOUR TIME OVER THERE, PULLMAN.
YOU DID TELL ME THAT, MR. CALLENDAR. AND I REPLIED AS FOLLOWS.
ERNIE COLE IS ABOUT THE ONE MAN IN LONDON THAT WILSON TAYLOR TRUSTS.
I DON'T REMEMBER GIVING YOU PERMISSION TO THINK FOR YOURSELF.
SORRY. I'M JUST FOLLOWING A HUNCH. I'LL BE AT FOLEY'S WHEN THE TIME COMES.
YES. YOU WILL. A FAKE TOMMY TAYLOR NOVEL--THAT'S POISON IN THE WELL. WILSON HAS TO SHOW.
IN THE MEANTIME, WE'VE GOT A LINE ON THE OTHER TAYLOR. THE EPONYMOUS THOMAS.
HEY! HEY, YOU!
YOU'RE NOT SUPPOSED TO BE UP HERE! THIS IS PRIVATE!
HAH. SO HE DIDN'T DIE AT THE PRISON.
NO. YOU WERE RIGHT ABOUT THAT. SKATE DROPPED THE BALL.
WHERE WAS THE PUPPY DOG SIGHTED?
HE WASN'T. BUT SOMEONE ACCESSED THE GRID VIA A DICKENS NOVEL.
OUR MUTUAL FRIEND. IT HAS A CHARACTER IN IT NAMED LIZZIE HEXAM.

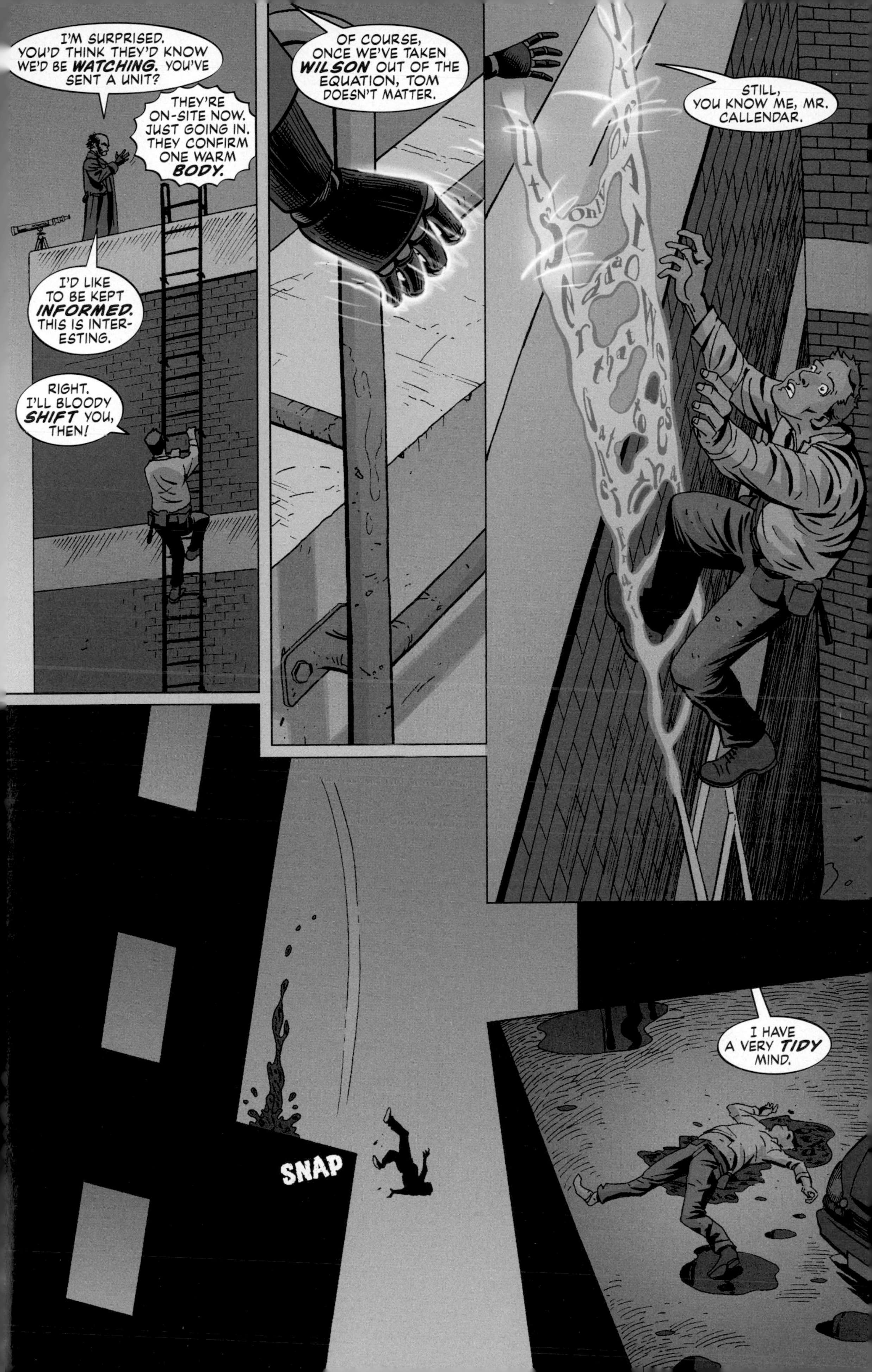
I'M SURPRISED. YOU'D THINK THEY'D KNOW WE'D BE WATCHING. YOU'VE SENT A UNIT?
THEY'RE ON-SITE NOW. JUST GOING IN. THEY CONFIRM ONE WARM BODY.
I'D LIKE TO BE KEPT INFORMED. THIS IS INTER-ESTING.
RIGHT. I'LL BLOODY SHIFT YOU, THEN!
OF COURSE, ONCE WE'VE TAKEN WILSON OUT OF THE EQUATION, TOM DOESN'T MATTER.
STILL, YOU KNOW ME, MR. CALLENDAR.
SNAP
I HAVE A VERY TIDY MIND.

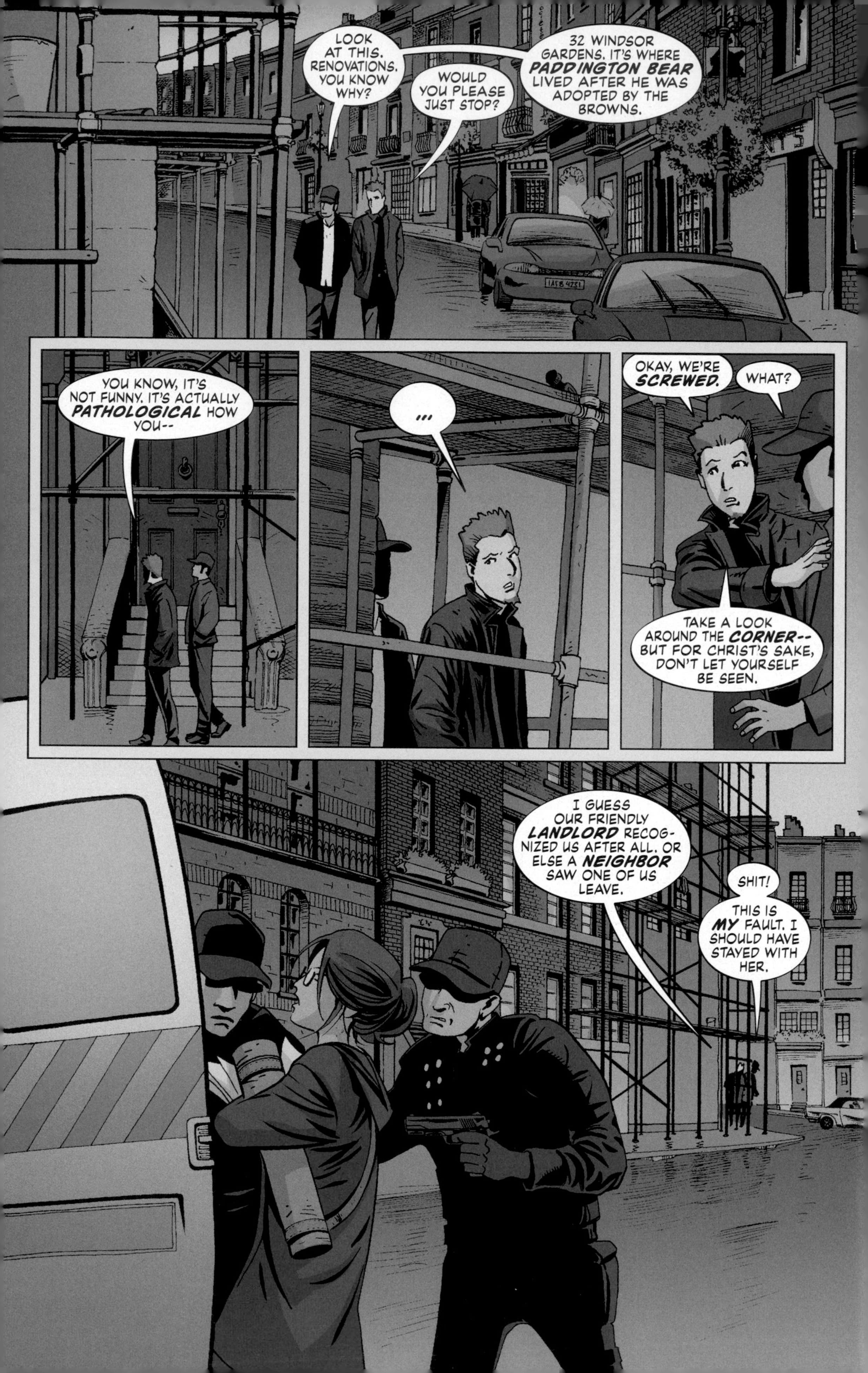
LOOK AT THIS. RENOVATIONS. YOU KNOW WHY?
32 WINDSOR GARDENS. IT'S WHERE PADDINGTON BEAR LIVED AFTER HE WAS ADOPTED BY THE BROWNS.
WOULD YOU PLEASE JUST STOP?
YOU KNOW, IT'S NOT FUNNY. IT'S ACTUALLY PATHOLOGICAL HOW YOU--
...
OKAY, WE'RE SCREWED.
WHAT?
TAKE A LOOK AROUND THE CORNER-- BUT FOR CHRIST'S SAKE, DON'T LET YOURSELF BE SEEN.
I GUESS OUR FRIENDLY LANDLORD RECOGNIZED US AFTER ALL. OR ELSE A NEIGHBOR SAW ONE OF US LEAVE.
SHIT!
THIS IS MY FAULT. I SHOULD HAVE STAYED WITH HER.

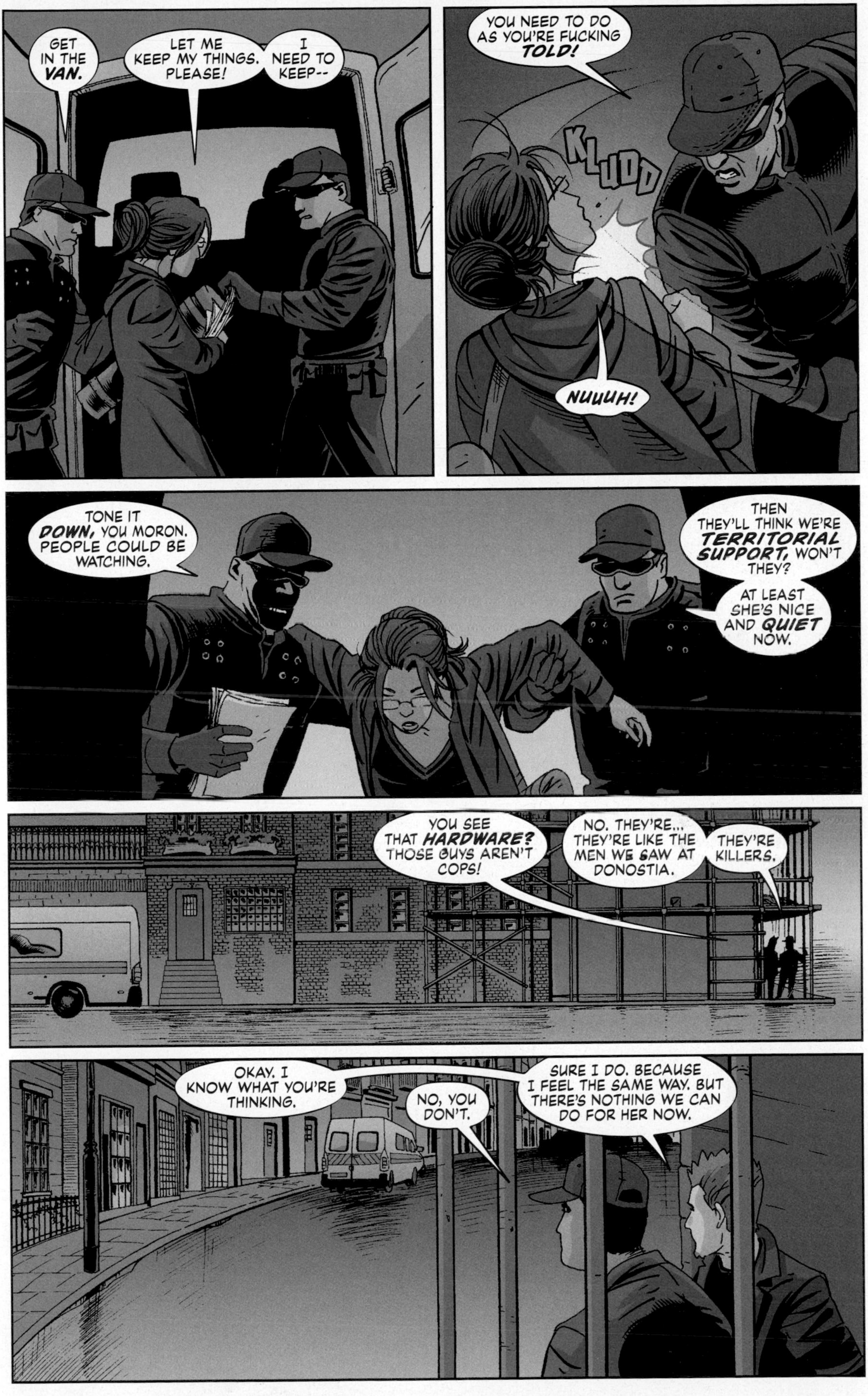

GET IN THE VAN.
LET ME KEEP MY THINGS. PLEASE!
I NEED TO KEEP--
YOU NEED TO DO AS YOU'RE FUCKING TOLD!
KLUDD
NUUUH!
TONE IT DOWN, YOU MORON. PEOPLE COULD BE WATCHING.
THEN THEY'LL THINK WE'RE TERRITORIAL SUPPORT, WON'T THEY?
AT LEAST SHE'S NICE AND QUIET NOW.
YOU SEE THAT HARDWARE? THOSE GUYS AREN'T COPS!
NO. THEY'RE... THEY'RE LIKE THE MEN WE SAW AT DONOSTIA.
THEY'RE KILLERS.
OKAY. I KNOW WHAT YOU'RE THINKING.
NO, YOU DON'T.
SURE I DO. BECAUSE I FEEL THE SAME WAY. BUT THERE'S NOTHING WE CAN DO FOR HER NOW.

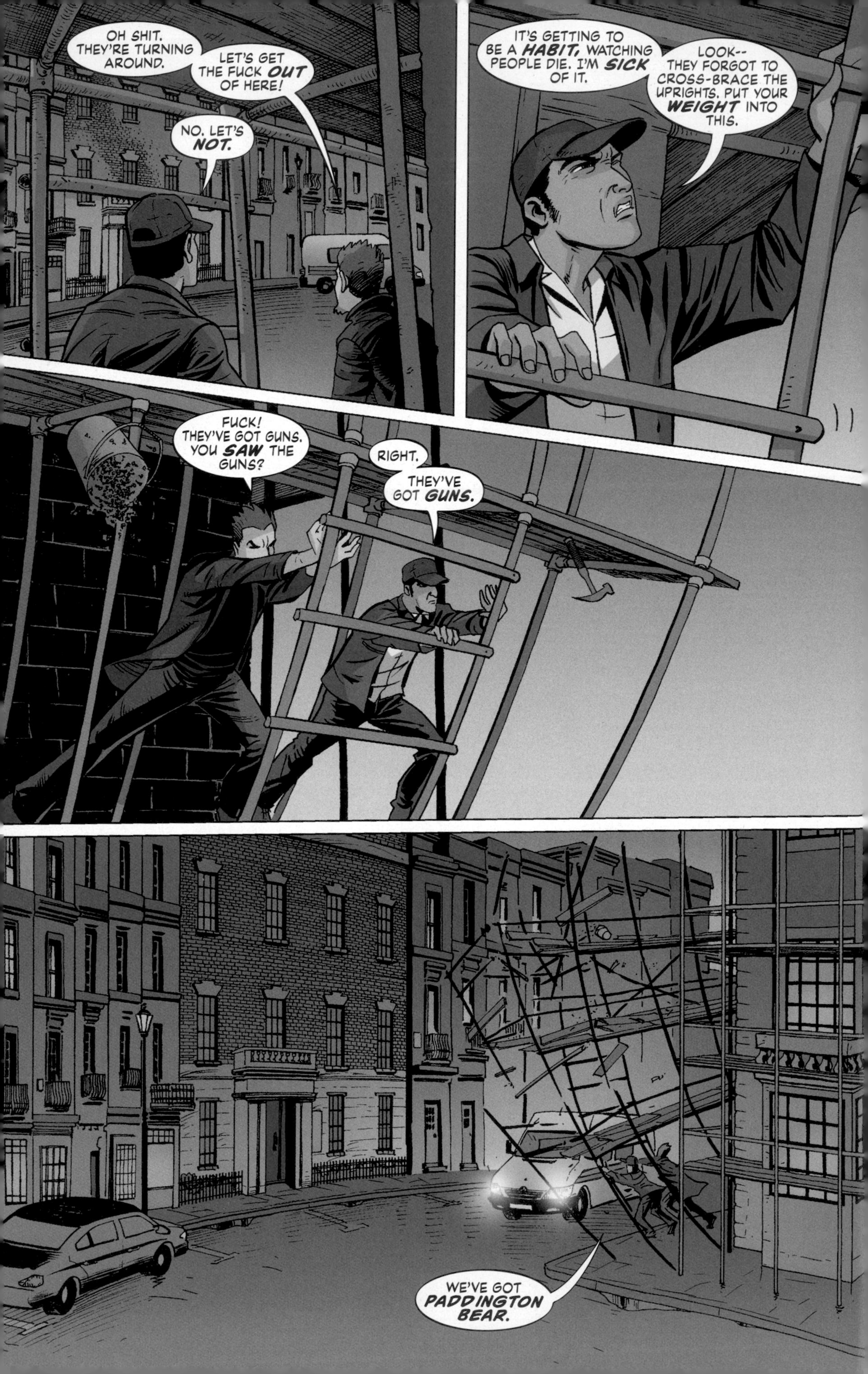
OH SHIT. THEY'RE TURNING AROUND.
LET'S GET THE FUCK OUT OF HERE!
NO. LET'S NOT.
IT'S GETTING TO BE A HABIT, WATCHING PEOPLE DIE. I'M SICK OF IT.
LOOK-- THEY FORGOT TO CROSS-BRACE THE UPRIGHTS. PUT YOUR WEIGHT INTO THIS.
FUCK! THEY'VE GOT GUNS. YOU SAW THE GUNS?
RIGHT.
THEY'VE GOT GUNS.
WE'VE GOT PADDINGTON BEAR.

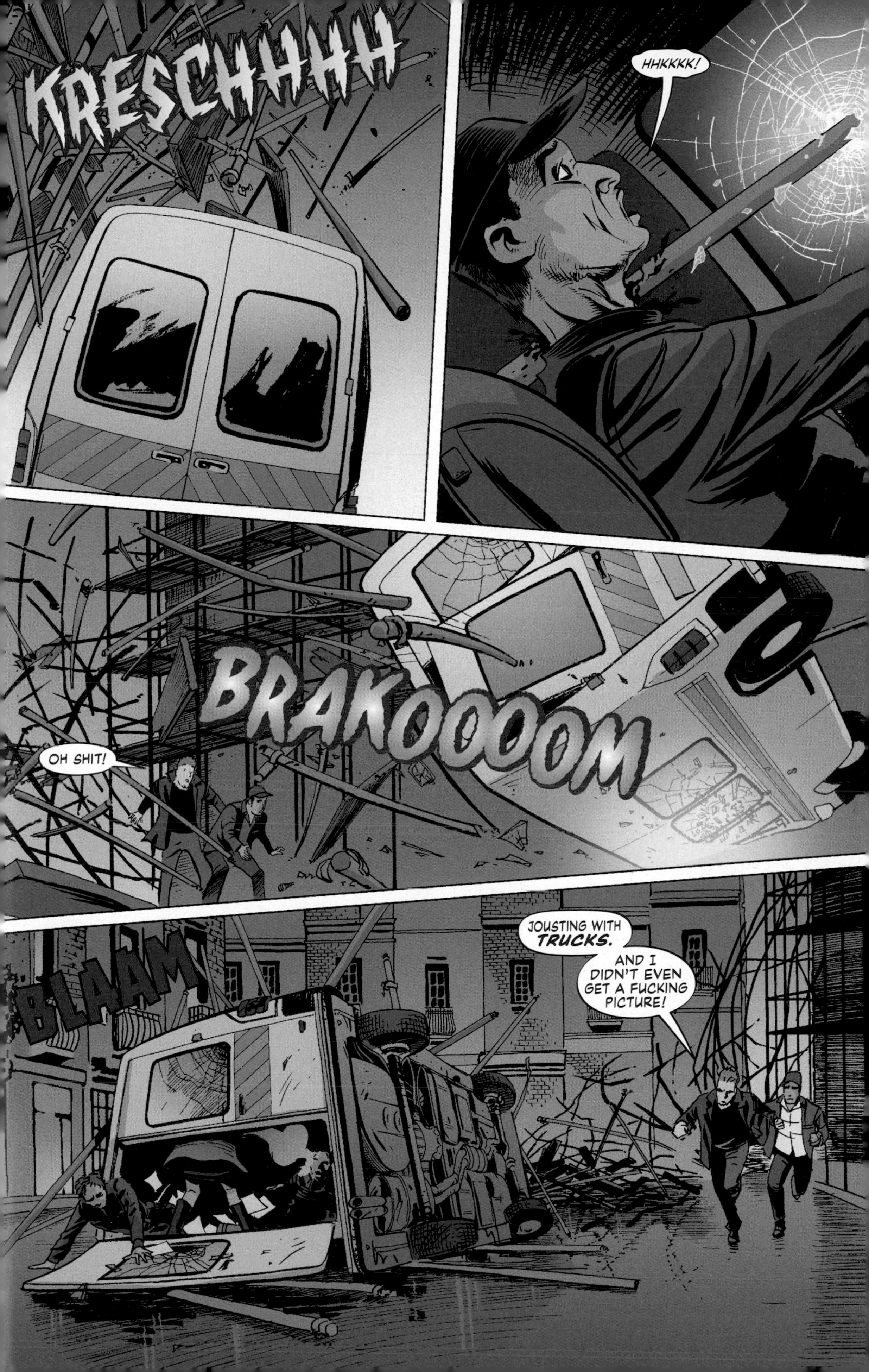
KRESCHHHH
HHKKKK!
BRAKOOOOM
OH SHIT!
BLAAM
JOUSTING WITH TRUCKS.
AND I DIDN'T EVEN GET A FUCKING PICTURE!

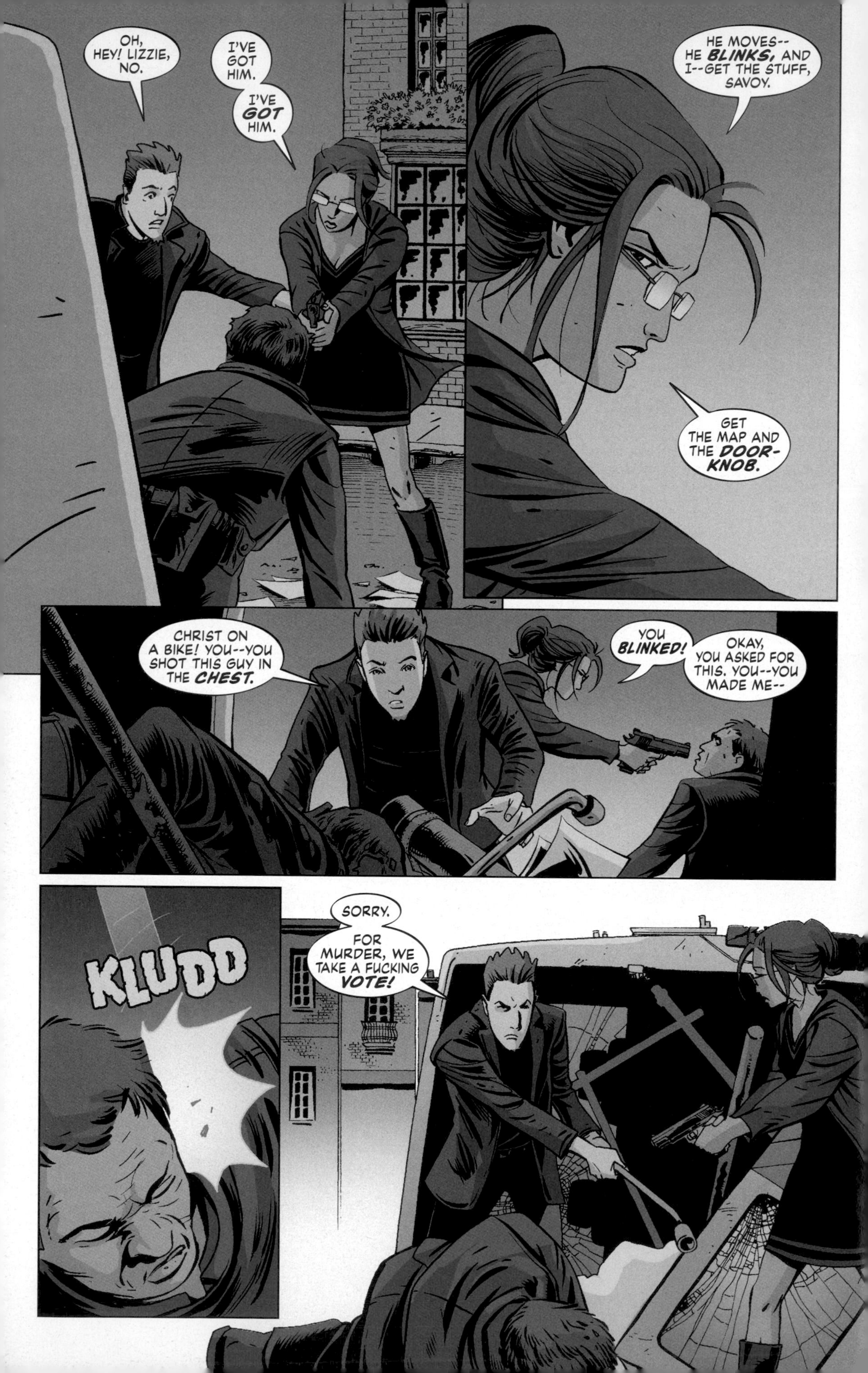
OH, HEY! LIZZIE, NO.
I'VE GOT HIM.
I'VE GOT HIM.
HE MOVES-- HE BLINKS, AND I--GET THE STUFF, SAVOY.
GET THE MAP AND THE DOOR-KNOB.
CHRIST ON A BIKE! YOU--YOU SHOT THIS GUY IN THE CHEST.
YOU BLINKED!
OKAY, YOU ASKED FOR THIS. YOU--YOU MADE ME--
KLUDD
SORRY.
FOR MURDER, WE TAKE A FUCKING VOTE!

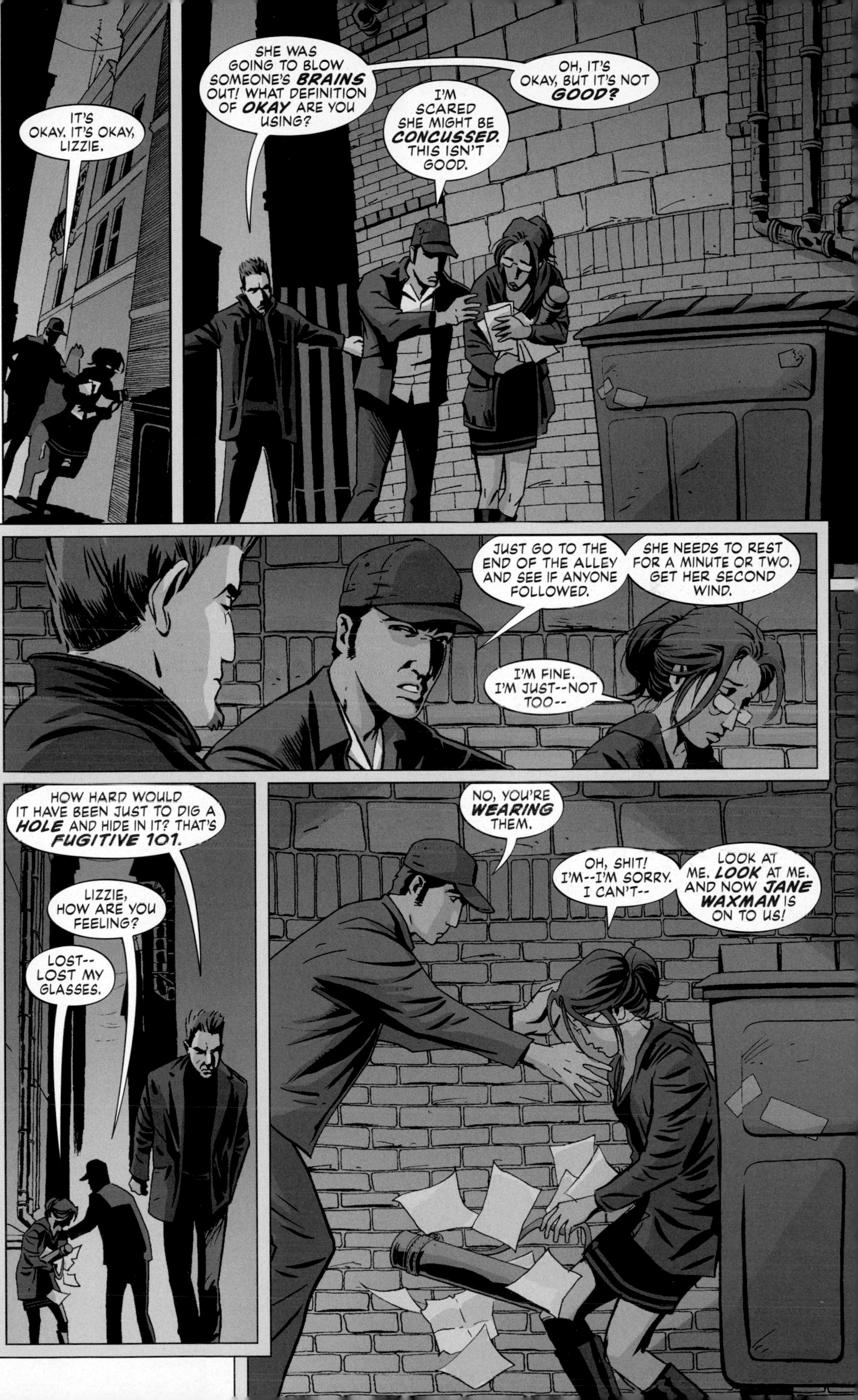
IT'S OKAY. IT'S OKAY, LIZZIE.
SHE WAS GOING TO BLOW SOMEONE'S **BRAINS** OUT! WHAT DEFINITION OF **OKAY** ARE YOU USING?
I'M SCARED SHE MIGHT BE **CONCUSSED.** THIS ISN'T GOOD.
OH, IT'S OKAY, BUT IT'S NOT **GOOD?**
JUST GO TO THE END OF THE ALLEY AND SEE IF ANYONE FOLLOWED.
SHE NEEDS TO REST FOR A MINUTE OR TWO. GET HER SECOND WIND.
I'M FINE. I'M JUST--NOT TOO--
HOW HARD WOULD IT HAVE BEEN JUST TO DIG A **HOLE** AND HIDE IN IT? THAT'S **FUGITIVE 101.**
LIZZIE, HOW ARE YOU FEELING?
LOST-- LOST MY GLASSES.
NO, YOU'RE **WEARING** THEM.
OH, SHIT! I'M--I'M SORRY. I CAN'T--
LOOK AT ME. **LOOK** AT ME. AND NOW **JANE WAXMAN** IS ON TO US!

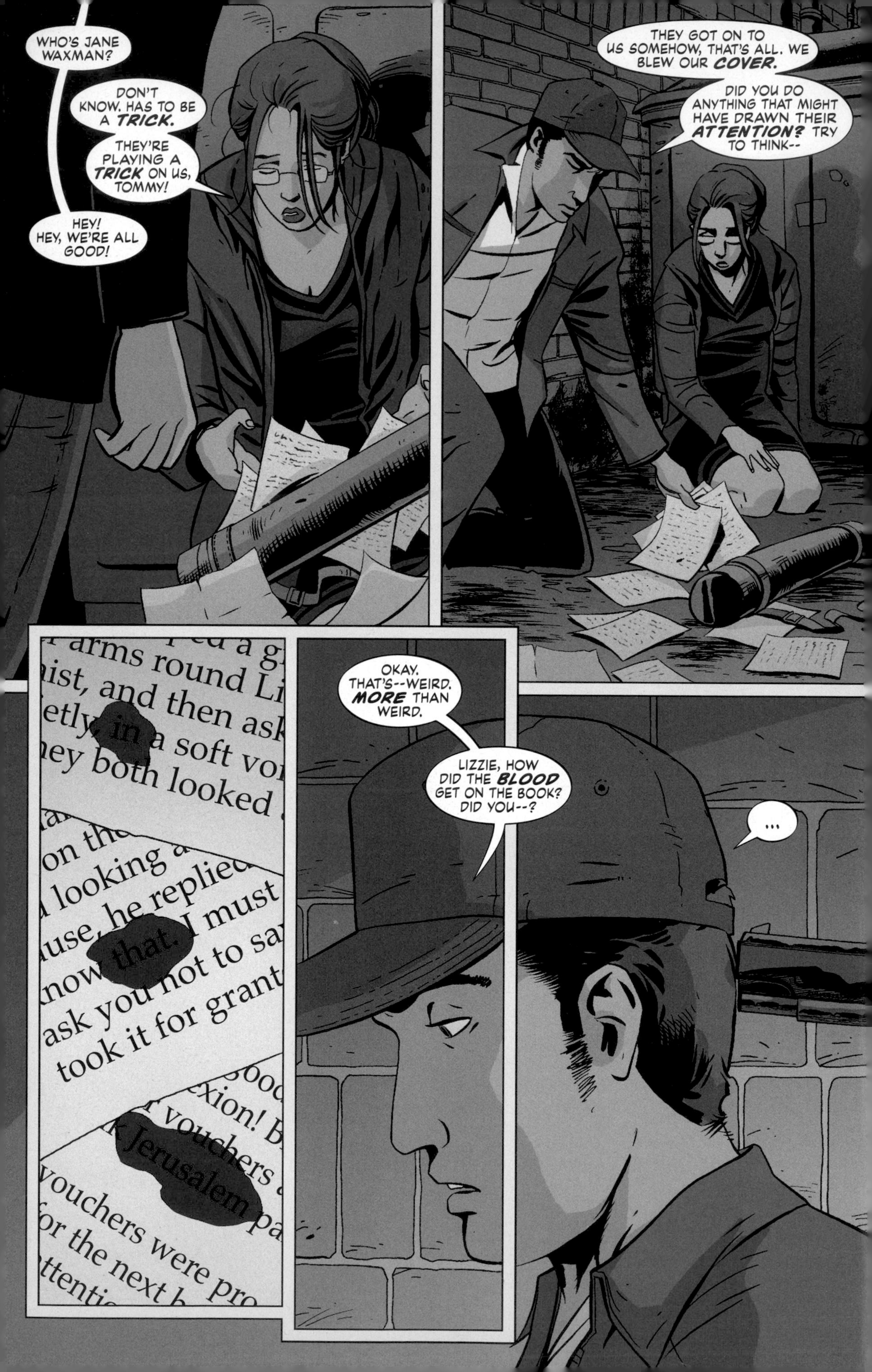
WHO'S JANE WAXMAN?
DON'T KNOW. HAS TO BE A TRICK.
THEY'RE PLAYING A TRICK ON US, TOMMY!
HEY! HEY, WE'RE ALL GOOD!
THEY GOT ON TO US SOMEHOW, THAT'S ALL. WE BLEW OUR COVER.
DID YOU DO ANYTHING THAT MIGHT HAVE DRAWN THEIR ATTENTION? TRY TO THINK--
OKAY. THAT'S--WEIRD. MORE THAN WEIRD.
LIZZIE, HOW DID THE BLOOD GET ON THE BOOK? DID YOU--?
...

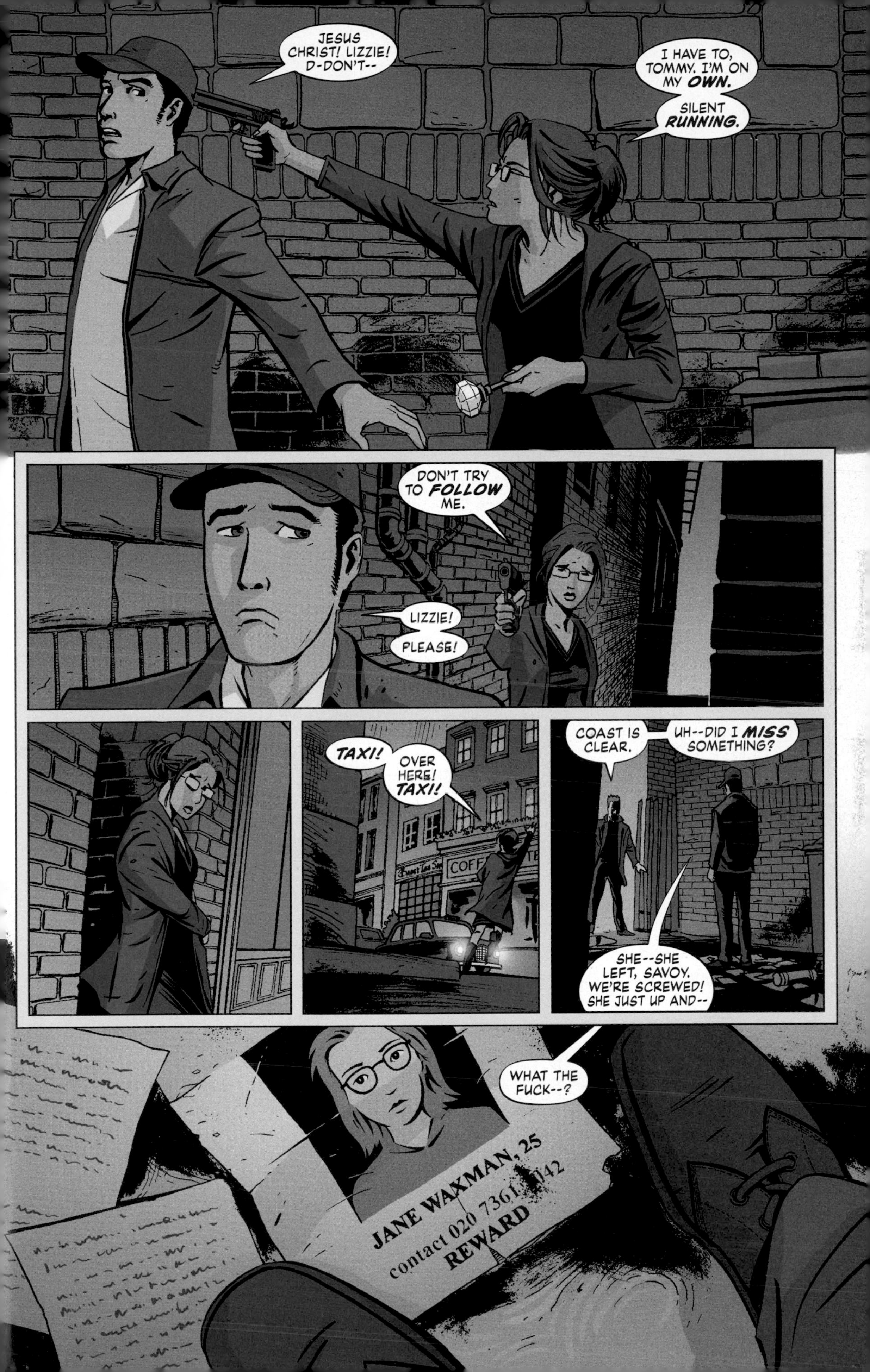
JESUS CHRIST! LIZZIE! D-DON'T--
I HAVE TO, TOMMY. I'M ON MY OWN.
SILENT RUNNING.
DON'T TRY TO FOLLOW ME.
LIZZIE!
PLEASE!
TAXI!
OVER HERE! TAXI!
COAST IS CLEAR.
UH--DID I MISS SOMETHING?
SHE--SHE LEFT, SAVOY. WE'RE SCREWED! SHE JUST UP AND--
WHAT THE FUCK--?
JANE WAXMAN, 25
contact 020 7361 042
REWARD

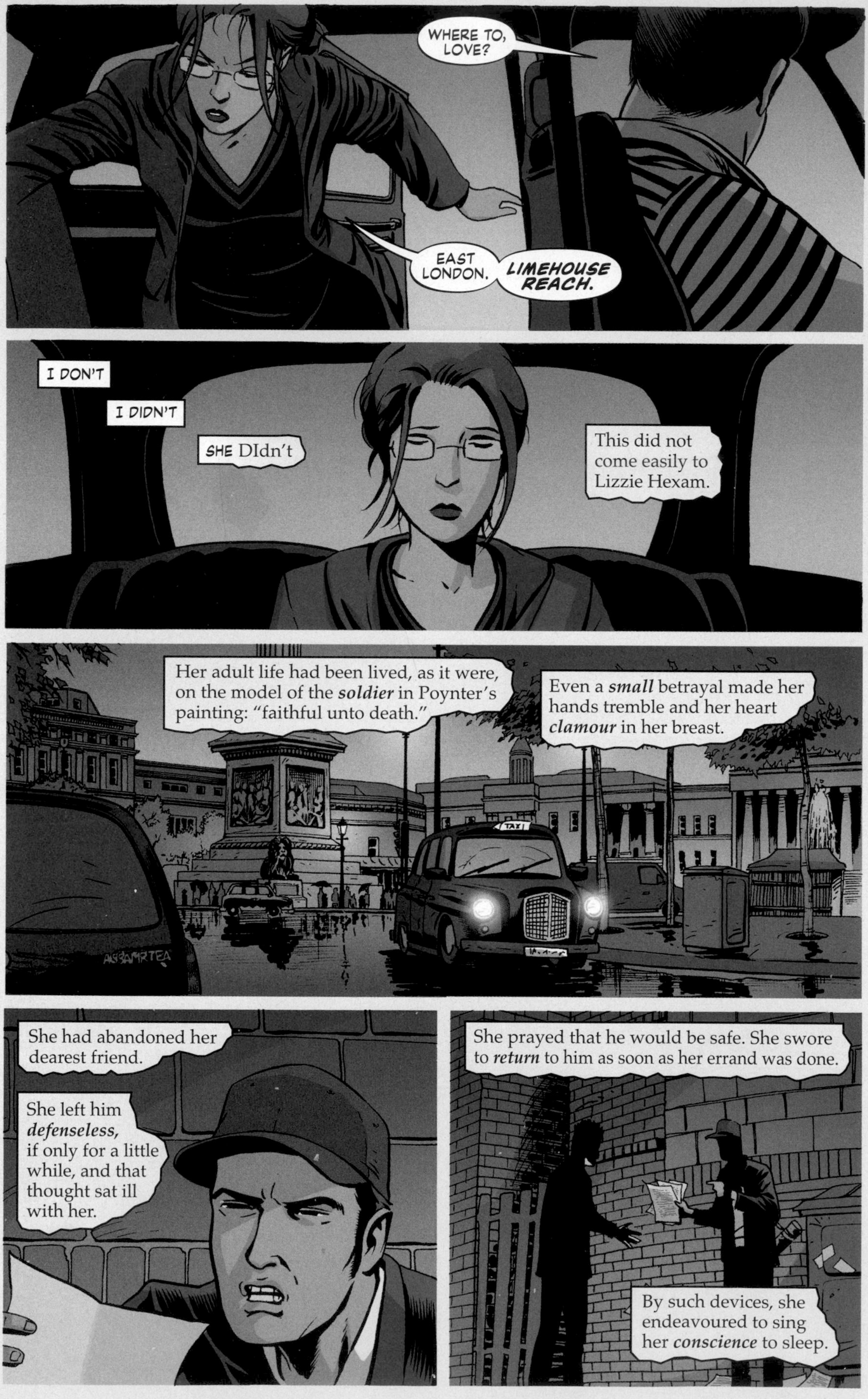

WHERE TO, LOVE?
EAST LONDON.
LIMEHOUSE REACH.
I DON'T
I DIDN'T
SHE DIdn't
This did not come easily to Lizzie Hexam.
Her adult life had been lived, as it were, on the model of the *soldier* in Poynter's painting: "faithful unto death."
Even a *small* betrayal made her hands tremble and her heart *clamour* in her breast.
TAXI
She had abandoned her dearest friend.
She left him *defenseless,* if only for a little while, and that thought sat ill with her.
She prayed that he would be safe. She swore to *return* to him as soon as her errand was done.
By such devices, she endeavoured to sing her *conscience* to sleep.

D'YOU WANT ME TO *WAIT,* SWEETHEART?

NO, THANK YOU.

I'M FINE.

She lied without *shame.* Without hesitation.

In truth she was *not* fine. Not well. Not thriving.

In her heart there was a worm of *doubt,* and it had a name: Jane Waxman.

This was the place where she was *born* — but oh, how changed!

She saw nothing here that spoke to her soul. No sight that greeted her as friend greets friend.

But there was one road left to her. One avenue kept tenuously *open.*

At great *cost,* it must be said.

And *now* seemed to be the time to use it.

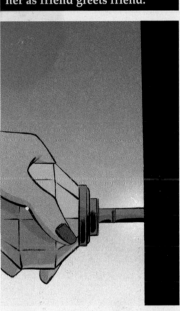

TAKE ME THERE.

TAKE ME THERE RIGHT *NOW.*

TAKE ME *HOME.*

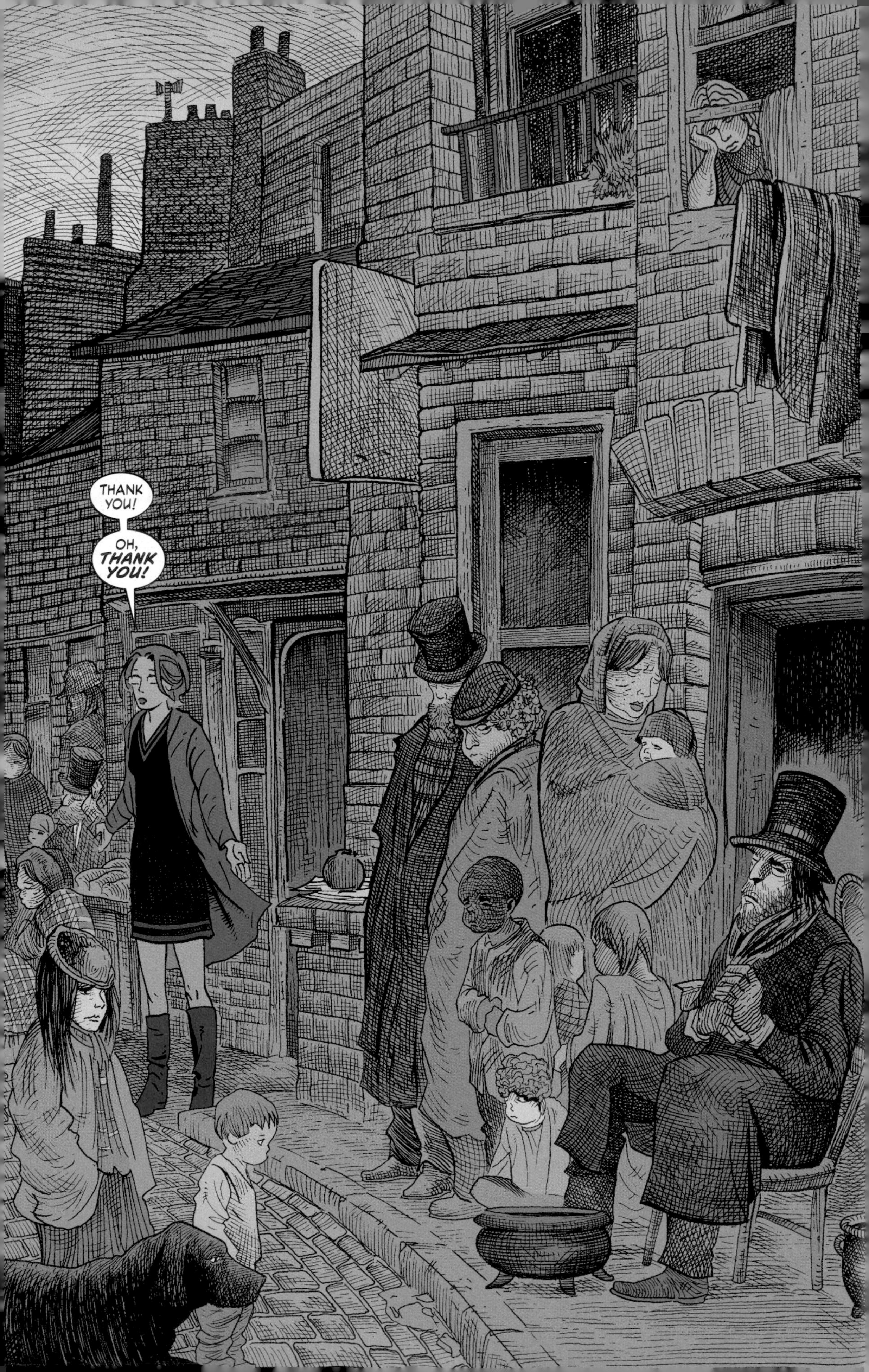
THANK YOU!
OH, THANK YOU!

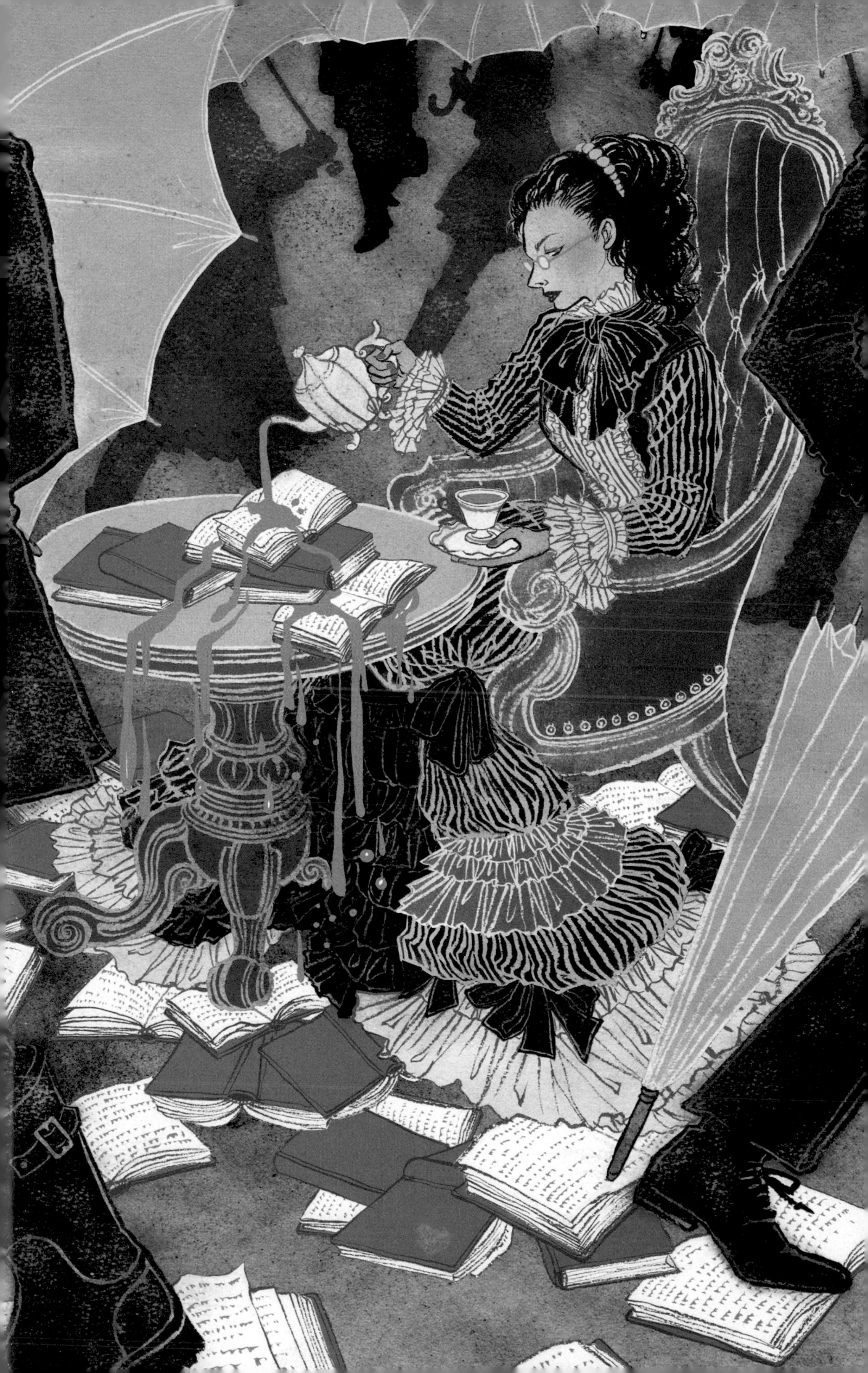

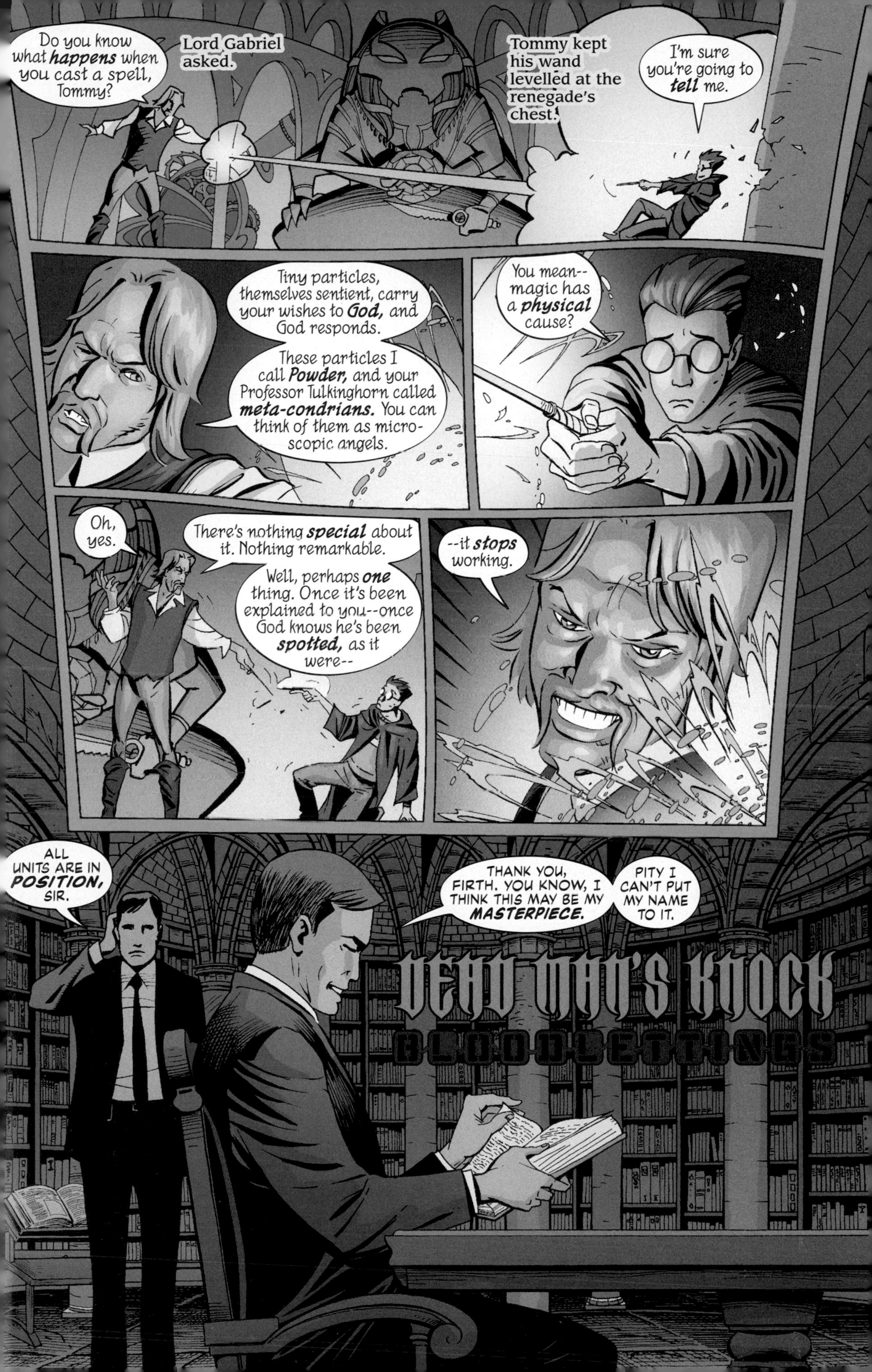
Do you know what happens when you cast a spell, Tommy?
Lord Gabriel asked.
Tommy kept his wand levelled at the renegade's chest.
I'm sure you're going to tell me.
Tiny particles, themselves sentient, carry your wishes to God, and God responds.
These particles I call Powder, and your Professor Tulkinghorn called meta-condrians. You can think of them as microscopic angels.
You mean--magic has a physical cause?
Oh, yes.
There's nothing special about it. Nothing remarkable.
Well, perhaps one thing. Once it's been explained to you--once God knows he's been spotted, as it were--
--it stops working.
ALL UNITS ARE IN POSITION, SIR.
THANK YOU, FIRTH. YOU KNOW, I THINK THIS MAY BE MY MASTERPIECE.
PITY I CAN'T PUT MY NAME TO IT.
DEAD MAN'S KNOCK
BLOODLETTINGS

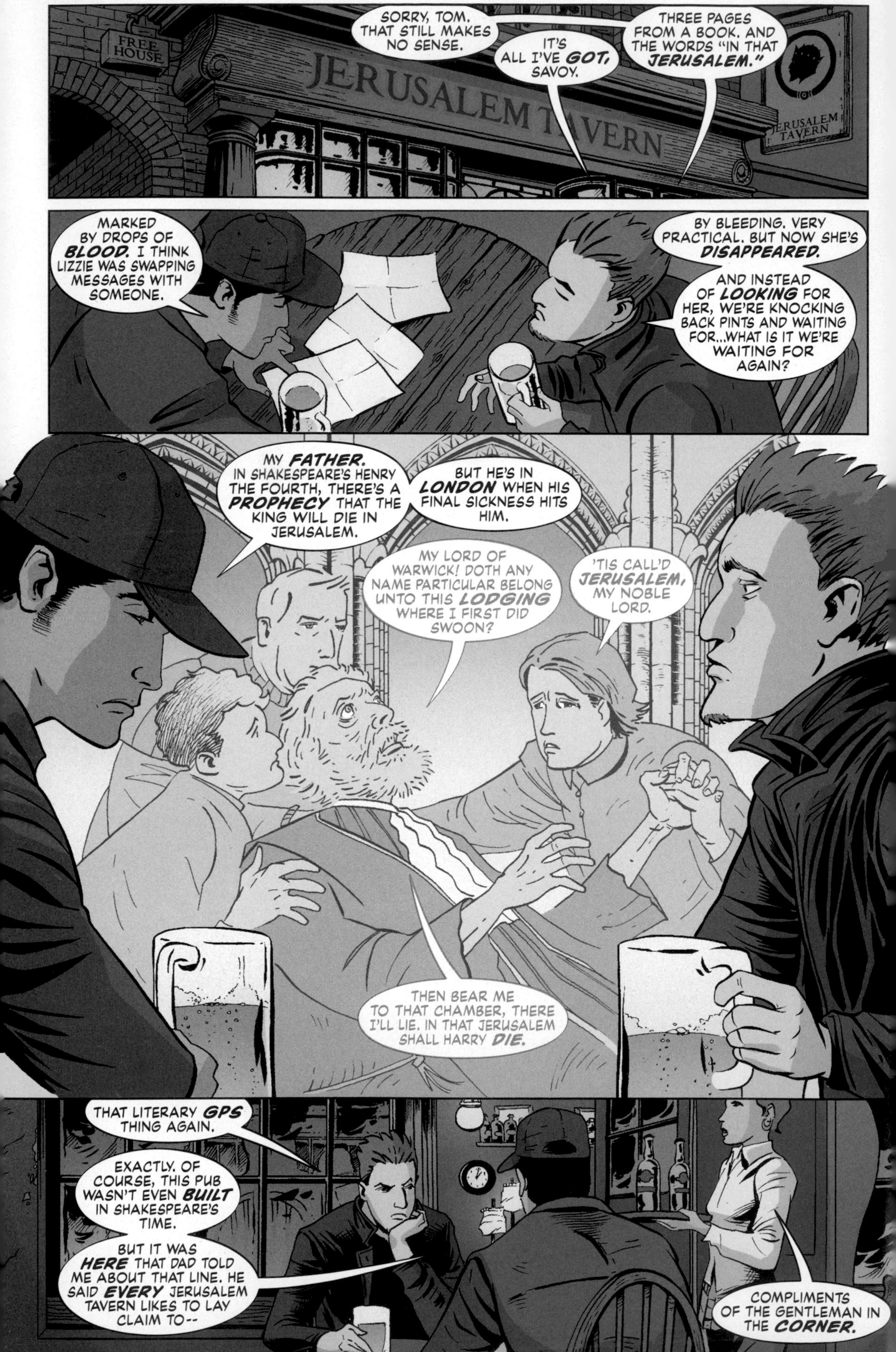
FREE HOUSE
JERUSALEM TAVERN
SORRY, TOM. THAT STILL MAKES NO SENSE.
THREE PAGES FROM A BOOK. AND THE WORDS "IN THAT JERUSALEM."
IT'S ALL I'VE GOT, SAVOY.
JERUSALEM TAVERN
MARKED BY DROPS OF BLOOD. I THINK LIZZIE WAS SWAPPING MESSAGES WITH SOMEONE.
BY BLEEDING. VERY PRACTICAL. BUT NOW SHE'S DISAPPEARED.
AND INSTEAD OF LOOKING FOR HER, WE'RE KNOCKING BACK PINTS AND WAITING FOR...WHAT IS IT WE'RE WAITING FOR AGAIN?
MY FATHER. IN SHAKESPEARE'S HENRY THE FOURTH, THERE'S A PROPHECY THAT THE KING WILL DIE IN JERUSALEM.
BUT HE'S IN LONDON WHEN HIS FINAL SICKNESS HITS HIM.
MY LORD OF WARWICK! DOTH ANY NAME PARTICULAR BELONG UNTO THIS LODGING WHERE I FIRST DID SWOON?
'TIS CALL'D JERUSALEM, MY NOBLE LORD.
THEN BEAR ME TO THAT CHAMBER, THERE I'LL LIE. IN THAT JERUSALEM SHALL HARRY DIE.
THAT LITERARY GPS THING AGAIN.
EXACTLY. OF COURSE, THIS PUB WASN'T EVEN BUILT IN SHAKESPEARE'S TIME.
BUT IT WAS HERE THAT DAD TOLD ME ABOUT THAT LINE. HE SAID EVERY JERUSALEM TAVERN LIKES TO LAY CLAIM TO--
COMPLIMENTS OF THE GENTLEMAN IN THE CORNER.

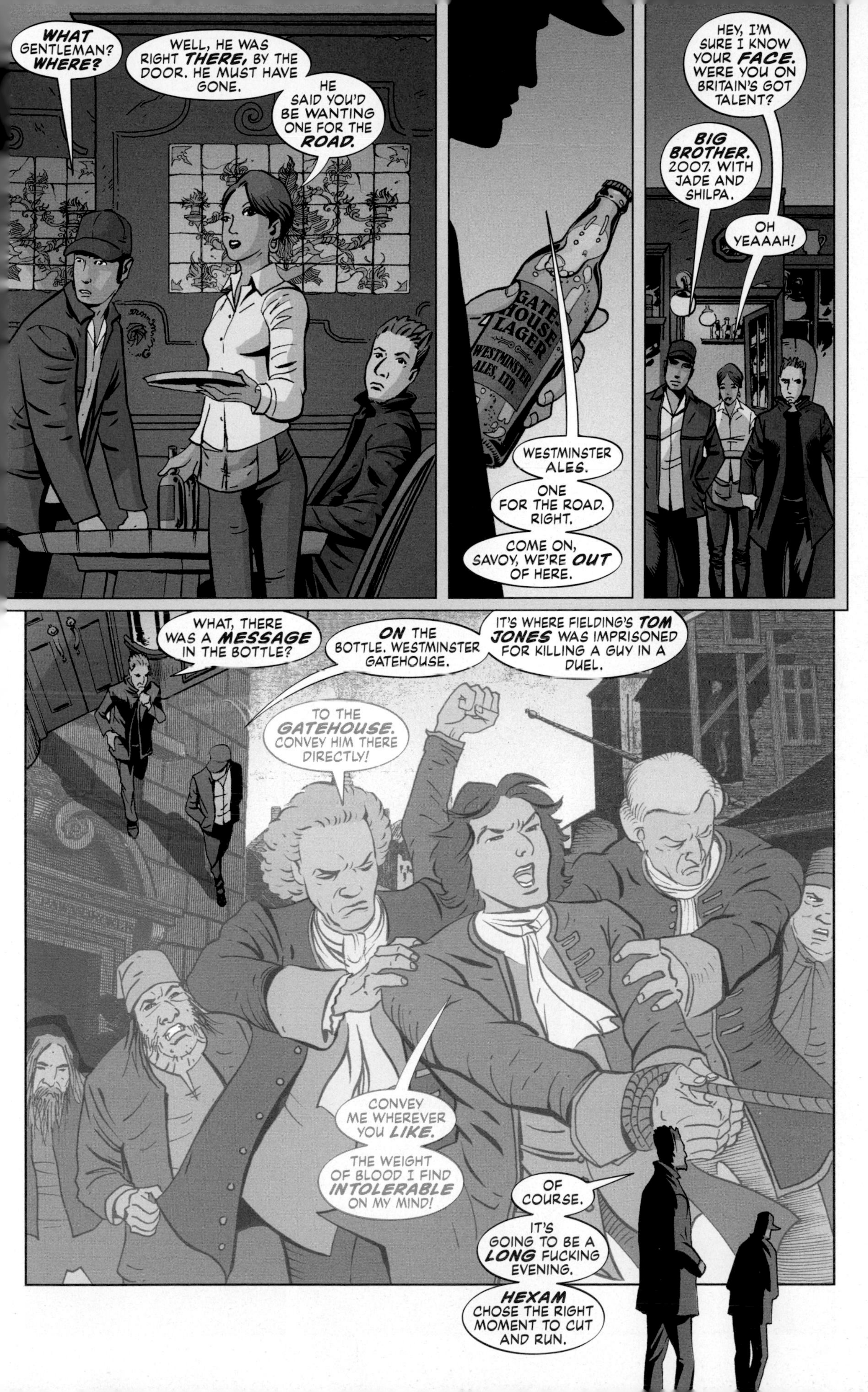
WHAT GENTLEMAN? WHERE?
WELL, HE WAS RIGHT THERE, BY THE DOOR. HE MUST HAVE GONE.
HE SAID YOU'D BE WANTING ONE FOR THE ROAD.
GATE-HOUSE LAGER WESTMINSTER ALES, LTD.
WESTMINSTER ALES.
ONE FOR THE ROAD. RIGHT.
COME ON, SAVOY, WE'RE OUT OF HERE.
HEY, I'M SURE I KNOW YOUR FACE. WERE YOU ON BRITAIN'S GOT TALENT?
BIG BROTHER. 2007. WITH JADE AND SHILPA.
OH YEAAAH!
WHAT, THERE WAS A MESSAGE IN THE BOTTLE?
ON THE BOTTLE. WESTMINSTER GATEHOUSE.
IT'S WHERE FIELDING'S TOM JONES WAS IMPRISONED FOR KILLING A GUY IN A DUEL.
TO THE GATEHOUSE. CONVEY HIM THERE DIRECTLY!
CONVEY ME WHEREVER YOU LIKE.
THE WEIGHT OF BLOOD I FIND INTOLERABLE ON MY MIND!
OF COURSE.
IT'S GOING TO BE A LONG FUCKING EVENING.
HEXAM CHOSE THE RIGHT MOMENT TO CUT AND RUN.

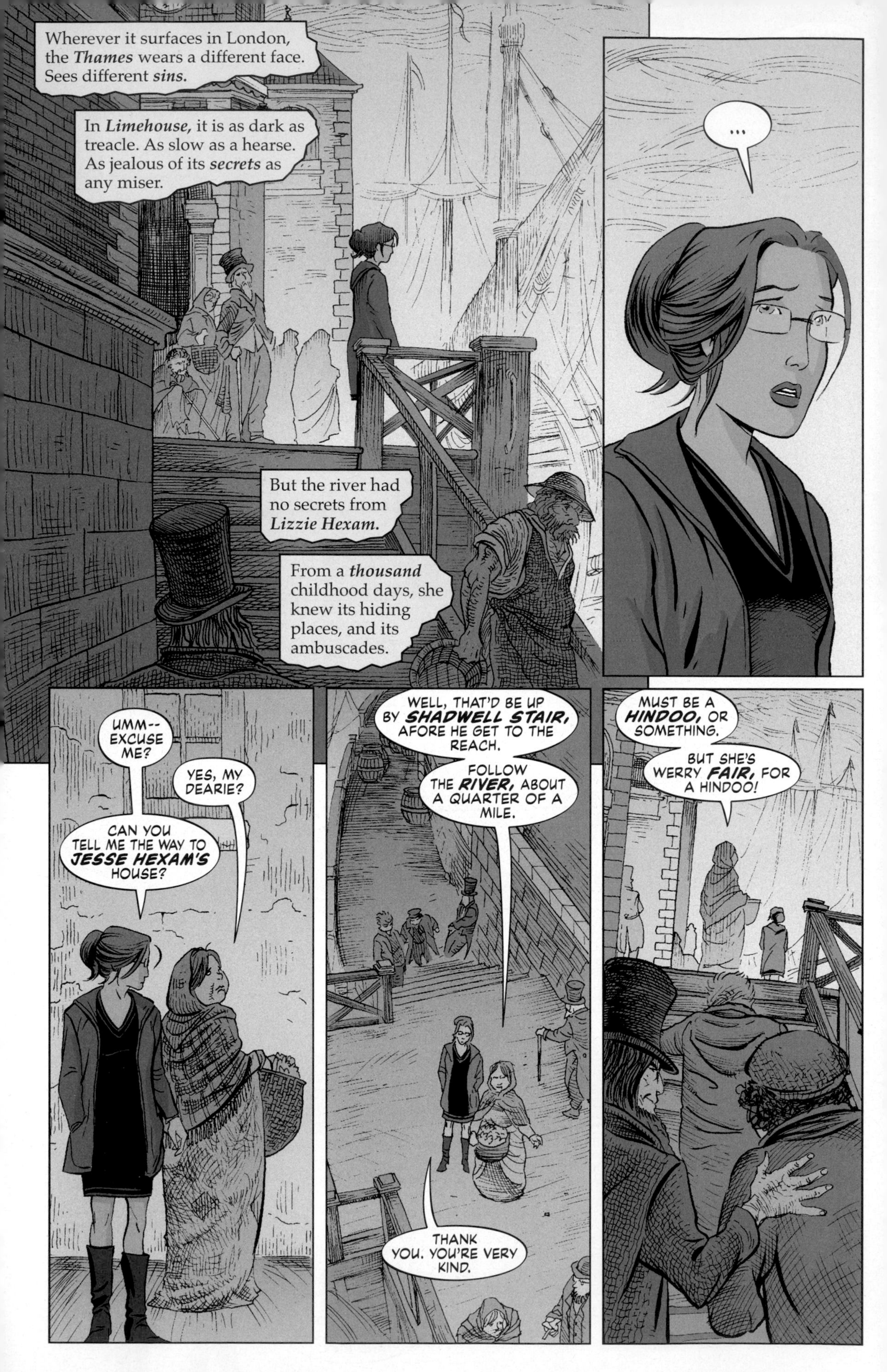
Wherever it surfaces in London, the *Thames* wears a different face. Sees different *sins.*
In *Limehouse,* it is as dark as treacle. As slow as a hearse. As jealous of its *secrets* as any miser.
But the river had no secrets from *Lizzie Hexam.*
From a *thousand* childhood days, she knew its hiding places, and its ambuscades.
...
UMM-- EXCUSE ME?
YES, MY DEARIE?
CAN YOU TELL ME THE WAY TO **JESSE HEXAM'S** HOUSE?
WELL, THAT'D BE UP BY **SHADWELL STAIR,** AFORE HE GET TO THE REACH.
FOLLOW THE **RIVER,** ABOUT A QUARTER OF A MILE.
THANK YOU. YOU'RE VERY KIND.
MUST BE A **HINDOO,** OR SOMETHING.
BUT SHE'S WERRY **FAIR,** FOR A HINDOO!

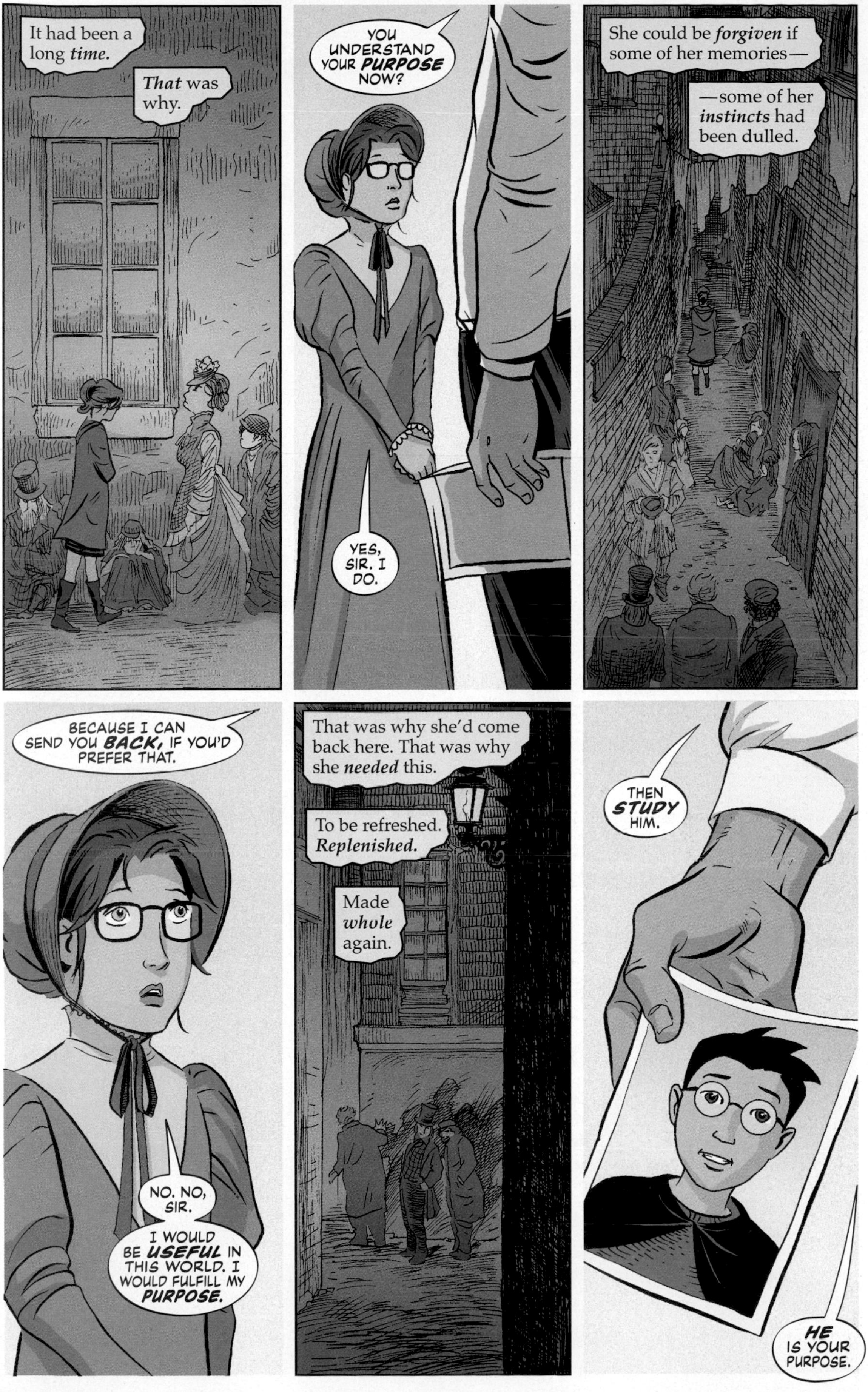
It had been a long *time.*
That was why.
YOU UNDERSTAND YOUR **PURPOSE** NOW?
YES, SIR. I DO.
She could be *forgiven* if some of her memories—
—some of her *instincts* had been dulled.
BECAUSE I CAN SEND YOU **BACK,** IF YOU'D PREFER THAT.
NO. NO, SIR.
I WOULD BE **USEFUL** IN THIS WORLD. I WOULD FULFILL MY **PURPOSE.**
That was why she'd come back here. That was why she *needed* this.
To be refreshed. *Replenished.*
Made *whole* again.
THEN **STUDY** HIM.
HE IS YOUR PURPOSE.

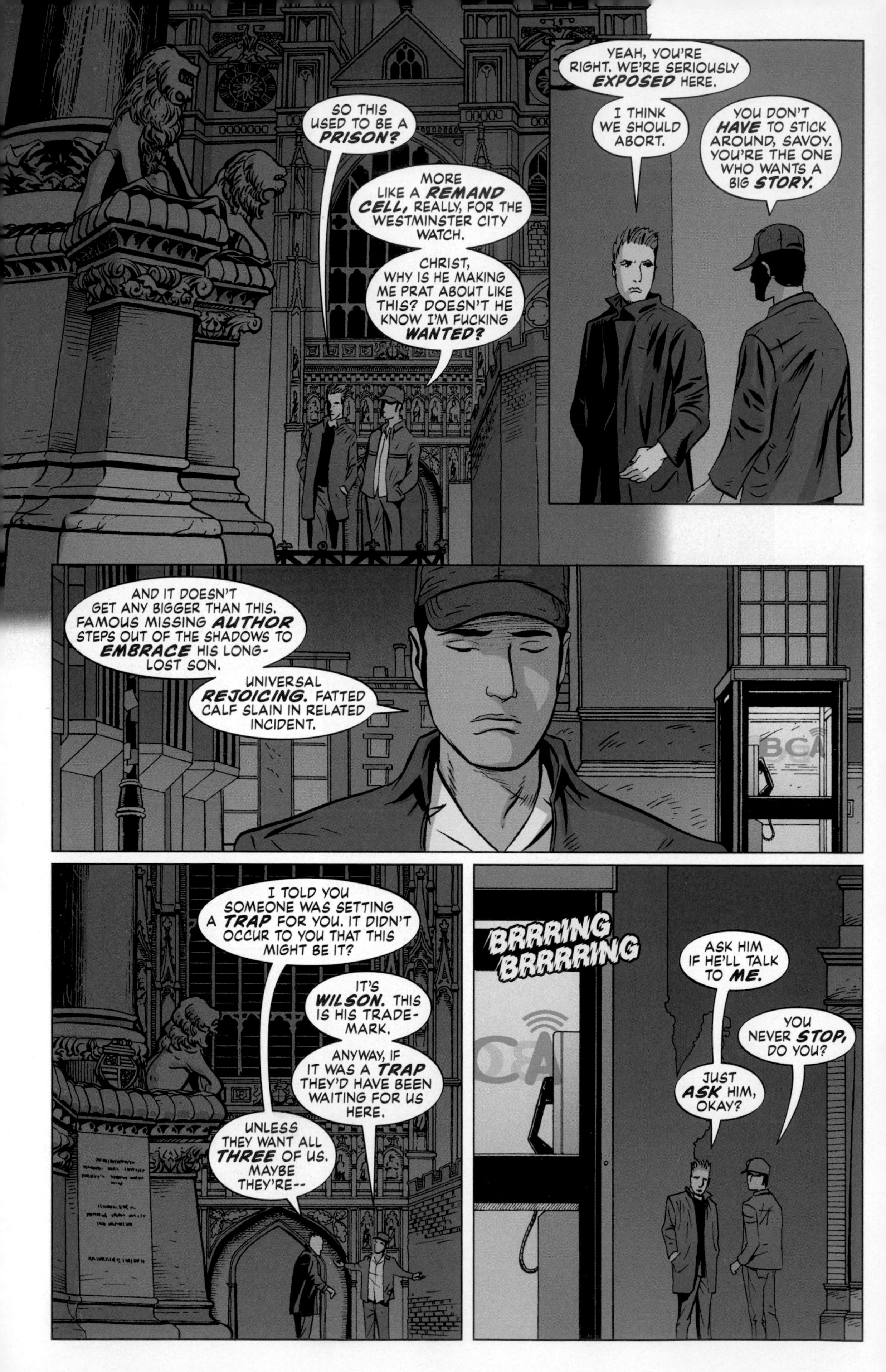
SO THIS USED TO BE A PRISON?
MORE LIKE A REMAND CELL, REALLY, FOR THE WESTMINSTER CITY WATCH.
CHRIST, WHY IS HE MAKING ME PRAT ABOUT LIKE THIS? DOESN'T HE KNOW I'M FUCKING WANTED?
YEAH, YOU'RE RIGHT. WE'RE SERIOUSLY EXPOSED HERE.
I THINK WE SHOULD ABORT.
YOU DON'T HAVE TO STICK AROUND, SAVOY. YOU'RE THE ONE WHO WANTS A BIG STORY.
AND IT DOESN'T GET ANY BIGGER THAN THIS. FAMOUS MISSING AUTHOR STEPS OUT OF THE SHADOWS TO EMBRACE HIS LONG-LOST SON.
UNIVERSAL REJOICING. FATTED CALF SLAIN IN RELATED INCIDENT.
BCA
I TOLD YOU SOMEONE WAS SETTING A TRAP FOR YOU. IT DIDN'T OCCUR TO YOU THAT THIS MIGHT BE IT?
IT'S WILSON. THIS IS HIS TRADE-MARK.
ANYWAY, IF IT WAS A TRAP THEY'D HAVE BEEN WAITING FOR US HERE.
UNLESS THEY WANT ALL THREE OF US. MAYBE THEY'RE--
BRRRING BRRRRING
ASK HIM IF HE'LL TALK TO ME.
YOU NEVER STOP, DO YOU?
JUST ASK HIM, OKAY?

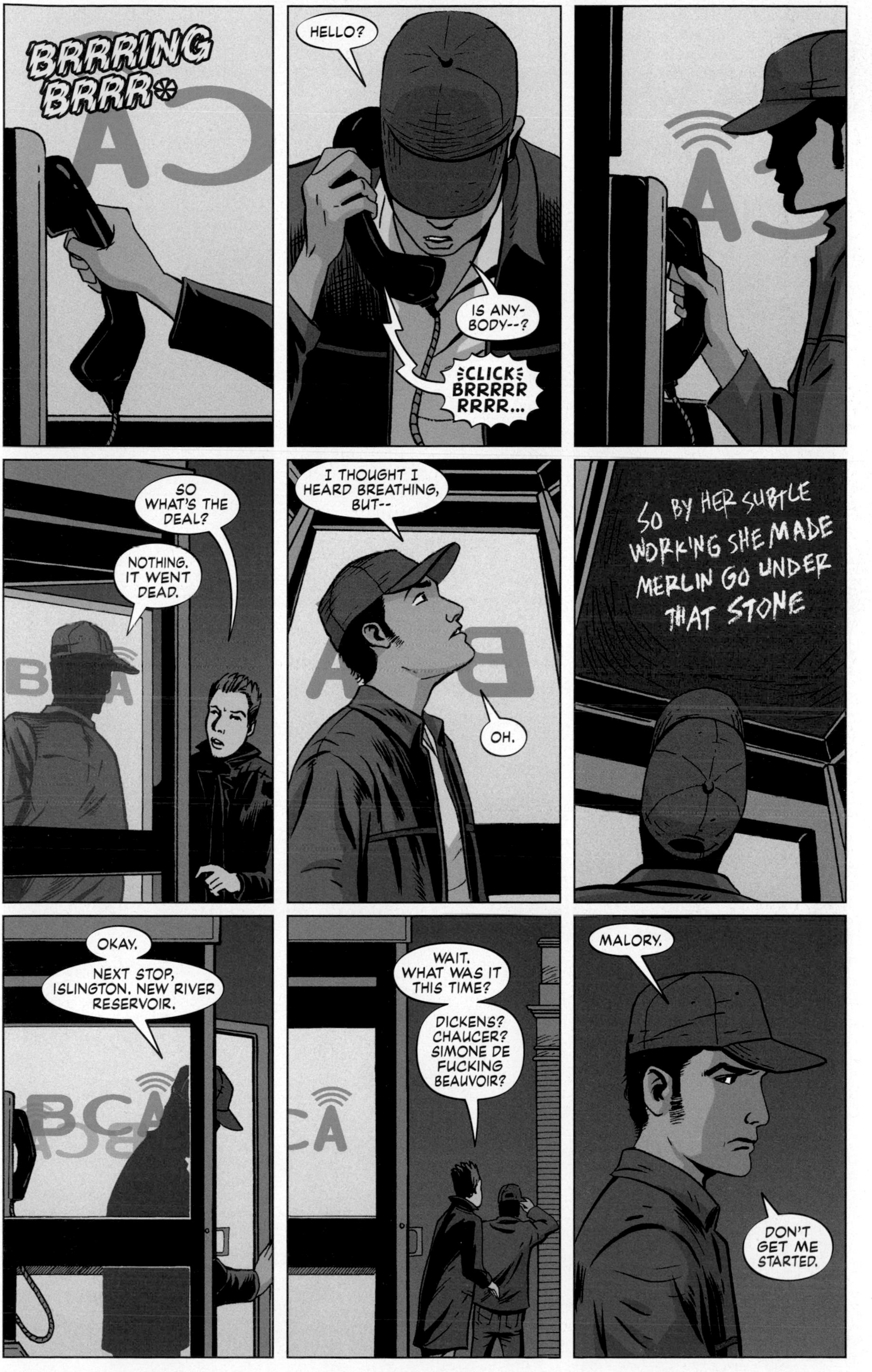
BRRRING BRRR*
HELLO?
IS ANY-BODY--?
CLICK BRRRRR RRRR...
SO WHAT'S THE DEAL?
NOTHING. IT WENT DEAD.
I THOUGHT I HEARD BREATHING, BUT--
OH.
SO BY HER SUBTLE WORKING SHE MADE MERLIN GO UNDER THAT STONE
OKAY.
NEXT STOP, ISLINGTON. NEW RIVER RESERVOIR.
WAIT. WHAT WAS IT THIS TIME?
DICKENS? CHAUCER? SIMONE DE FUCKING BEAUVOIR?
MALORY.
DON'T GET ME STARTED.

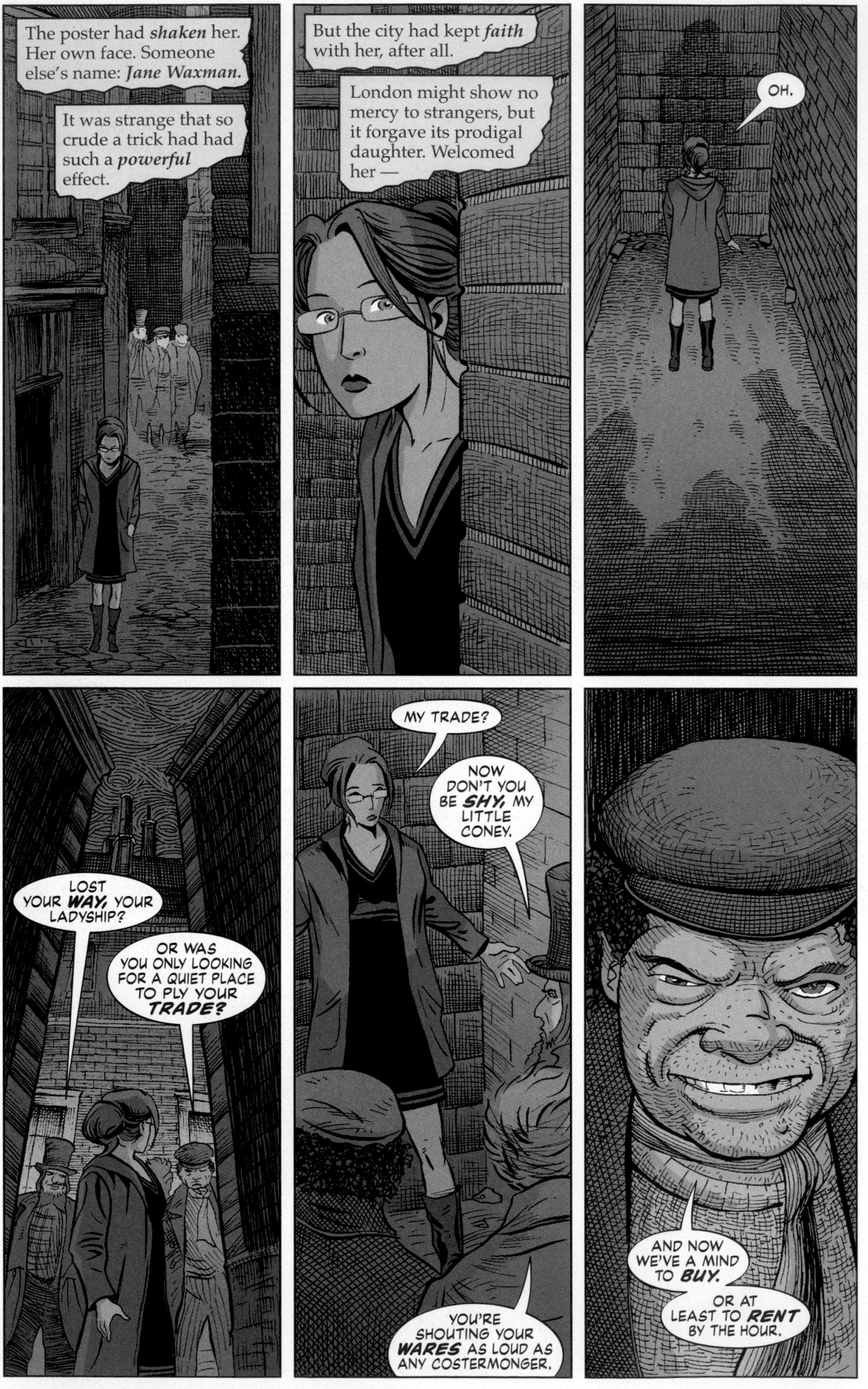

The poster had *shaken* her. Her own face. Someone else's name: *Jane Waxman.*
It was strange that so crude a trick had had such a *powerful* effect.
But the city had kept *faith* with her, after all.
London might show no mercy to strangers, but it forgave its prodigal daughter. Welcomed her —
OH.
LOST YOUR **WAY,** YOUR LADYSHIP?
OR WAS YOU ONLY LOOKING FOR A QUIET PLACE TO PLY YOUR **TRADE?**
MY TRADE?
NOW DON'T YOU BE **SHY,** MY LITTLE CONEY.
YOU'RE SHOUTING YOUR **WARES** AS LOUD AS ANY COSTERMONGER.
AND NOW WE'VE A MIND TO **BUY.**
OR AT LEAST TO **RENT** BY THE HOUR.

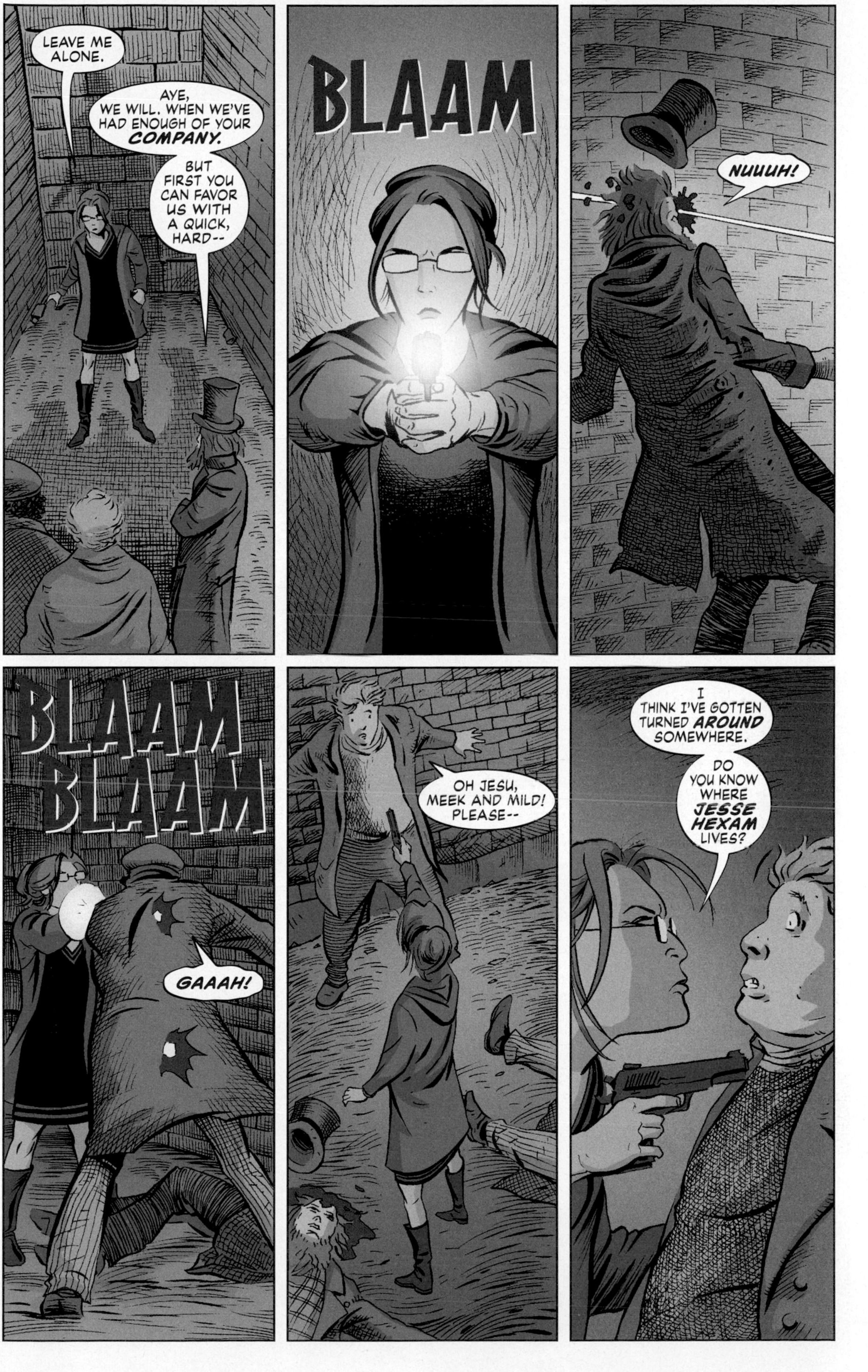
LEAVE ME ALONE.
AYE, WE WILL. WHEN WE'VE HAD ENOUGH OF YOUR COMPANY.
BUT FIRST YOU CAN FAVOR US WITH A QUICK, HARD--
BLAAM
NUUUH!
BLAAM BLAAM
GAAAH!
OH JESU, MEEK AND MILD! PLEASE--
I THINK I'VE GOTTEN TURNED AROUND SOMEWHERE.
DO YOU KNOW WHERE JESSE HEXAM LIVES?

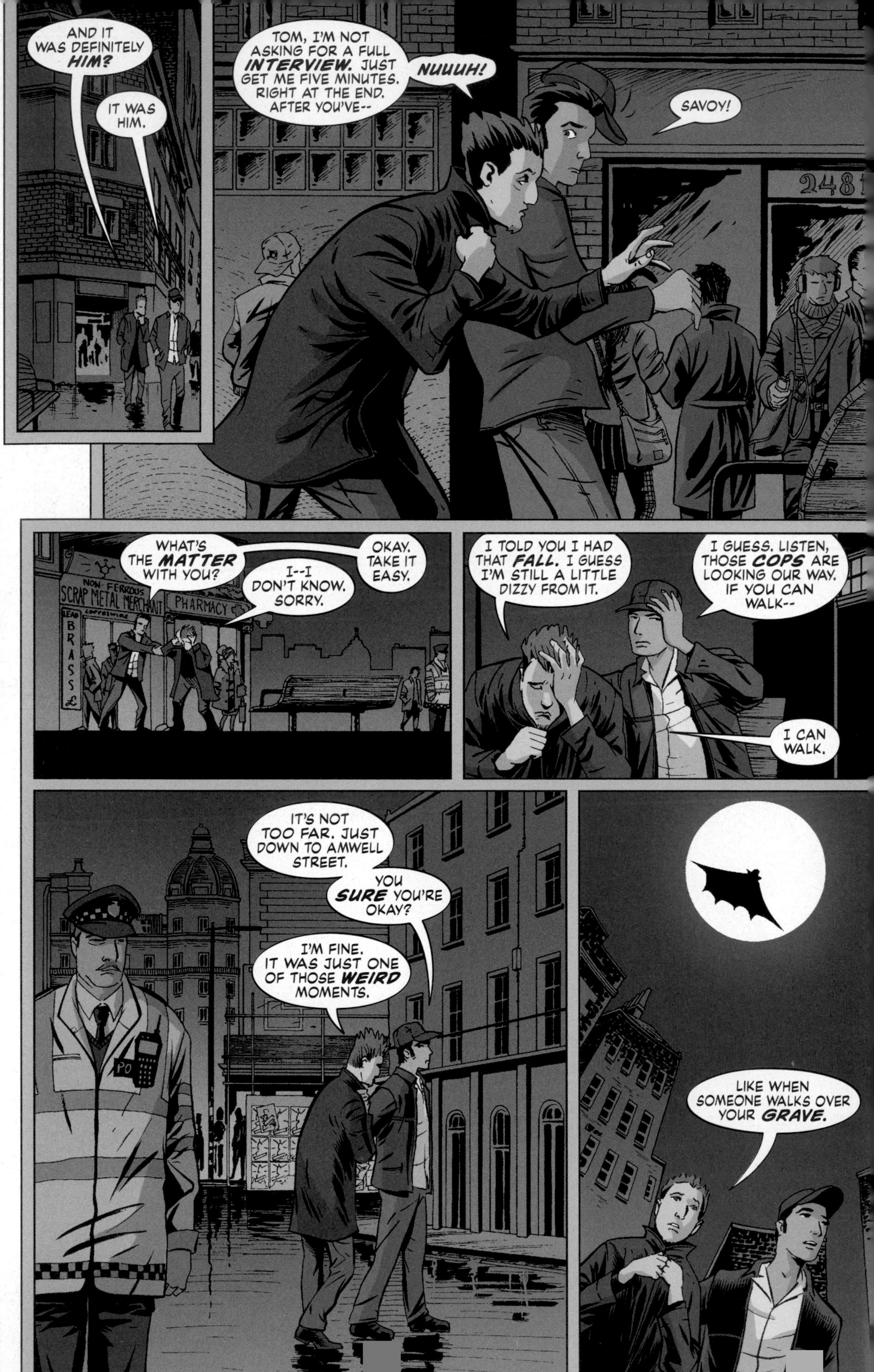
AND IT WAS DEFINITELY HIM?
IT WAS HIM.
TOM, I'M NOT ASKING FOR A FULL INTERVIEW. JUST GET ME FIVE MINUTES. RIGHT AT THE END. AFTER YOU'VE--
NUUUH!
SAVOY!
248
WHAT'S THE MATTER WITH YOU?
I--I DON'T KNOW. SORRY.
OKAY. TAKE IT EASY.
NON-FERROUS SCRAP METAL MERCHANT
PHARMACY
LEAD BRASS
I TOLD YOU I HAD THAT FALL. I GUESS I'M STILL A LITTLE DIZZY FROM IT.
I GUESS. LISTEN, THOSE COPS ARE LOOKING OUR WAY. IF YOU CAN WALK--
I CAN WALK.
IT'S NOT TOO FAR. JUST DOWN TO AMWELL STREET.
YOU SURE YOU'RE OKAY?
I'M FINE. IT WAS JUST ONE OF THOSE WEIRD MOMENTS.
PO
LIKE WHEN SOMEONE WALKS OVER YOUR GRAVE.

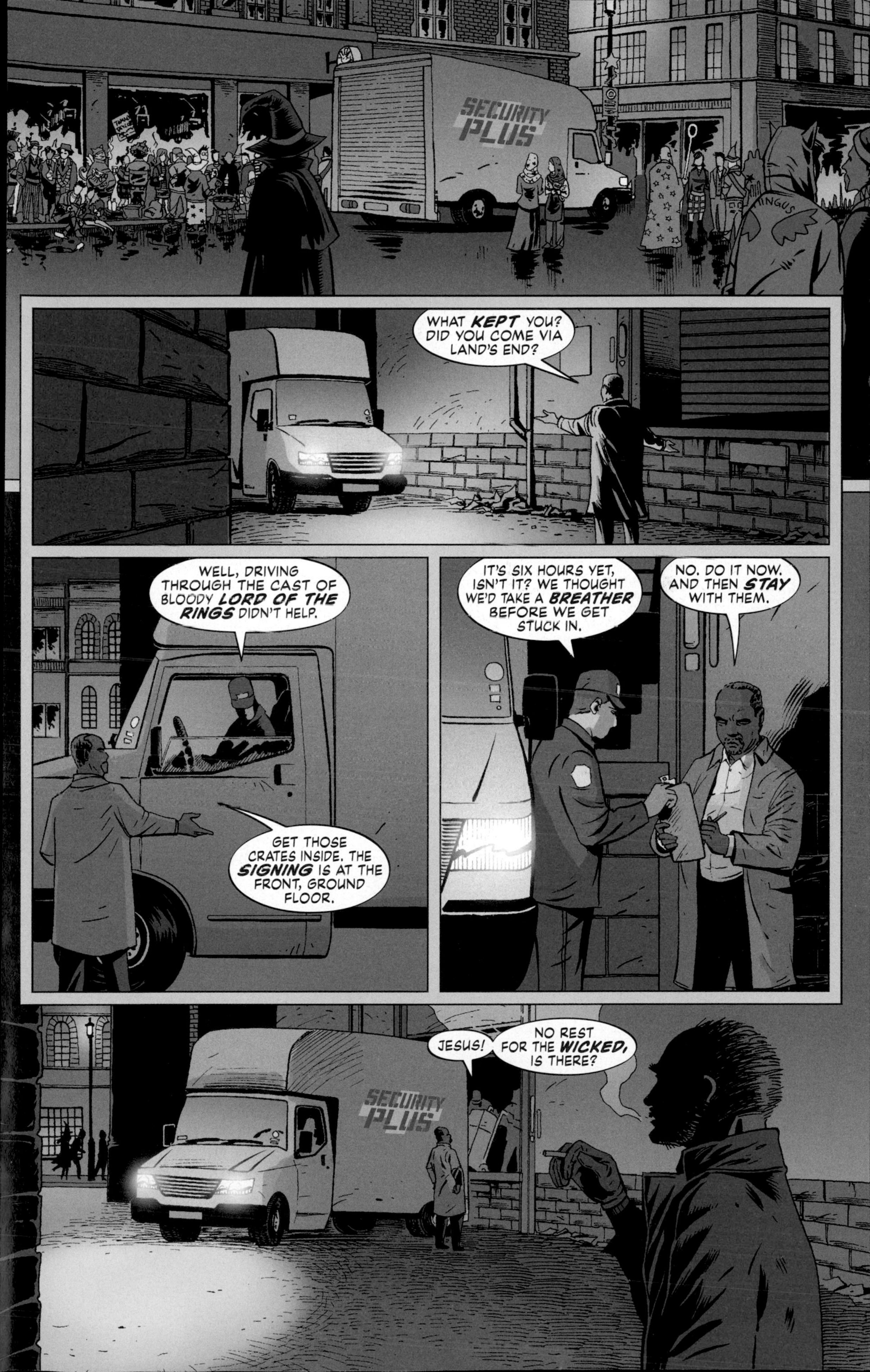
SECURITY PLUS
WHAT KEPT YOU? DID YOU COME VIA LAND'S END?
WELL, DRIVING THROUGH THE CAST OF BLOODY LORD OF THE RINGS DIDN'T HELP.
GET THOSE CRATES INSIDE. THE SIGNING IS AT THE FRONT, GROUND FLOOR.
IT'S SIX HOURS YET, ISN'T IT? WE THOUGHT WE'D TAKE A BREATHER BEFORE WE GET STUCK IN.
NO. DO IT NOW. AND THEN STAY WITH THEM.
JESUS!
NO REST FOR THE WICKED, IS THERE?
SECURITY PLUS

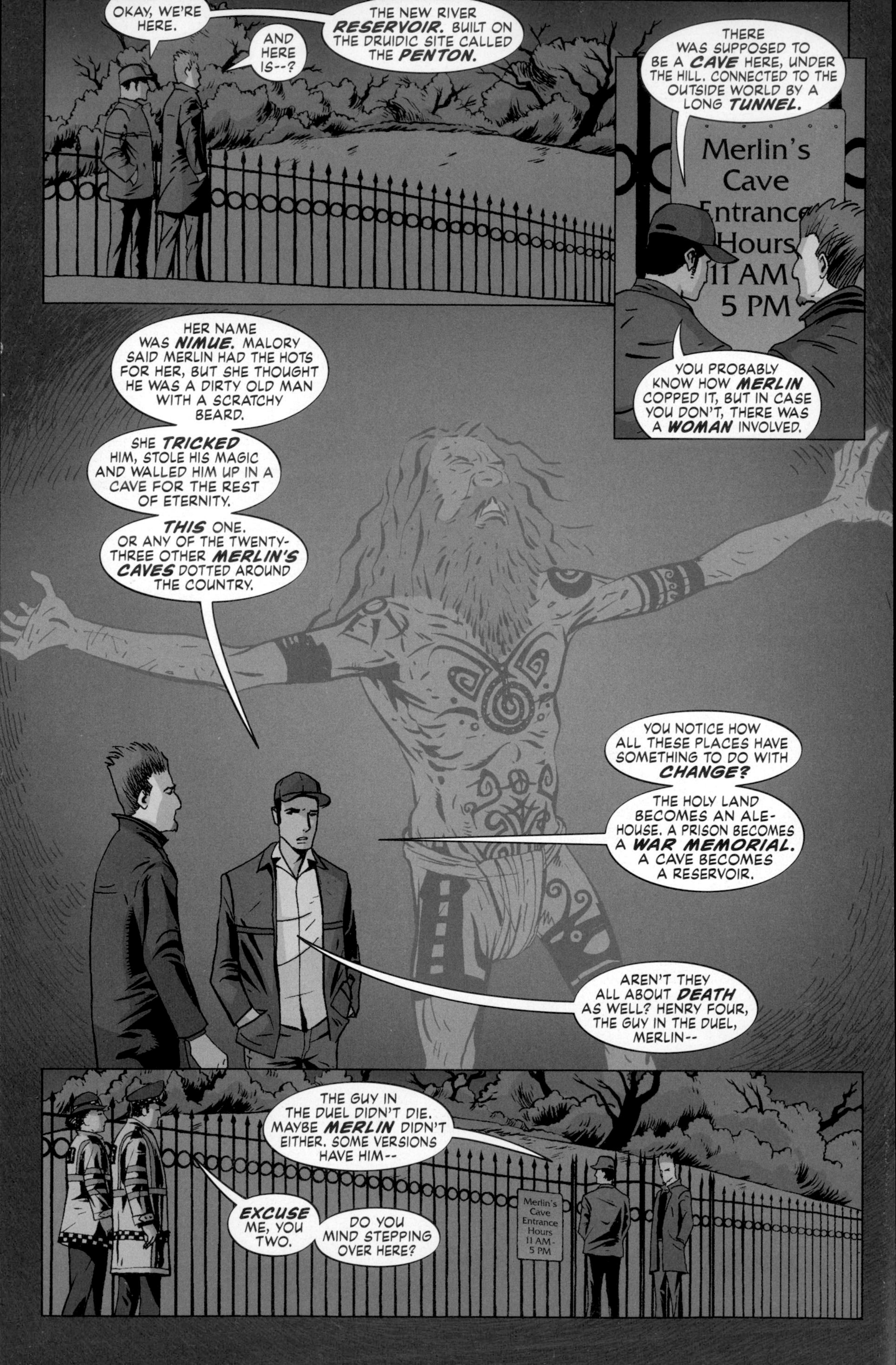
OKAY, WE'RE HERE.
AND HERE IS--?
THE NEW RIVER RESERVOIR. BUILT ON THE DRUIDIC SITE CALLED THE PENTON.
THERE WAS SUPPOSED TO BE A CAVE HERE, UNDER THE HILL. CONNECTED TO THE OUTSIDE WORLD BY A LONG TUNNEL.
Merlin's Cave Entrance Hours 11 AM 5 PM
YOU PROBABLY KNOW HOW MERLIN COPPED IT, BUT IN CASE YOU DON'T, THERE WAS A WOMAN INVOLVED.
HER NAME WAS NIMUE. MALORY SAID MERLIN HAD THE HOTS FOR HER, BUT SHE THOUGHT HE WAS A DIRTY OLD MAN WITH A SCRATCHY BEARD.
SHE TRICKED HIM, STOLE HIS MAGIC AND WALLED HIM UP IN A CAVE FOR THE REST OF ETERNITY.
THIS ONE. OR ANY OF THE TWENTY-THREE OTHER MERLIN'S CAVES DOTTED AROUND THE COUNTRY.
YOU NOTICE HOW ALL THESE PLACES HAVE SOMETHING TO DO WITH CHANGE?
THE HOLY LAND BECOMES AN ALE-HOUSE. A PRISON BECOMES A WAR MEMORIAL. A CAVE BECOMES A RESERVOIR.
AREN'T THEY ALL ABOUT DEATH AS WELL? HENRY FOUR, THE GUY IN THE DUEL, MERLIN--
THE GUY IN THE DUEL DIDN'T DIE. MAYBE MERLIN DIDN'T EITHER. SOME VERSIONS HAVE HIM--
EXCUSE ME, YOU TWO.
DO YOU MIND STEPPING OVER HERE?
Merlin's Cave Entrance Hours 11 AM - 5 PM

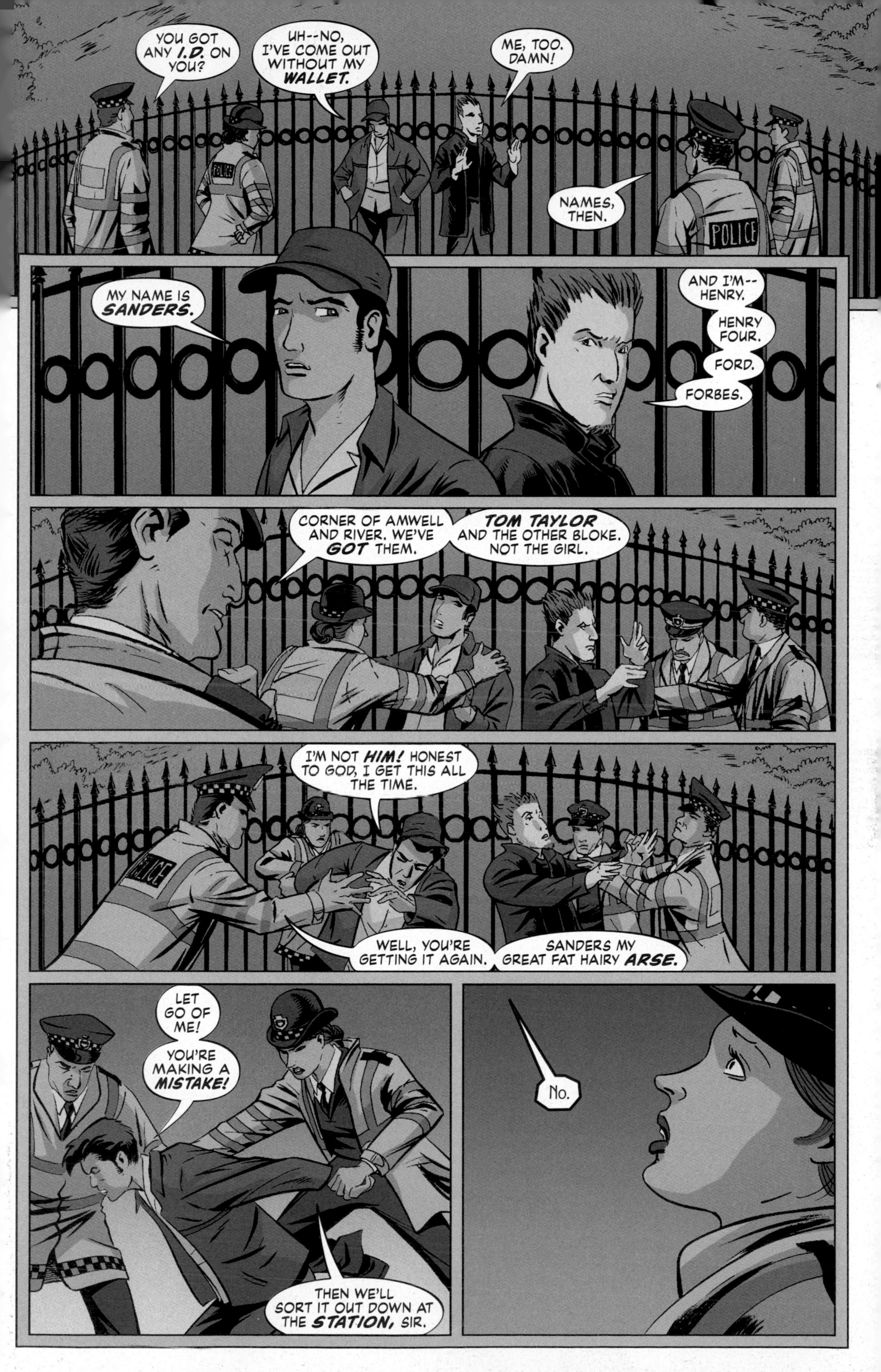
YOU GOT ANY I.D. ON YOU?
UH--NO, I'VE COME OUT WITHOUT MY WALLET.
ME, TOO. DAMN!
NAMES, THEN.
MY NAME IS SANDERS.
AND I'M-- HENRY.
HENRY FOUR.
FORD.
FORBES.
CORNER OF AMWELL AND RIVER. WE'VE GOT THEM.
TOM TAYLOR AND THE OTHER BLOKE. NOT THE GIRL.
I'M NOT HIM! HONEST TO GOD, I GET THIS ALL THE TIME.
WELL, YOU'RE GETTING IT AGAIN.
SANDERS MY GREAT FAT HAIRY ARSE.
LET GO OF ME!
YOU'RE MAKING A MISTAKE!
THEN WE'LL SORT IT OUT DOWN AT THE STATION, SIR.
No.

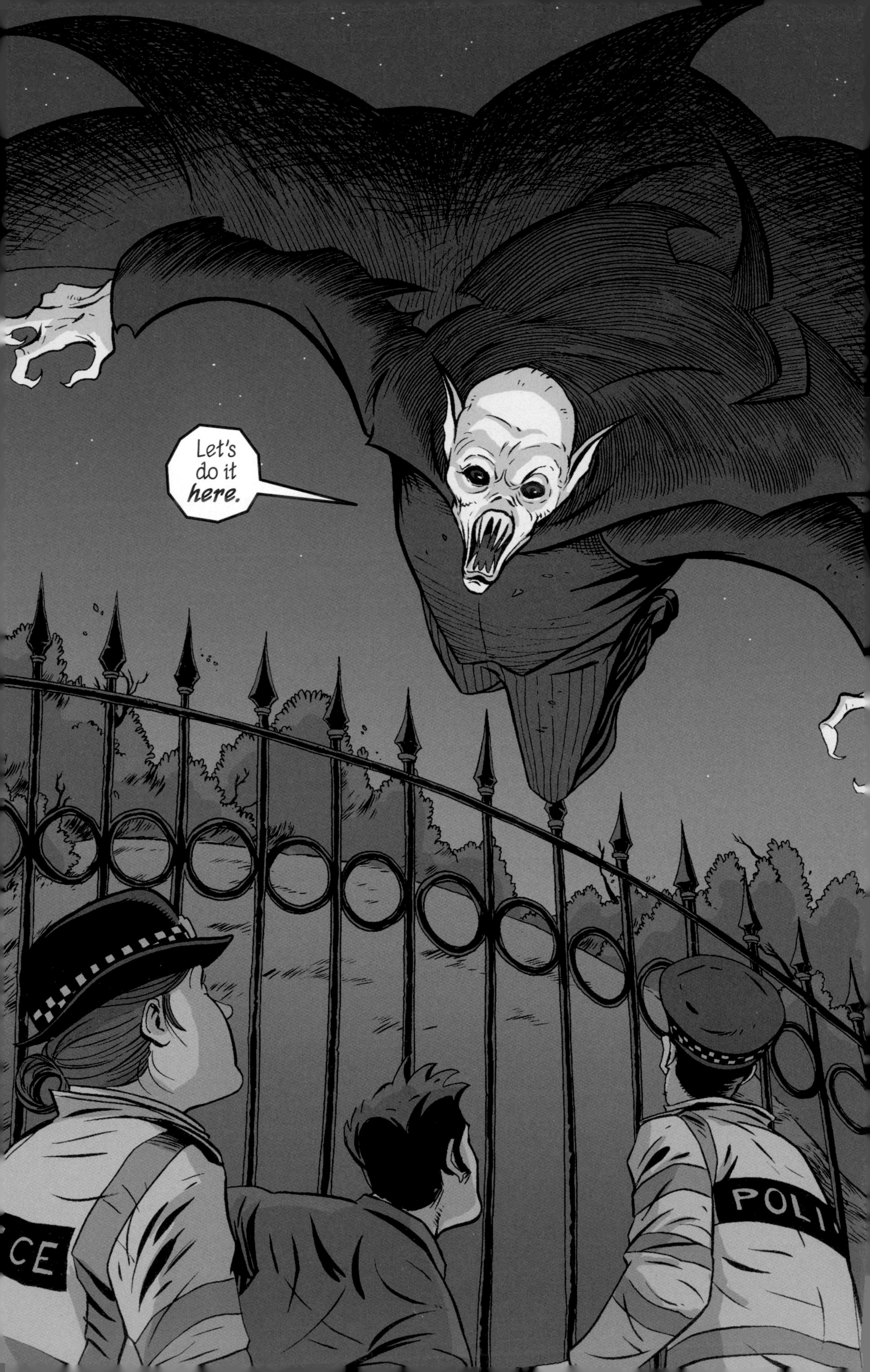
Let's do it *here.*
CE
POLI

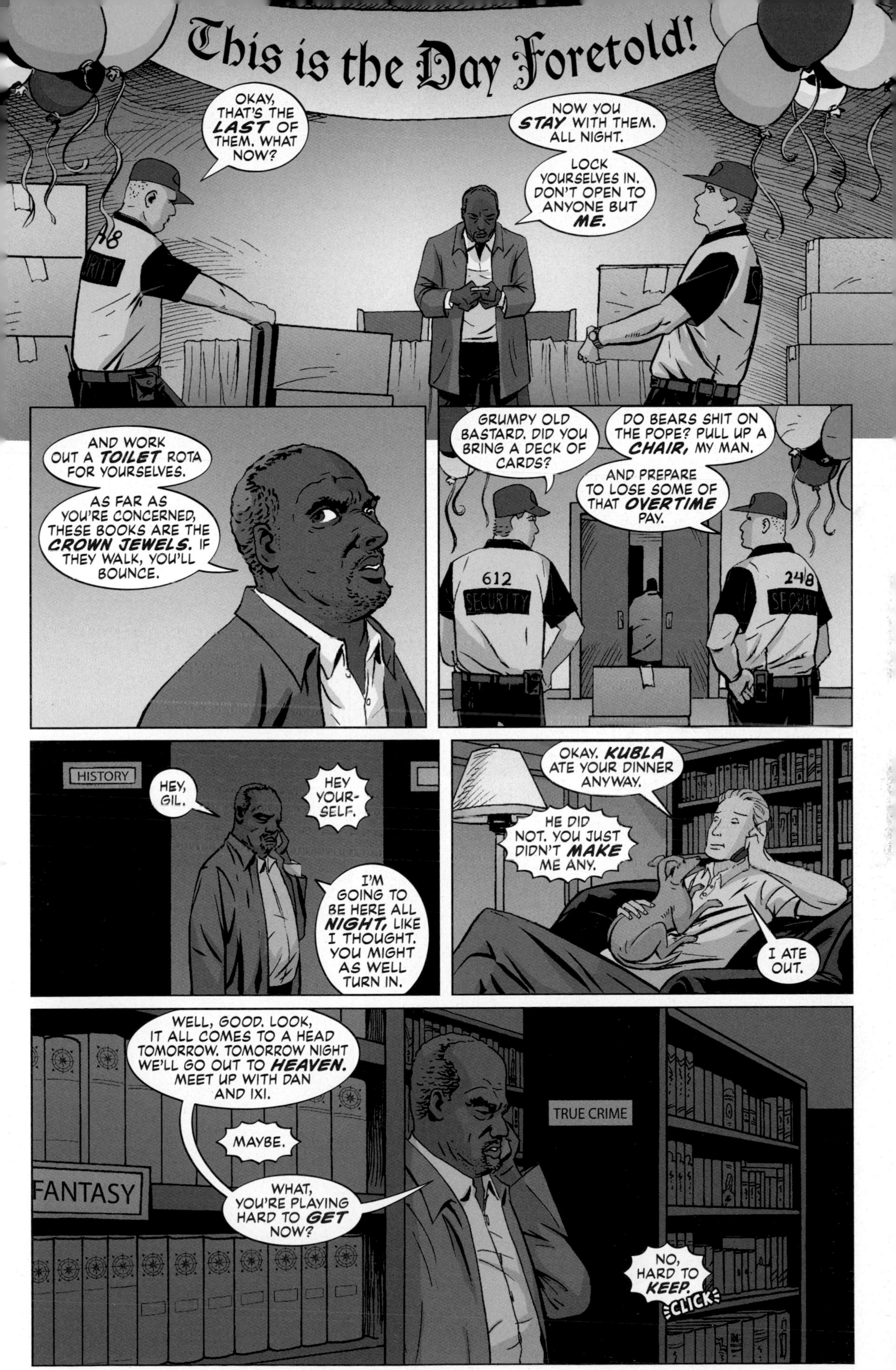
This is the Day Foretold!
OKAY, THAT'S THE LAST OF THEM. WHAT NOW?
NOW YOU STAY WITH THEM. ALL NIGHT.
LOCK YOURSELVES IN. DON'T OPEN TO ANYONE BUT ME.
AND WORK OUT A TOILET ROTA FOR YOURSELVES.
AS FAR AS YOU'RE CONCERNED, THESE BOOKS ARE THE CROWN JEWELS. IF THEY WALK, YOU'LL BOUNCE.
GRUMPY OLD BASTARD. DID YOU BRING A DECK OF CARDS?
DO BEARS SHIT ON THE POPE? PULL UP A CHAIR, MY MAN.
AND PREPARE TO LOSE SOME OF THAT OVERTIME PAY.
612
SECURITY
248
HISTORY
HEY, GIL.
HEY YOURSELF.
I'M GOING TO BE HERE ALL NIGHT, LIKE I THOUGHT. YOU MIGHT AS WELL TURN IN.
OKAY. KUBLA ATE YOUR DINNER ANYWAY.
HE DID NOT. YOU JUST DIDN'T MAKE ME ANY.
I ATE OUT.
WELL, GOOD. LOOK, IT ALL COMES TO A HEAD TOMORROW. TOMORROW NIGHT WE'LL GO OUT TO HEAVEN. MEET UP WITH DAN AND IXI.
MAYBE.
WHAT, YOU'RE PLAYING HARD TO GET NOW?
FANTASY
TRUE CRIME
NO, HARD TO KEEP.
CLICK

WELL, THAT'S THE BIG *QUESTION*, ISN'T IT?

HUH?

FUCK. THIS BETTER BE WORTH IT, WILSON.

THIS BETTER BE FUCKING *WORTH* IT.

I THINK MAYBE WE SHOULD EXPLORE IT *TOGETHER*.

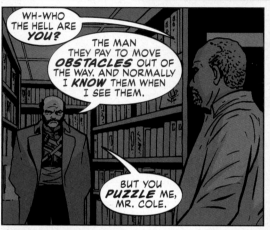

WH-WHO THE HELL ARE *YOU*?

THE MAN THEY PAY TO MOVE *OBSTACLES* OUT OF THE WAY. AND NORMALLY I *KNOW* THEM WHEN I SEE THEM.

BUT YOU *PUZZLE* ME, MR. COLE.

YOU'RE REALLY *SCARED*. WHICH I SUPPOSE IS UNDERSTANDABLE, GIVEN THE ATROCITY YOU'RE ABOUT TO PERPETRATE ON THE BOOK-BUYING PUBLIC. BUT IT HAS THE WRONG *FEEL* TO IT, SOMEHOW.

YOU'RE SCARED ABOUT SOMETHING I CAN'T *SEE*. AND I'D LIKE TO KNOW WHAT IT IS.

I DON'T KNOW WHAT YOU'RE-- ¡UKKKKK!¡

YEAH, YOU DO. BUT IT'S A *SECRET*. I GET THAT.

MAYBE IT INVOLVES A PROMISE TO A *FRIEND* OR SOMETHING.

WE JUST NEED A LITTLE *VIOLENCE* TO TEASE IT OUT.

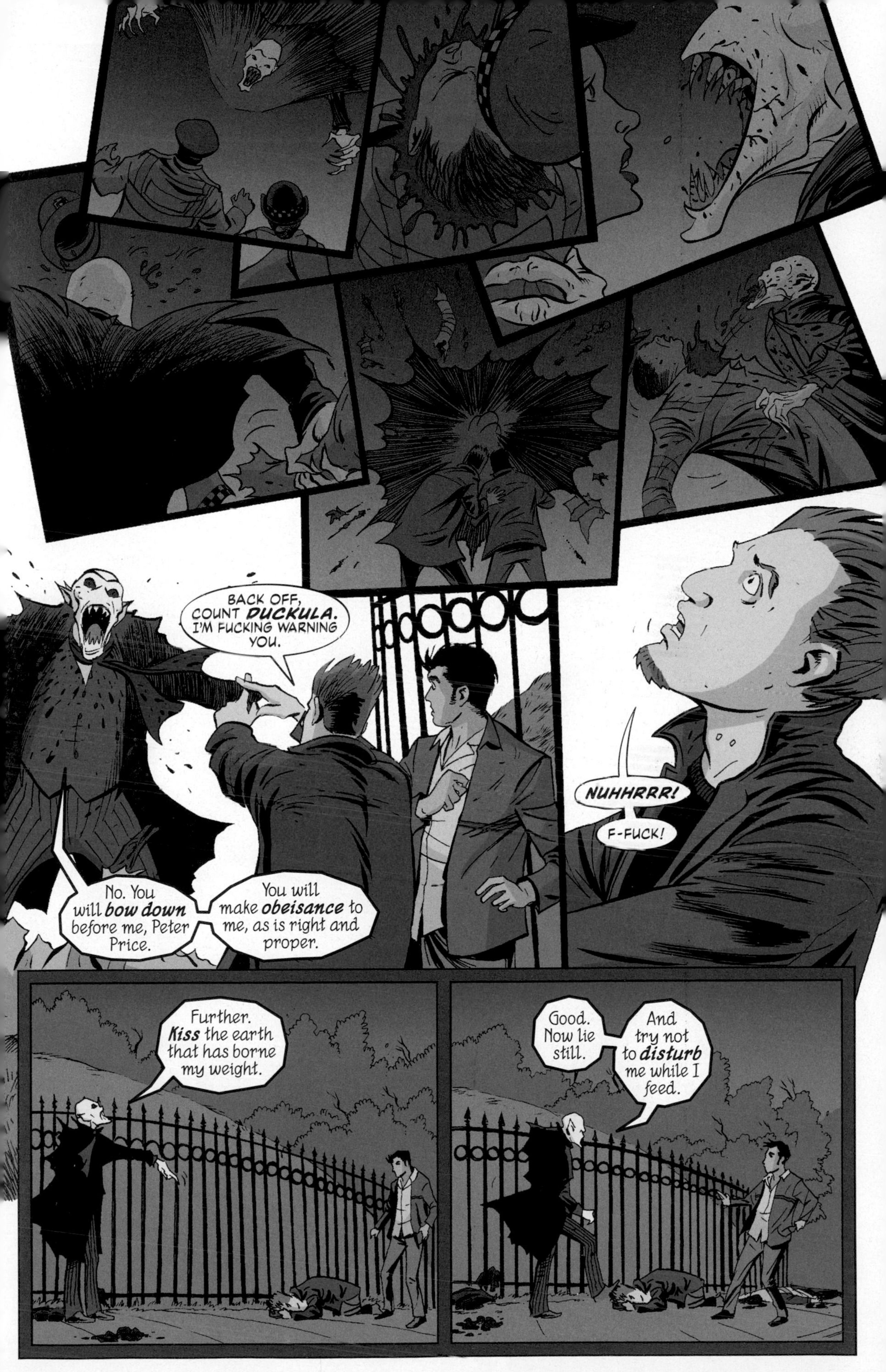

BACK OFF, COUNT DUCKULA. I'M FUCKING WARNING YOU.
No. You will bow down before me, Peter Price.
You will make obeisance to me, as is right and proper.
NUHHRRR!
F-FUCK!
Further. Kiss the earth that has borne my weight.
Good. Now lie still.
And try not to disturb me while I feed.

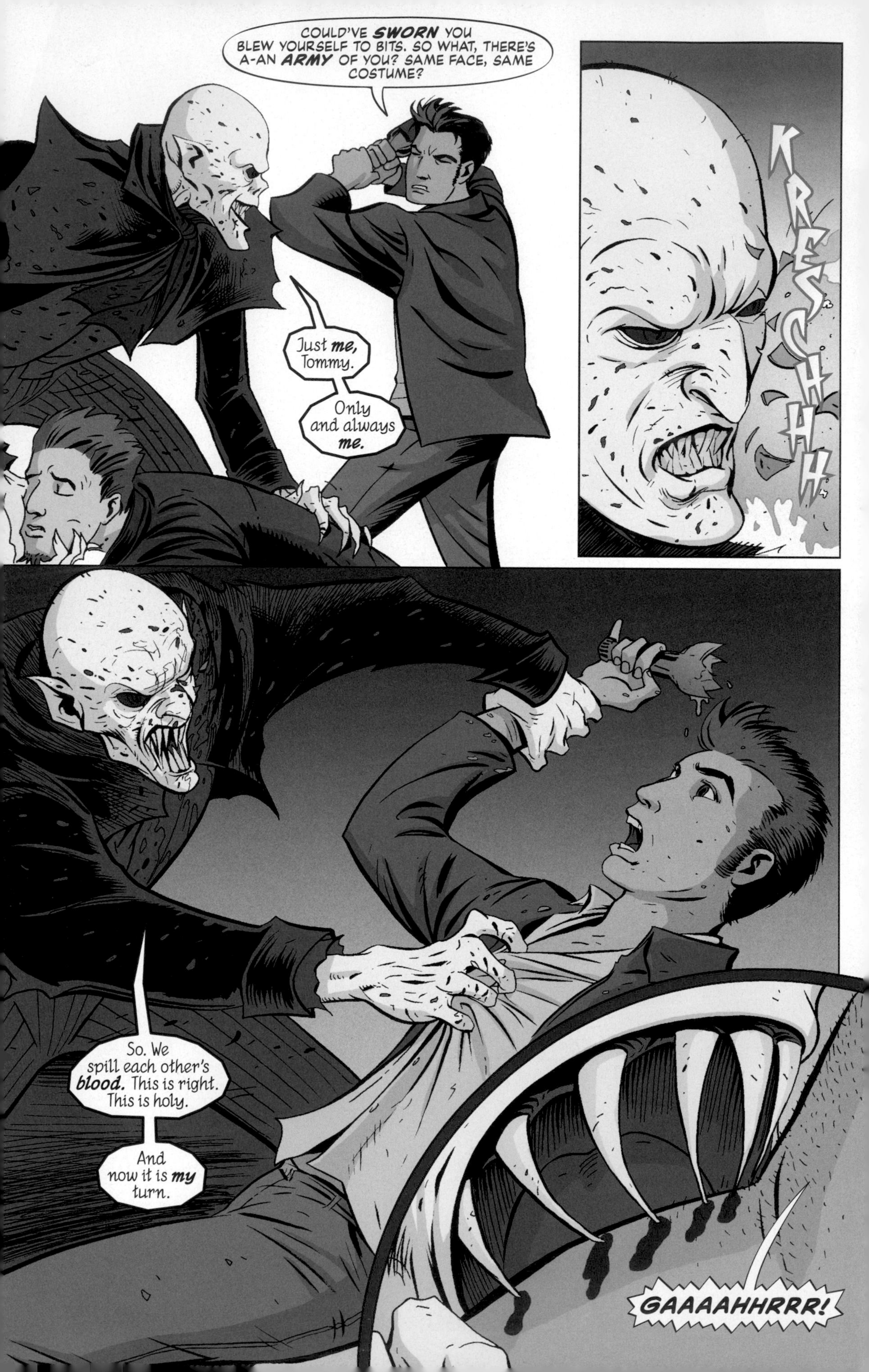
COULD'VE SWORN YOU BLEW YOURSELF TO BITS. SO WHAT, THERE'S A-AN ARMY OF YOU? SAME FACE, SAME COSTUME?
Just me, Tommy.
Only and always me.
KRESCHHH
So. We spill each other's blood. This is right. This is holy.
And now it is my turn.
GAAAAHHRRR!

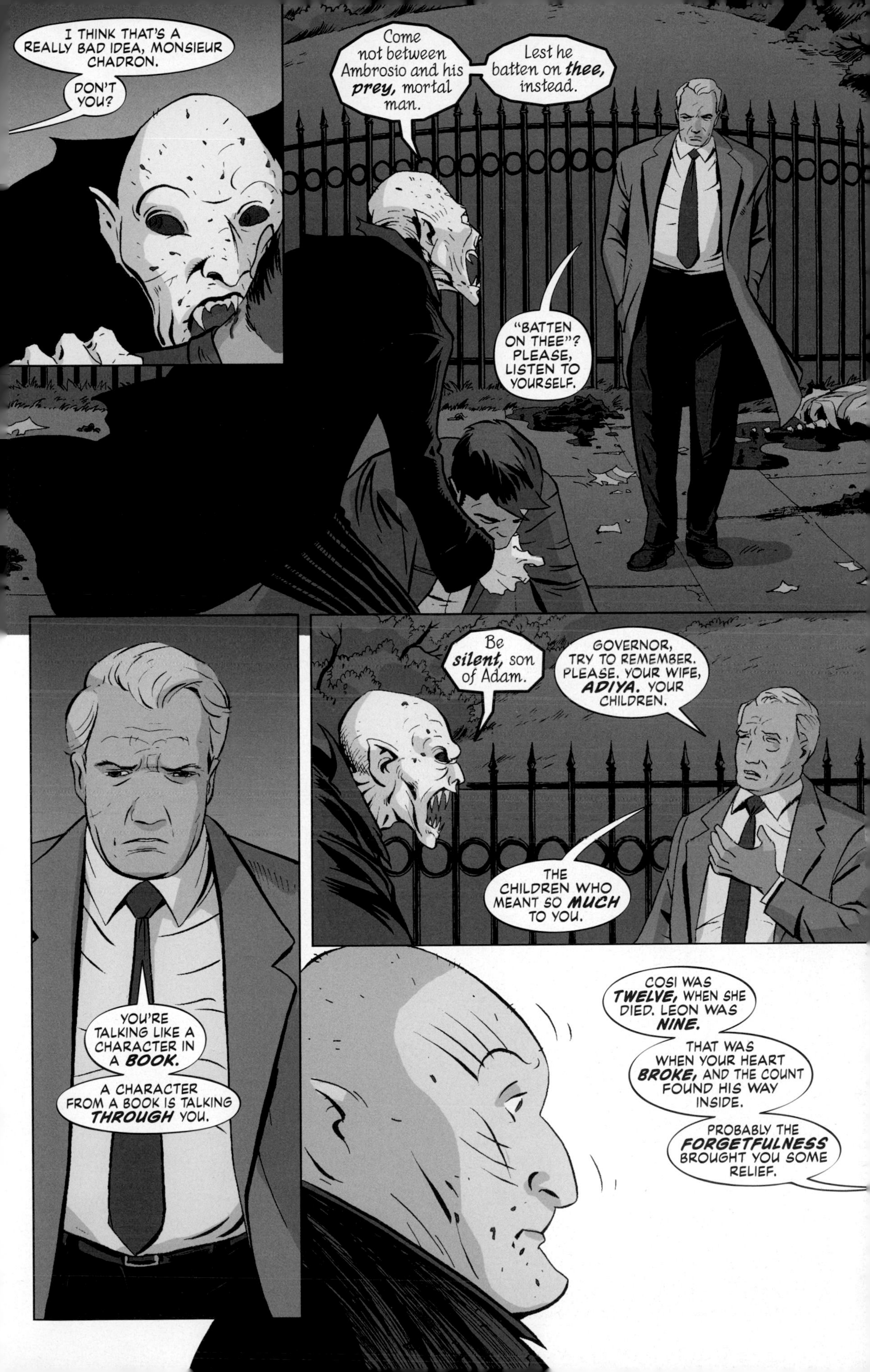

I THINK THAT'S A REALLY BAD IDEA, MONSIEUR CHADRON.
DON'T YOU?
Come not between Ambrosio and his *prey*, mortal man.
Lest he batten on *thee*, instead.
"BATTEN ON THEE"? PLEASE, LISTEN TO YOURSELF.
YOU'RE TALKING LIKE A CHARACTER IN A *BOOK*.
A CHARACTER FROM A BOOK IS TALKING *THROUGH* YOU.
Be *silent*, son of Adam.
GOVERNOR, TRY TO REMEMBER. PLEASE. YOUR WIFE, *ADIYA*. YOUR CHILDREN.
THE CHILDREN WHO MEANT SO *MUCH* TO YOU.
COSI WAS *TWELVE*, WHEN SHE DIED. LEON WAS *NINE*.
THAT WAS WHEN YOUR HEART *BROKE*, AND THE COUNT FOUND HIS WAY INSIDE.
PROBABLY THE *FORGETFULNESS* BROUGHT YOU SOME RELIEF.

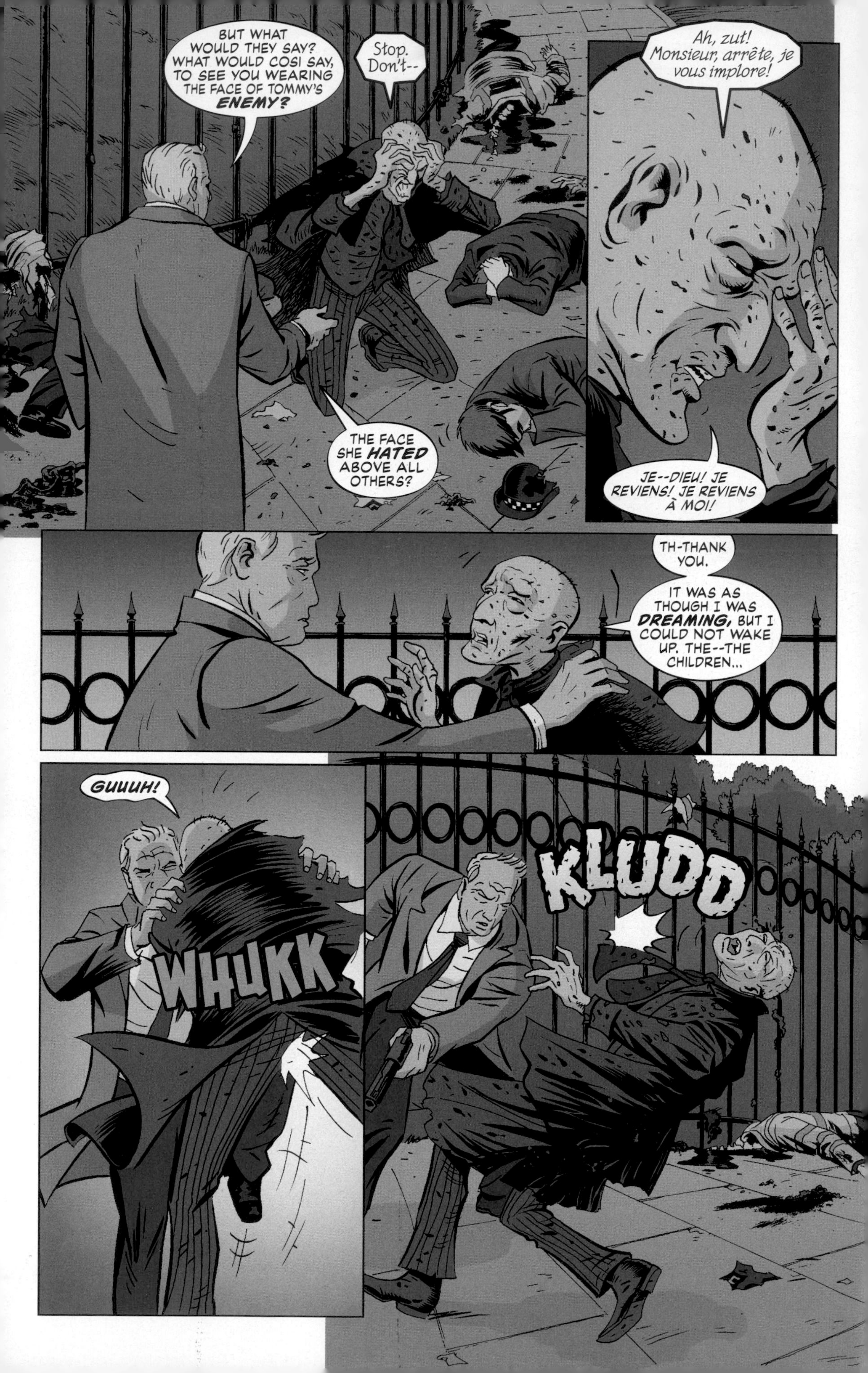
BUT WHAT WOULD THEY SAY? WHAT WOULD COSI SAY, TO SEE YOU WEARING THE FACE OF TOMMY'S ENEMY?
Stop. Don't--
THE FACE SHE HATED ABOVE ALL OTHERS?
Ah, zut! Monsieur, arrête, je vous implore!
JE--DIEU! JE REVIENS! JE REVIENS À MOI!
TH-THANK YOU.
IT WAS AS THOUGH I WAS DREAMING, BUT I COULD NOT WAKE UP. THE--THE CHILDREN...
GUUUH!
WHUKK
KLUDD

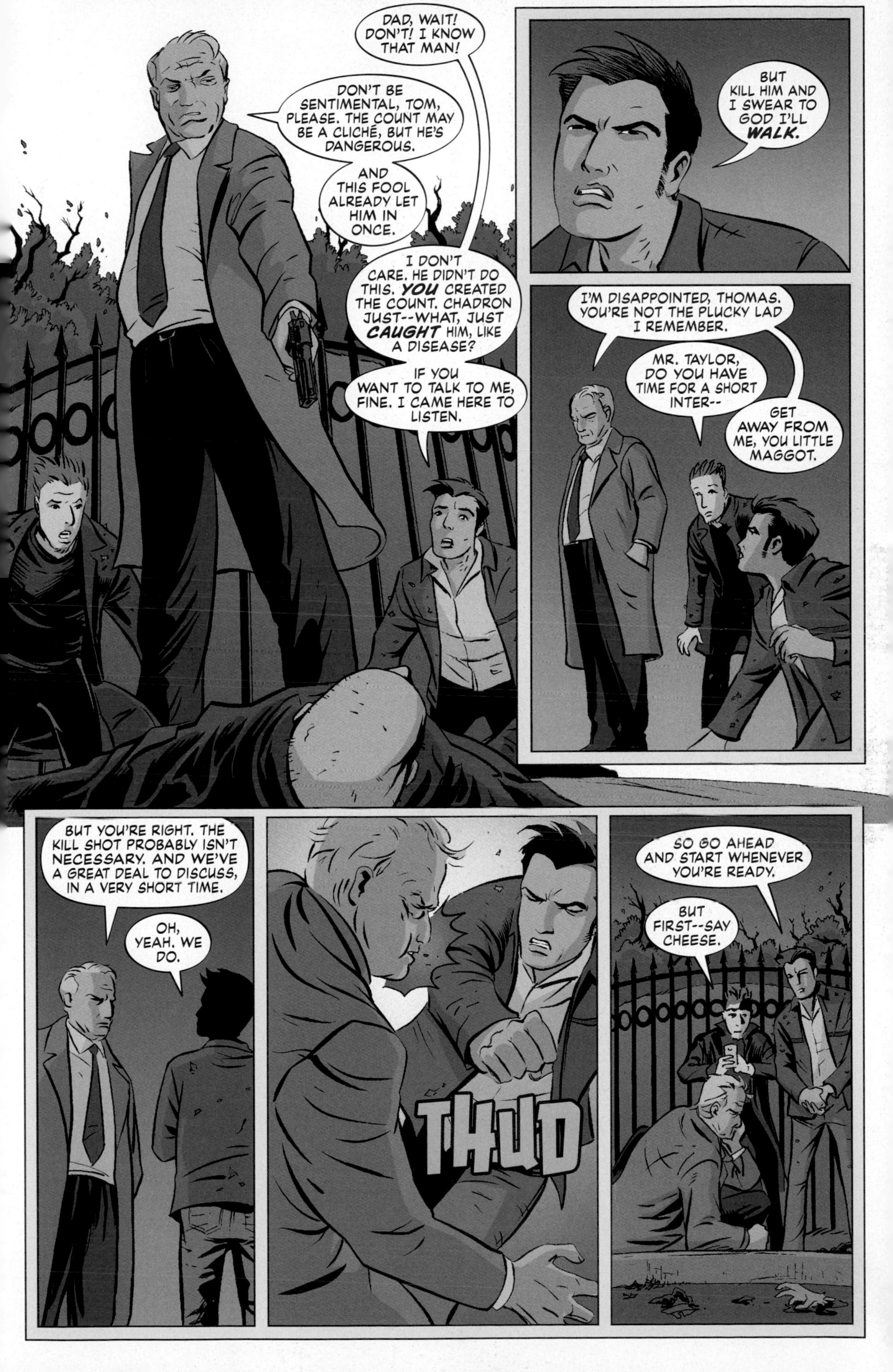
DAD, WAIT! DON'T! I KNOW THAT MAN!
DON'T BE SENTIMENTAL, TOM, PLEASE. THE COUNT MAY BE A CLICHÉ, BUT HE'S DANGEROUS.
AND THIS FOOL ALREADY LET HIM IN ONCE.
I DON'T CARE. HE DIDN'T DO THIS. YOU CREATED THE COUNT. CHADRON JUST--WHAT, JUST CAUGHT HIM, LIKE A DISEASE?
IF YOU WANT TO TALK TO ME, FINE. I CAME HERE TO LISTEN.
BUT KILL HIM AND I SWEAR TO GOD I'LL WALK.
I'M DISAPPOINTED, THOMAS. YOU'RE NOT THE PLUCKY LAD I REMEMBER.
MR. TAYLOR, DO YOU HAVE TIME FOR A SHORT INTER--
GET AWAY FROM ME, YOU LITTLE MAGGOT.
BUT YOU'RE RIGHT. THE KILL SHOT PROBABLY ISN'T NECESSARY. AND WE'VE A GREAT DEAL TO DISCUSS, IN A VERY SHORT TIME.
OH, YEAH. WE DO.
THUD
SO GO AHEAD AND START WHENEVER YOU'RE READY.
BUT FIRST--SAY CHEESE.

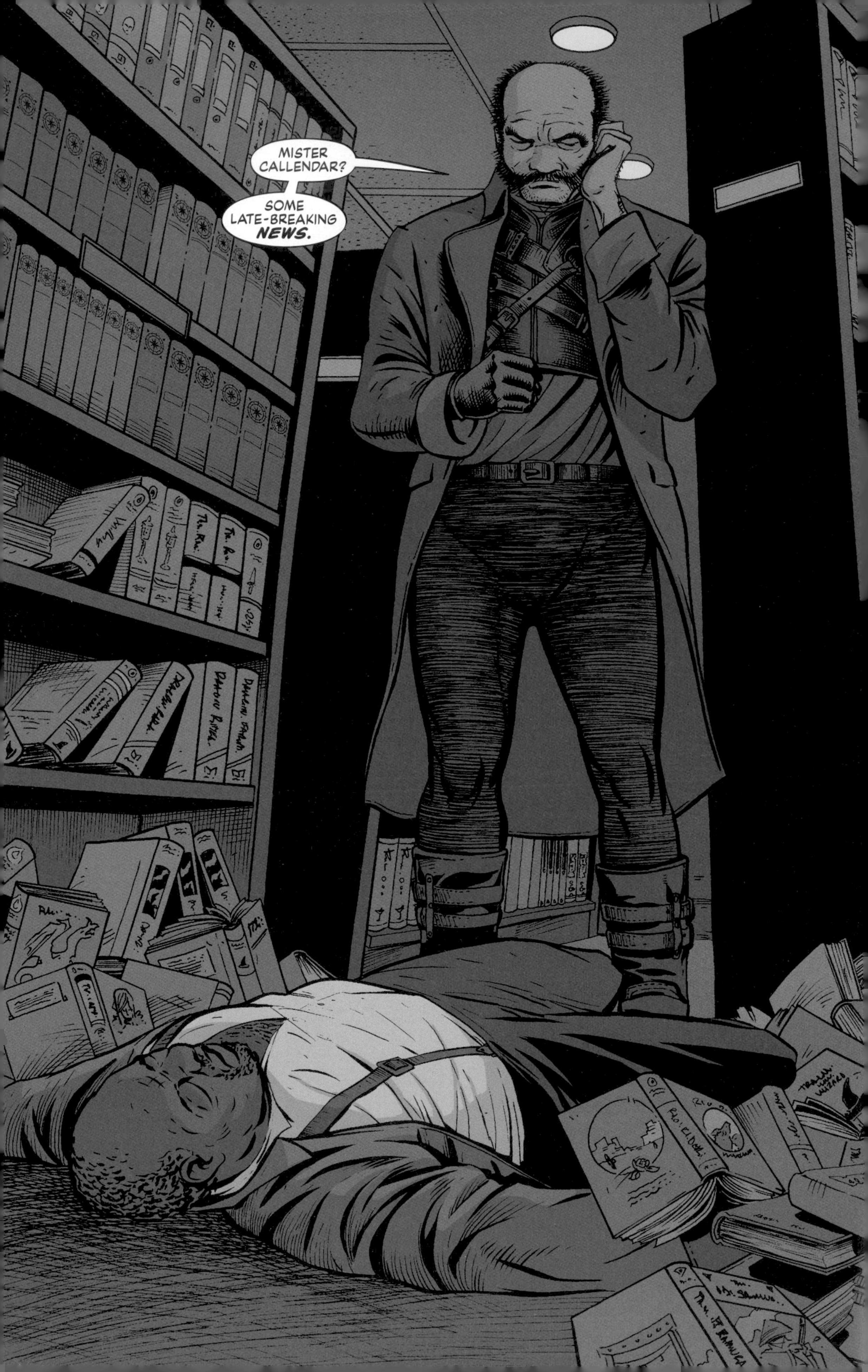
MISTER CALLENDAR?
SOME LATE-BREAKING NEWS.

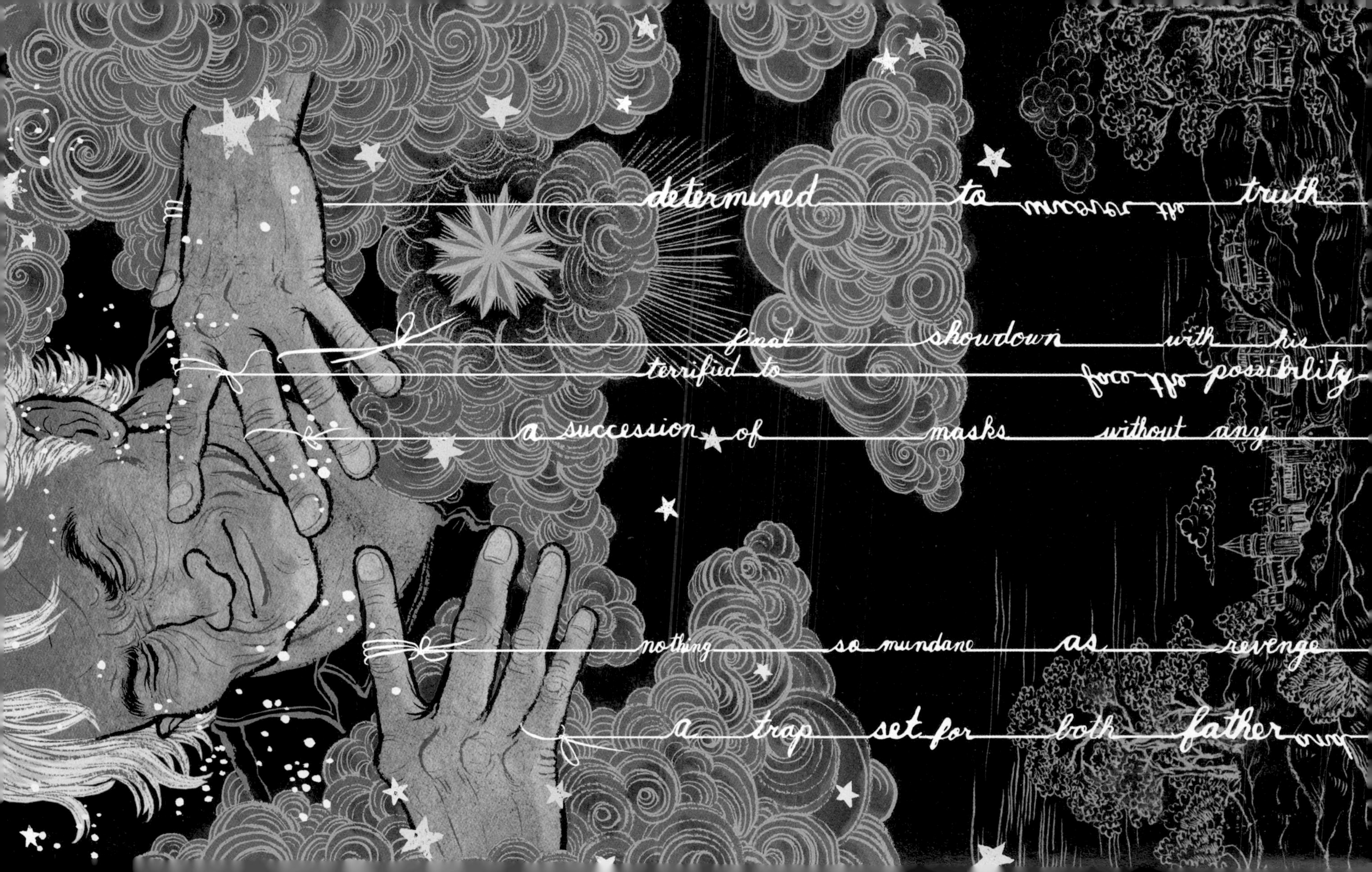
determined to uncover the truth
final showdown with his
terrified to face the possibility
a succession of masks without any
nothing so mundane as revenge
a trap set for both father and

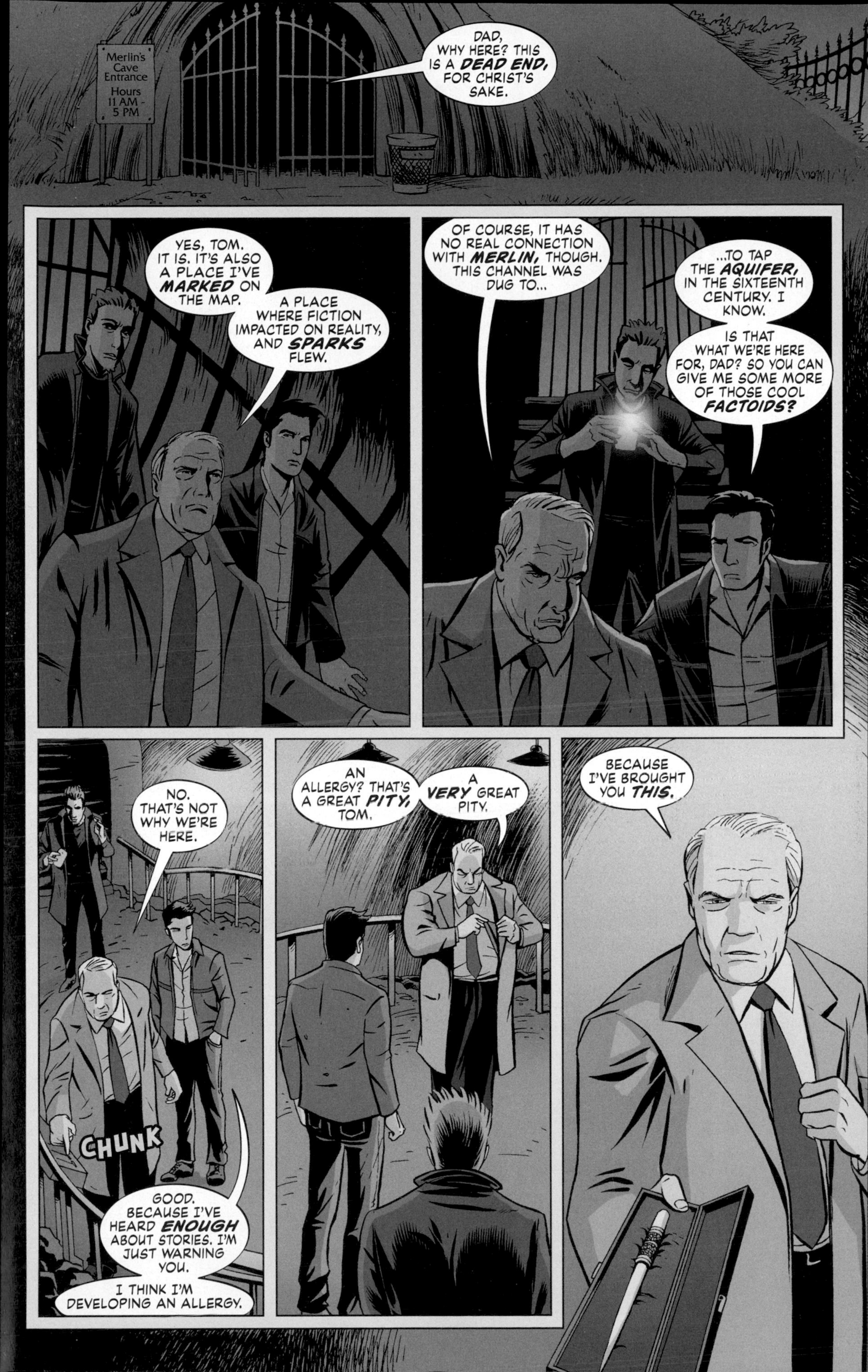
Merlin's Cave Entrance
Hours 11 AM - 5 PM
DAD, WHY HERE? THIS IS A ***DEAD END,*** FOR CHRIST'S SAKE.
YES, TOM. IT IS. IT'S ALSO A PLACE I'VE ***MARKED*** ON THE MAP.
A PLACE WHERE FICTION IMPACTED ON REALITY, AND ***SPARKS*** FLEW.
OF COURSE, IT HAS NO REAL CONNECTION WITH ***MERLIN,*** THOUGH. THIS CHANNEL WAS DUG TO...
...TO TAP THE ***AQUIFER,*** IN THE SIXTEENTH CENTURY. I KNOW.
IS THAT WHAT WE'RE HERE FOR, DAD? SO YOU CAN GIVE ME SOME MORE OF THOSE COOL ***FACTOIDS?***
NO. THAT'S NOT WHY WE'RE HERE.
CHUNK
GOOD. BECAUSE I'VE HEARD ***ENOUGH*** ABOUT STORIES. I'M JUST WARNING YOU.
I THINK I'M DEVELOPING AN ALLERGY.
AN ALLERGY? THAT'S A GREAT ***PITY,*** TOM.
A ***VERY*** GREAT PITY.
BECAUSE I'VE BROUGHT YOU ***THIS.***

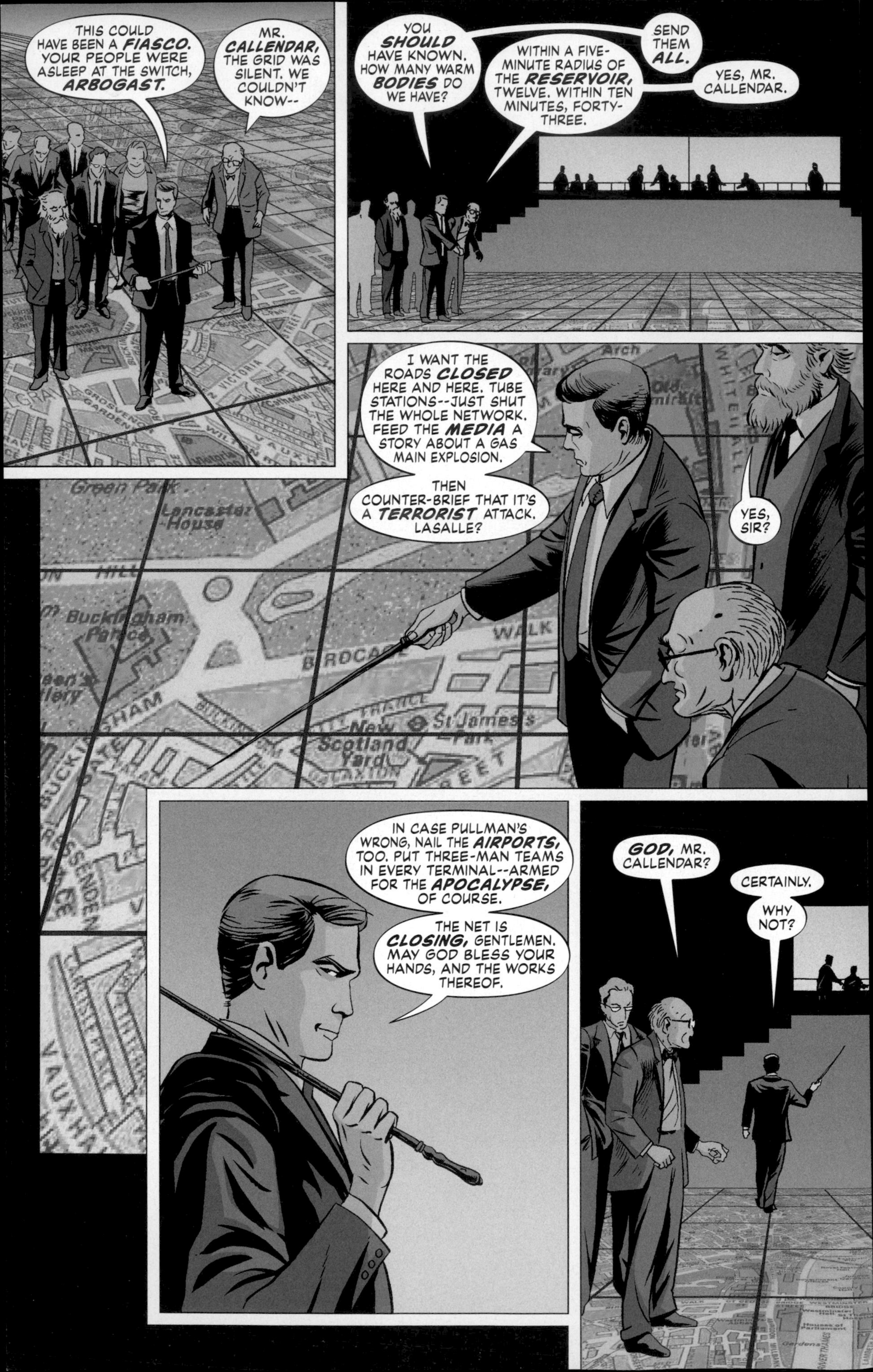
THIS COULD HAVE BEEN A FIASCO. YOUR PEOPLE WERE ASLEEP AT THE SWITCH, ARBOGAST.
MR. CALLENDAR, THE GRID WAS SILENT. WE COULDN'T KNOW--
YOU SHOULD HAVE KNOWN. HOW MANY WARM BODIES DO WE HAVE?
WITHIN A FIVE-MINUTE RADIUS OF THE RESERVOIR, TWELVE. WITHIN TEN MINUTES, FORTY-THREE.
SEND THEM ALL.
YES, MR. CALLENDAR.
I WANT THE ROADS CLOSED HERE AND HERE. TUBE STATIONS--JUST SHUT THE WHOLE NETWORK. FEED THE MEDIA A STORY ABOUT A GAS MAIN EXPLOSION.
THEN COUNTER-BRIEF THAT IT'S A TERRORIST ATTACK. LASALLE?
YES, SIR?
IN CASE PULLMAN'S WRONG, NAIL THE AIRPORTS, TOO. PUT THREE-MAN TEAMS IN EVERY TERMINAL--ARMED FOR THE APOCALYPSE, OF COURSE.
THE NET IS CLOSING, GENTLEMEN. MAY GOD BLESS YOUR HANDS, AND THE WORKS THEREOF.
GOD, MR. CALLENDAR?
CERTAINLY.
WHY NOT?

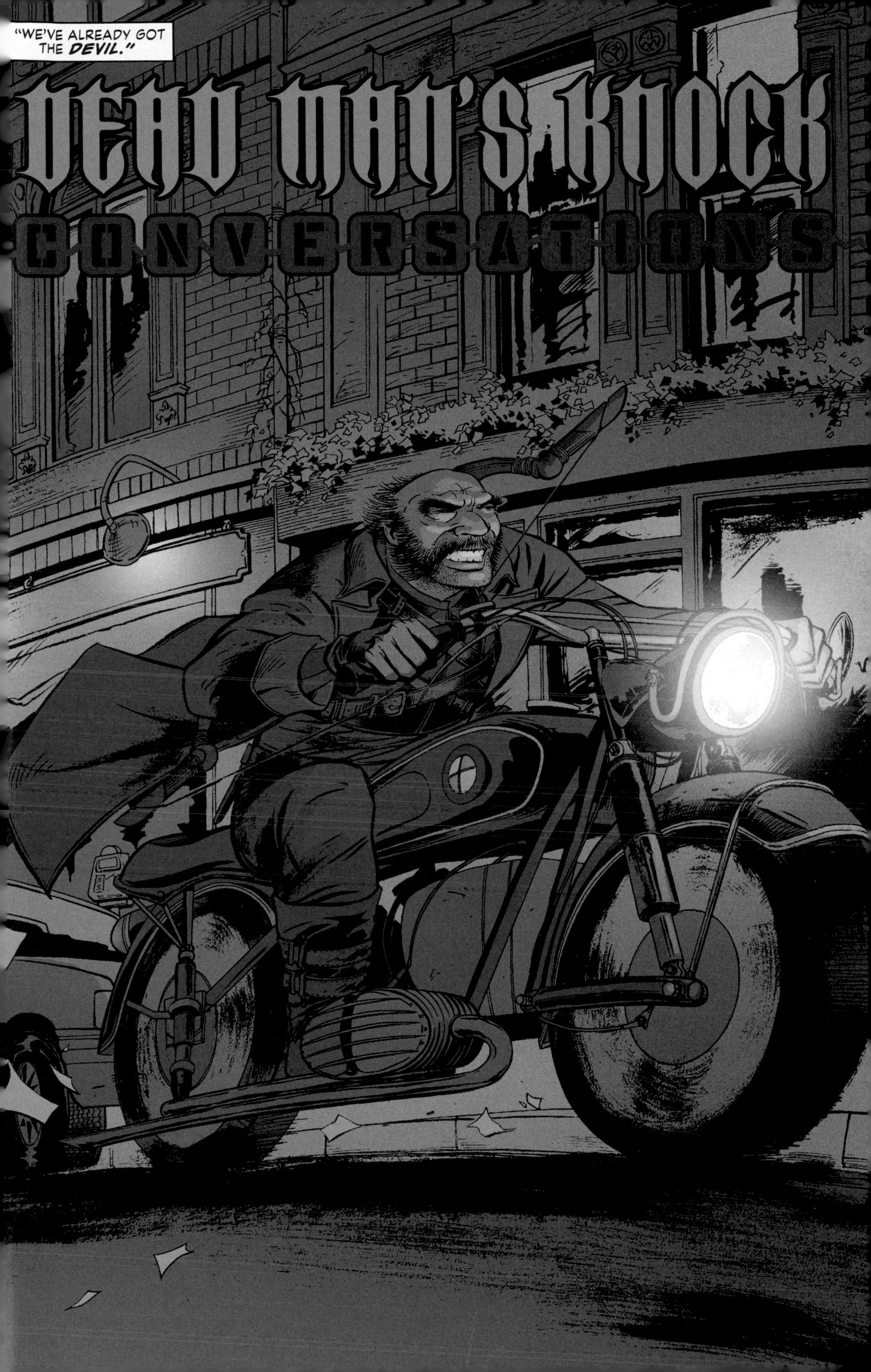
"WE'VE ALREADY GOT THE *DEVIL.*"
DEAD MAN'S KNOCK
CONVERSATIONS

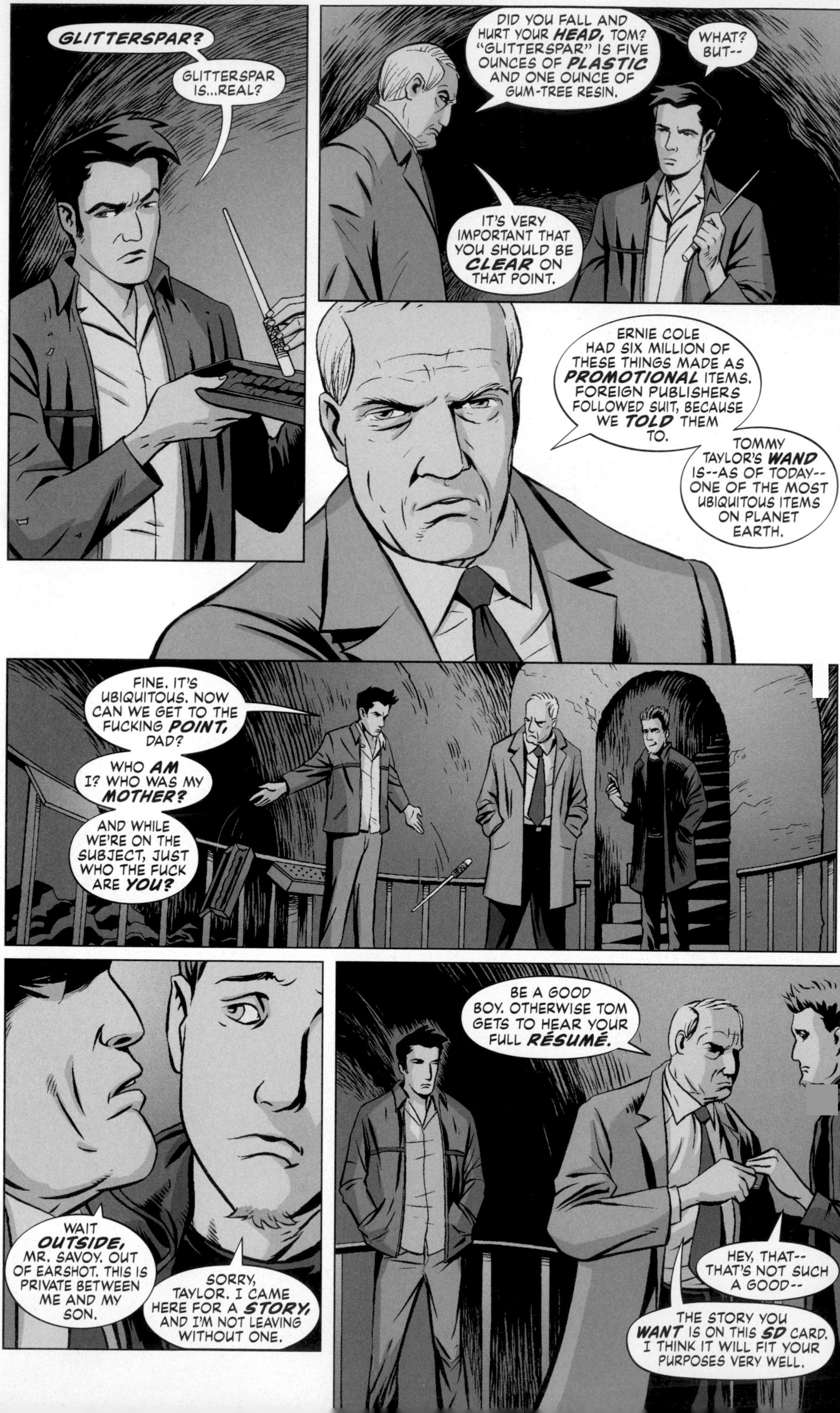
GLITTERSPAR?
GLITTERSPAR IS...REAL?
DID YOU FALL AND HURT YOUR HEAD, TOM? "GLITTERSPAR" IS FIVE OUNCES OF PLASTIC AND ONE OUNCE OF GUM-TREE RESIN.
WHAT? BUT--
IT'S VERY IMPORTANT THAT YOU SHOULD BE CLEAR ON THAT POINT.
ERNIE COLE HAD SIX MILLION OF THESE THINGS MADE AS PROMOTIONAL ITEMS. FOREIGN PUBLISHERS FOLLOWED SUIT, BECAUSE WE TOLD THEM TO.
TOMMY TAYLOR'S WAND IS--AS OF TODAY--ONE OF THE MOST UBIQUITOUS ITEMS ON PLANET EARTH.
FINE. IT'S UBIQUITOUS. NOW CAN WE GET TO THE FUCKING POINT, DAD?
WHO AM I? WHO WAS MY MOTHER?
AND WHILE WE'RE ON THE SUBJECT, JUST WHO THE FUCK ARE YOU?
WAIT OUTSIDE, MR. SAVOY. OUT OF EARSHOT. THIS IS PRIVATE BETWEEN ME AND MY SON.
SORRY, TAYLOR. I CAME HERE FOR A STORY, AND I'M NOT LEAVING WITHOUT ONE.
BE A GOOD BOY. OTHERWISE TOM GETS TO HEAR YOUR FULL RÉSUMÉ.
HEY, THAT--THAT'S NOT SUCH A GOOD--
THE STORY YOU WANT IS ON THIS SD CARD. I THINK IT WILL FIT YOUR PURPOSES VERY WELL.

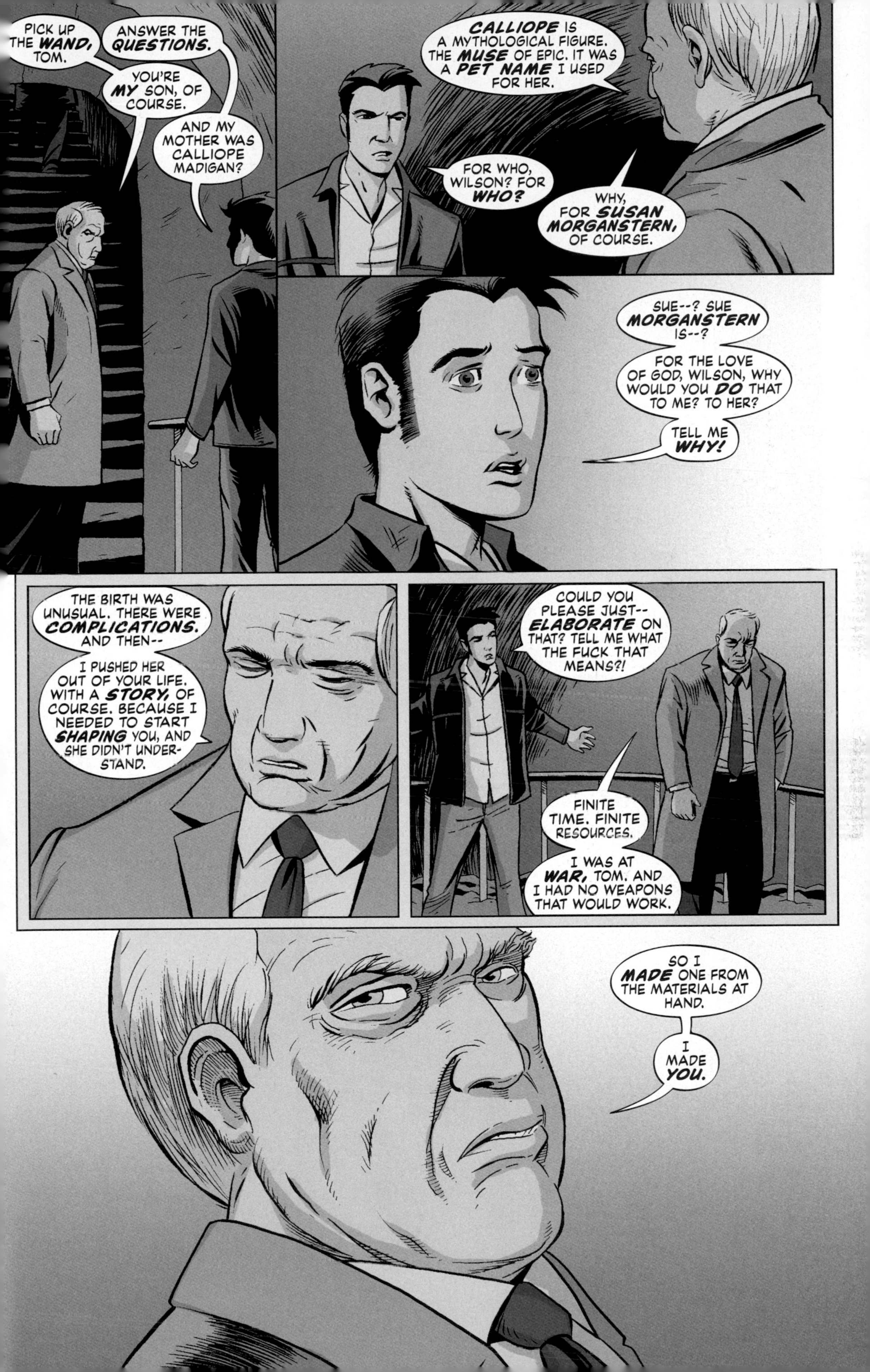
PICK UP THE WAND, TOM.
ANSWER THE QUESTIONS.
YOU'RE MY SON, OF COURSE.
AND MY MOTHER WAS CALLIOPE MADIGAN?
CALLIOPE IS A MYTHOLOGICAL FIGURE. THE MUSE OF EPIC. IT WAS A PET NAME I USED FOR HER.
FOR WHO, WILSON? FOR WHO?
WHY, FOR SUSAN MORGANSTERN, OF COURSE.
SUE--? SUE MORGANSTERN IS--?
FOR THE LOVE OF GOD, WILSON, WHY WOULD YOU DO THAT TO ME? TO HER?
TELL ME WHY!
THE BIRTH WAS UNUSUAL. THERE WERE COMPLICATIONS. AND THEN--
I PUSHED HER OUT OF YOUR LIFE. WITH A STORY, OF COURSE. BECAUSE I NEEDED TO START SHAPING YOU, AND SHE DIDN'T UNDER-STAND.
COULD YOU PLEASE JUST-- ELABORATE ON THAT? TELL ME WHAT THE FUCK THAT MEANS?!
FINITE TIME. FINITE RESOURCES.
I WAS AT WAR, TOM. AND I HAD NO WEAPONS THAT WOULD WORK.
SO I MADE ONE FROM THE MATERIALS AT HAND.
I MADE YOU.

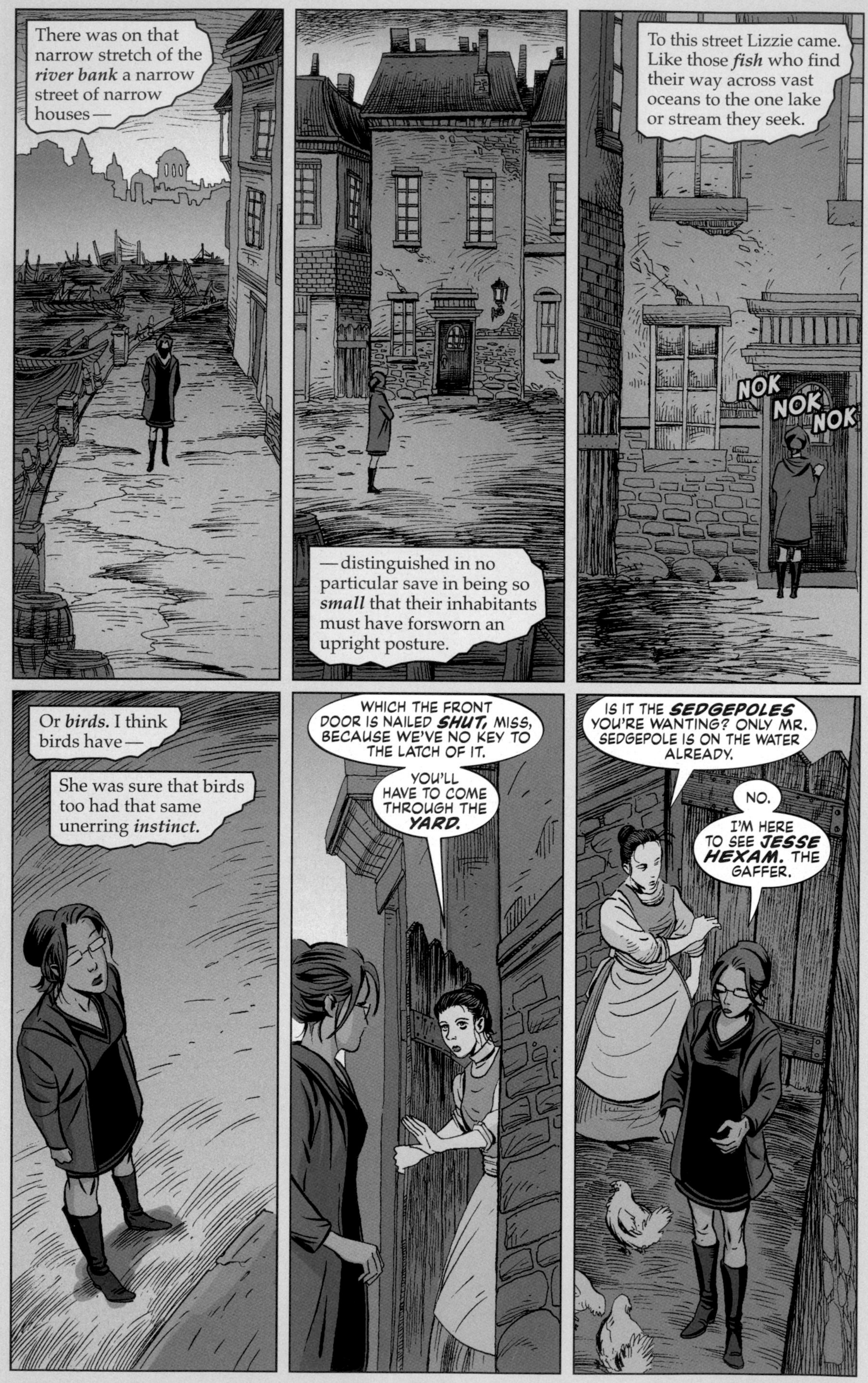
There was on that narrow stretch of the *river bank* a narrow street of narrow houses —
— distinguished in no particular save in being so *small* that their inhabitants must have forsworn an upright posture.
To this street Lizzie came. Like those *fish* who find their way across vast oceans to the one lake or stream they seek.
NOK NOK NOK
Or *birds.* I think birds have —
She was sure that birds too had that same unerring *instinct.*
WHICH THE FRONT DOOR IS NAILED ***SHUT,*** MISS, BECAUSE WE'VE NO KEY TO THE LATCH OF IT.
YOU'LL HAVE TO COME THROUGH THE ***YARD.***
IS IT THE ***SEDGEPOLES*** YOU'RE WANTING? ONLY MR. SEDGEPOLE IS ON THE WATER ALREADY.
NO.
I'M HERE TO SEE ***JESSE HEXAM.*** THE GAFFER.

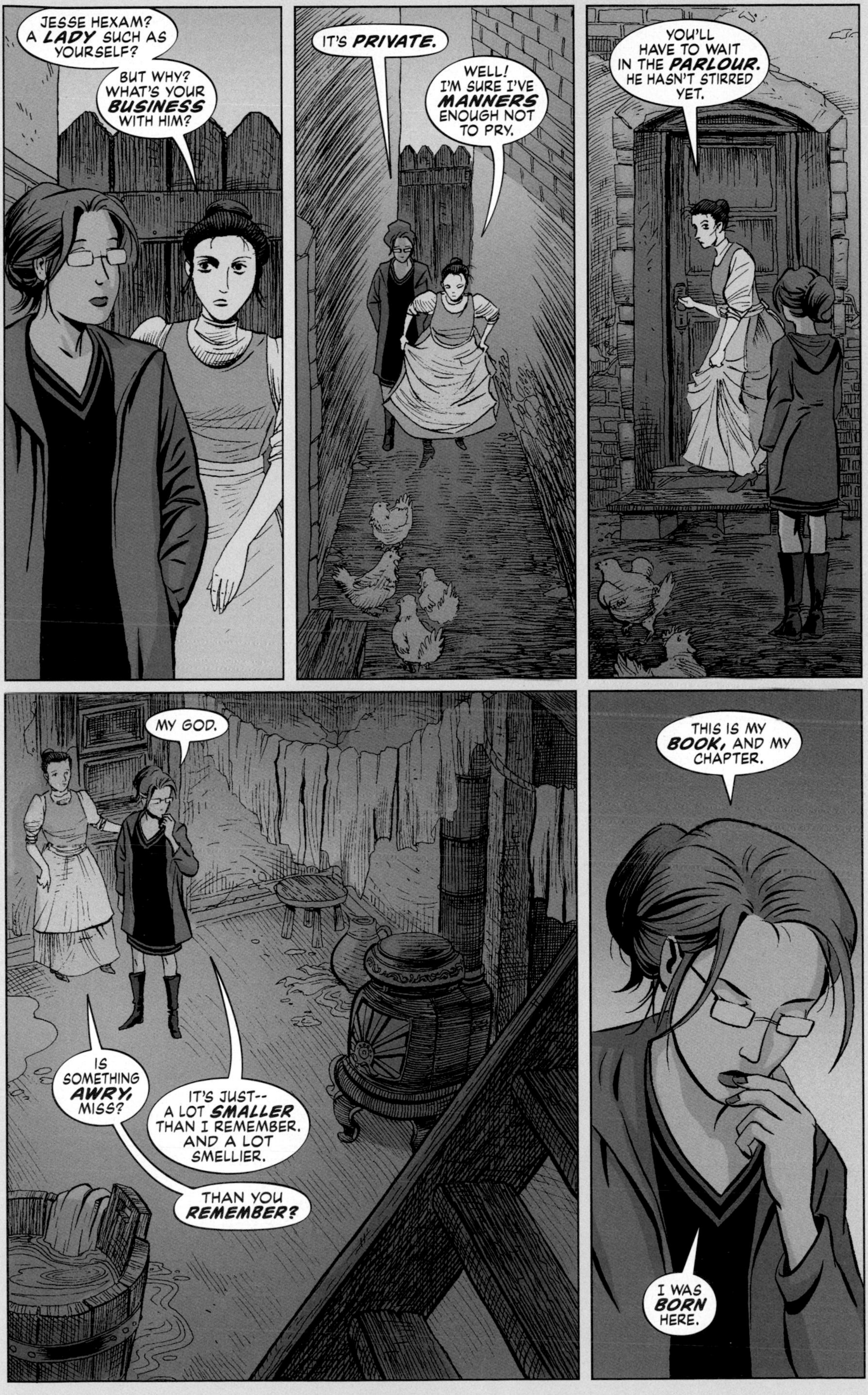
JESSE HEXAM? A LADY SUCH AS YOURSELF?
BUT WHY? WHAT'S YOUR BUSINESS WITH HIM?
IT'S PRIVATE.
WELL! I'M SURE I'VE MANNERS ENOUGH NOT TO PRY.
YOU'LL HAVE TO WAIT IN THE PARLOUR. HE HASN'T STIRRED YET.
MY GOD.
IS SOMETHING AWRY, MISS?
IT'S JUST-- A LOT SMALLER THAN I REMEMBER. AND A LOT SMELLIER.
THAN YOU REMEMBER?
THIS IS MY BOOK, AND MY CHAPTER.
I WAS BORN HERE.

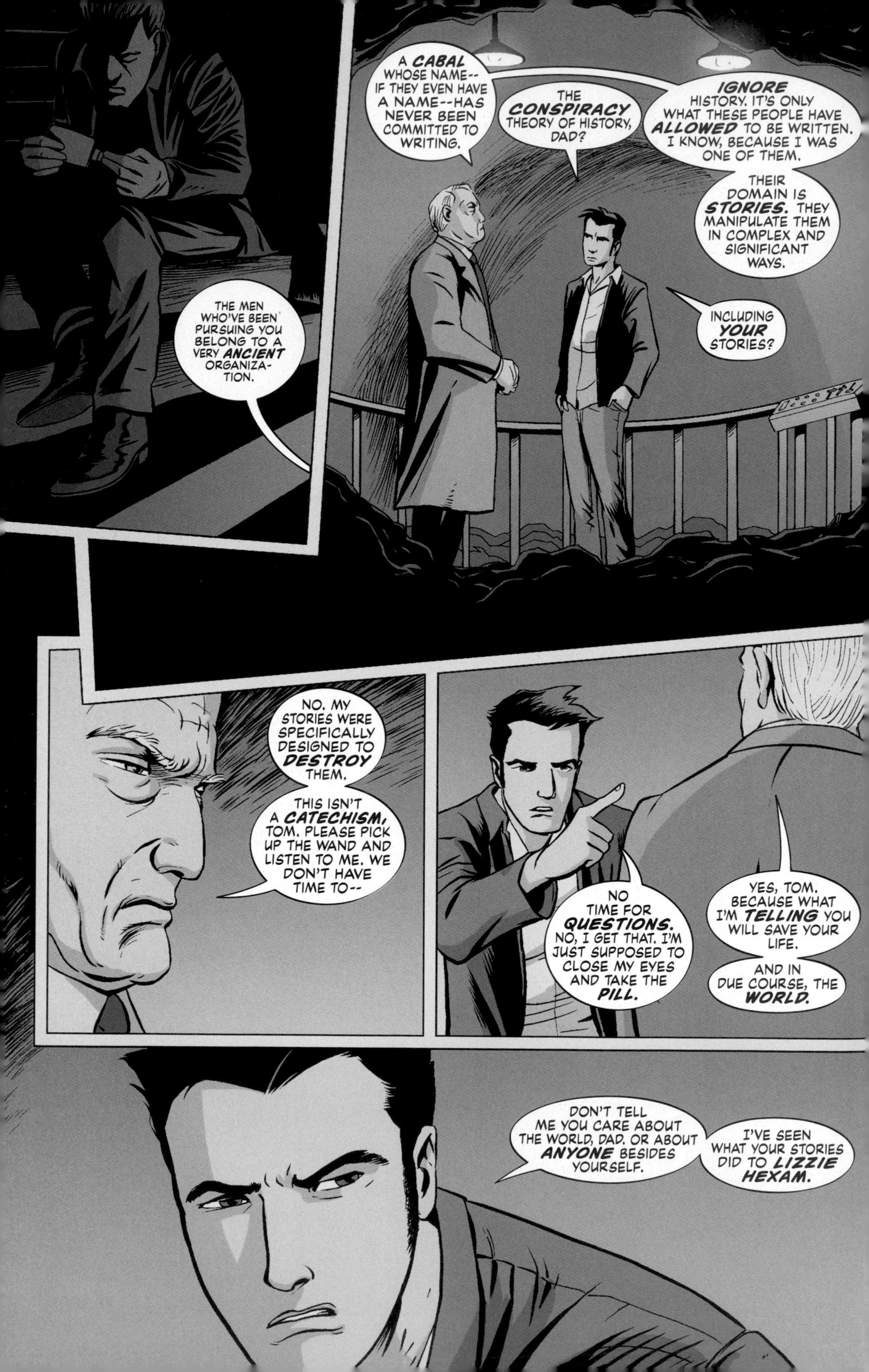

THE MEN WHO'VE BEEN PURSUING YOU BELONG TO A VERY ANCIENT ORGANIZATION.
A CABAL WHOSE NAME-- IF THEY EVEN HAVE A NAME--HAS NEVER BEEN COMMITTED TO WRITING.
THE CONSPIRACY THEORY OF HISTORY, DAD?
IGNORE HISTORY. IT'S ONLY WHAT THESE PEOPLE HAVE ALLOWED TO BE WRITTEN. I KNOW, BECAUSE I WAS ONE OF THEM.
THEIR DOMAIN IS STORIES. THEY MANIPULATE THEM IN COMPLEX AND SIGNIFICANT WAYS.
INCLUDING YOUR STORIES?
NO. MY STORIES WERE SPECIFICALLY DESIGNED TO DESTROY THEM.
THIS ISN'T A CATECHISM, TOM. PLEASE PICK UP THE WAND AND LISTEN TO ME. WE DON'T HAVE TIME TO--
NO TIME FOR QUESTIONS. NO, I GET THAT. I'M JUST SUPPOSED TO CLOSE MY EYES AND TAKE THE PILL.
YES, TOM. BECAUSE WHAT I'M TELLING YOU WILL SAVE YOUR LIFE.
AND IN DUE COURSE, THE WORLD.
DON'T TELL ME YOU CARE ABOUT THE WORLD, DAD. OR ABOUT ANYONE BESIDES YOURSELF.
I'VE SEEN WHAT YOUR STORIES DID TO LIZZIE HEXAM.

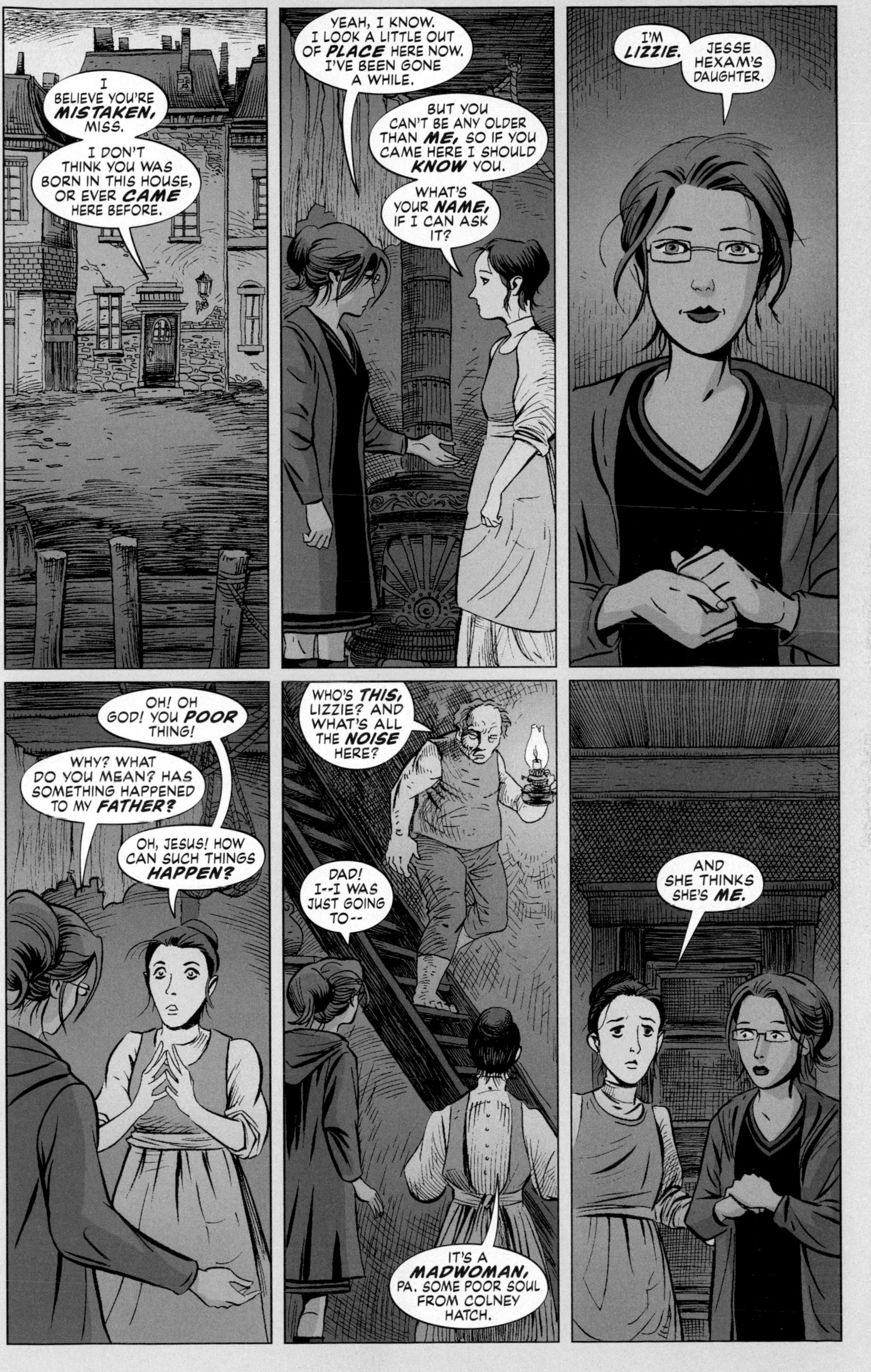
I BELIEVE YOU'RE MISTAKEN, MISS.
I DON'T THINK YOU WAS BORN IN THIS HOUSE, OR EVER CAME HERE BEFORE.
YEAH, I KNOW. I LOOK A LITTLE OUT OF PLACE HERE NOW. I'VE BEEN GONE A WHILE.
BUT YOU CAN'T BE ANY OLDER THAN ME, SO IF YOU CAME HERE I SHOULD KNOW YOU.
WHAT'S YOUR NAME, IF I CAN ASK IT?
I'M LIZZIE.
JESSE HEXAM'S DAUGHTER.
OH! OH GOD! YOU POOR THING!
WHY? WHAT DO YOU MEAN? HAS SOMETHING HAPPENED TO MY FATHER?
OH, JESUS! HOW CAN SUCH THINGS HAPPEN?
WHO'S THIS, LIZZIE? AND WHAT'S ALL THE NOISE HERE?
DAD! I--I WAS JUST GOING TO--
IT'S A MADWOMAN, PA. SOME POOR SOUL FROM COLNEY HATCH.
AND SHE THINKS SHE'S ME.

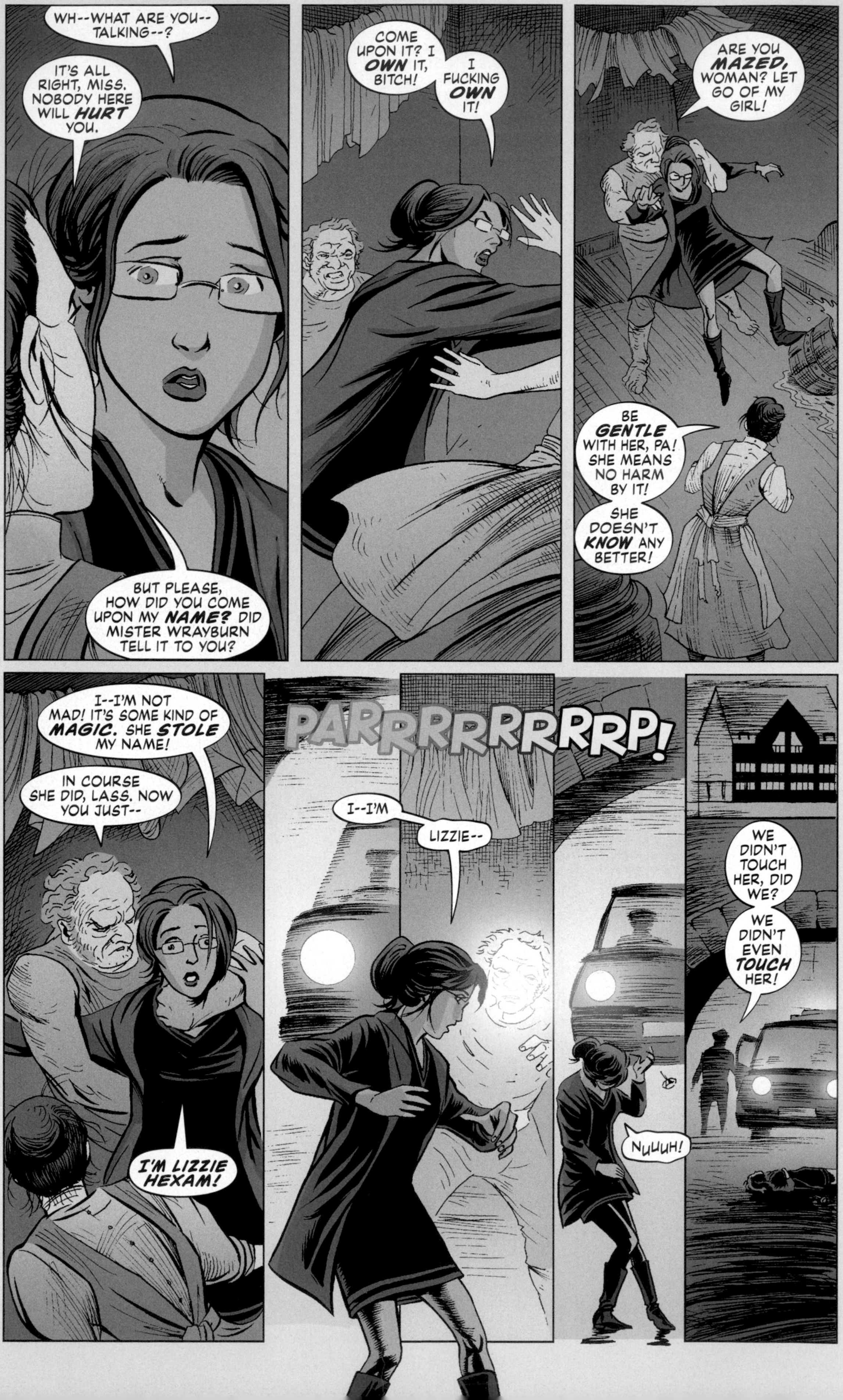
WH--WHAT ARE YOU--TALKING--?
IT'S ALL RIGHT, MISS. NOBODY HERE WILL HURT YOU.
BUT PLEASE, HOW DID YOU COME UPON MY NAME? DID MISTER WRAYBURN TELL IT TO YOU?
COME UPON IT? I OWN IT, BITCH!
I FUCKING OWN IT!
ARE YOU MAZED, WOMAN? LET GO OF MY GIRL!
BE GENTLE WITH HER, PA! SHE MEANS NO HARM BY IT!
SHE DOESN'T KNOW ANY BETTER!
I--I'M NOT MAD! IT'S SOME KIND OF MAGIC. SHE STOLE MY NAME!
IN COURSE SHE DID, LASS. NOW YOU JUST--
I'M LIZZIE HEXAM!
PARRRRRRRRP!
I--I'M
LIZZIE--
NUUUH!
WE DIDN'T TOUCH HER, DID WE?
WE DIDN'T EVEN TOUCH HER!

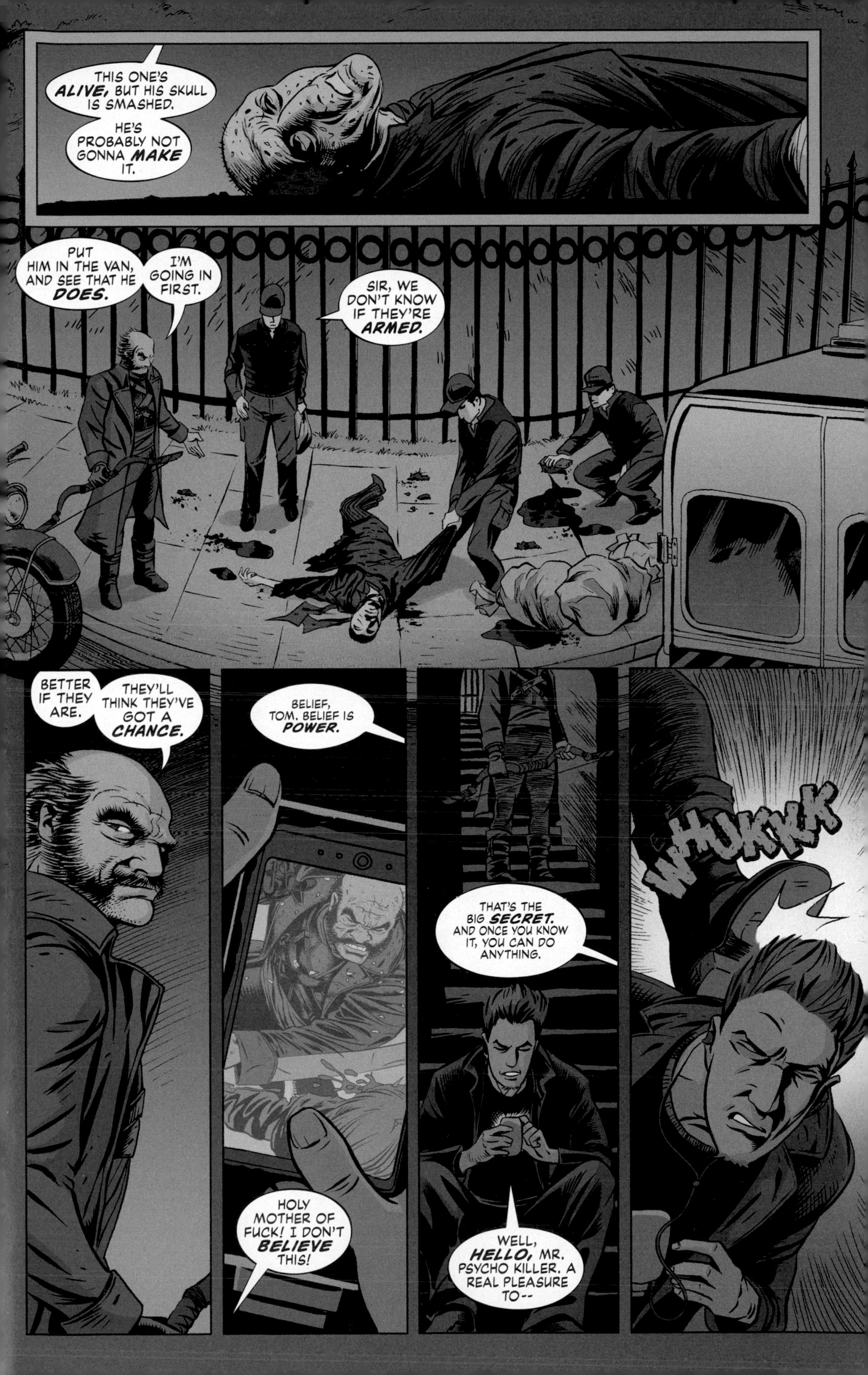
THIS ONE'S ALIVE, BUT HIS SKULL IS SMASHED.
HE'S PROBABLY NOT GONNA MAKE IT.
PUT HIM IN THE VAN, AND SEE THAT HE DOES.
I'M GOING IN FIRST.
SIR, WE DON'T KNOW IF THEY'RE ARMED.
BETTER IF THEY ARE.
THEY'LL THINK THEY'VE GOT A CHANCE.
BELIEF, TOM. BELIEF IS POWER.
HOLY MOTHER OF FUCK! I DON'T BELIEVE THIS!
THAT'S THE BIG SECRET. AND ONCE YOU KNOW IT, YOU CAN DO ANYTHING.
WELL, HELLO, MR. PSYCHO KILLER. A REAL PLEASURE TO--
WHUKKK

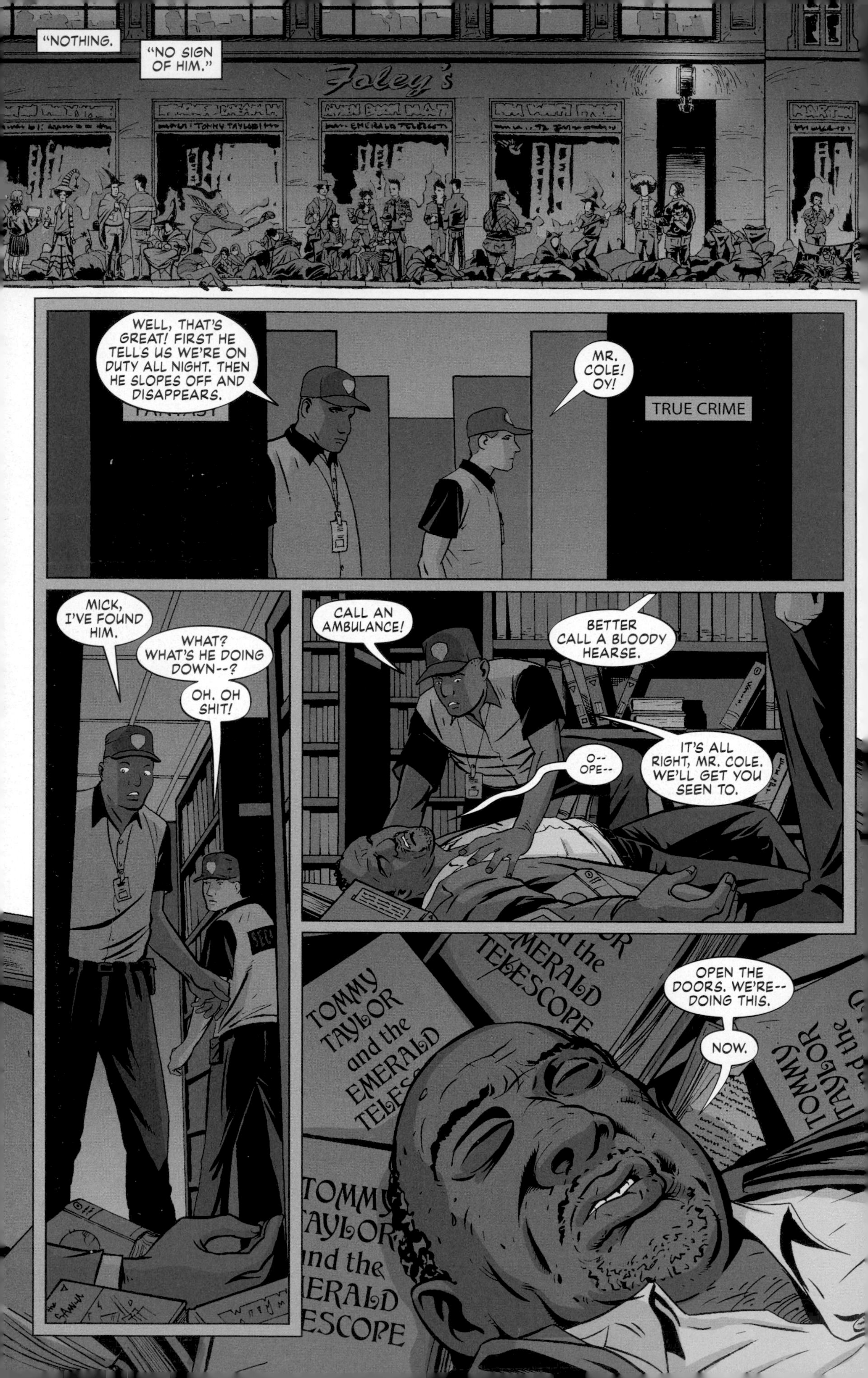
"NOTHING.
"NO SIGN OF HIM."
Foley's
TRUE CRIME
WELL, THAT'S GREAT! FIRST HE TELLS US WE'RE ON DUTY ALL NIGHT. THEN HE SLOPES OFF AND DISAPPEARS.
MR. COLE! OY!
MICK, I'VE FOUND HIM.
WHAT? WHAT'S HE DOING DOWN--?
OH. OH SHIT!
CALL AN AMBULANCE!
BETTER CALL A BLOODY HEARSE.
IT'S ALL RIGHT, MR. COLE. WE'LL GET YOU SEEN TO.
O-- OPE--
TOMMY TAYLOR and the EMERALD TELESCOPE
OPEN THE DOORS. WE'RE-- DOING THIS.
NOW.

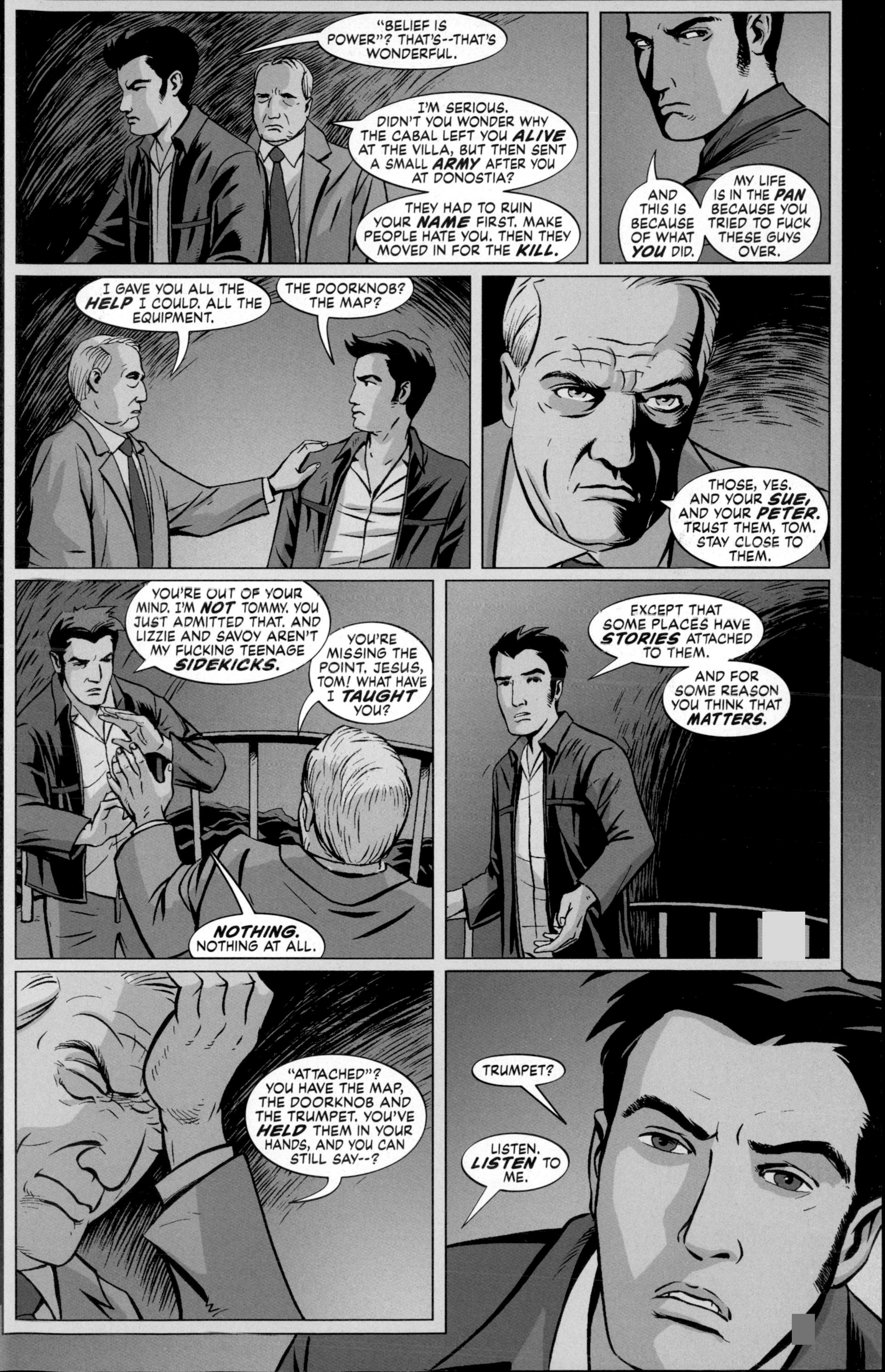
"BELIEF IS POWER"? THAT'S--THAT'S WONDERFUL.
I'M SERIOUS. DIDN'T YOU WONDER WHY THE CABAL LEFT YOU ALIVE AT THE VILLA, BUT THEN SENT A SMALL ARMY AFTER YOU AT DONOSTIA?
THEY HAD TO RUIN YOUR NAME FIRST. MAKE PEOPLE HATE YOU. THEN THEY MOVED IN FOR THE KILL.
AND THIS IS BECAUSE OF WHAT YOU DID.
MY LIFE IS IN THE PAN BECAUSE YOU TRIED TO FUCK THESE GUYS OVER.
I GAVE YOU ALL THE HELP I COULD. ALL THE EQUIPMENT.
THE DOORKNOB? THE MAP?
THOSE, YES. AND YOUR SUE, AND YOUR PETER. TRUST THEM, TOM. STAY CLOSE TO THEM.
YOU'RE OUT OF YOUR MIND. I'M NOT TOMMY. YOU JUST ADMITTED THAT. AND LIZZIE AND SAVOY AREN'T MY FUCKING TEENAGE SIDEKICKS.
YOU'RE MISSING THE POINT. JESUS, TOM! WHAT HAVE I TAUGHT YOU?
NOTHING. NOTHING AT ALL.
EXCEPT THAT SOME PLACES HAVE STORIES ATTACHED TO THEM.
AND FOR SOME REASON YOU THINK THAT MATTERS.
"ATTACHED"? YOU HAVE THE MAP, THE DOORKNOB AND THE TRUMPET. YOU'VE HELD THEM IN YOUR HANDS, AND YOU CAN STILL SAY--?
TRUMPET?
LISTEN. LISTEN TO ME.

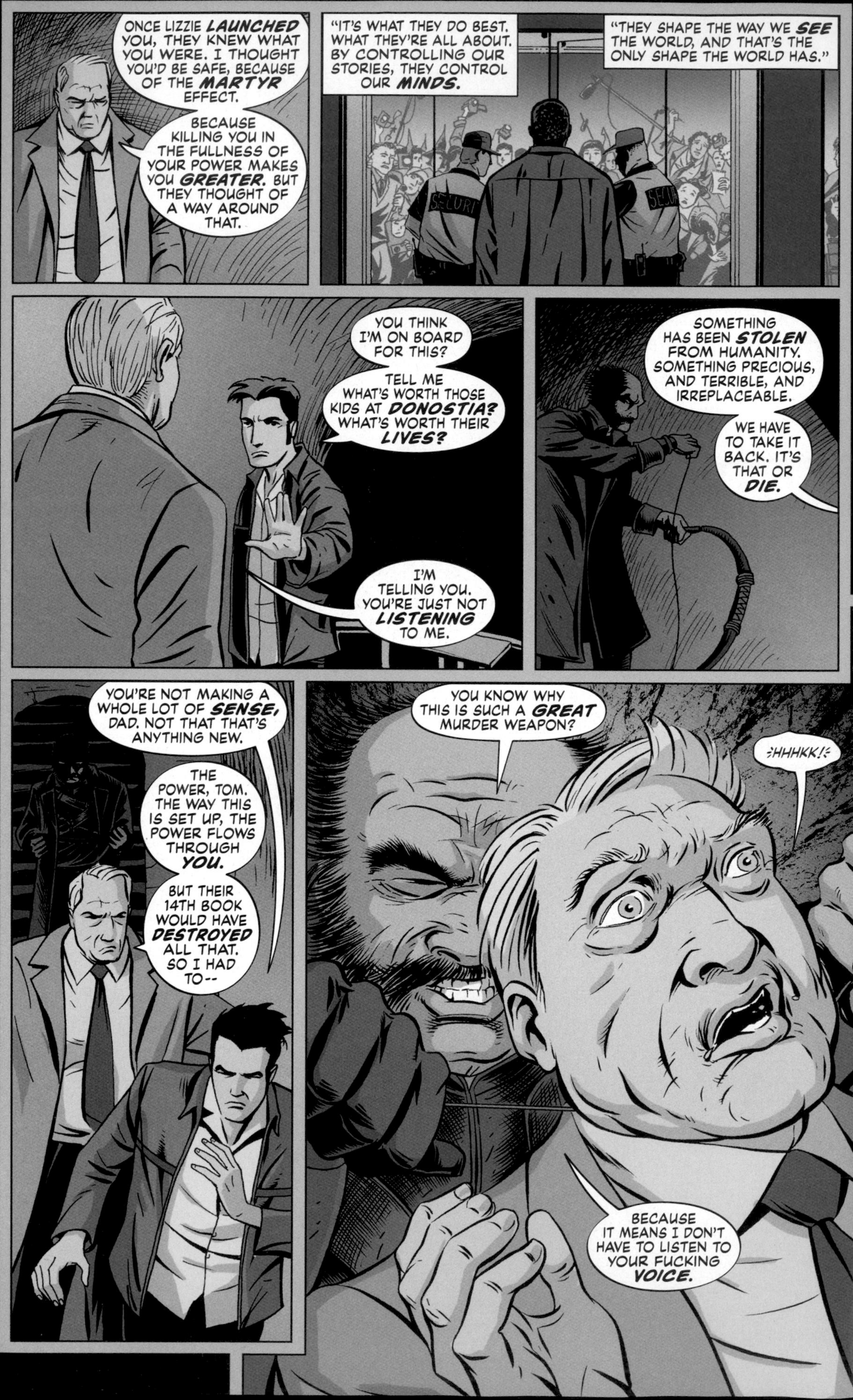

ONCE LIZZIE LAUNCHED YOU, THEY KNEW WHAT YOU WERE. I THOUGHT YOU'D BE SAFE, BECAUSE OF THE MARTYR EFFECT.
BECAUSE KILLING YOU IN THE FULLNESS OF YOUR POWER MAKES YOU GREATER. BUT THEY THOUGHT OF A WAY AROUND THAT.
"IT'S WHAT THEY DO BEST. WHAT THEY'RE ALL ABOUT. BY CONTROLLING OUR STORIES, THEY CONTROL OUR MINDS.
"THEY SHAPE THE WAY WE SEE THE WORLD, AND THAT'S THE ONLY SHAPE THE WORLD HAS."
SECURI
SECU
YOU THINK I'M ON BOARD FOR THIS?
TELL ME WHAT'S WORTH THOSE KIDS AT DONOSTIA? WHAT'S WORTH THEIR LIVES?
I'M TELLING YOU. YOU'RE JUST NOT LISTENING TO ME.
SOMETHING HAS BEEN STOLEN FROM HUMANITY. SOMETHING PRECIOUS, AND TERRIBLE, AND IRREPLACEABLE.
WE HAVE TO TAKE IT BACK. IT'S THAT OR DIE.
YOU'RE NOT MAKING A WHOLE LOT OF SENSE, DAD. NOT THAT THAT'S ANYTHING NEW.
THE POWER, TOM. THE WAY THIS IS SET UP, THE POWER FLOWS THROUGH YOU.
BUT THEIR 14TH BOOK WOULD HAVE DESTROYED ALL THAT. SO I HAD TO--
YOU KNOW WHY THIS IS SUCH A GREAT MURDER WEAPON?
HHHKK!
BECAUSE IT MEANS I DON'T HAVE TO LISTEN TO YOUR FUCKING VOICE.

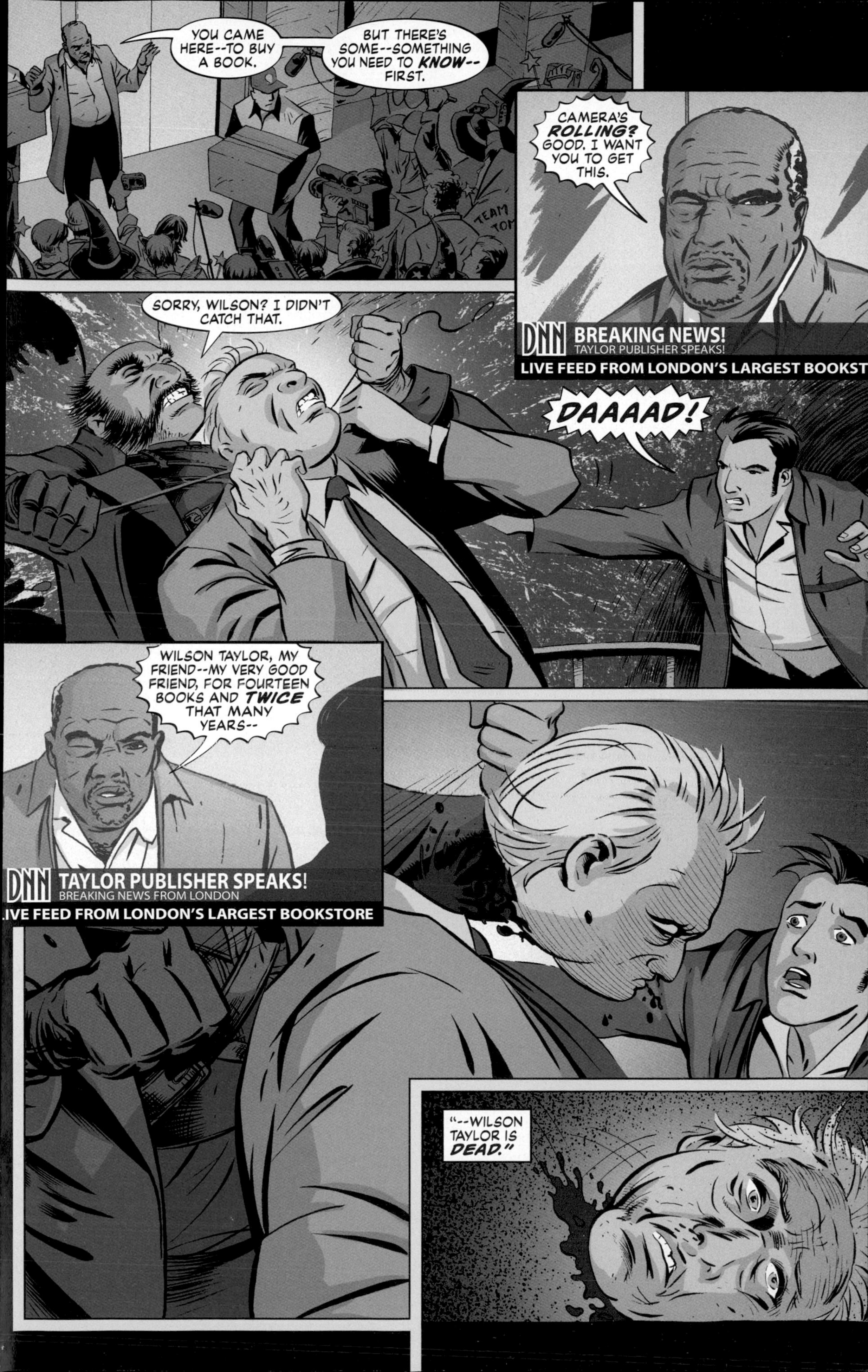
YOU CAME HERE--TO BUY A BOOK.
BUT THERE'S SOME--SOMETHING YOU NEED TO KNOW-- FIRST.
TEAM TOM
CAMERA'S ROLLING? GOOD. I WANT YOU TO GET THIS.
DNN BREAKING NEWS!
TAYLOR PUBLISHER SPEAKS!
LIVE FEED FROM LONDON'S LARGEST BOOKST
SORRY, WILSON? I DIDN'T CATCH THAT.
DAAAAD!
WILSON TAYLOR, MY FRIEND--MY VERY GOOD FRIEND, FOR FOURTEEN BOOKS AND TWICE THAT MANY YEARS--
DNN TAYLOR PUBLISHER SPEAKS!
BREAKING NEWS FROM LONDON
LIVE FEED FROM LONDON'S LARGEST BOOKSTORE
"--WILSON TAYLOR IS DEAD."

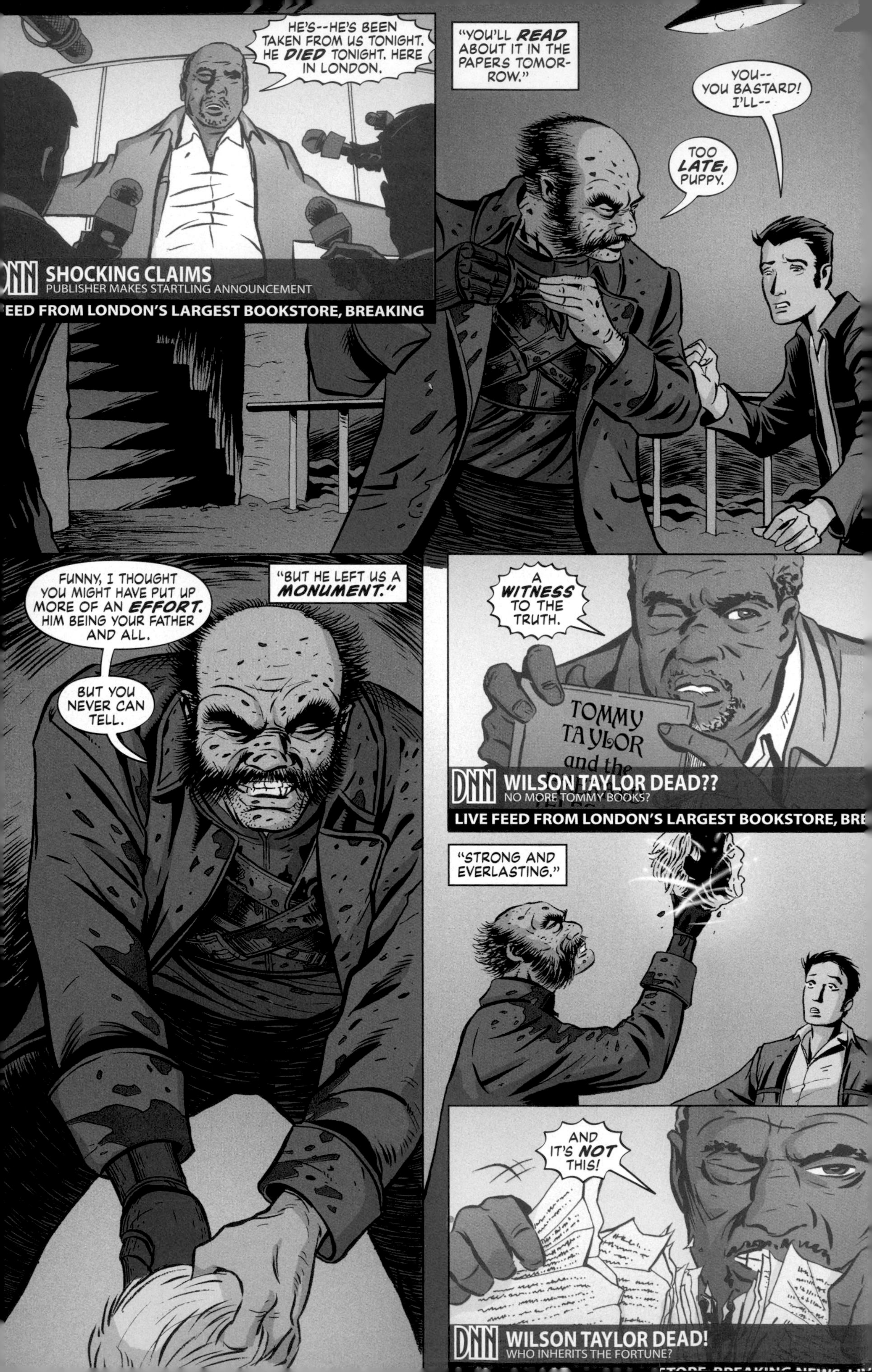
HE'S--HE'S BEEN TAKEN FROM US TONIGHT. HE DIED TONIGHT. HERE IN LONDON.
DNN SHOCKING CLAIMS
PUBLISHER MAKES STARTLING ANNOUNCEMENT
EED FROM LONDON'S LARGEST BOOKSTORE, BREAKING
"YOU'LL READ ABOUT IT IN THE PAPERS TOMORROW."
YOU-- YOU BASTARD! I'LL--
TOO LATE, PUPPY.
FUNNY, I THOUGHT YOU MIGHT HAVE PUT UP MORE OF AN EFFORT. HIM BEING YOUR FATHER AND ALL.
BUT YOU NEVER CAN TELL.
"BUT HE LEFT US A MONUMENT."
A WITNESS TO THE TRUTH.
TOMMY TAYLOR and the
DNN WILSON TAYLOR DEAD??
NO MORE TOMMY BOOKS?
LIVE FEED FROM LONDON'S LARGEST BOOKSTORE, BRE
"STRONG AND EVERLASTING."
AND IT'S NOT THIS!
DNN WILSON TAYLOR DEAD!
WHO INHERITS THE FORTUNE?

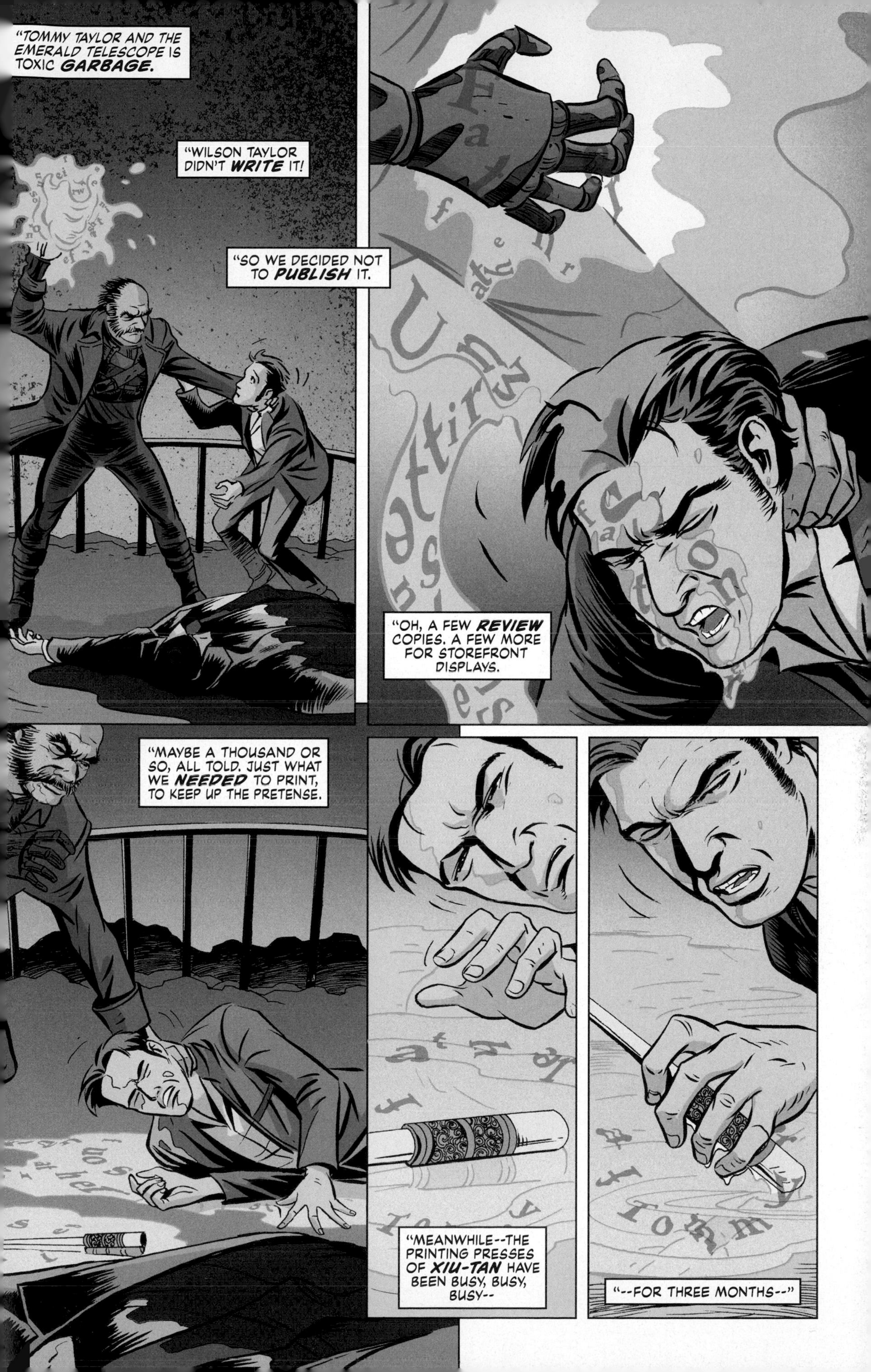
"TOMMY TAYLOR AND THE EMERALD TELESCOPE IS TOXIC GARBAGE.
"WILSON TAYLOR DIDN'T WRITE IT!
"SO WE DECIDED NOT TO PUBLISH IT.
"OH, A FEW REVIEW COPIES. A FEW MORE FOR STOREFRONT DISPLAYS.
"MAYBE A THOUSAND OR SO, ALL TOLD. JUST WHAT WE NEEDED TO PRINT, TO KEEP UP THE PRETENSE.
"MEANWHILE--THE PRINTING PRESSES OF XIU-TAN HAVE BEEN BUSY, BUSY, BUSY--
"--FOR THREE MONTHS--"

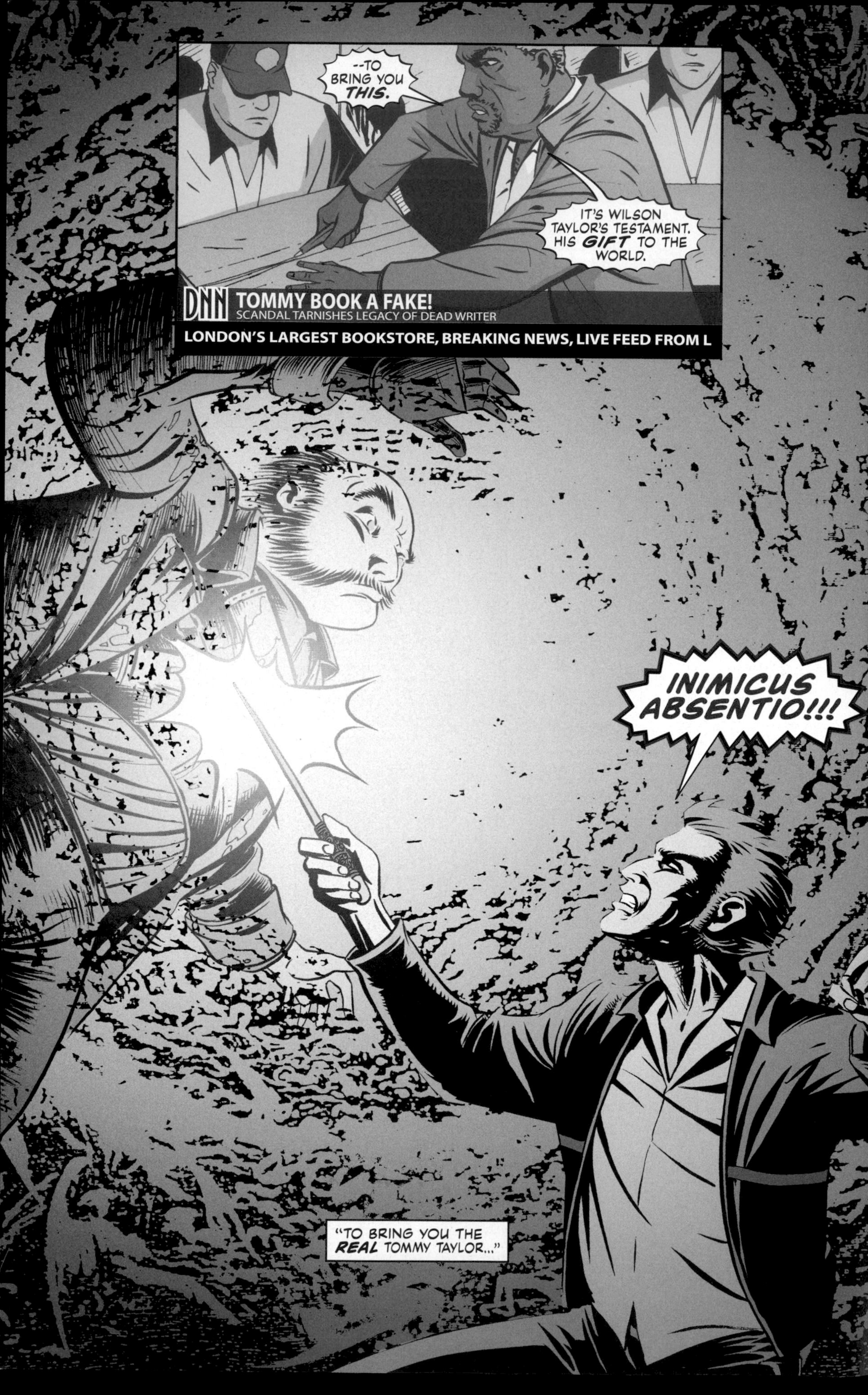
--TO BRING YOU THIS.
IT'S WILSON TAYLOR'S TESTAMENT. HIS GIFT TO THE WORLD.
DNN
TOMMY BOOK A FAKE!
SCANDAL TARNISHES LEGACY OF DEAD WRITER
LONDON'S LARGEST BOOKSTORE, BREAKING NEWS, LIVE FEED FROM L
INIMICUS ABSENTIO!!!
"TO BRING YOU THE REAL TOMMY TAYLOR..."

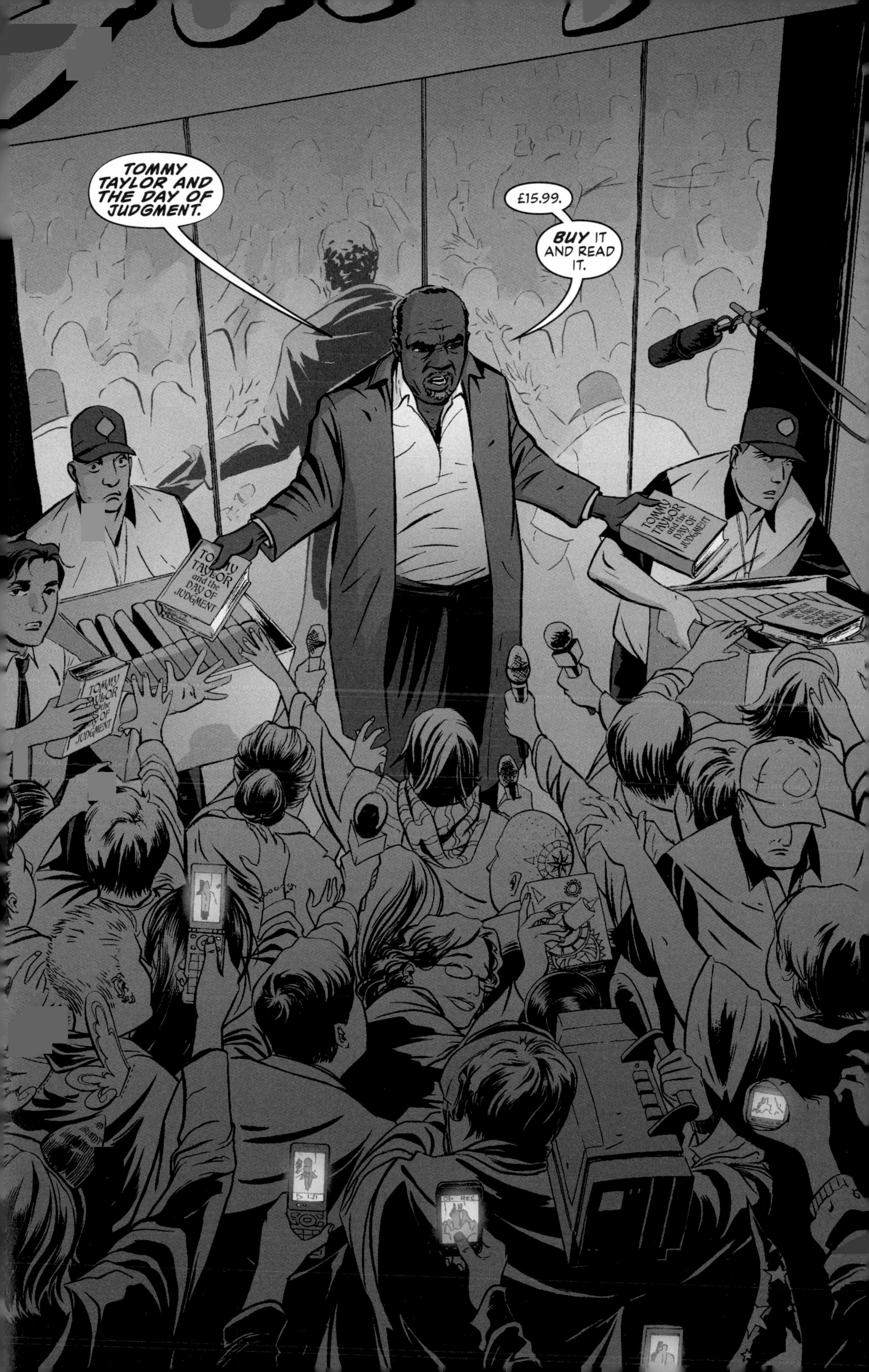
TOMMY TAYLOR AND THE DAY OF JUDGMENT.
£15.99.
BUY IT AND READ IT.
TOMMY TAYLOR and the DAY OF JUDGMENT

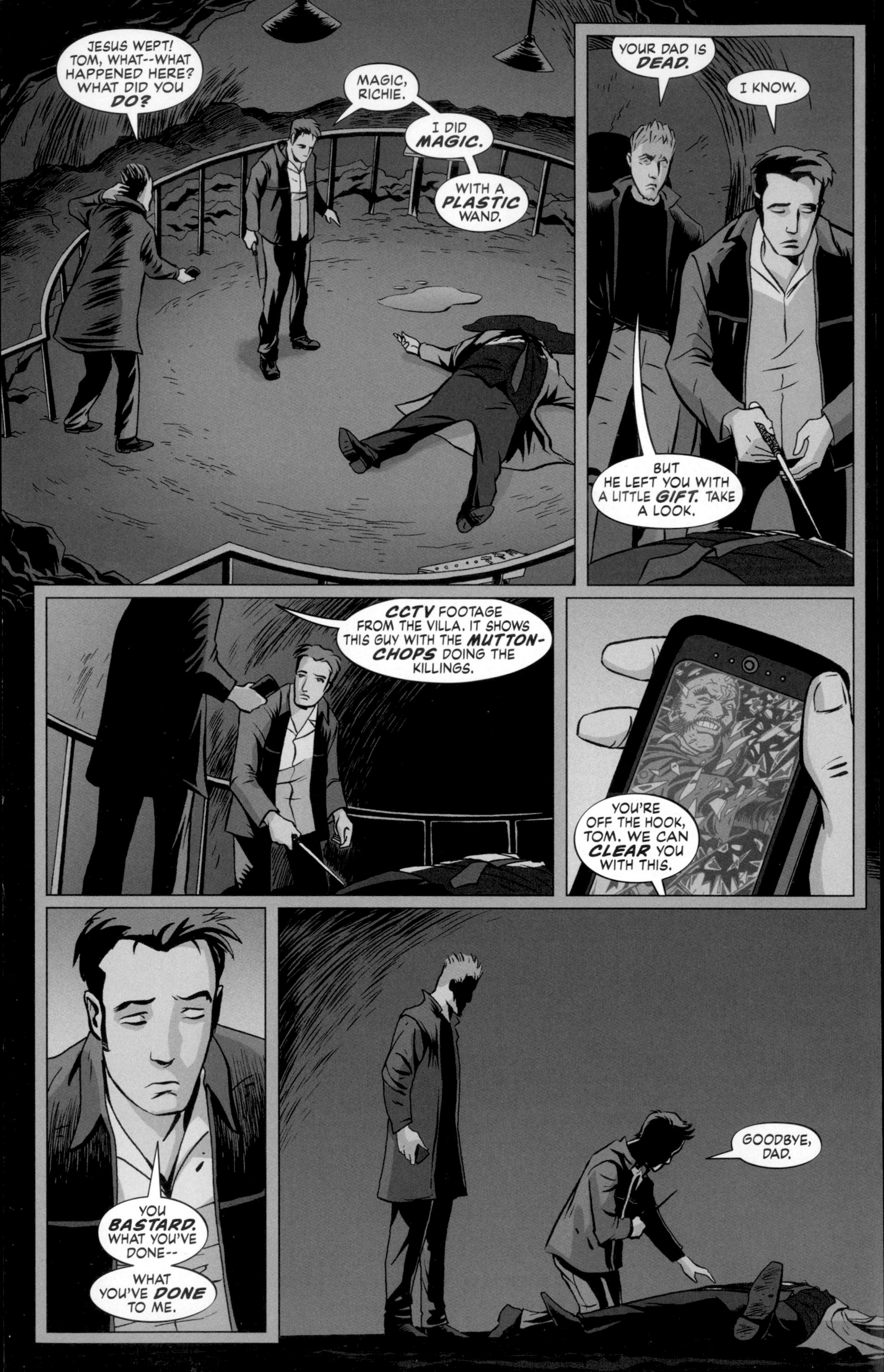
JESUS WEPT! TOM, WHAT--WHAT HAPPENED HERE? WHAT DID YOU DO?
MAGIC, RICHIE.
I DID MAGIC.
WITH A PLASTIC WAND.
YOUR DAD IS DEAD.
I KNOW.
BUT HE LEFT YOU WITH A LITTLE GIFT. TAKE A LOOK.
CCTV FOOTAGE FROM THE VILLA. IT SHOWS THIS GUY WITH THE MUTTON-CHOPS DOING THE KILLINGS.
YOU'RE OFF THE HOOK, TOM. WE CAN CLEAR YOU WITH THIS.
YOU BASTARD. WHAT YOU'VE DONE--
WHAT YOU'VE DONE TO ME.
GOODBYE, DAD.

All the news that's fit to post.

| Home | News | Sports | Weather | Lifestyle | Arts |

Africa
Americas
Asia-Pacific
Europe
Middle East
South Asia

14TH TOMMY "A REVELATION"

After the violent death of its author, and the extraordinary maneuvering of publishers Queensberry in passing off a fake Tommy Taylor book on reviewers, then revealing a different book on the actual day of the launch, it would perhaps not be surprising if the book itself failed to live up to the real-life drama of its genesis.

Nothing could be further from the truth. Critics and fans alike are hailing this as Wilson Taylor's definitive masterpiece – a poignant and powerful reflection on truth, eternity and the value of human striving.

Casting his wizard hero as a savior bringing a new gospel to a troubled world, Taylor might have lapsed into pretension and grandiloquence. But in powerful and simple speeches, Tommy addresses us as his contemporaries, his countrymen, and we respond.

We respond with

CULT OF TOMMY EXPLODES

by: Barb L.G.

The fringe cults hailing Tom Taylor, namesake of the boy wizard hero of his father's best-selling books, as a potential savior of humankind fell into eclipse after Taylor was arrested on multiple counts of murder after the Villa Diodati slayings. Taylor's death in the Donostia fire of last December was mourned by few.

But now that new evidence has led to a posthumous dropping of all charges, the cult of Tommy has found a new lease on life. Fueled by the messianic tone of the new novel, Tommy Taylor and the Day of Judgment, the pseudo-religion of Tommyism has now moved out of the fringe into the mainstream.

With 700,000 adherents in the US alone, the cult is starting to cause alarm in some circles. "It can't be healthy for so many people to be looking to a fallible human being to change their lives and their world," said Cardinal Desmond Connell, of the Irish Catholic Church. "That's a recipe for

---

The News Times

◀ ▶ ☆ Ω | Ⓣ http://www.TheNewsTimes.com/world/TommyGoesDarkbutFindstheLight/.

HOME PAGE   TODAY'S PAPER   VIDEO   MOST POPULAR   TIMES TOPICS

| WORLD | U.S. | N.Y. / REGION | BUSINESS | TECHNOLOGY | SCIENCE | HEALTH | SPORTS | OPINION |

Tommy Goes Dark – but Finds the Light

Readers across the world have waited patiently for years to read the conclusion of Wilson Taylor's fictional epic. But critics were left bemused at the shift in tone as the fourteenth and purportedly final novel, Day of Judgment, went on sale across the world yesterday.

The bizarre expedient of trailing a different book for review purposes – allegedly to minimize the risk of piracy and illegal downloads – had already created widespread controversy. But that discussion was washed away in an instant by the broader debate about the book itself.

In some ways darker and more mature in tone than the rest of Taylor's beloved fantasies, Day of Judgment is also unashamedly messianic and utopian. Returned from the dead, boy wizard Tommy Taylor has become a holy figure, a soothsayer, a spokesman for eternal values.

But while the strange gear-change baffled some, others – in numbers that can only be called vast – have embraced and welcomed it. "The change in the Tommy books reflects our changing status quo," said media guru Edward Lutycns. "These books are like a kaleidoscope through which we see the zeitgeist: in dark times, of course they become dark."

Lucas Filby, president of one of the many Tommy Taylor fan clubs, was even more categorical. "The darkness you see is in your own eye. Trust in Tommy, and he'll take you into the light. How many times do you need to be told?"

Around the world, spontaneous "Tommy-fests" involving tens of thousands of fans have been

---

◀ ▶ ☆ Ω | http://www.figmentsandfantasias/forum/. ~ | ? ▾

Author	Message

appycat | 🗎 Posted: 1:03 am   quote

Tommy is still out there. They never found his body after that fire.

ck to top   profile   pm

unk Moreland | 🗎 Posted: 1:10 am   quote

You mean Tom. Tom Taylor is still out there.

...dude

ck to top   profile   pm

wordsman55 | 🗎 Posted: 1:12 am   quote

Haven't you read the book? "He put on new clothes, new flesh. He went out to meet them."

ck to top   profile   pm

lappycat | 🗎 Posted: 1:20 am   quote

Don't stop there, S55! "When they saw him, they didn't know him at first. He looked like someone they'd always known and never really seen until now."

ck to top   profile   pm

true | 🗎 Posted: 1:38 pm   quote

forever

So what do we do?

ck to top   profile   pm

Malinky Robot | 🗎 Posted: 1:43 pm   quote

We wait. We wait for him to tell us what he wants.

ck to top

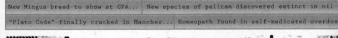

◀ ▶ ☆ Ω | http://thePOSTnation.com/video

New Mingus breed to show at CFA...   New species of pelican discovered extinct in oil
"Plato Code" finally cracked in Manches...   Homeopath found in self-medicated overdos

The POSTnation

When all else fails, read everything.

| HOME | BREAKING NEWS | POLITICS | BUSINESS | WORLD | MEDIA | TECHNOLOGY | ENTERTAIN |
| ARTS | LIVING | STYLE | VIDEO | BLOGS | LINKS | | |

Death of a Great Master

Filed by: Margaret Guttmann

When the Thane of Cawdor dies, in the Shakespeare play Macbeth, even those who have fought against him have to admit that "Nothing in his life became him like the leaving it."

The opposite appears to be the case for author Wilson Taylor. In his lifetime he brought joy to uncountable millions through his best-selling Tommy Taylor novels. His death, by contrast, is a bleak, hole-in-corner affair dogged by anomalies and unanswered questions.

DNA evidence has confirmed beyond doubt that the headless body found at the Merlin's Cave tourist attraction in Islington, London, was that of the author, who had not made any public appearances during the last decade of his life. But police have still failed to find his head, or the weapon that was used to sever it, or any substantial clues to the identity of his murderer.

An early rumor that Taylor's estranged son, Tom, might have been present at the killing and indeed involved with it, has foundered both on a lack of physical evidence and on the CCTV footage from the Villa Diodati which appears to show that Tom Taylor has already been the victim of one miscarriage of justice. Officially, Tom remains missing, presumed dead after the fire at Donostia jail which

MINKIES PIZZA

So good,
your cat
wants
some!

"We don't know w
worst thing to ev

- Britt Mingbo, fa

嵐

TOMMY TAILO
RACE
for KIDS!
Help fight
JUVENILE DIABE

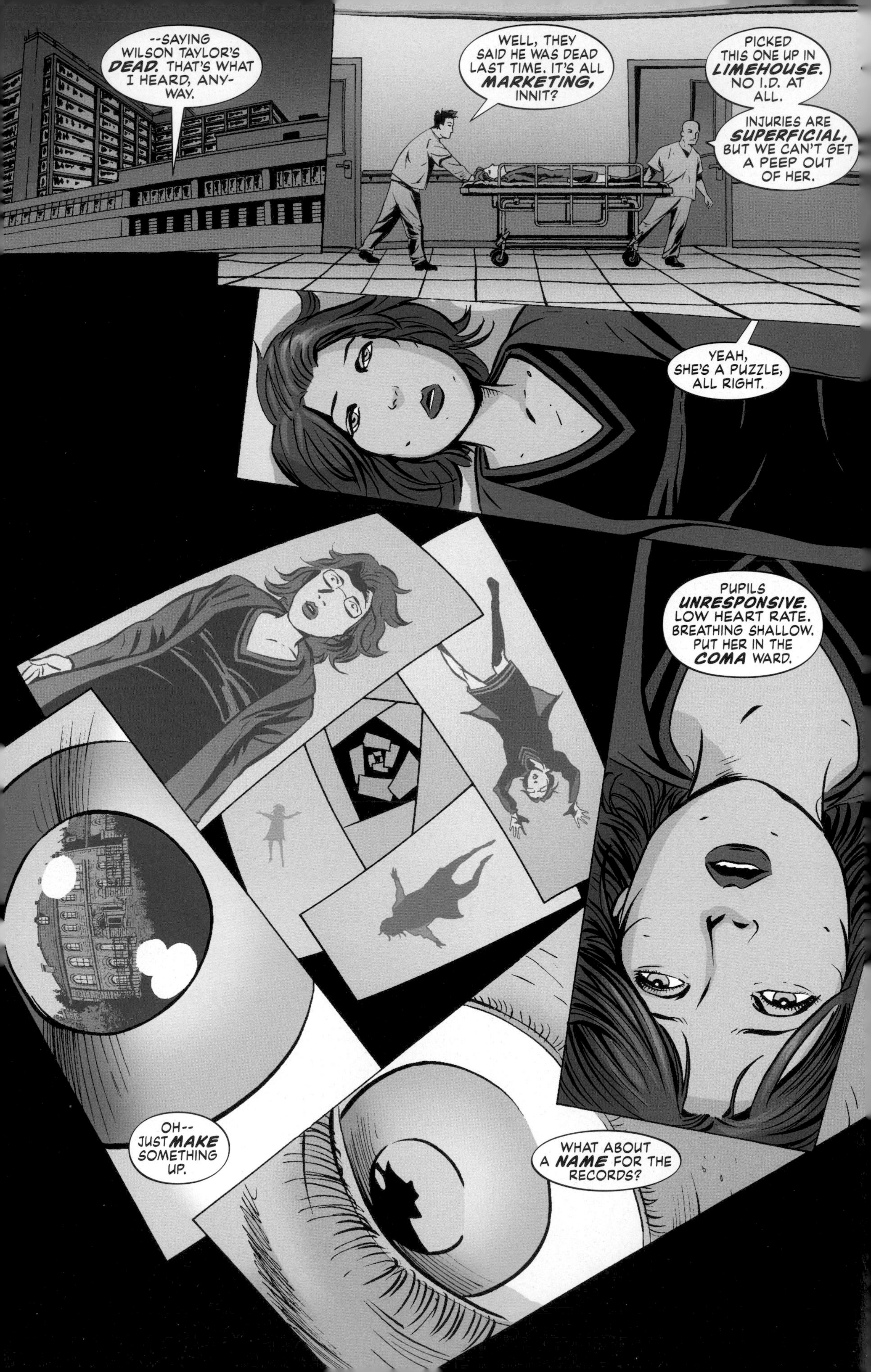
--SAYING WILSON TAYLOR'S DEAD. THAT'S WHAT I HEARD, ANY-WAY.
WELL, THEY SAID HE WAS DEAD LAST TIME. IT'S ALL MARKETING, INNIT?
PICKED THIS ONE UP IN LIMEHOUSE. NO I.D. AT ALL.
INJURIES ARE SUPERFICIAL, BUT WE CAN'T GET A PEEP OUT OF HER.
YEAH, SHE'S A PUZZLE, ALL RIGHT.
PUPILS UNRESPONSIVE. LOW HEART RATE. BREATHING SHALLOW. PUT HER IN THE COMA WARD.
WHAT ABOUT A NAME FOR THE RECORDS?
OH-- JUST MAKE SOMETHING UP.

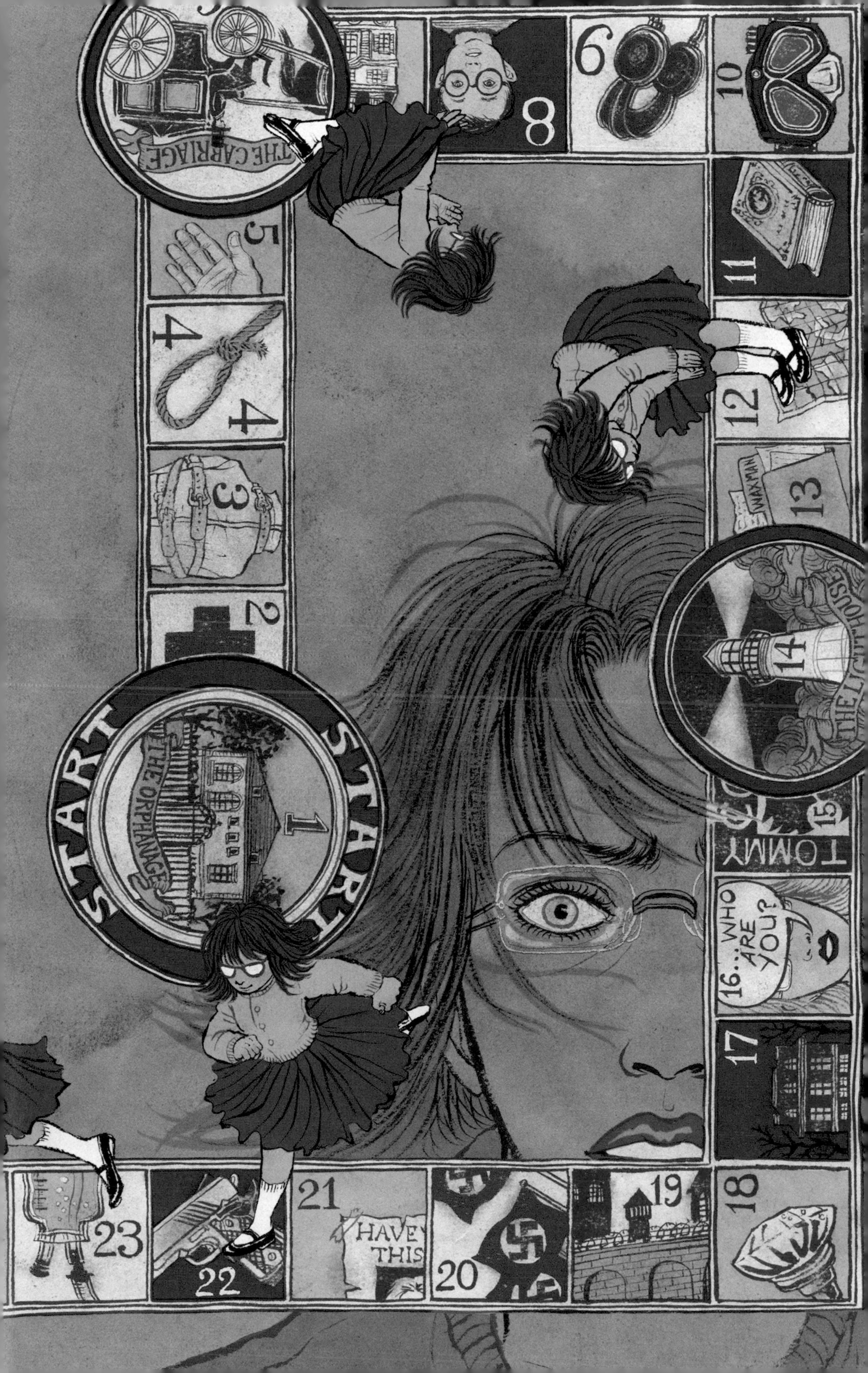

START
THE ORPHANAGE
1
2
3
4
4
4
5
THE CARRIAGE
8
9
10
11
12
WAXMAN
13
14
THE LIGHTHOUSE
15
TOMMY
16... WHO ARE YOU?
17
18
19
20
21
HAVE THIS
22
23
START

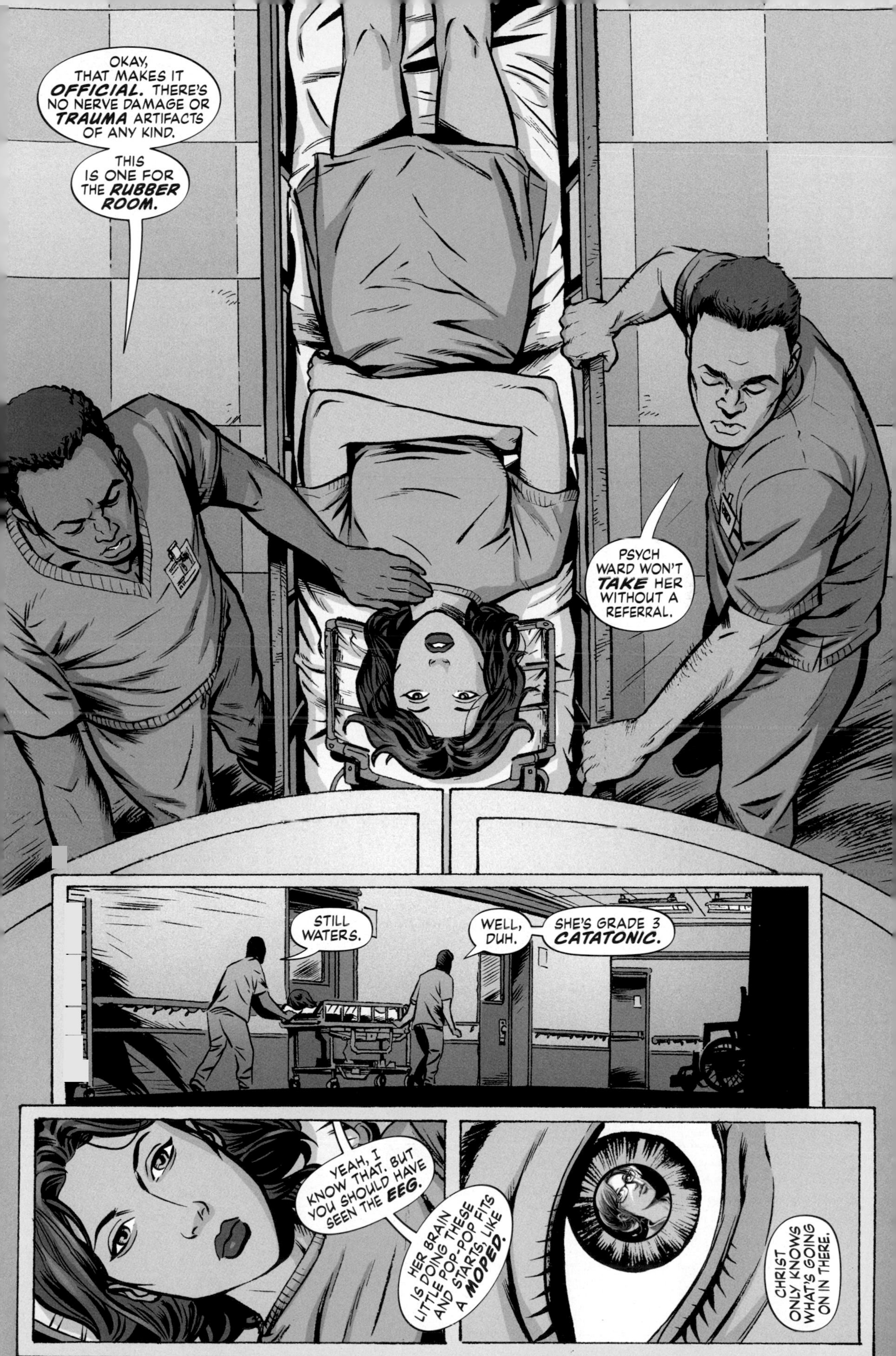
OKAY, THAT MAKES IT OFFICIAL. THERE'S NO NERVE DAMAGE OR TRAUMA ARTIFACTS OF ANY KIND.
THIS IS ONE FOR THE RUBBER ROOM.
PSYCH WARD WON'T TAKE HER WITHOUT A REFERRAL.
STILL WATERS.
WELL, DUH.
SHE'S GRADE 3 CATATONIC.
YEAH, I KNOW THAT. BUT YOU SHOULD HAVE SEEN THE EEG.
HER BRAIN IS DOING THESE LITTLE POP-POP FITS AND STARTS, LIKE A MOPED.
CHRIST ONLY KNOWS WHAT'S GOING ON IN THERE.

Lizzie Hexam is a girl with a strange destiny – and it's up to **you** to choose it!

Tom Taylor's life has been thrown into turmoil, and Lizzie Hexam has to help him survive. But Lizzie has secrets of her own. Where does she come from? What is her link to mysterious recluse Wilson Taylor? Is Lizzie even her real name?

Shape Lizzie's life! Bring her to the fateful moment when she meets Tom Taylor! Uncover the mysteries that lie in her past, and launch her into a new future! Or fail, and see her fall. The power, and the choice, lie with you…

– INSTRUCTIONS –

When you read a Pick-a-Story® book, you steer the characters through a unique adventure that takes its shape as you make your choices. It's easy and fun, so long as you follow these simple instructions:

DON'T read the pages in numerical order. Follow the numbers at the bottom of each page to find your way through the story.

A GREEN number means **GO TO THIS PAGE!**

RED numbers mean **CHOOSE ONE OF THESE OPTIONS!**

If you get to the words **THE END**, the story's over – but if you don't like the ending, you can just begin again at page 1!

Time to get started. Choose wisely, and live well…

The MANY LIVES of LIZZIE HEXAM

By Lizzie Hexam

A Pick-a-Story® Book!

Tommy Taylor and The Ship Ring Bank Five
The Tulkinghorn Ragers in the C y —of

Our Mutual Friend

had five hundred and…… …e saw
students and more than…… …a step outside that caught
In this hive of ceaseless activity staff…… was a soft knock at the
boy Tommy led a mostly three…… …and there within her reach,
childhood. He had a dozen happy…… …at a handle laugh: 'Now here,
and fathers, half a hundred mothers…… …pulling up a grown-up that's my particu-
and sisters. ……door, said, is a Lizzie Hexam in a black
……ance,' and Lizzie Hexam in a black
His playground wa…… the s……friend! and entered the room.
quarte……arts t……no longer……dress
……e……no one….se.

…e……mbered or visited by its current
……habitants.

…he students were another breed, 'There, there, there, Liz, all right my dear. See! Here's Mr. Headstone come with me.'
…stant and aloof. The masters,
…en more so. Tommy's friends Her eyes met those of the schoolmaster,
ere the children of the other who had evidently expected to see a very
rvants, and his best friend of all different sort of person, and a murmured
word or two of salutation passed between
them. She was a little flurried by the unex-

'Charley! You!'

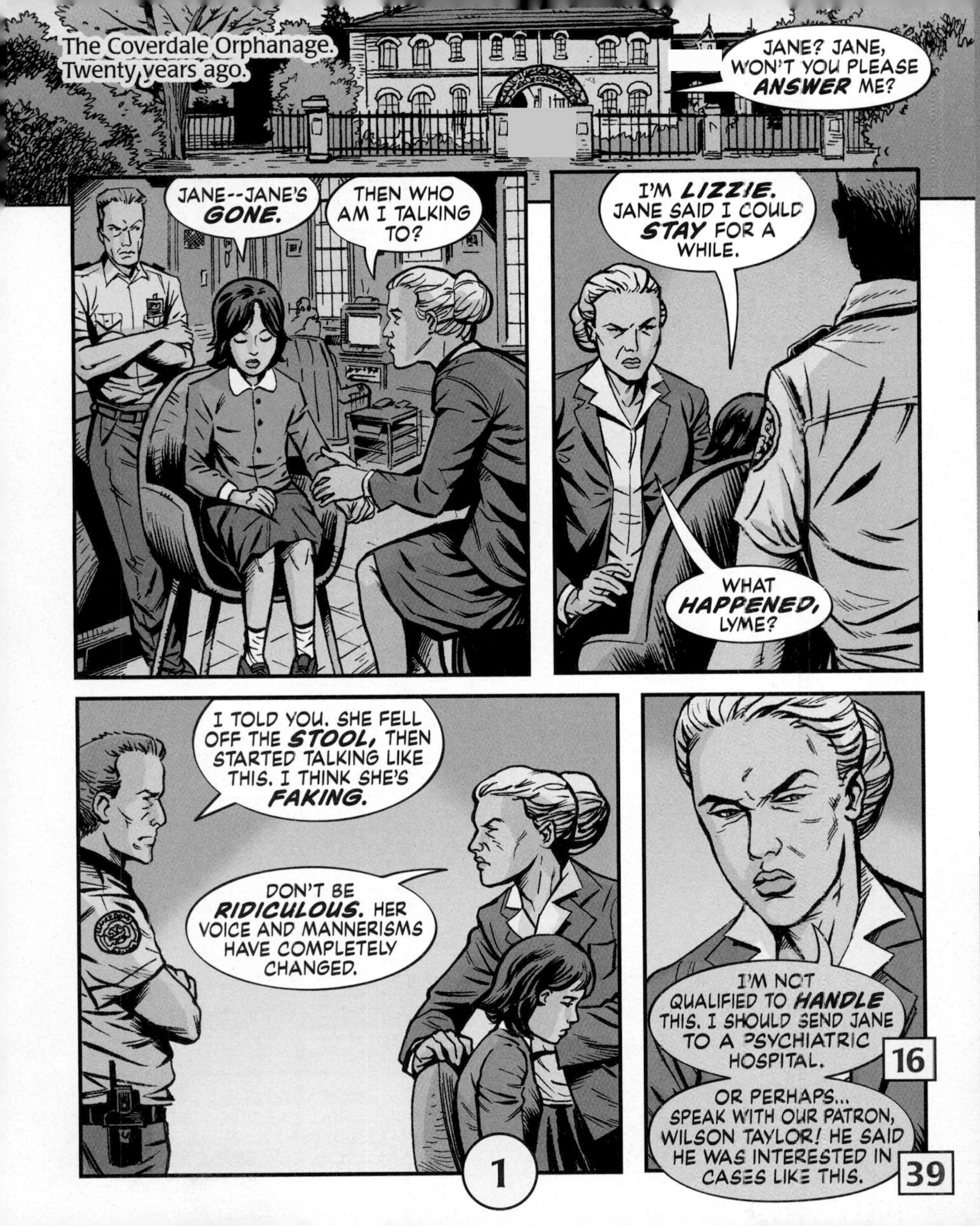
The Coverdale Orphanage.
Twenty years ago.
JANE? JANE, WON'T YOU PLEASE ANSWER ME?
JANE--JANE'S GONE.
THEN WHO AM I TALKING TO?
I'M LIZZIE. JANE SAID I COULD STAY FOR A WHILE.
WHAT HAPPENED, LYME?
I TOLD YOU. SHE FELL OFF THE STOOL, THEN STARTED TALKING LIKE THIS. I THINK SHE'S FAKING.
DON'T BE RIDICULOUS. HER VOICE AND MANNERISMS HAVE COMPLETELY CHANGED.
I'M NOT QUALIFIED TO HANDLE THIS. I SHOULD SEND JANE TO A PSYCHIATRIC HOSPITAL.
16
OR PERHAPS... SPEAK WITH OUR PATRON, WILSON TAYLOR! HE SAID HE WAS INTERESTED IN CASES LIKE THIS.
39
1

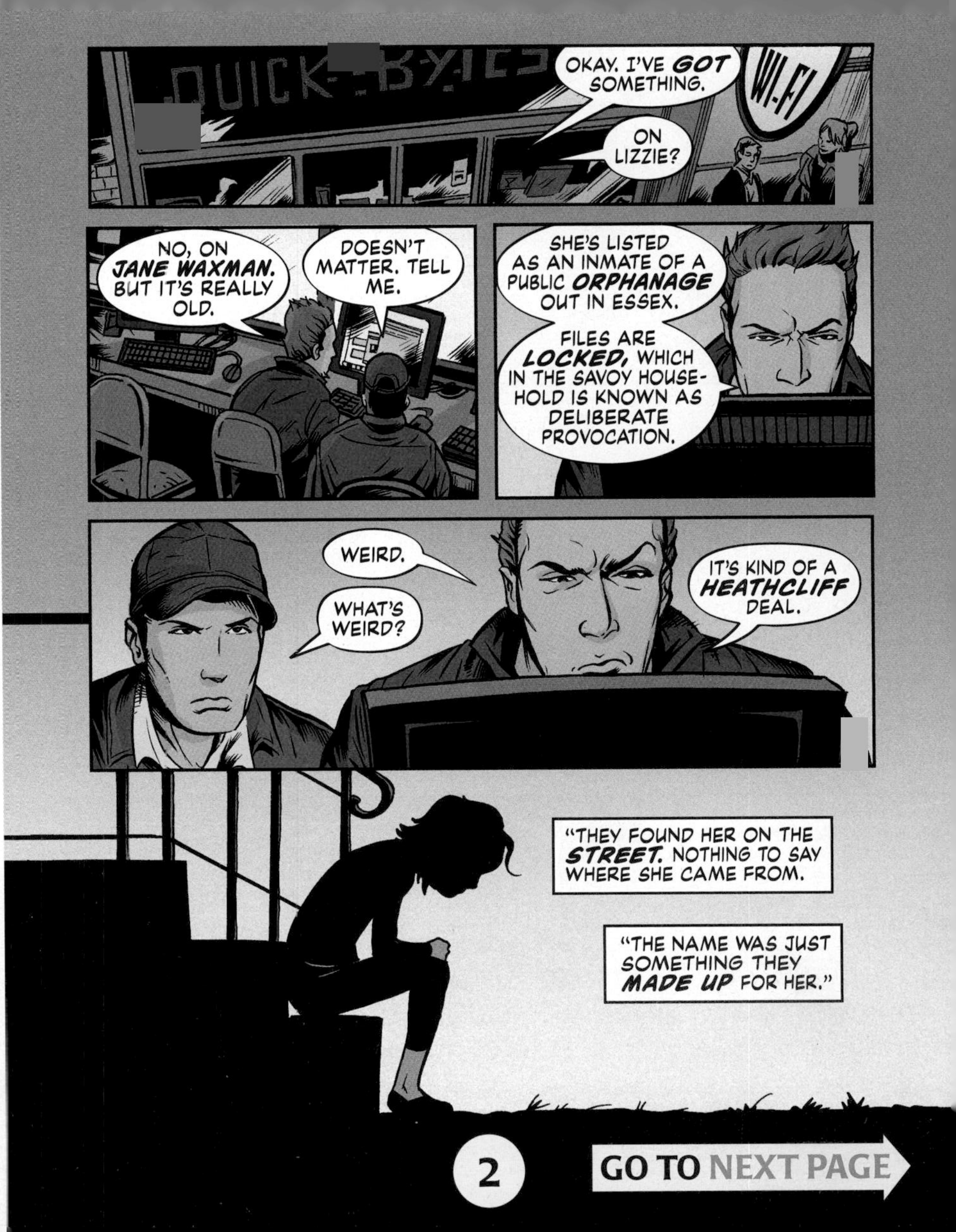
OKAY. I'VE GOT SOMETHING.
ON LIZZIE?
WI-FI
NO, ON JANE WAXMAN. BUT IT'S REALLY OLD.
DOESN'T MATTER. TELL ME.
SHE'S LISTED AS AN INMATE OF A PUBLIC ORPHANAGE OUT IN ESSEX.
FILES ARE LOCKED, WHICH IN THE SAVOY HOUSEHOLD IS KNOWN AS DELIBERATE PROVOCATION.
WEIRD.
WHAT'S WEIRD?
IT'S KIND OF A HEATHCLIFF DEAL.
"THEY FOUND HER ON THE STREET. NOTHING TO SAY WHERE SHE CAME FROM.
"THE NAME WAS JUST SOMETHING THEY MADE UP FOR HER."
2
GO TO NEXT PAGE

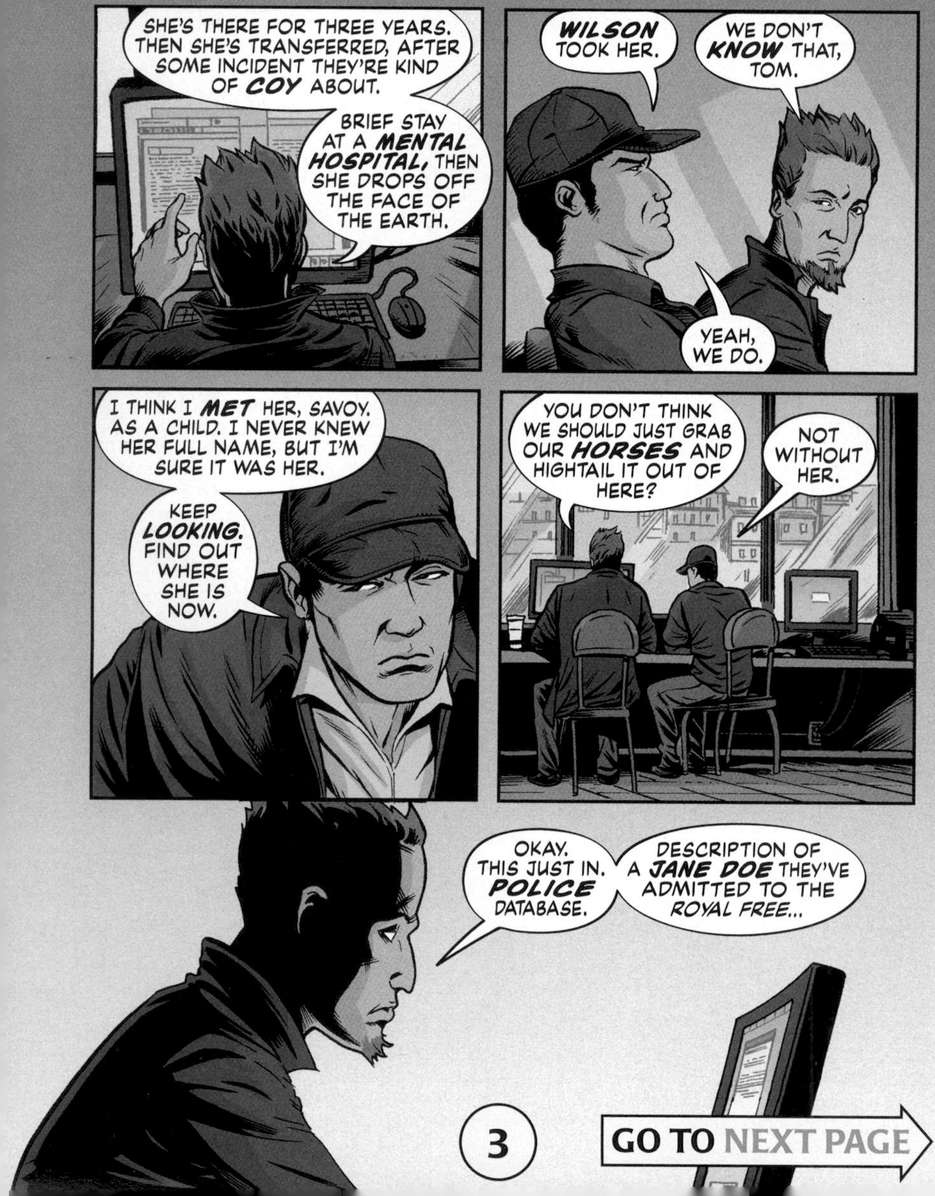

SHE'S THERE FOR THREE YEARS. THEN SHE'S TRANSFERRED, AFTER SOME INCIDENT THEY'RE KIND OF COY ABOUT.
BRIEF STAY AT A MENTAL HOSPITAL, THEN SHE DROPS OFF THE FACE OF THE EARTH.
WILSON TOOK HER.
WE DON'T KNOW THAT, TOM.
YEAH, WE DO.
I THINK I MET HER, SAVOY. AS A CHILD. I NEVER KNEW HER FULL NAME, BUT I'M SURE IT WAS HER.
KEEP LOOKING. FIND OUT WHERE SHE IS NOW.
YOU DON'T THINK WE SHOULD JUST GRAB OUR HORSES AND HIGHTAIL IT OUT OF HERE?
NOT WITHOUT HER.
OKAY. THIS JUST IN. POLICE DATABASE.
DESCRIPTION OF A JANE DOE THEY'VE ADMITTED TO THE ROYAL FREE...

GO TO NEXT PAGE

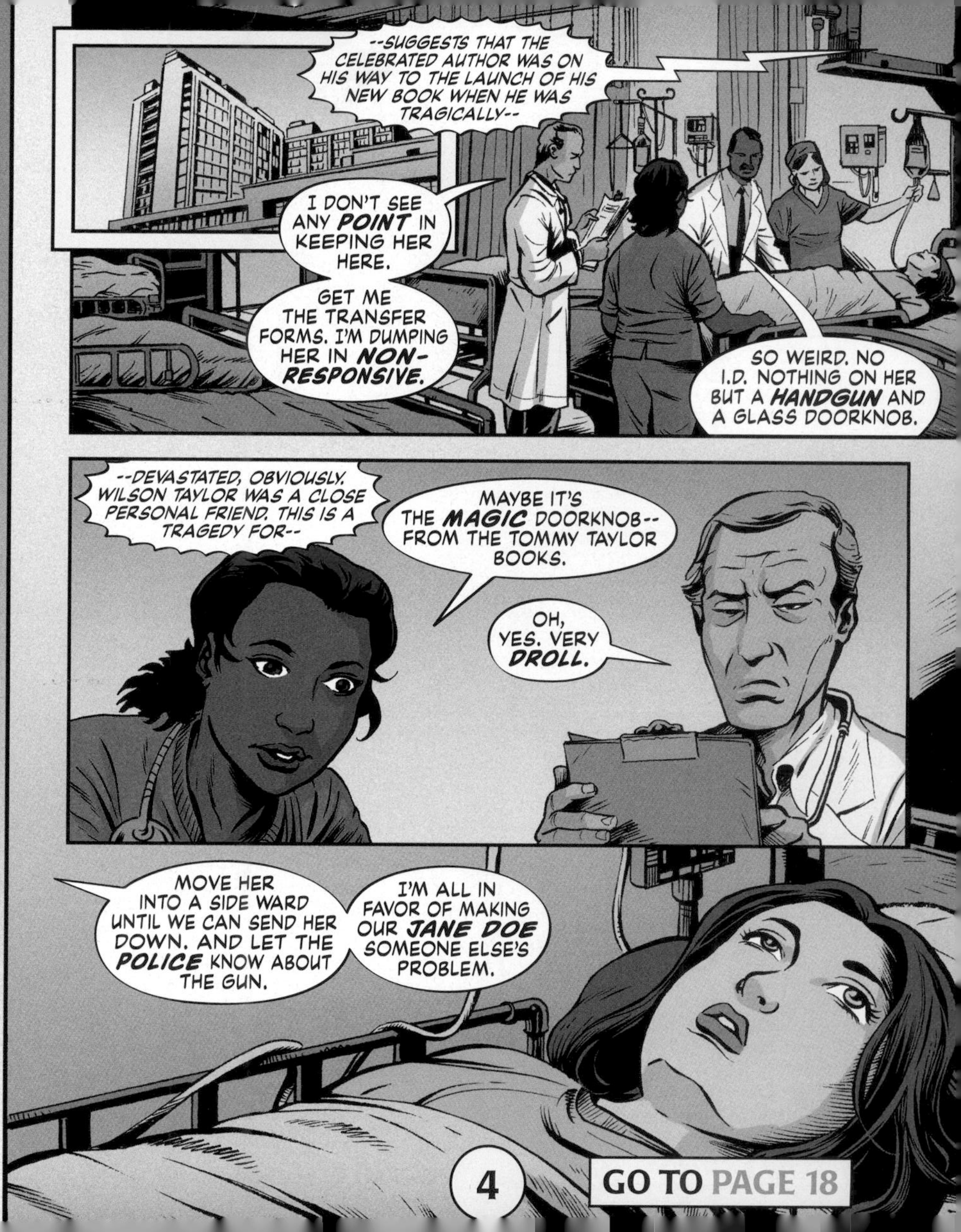

--SUGGESTS THAT THE CELEBRATED AUTHOR WAS ON HIS WAY TO THE LAUNCH OF HIS NEW BOOK WHEN HE WAS TRAGICALLY--
I DON'T SEE ANY POINT IN KEEPING HER HERE.
GET ME THE TRANSFER FORMS. I'M DUMPING HER IN NON-RESPONSIVE.
SO WEIRD. NO I.D. NOTHING ON HER BUT A HANDGUN AND A GLASS DOORKNOB.
--DEVASTATED, OBVIOUSLY. WILSON TAYLOR WAS A CLOSE PERSONAL FRIEND. THIS IS A TRAGEDY FOR--
MAYBE IT'S THE MAGIC DOORKNOB-- FROM THE TOMMY TAYLOR BOOKS.
OH, YES. VERY DROLL.
MOVE HER INTO A SIDE WARD UNTIL WE CAN SEND HER DOWN. AND LET THE POLICE KNOW ABOUT THE GUN.
I'M ALL IN FAVOR OF MAKING OUR JANE DOE SOMEONE ELSE'S PROBLEM.

GO TO PAGE 18

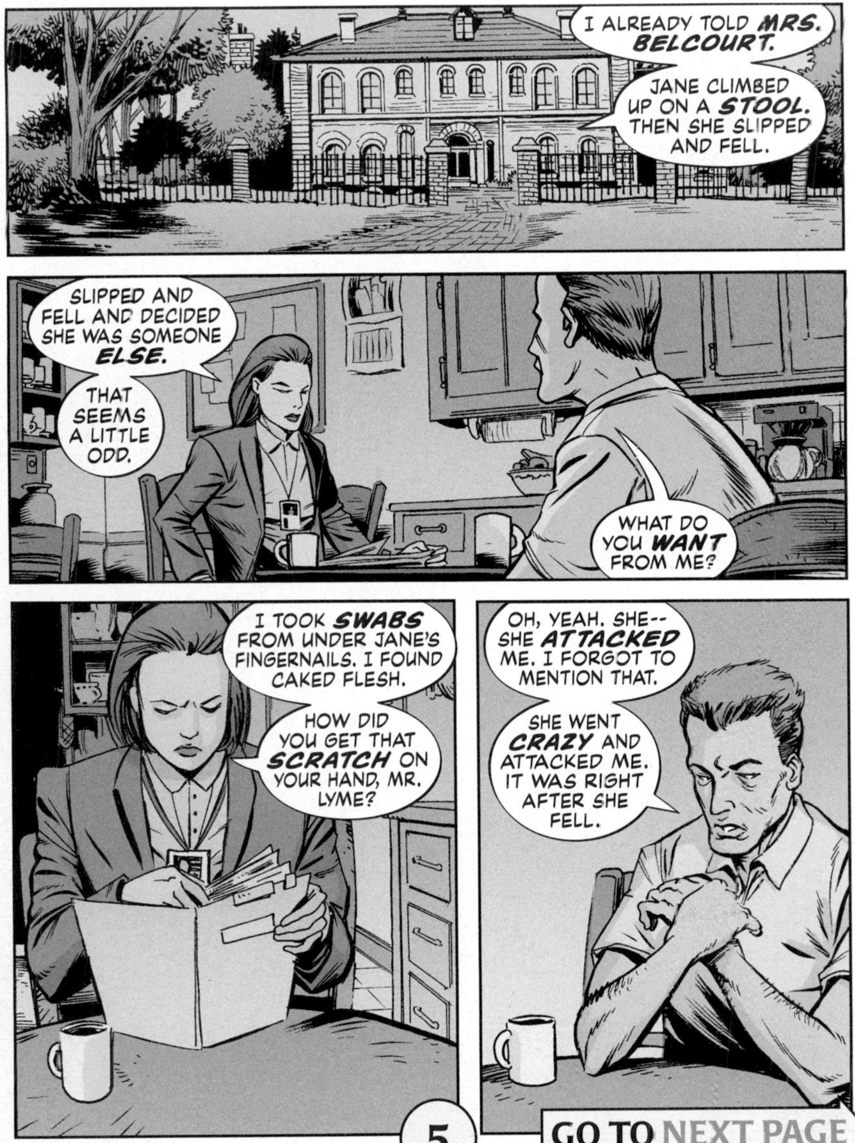
I ALREADY TOLD MRS. BELCOURT.
JANE CLIMBED UP ON A STOOL. THEN SHE SLIPPED AND FELL.
SLIPPED AND FELL AND DECIDED SHE WAS SOMEONE ELSE.
THAT SEEMS A LITTLE ODD.
WHAT DO YOU WANT FROM ME?
I TOOK SWABS FROM UNDER JANE'S FINGERNAILS. I FOUND CAKED FLESH.
HOW DID YOU GET THAT SCRATCH ON YOUR HAND, MR. LYME?
OH, YEAH. SHE-- SHE ATTACKED ME. I FORGOT TO MENTION THAT.
SHE WENT CRAZY AND ATTACKED ME. IT WAS RIGHT AFTER SHE FELL.

5

GO TO NEXT PAGE

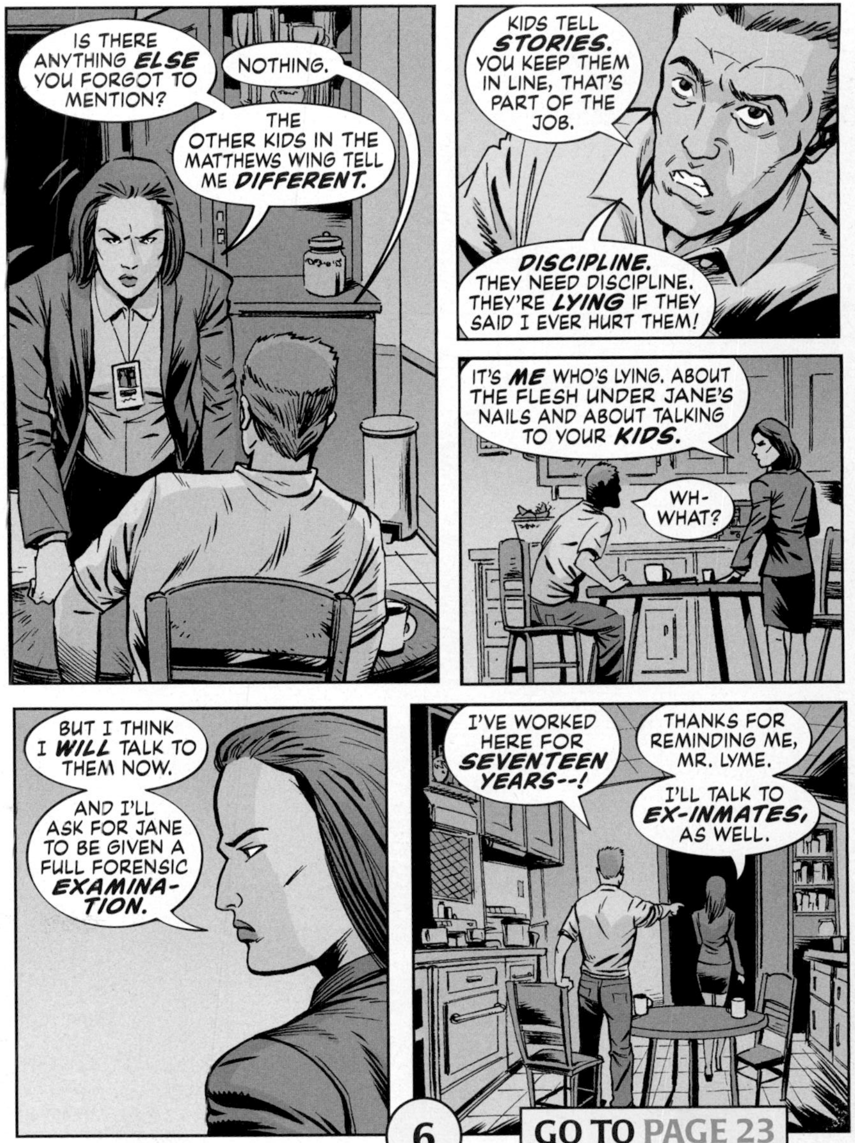
IS THERE ANYTHING ELSE YOU FORGOT TO MENTION?
NOTHING.
THE OTHER KIDS IN THE MATTHEWS WING TELL ME DIFFERENT.
KIDS TELL STORIES. YOU KEEP THEM IN LINE, THAT'S PART OF THE JOB.
DISCIPLINE. THEY NEED DISCIPLINE. THEY'RE LYING IF THEY SAID I EVER HURT THEM!
IT'S ME WHO'S LYING. ABOUT THE FLESH UNDER JANE'S NAILS AND ABOUT TALKING TO YOUR KIDS.
WH-WHAT?
BUT I THINK I WILL TALK TO THEM NOW.
AND I'LL ASK FOR JANE TO BE GIVEN A FULL FORENSIC EXAMINA-TION.
I'VE WORKED HERE FOR SEVENTEEN YEARS--!
THANKS FOR REMINDING ME, MR. LYME.
I'LL TALK TO EX-INMATES, AS WELL.

6

GO TO PAGE 23

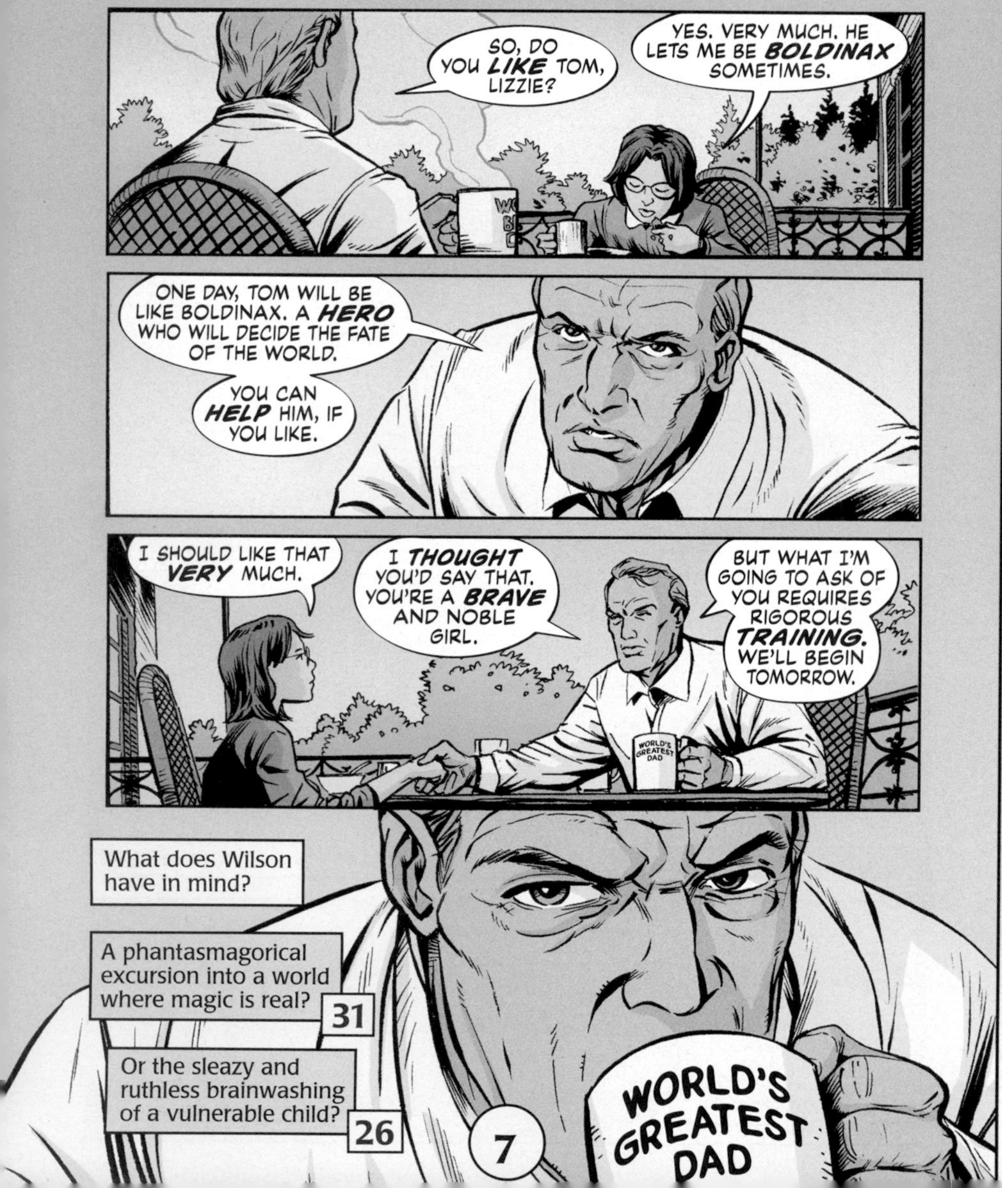
SO, DO YOU LIKE TOM, LIZZIE?
YES. VERY MUCH. HE LETS ME BE BOLDINAX SOMETIMES.
ONE DAY, TOM WILL BE LIKE BOLDINAX. A HERO WHO WILL DECIDE THE FATE OF THE WORLD.
YOU CAN HELP HIM, IF YOU LIKE.
I SHOULD LIKE THAT VERY MUCH.
I THOUGHT YOU'D SAY THAT. YOU'RE A BRAVE AND NOBLE GIRL.
BUT WHAT I'M GOING TO ASK OF YOU REQUIRES RIGOROUS TRAINING. WE'LL BEGIN TOMORROW.
WORLD'S GREATEST DAD
What does Wilson have in mind?
A phantasmagorical excursion into a world where magic is real? 31
Or the sleazy and ruthless brainwashing of a vulnerable child? 26
7

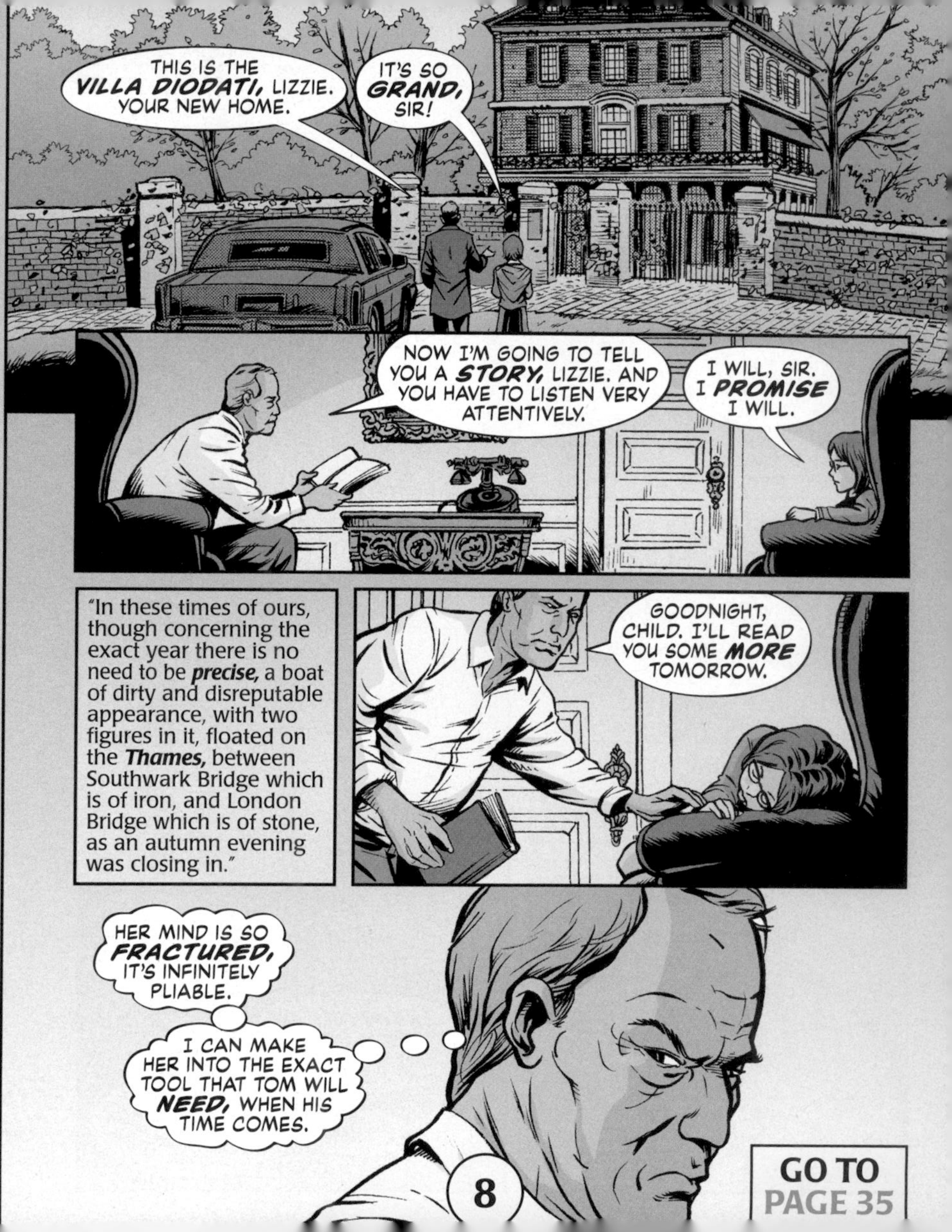
THIS IS THE VILLA DIODATI, LIZZIE. YOUR NEW HOME.
IT'S SO GRAND, SIR!
NOW I'M GOING TO TELL YOU A STORY, LIZZIE. AND YOU HAVE TO LISTEN VERY ATTENTIVELY.
I WILL, SIR. I PROMISE I WILL.
"In these times of ours, though concerning the exact year there is no need to be precise, a boat of dirty and disreputable appearance, with two figures in it, floated on the Thames, between Southwark Bridge which is of iron, and London Bridge which is of stone, as an autumn evening was closing in."
GOODNIGHT, CHILD. I'LL READ YOU SOME MORE TOMORROW.
HER MIND IS SO FRACTURED, IT'S INFINITELY PLIABLE.
I CAN MAKE HER INTO THE EXACT TOOL THAT TOM WILL NEED, WHEN HIS TIME COMES.
8
GO TO PAGE 35

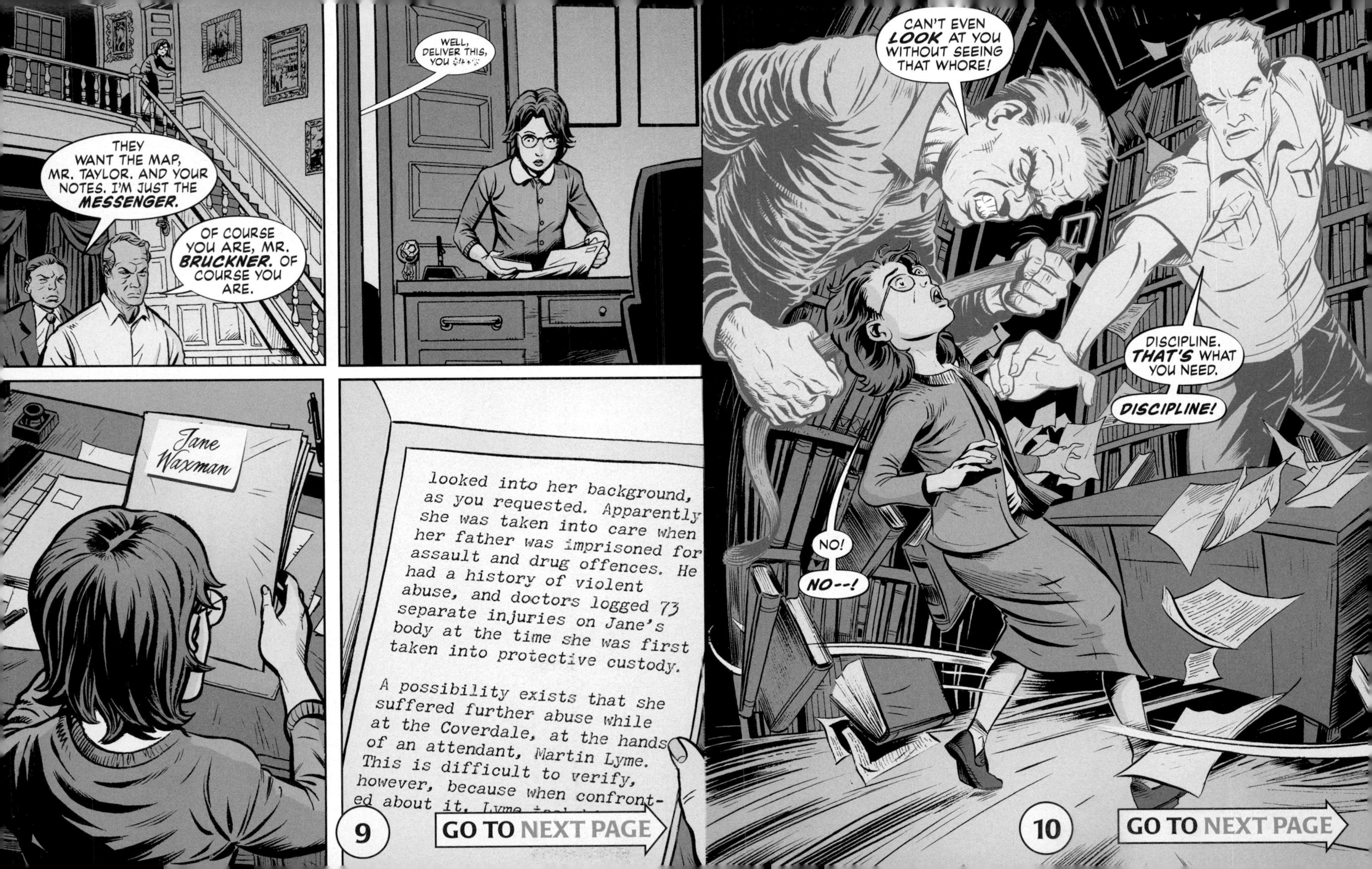
THEY WANT THE MAP, MR. TAYLOR. AND YOUR NOTES. I'M JUST THE MESSENGER.
OF COURSE YOU ARE, MR. BRUCKNER. OF COURSE YOU ARE.
WELL, DELIVER THIS, YOU $#*%
Jane Waxman
looked into her background, as you requested. Apparently she was taken into care when her father was imprisoned for assault and drug offences. He had a history of violent abuse, and doctors logged 73 separate injuries on Jane's body at the time she was first taken into protective custody.
A possibility exists that she suffered further abuse while at the Coverdale, at the hands of an attendant, Martin Lyme. This is difficult to verify, however, because when confront-ed about it,
9
GO TO NEXT PAGE
CAN'T EVEN LOOK AT YOU WITHOUT SEEING THAT WHORE!
DISCIPLINE. THAT'S WHAT YOU NEED.
DISCIPLINE!
NO!
NO--!
10
GO TO NEXT PAGE

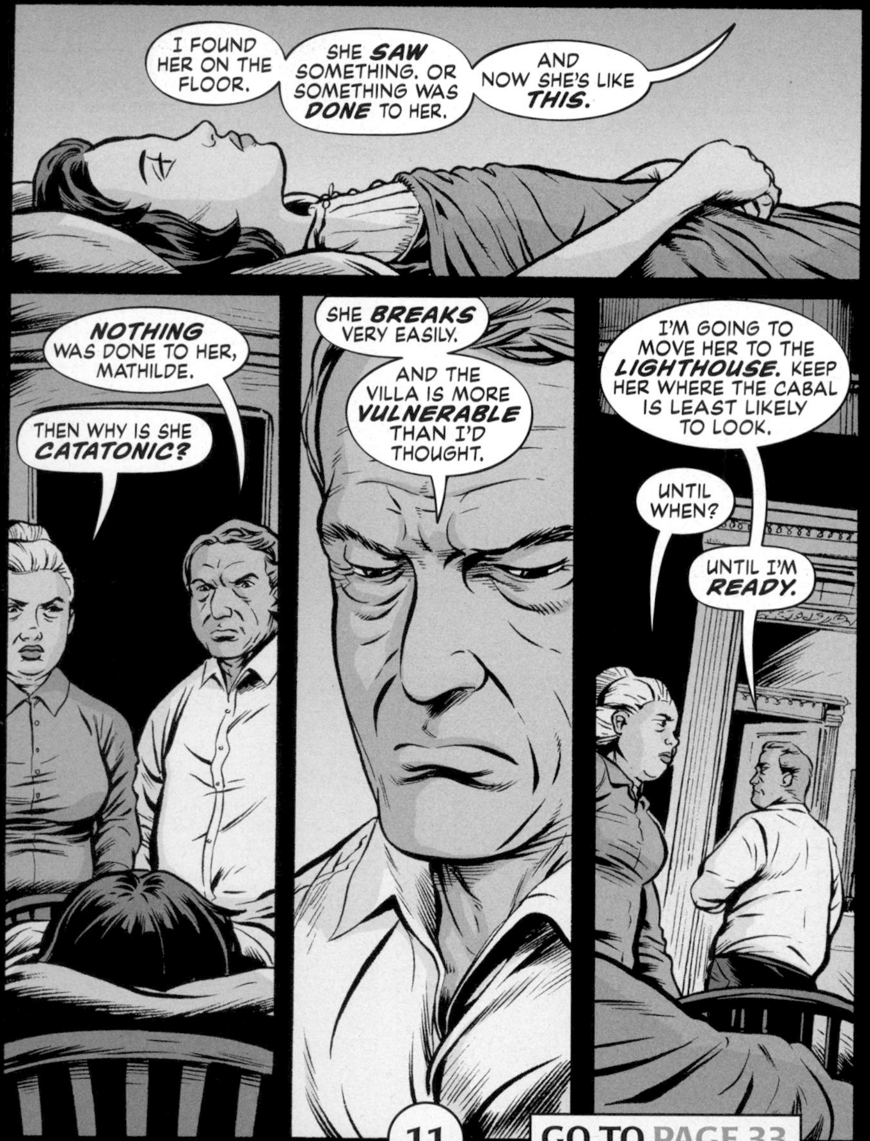
I FOUND HER ON THE FLOOR.
SHE SAW SOMETHING. OR SOMETHING WAS DONE TO HER.
AND NOW SHE'S LIKE THIS.
NOTHING WAS DONE TO HER, MATHILDE.
THEN WHY IS SHE CATATONIC?
SHE BREAKS VERY EASILY.
AND THE VILLA IS MORE VULNERABLE THAN I'D THOUGHT.
I'M GOING TO MOVE HER TO THE LIGHTHOUSE. KEEP HER WHERE THE CABAL IS LEAST LIKELY TO LOOK.
UNTIL WHEN?
UNTIL I'M READY.

GO TO PAGE 33

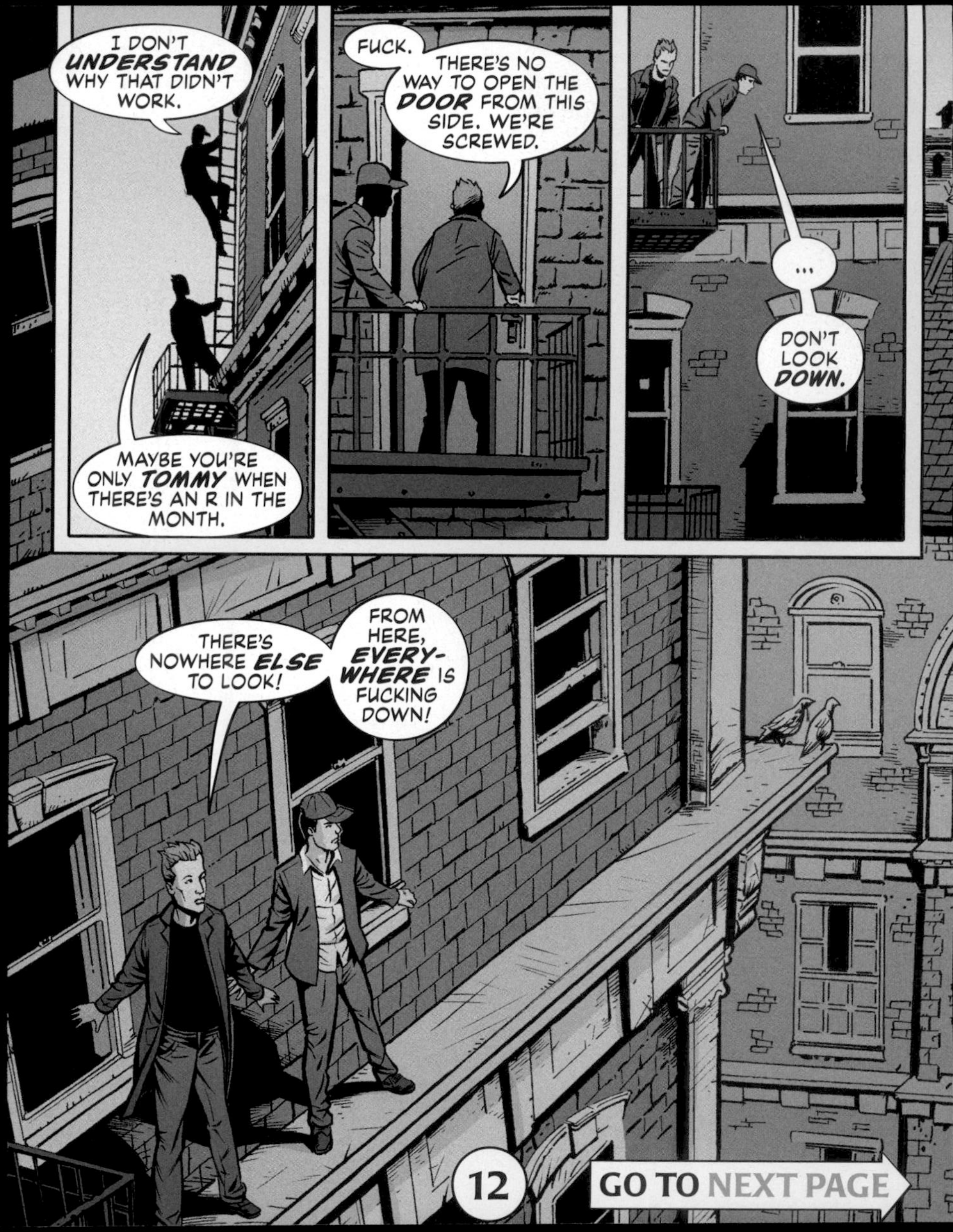
I DON'T UNDERSTAND WHY THAT DIDN'T WORK.
MAYBE YOU'RE ONLY TOMMY WHEN THERE'S AN R IN THE MONTH.
FUCK.
THERE'S NO WAY TO OPEN THE DOOR FROM THIS SIDE. WE'RE SCREWED.
...
DON'T LOOK DOWN.
THERE'S NOWHERE ELSE TO LOOK!
FROM HERE, EVERYWHERE IS FUCKING DOWN!

GO TO NEXT PAGE

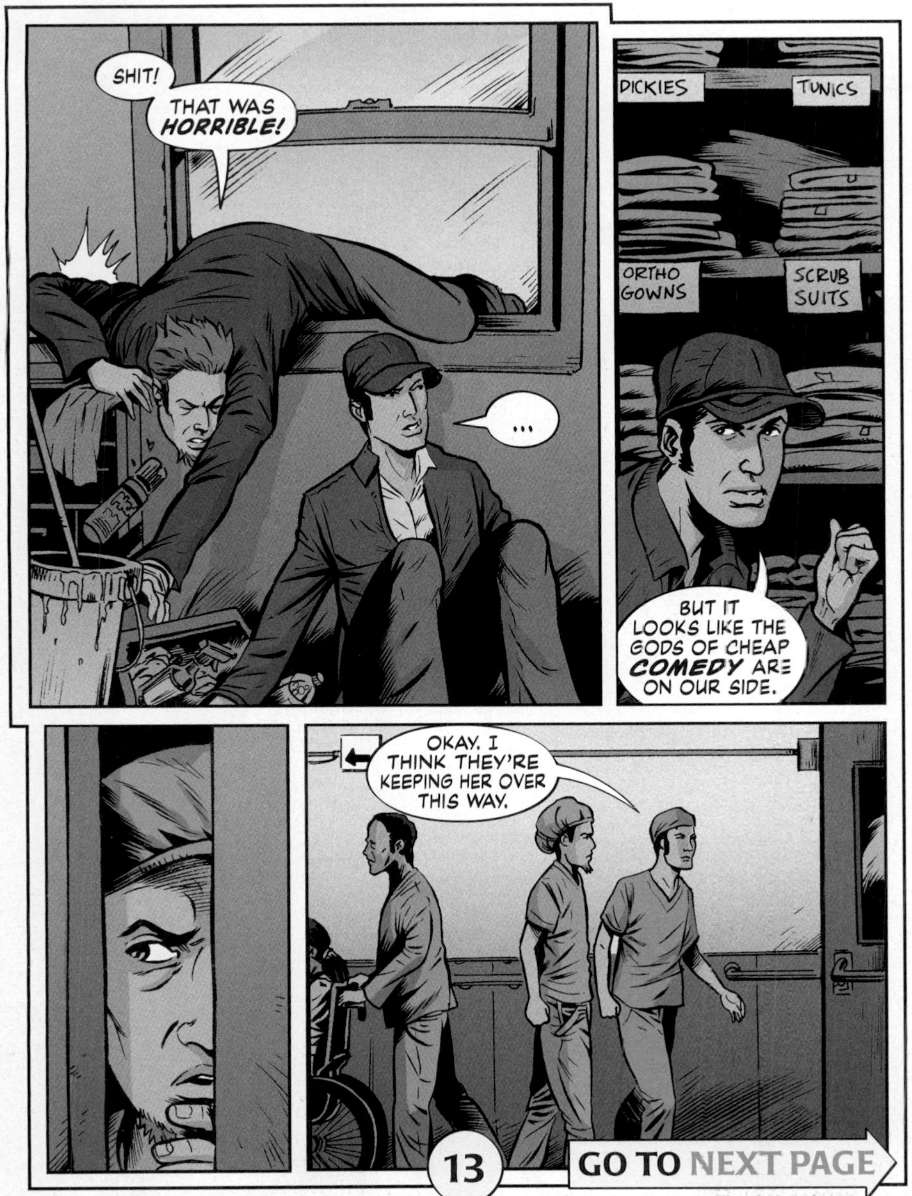
SHIT!
THAT WAS HORRIBLE!
...
DICKIES
TUNICS
ORTHO GOWNS
SCRUB SUITS
BUT IT LOOKS LIKE THE GODS OF CHEAP COMEDY ARE ON OUR SIDE.
OKAY. I THINK THEY'RE KEEPING HER OVER THIS WAY.
13
GO TO NEXT PAGE

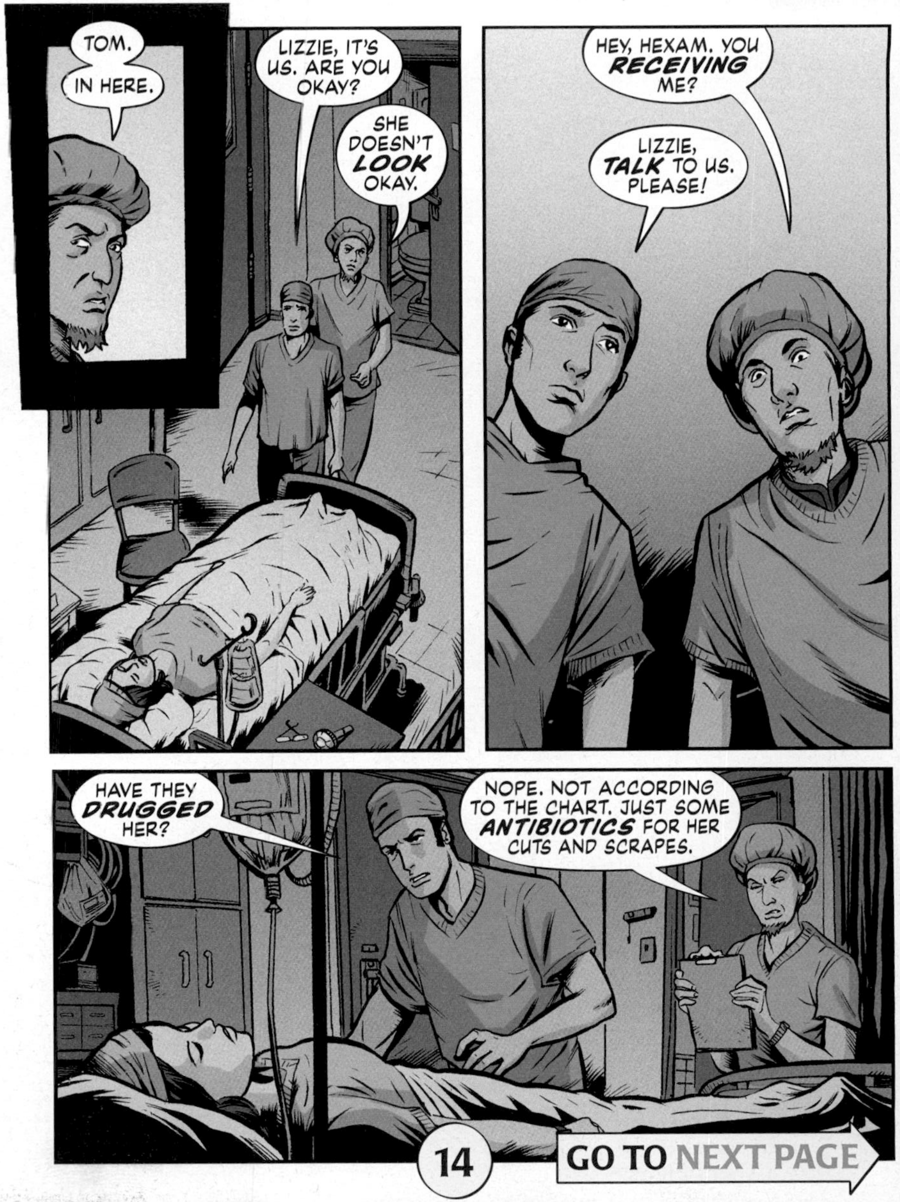
TOM.
IN HERE.
LIZZIE, IT'S US. ARE YOU OKAY?
SHE DOESN'T LOOK OKAY.
HEY, HEXAM. YOU RECEIVING ME?
LIZZIE, TALK TO US. PLEASE!
HAVE THEY DRUGGED HER?
NOPE. NOT ACCORDING TO THE CHART. JUST SOME ANTIBIOTICS FOR HER CUTS AND SCRAPES.
14
GO TO NEXT PAGE

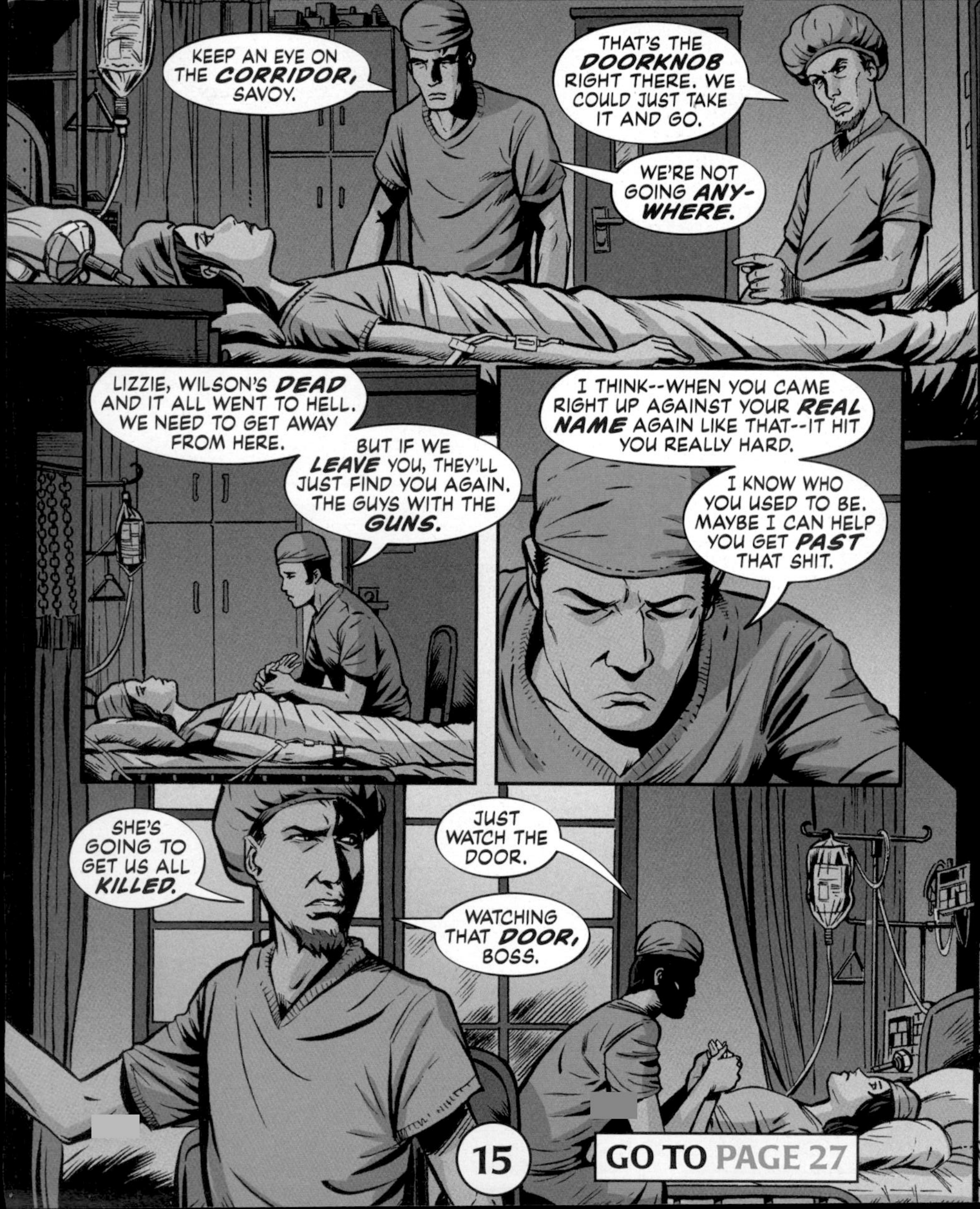
KEEP AN EYE ON THE CORRIDOR, SAVOY.
THAT'S THE DOORKNOB RIGHT THERE. WE COULD JUST TAKE IT AND GO.
WE'RE NOT GOING ANY-WHERE.
LIZZIE, WILSON'S DEAD AND IT ALL WENT TO HELL. WE NEED TO GET AWAY FROM HERE.
BUT IF WE LEAVE YOU, THEY'LL JUST FIND YOU AGAIN. THE GUYS WITH THE GUNS.
I THINK--WHEN YOU CAME RIGHT UP AGAINST YOUR REAL NAME AGAIN LIKE THAT--IT HIT YOU REALLY HARD.
I KNOW WHO YOU USED TO BE. MAYBE I CAN HELP YOU GET PAST THAT SHIT.
SHE'S GOING TO GET US ALL KILLED.
JUST WATCH THE DOOR.
WATCHING THAT DOOR, BOSS.

GO TO PAGE 27

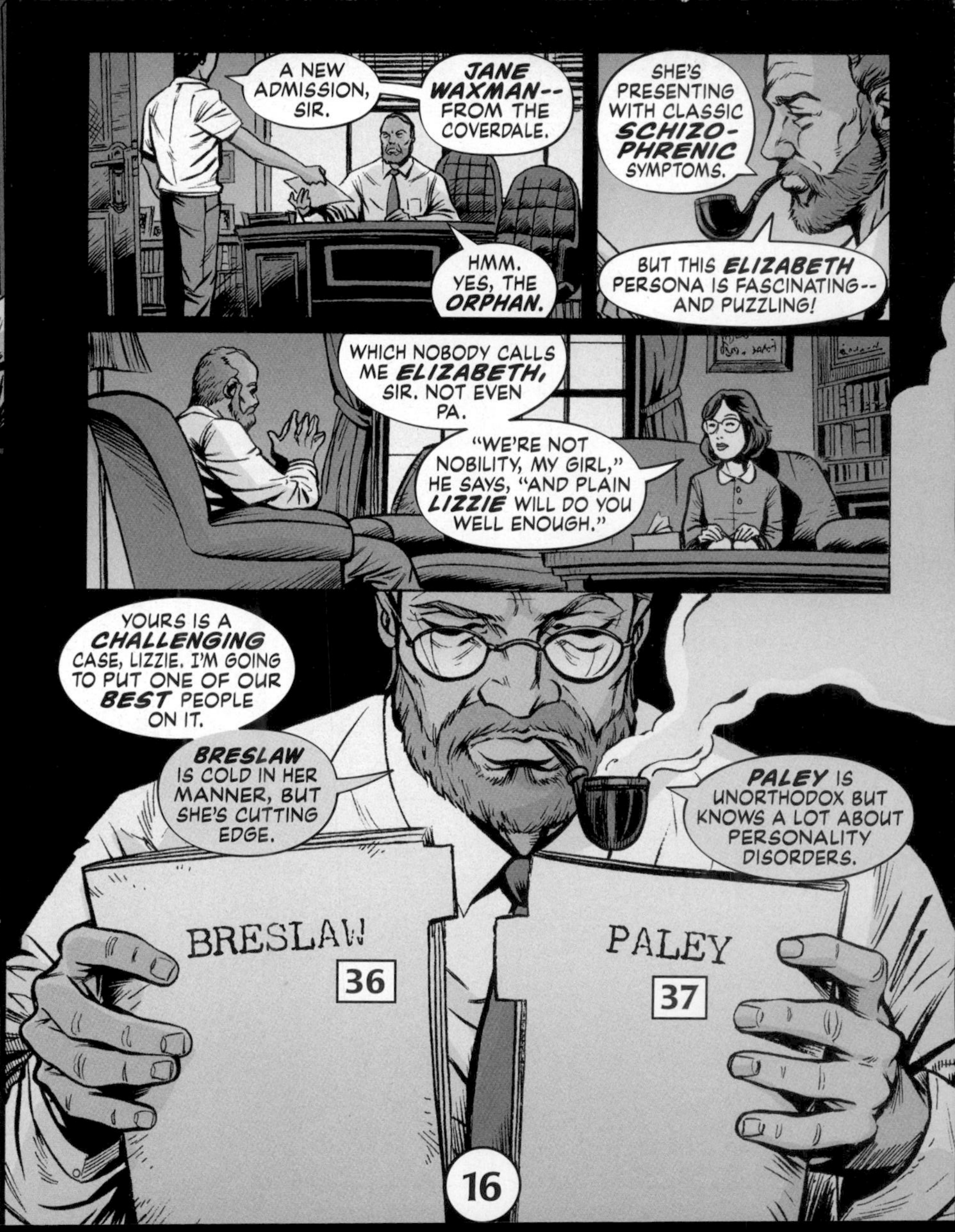
A NEW ADMISSION, SIR.
JANE WAXMAN-- FROM THE COVERDALE.
HMM. YES, THE ORPHAN.
SHE'S PRESENTING WITH CLASSIC SCHIZO-PHRENIC SYMPTOMS.
BUT THIS ELIZABETH PERSONA IS FASCINATING-- AND PUZZLING!
WHICH NOBODY CALLS ME ELIZABETH, SIR. NOT EVEN PA.
"WE'RE NOT NOBILITY, MY GIRL," HE SAYS, "AND PLAIN LIZZIE WILL DO YOU WELL ENOUGH."
YOURS IS A CHALLENGING CASE, LIZZIE. I'M GOING TO PUT ONE OF OUR BEST PEOPLE ON IT.
BRESLAW IS COLD IN HER MANNER, BUT SHE'S CUTTING EDGE.
PALEY IS UNORTHODOX BUT KNOWS A LOT ABOUT PERSONALITY DISORDERS.
BRESLAW
36
PALEY
37

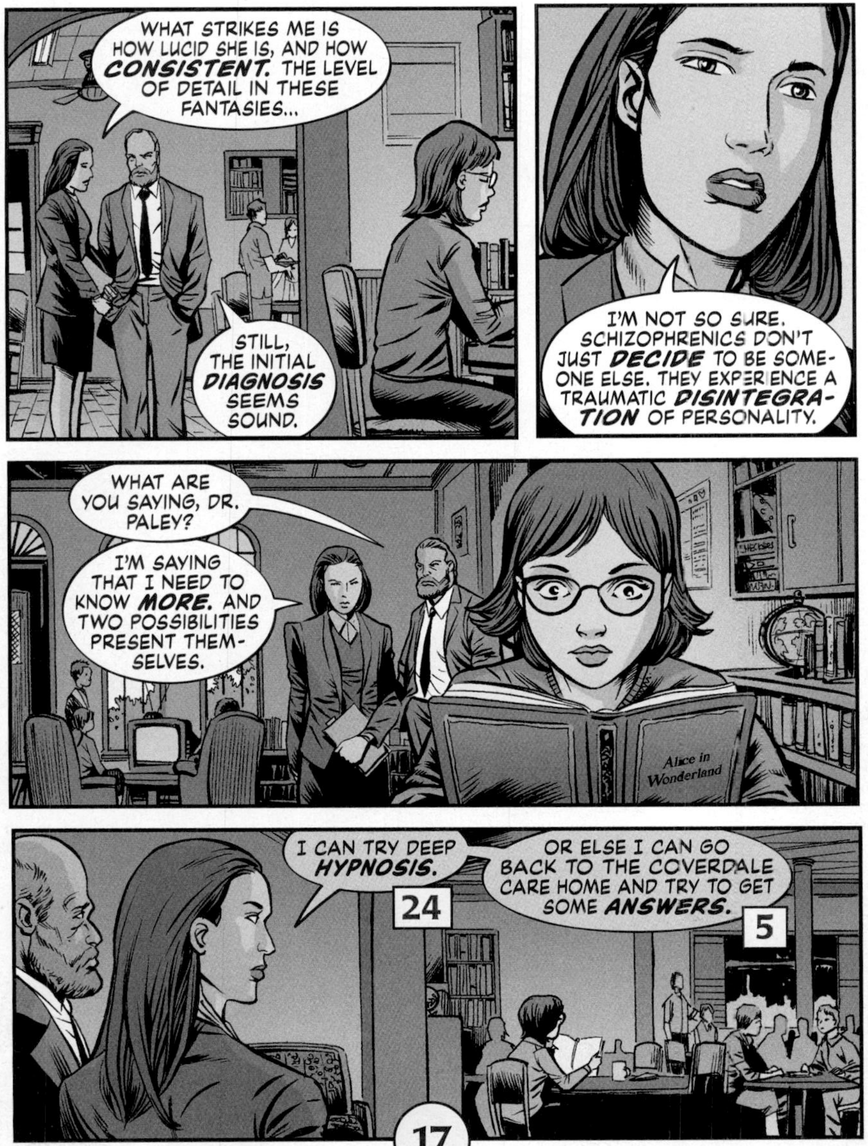
WHAT STRIKES ME IS HOW LUCID SHE IS, AND HOW CONSISTENT. THE LEVEL OF DETAIL IN THESE FANTASIES...
STILL, THE INITIAL DIAGNOSIS SEEMS SOUND.
I'M NOT SO SURE. SCHIZOPHRENICS DON'T JUST DECIDE TO BE SOME-ONE ELSE. THEY EXPERIENCE A TRAUMATIC DISINTEGRA-TION OF PERSONALITY.
WHAT ARE YOU SAYING, DR. PALEY?
I'M SAYING THAT I NEED TO KNOW MORE. AND TWO POSSIBILITIES PRESENT THEM-SELVES.
Alice in Wonderland
I CAN TRY DEEP HYPNOSIS.
24
OR ELSE I CAN GO BACK TO THE COVERDALE CARE HOME AND TRY TO GET SOME ANSWERS.
5

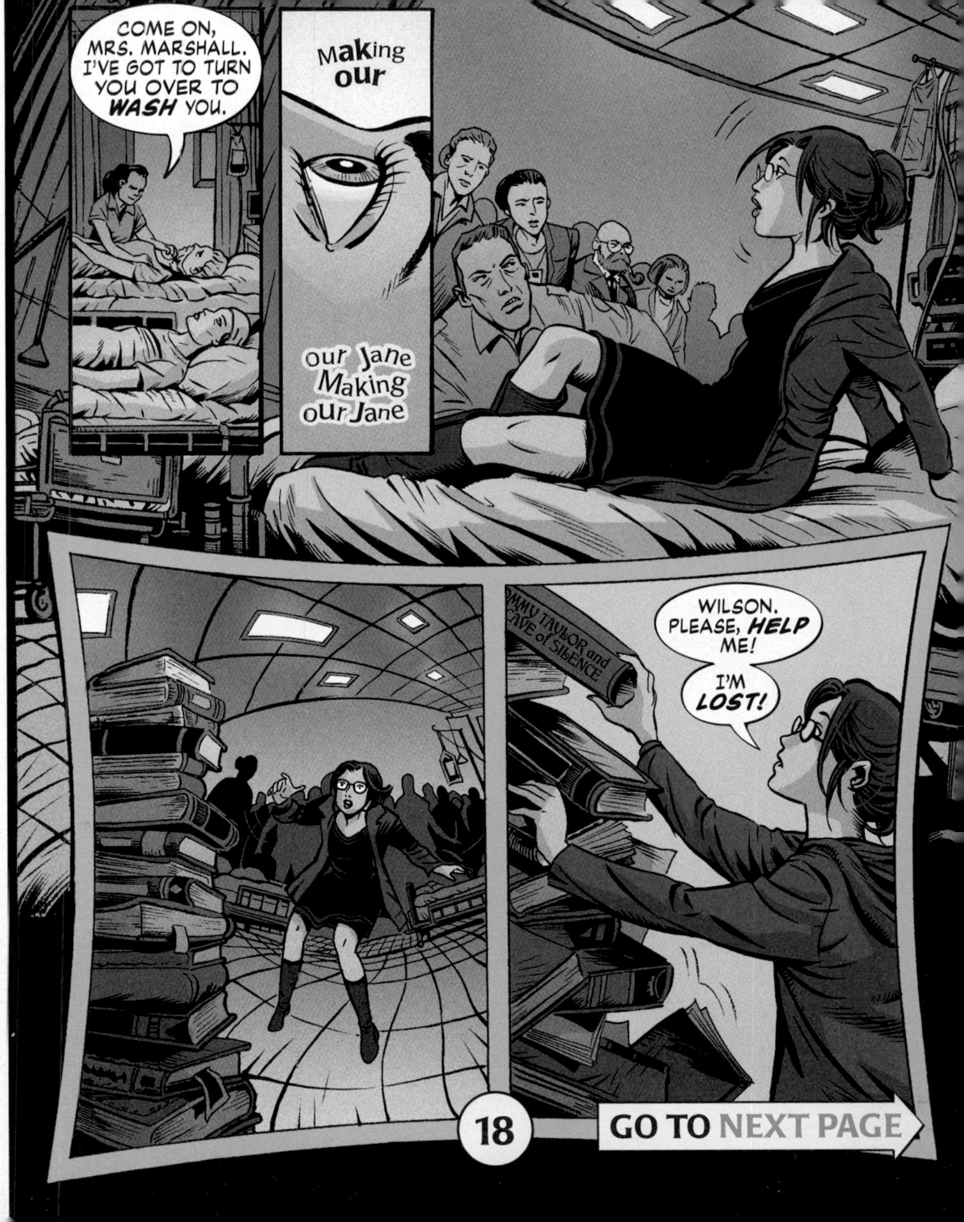
COME ON, MRS. MARSHALL. I'VE GOT TO TURN YOU OVER TO WASH YOU.
Making our
our Jane Making our Jane
WILSON. PLEASE, HELP ME!
I'M LOST!

GO TO NEXT PAGE

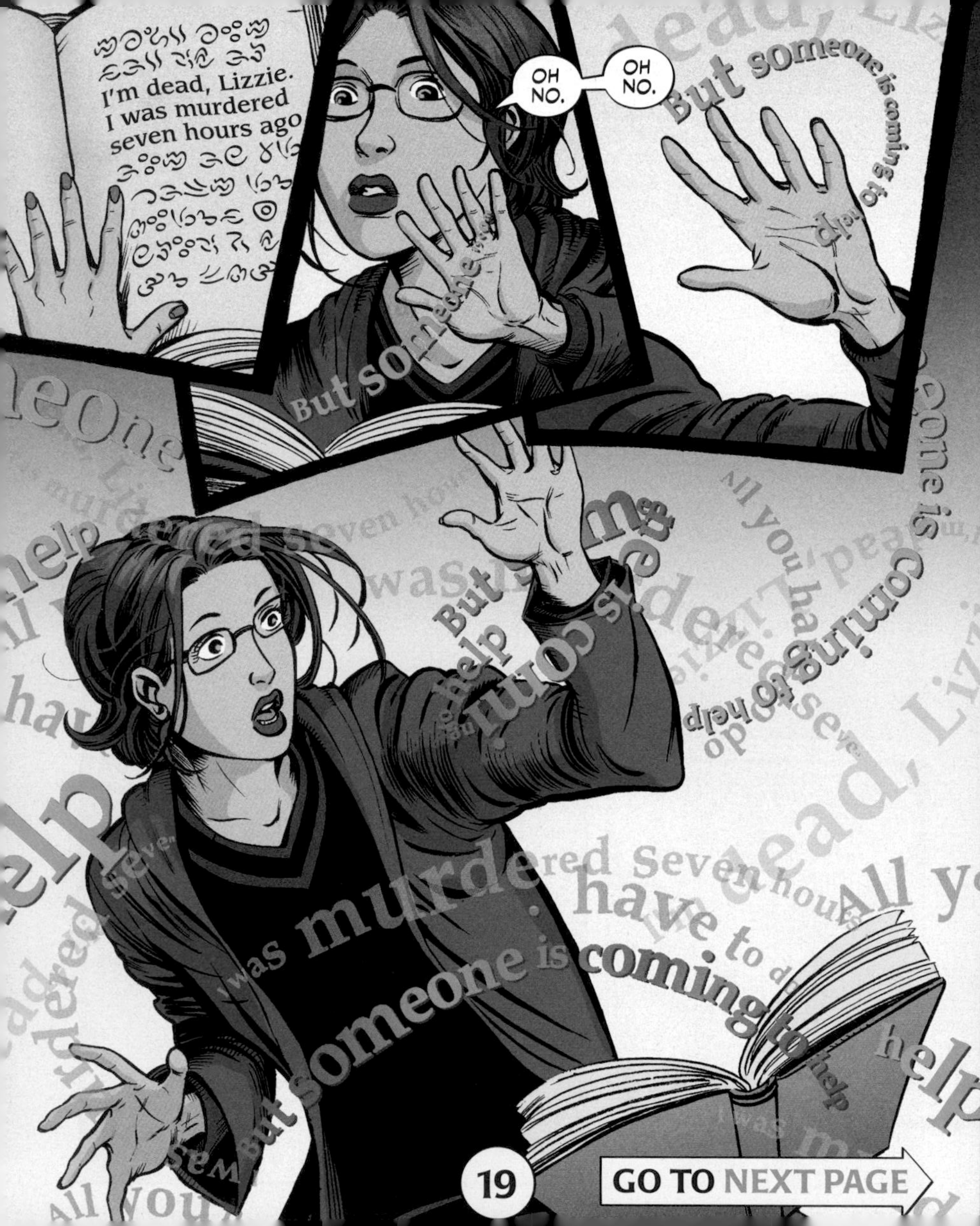
I'm dead, Lizzie. I was murdered seven hours ago
OH NO.
OH NO.
But someone is coming to help

GO TO NEXT PAGE

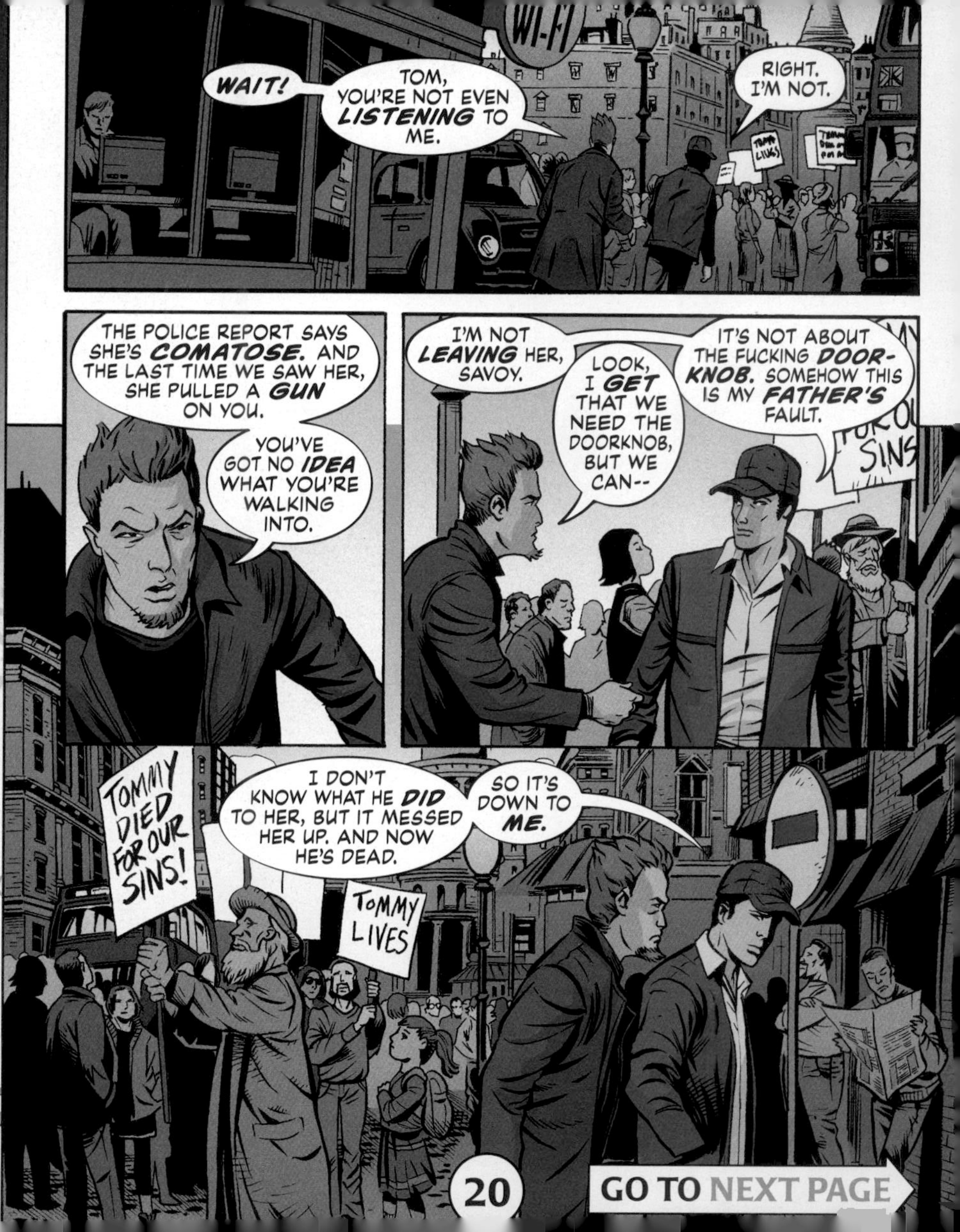
WAIT!
TOM, YOU'RE NOT EVEN LISTENING TO ME.
RIGHT. I'M NOT.
THE POLICE REPORT SAYS SHE'S COMATOSE. AND THE LAST TIME WE SAW HER, SHE PULLED A GUN ON YOU.
YOU'VE GOT NO IDEA WHAT YOU'RE WALKING INTO.
I'M NOT LEAVING HER, SAVOY.
LOOK, I GET THAT WE NEED THE DOORKNOB, BUT WE CAN--
IT'S NOT ABOUT THE FUCKING DOORKNOB. SOMEHOW THIS IS MY FATHER'S FAULT.
TOMMY DIED FOR OUR SINS!
TOMMY LIVES
I DON'T KNOW WHAT HE DID TO HER, BUT IT MESSED HER UP. AND NOW HE'S DEAD.
SO IT'S DOWN TO ME.

GO TO NEXT PAGE

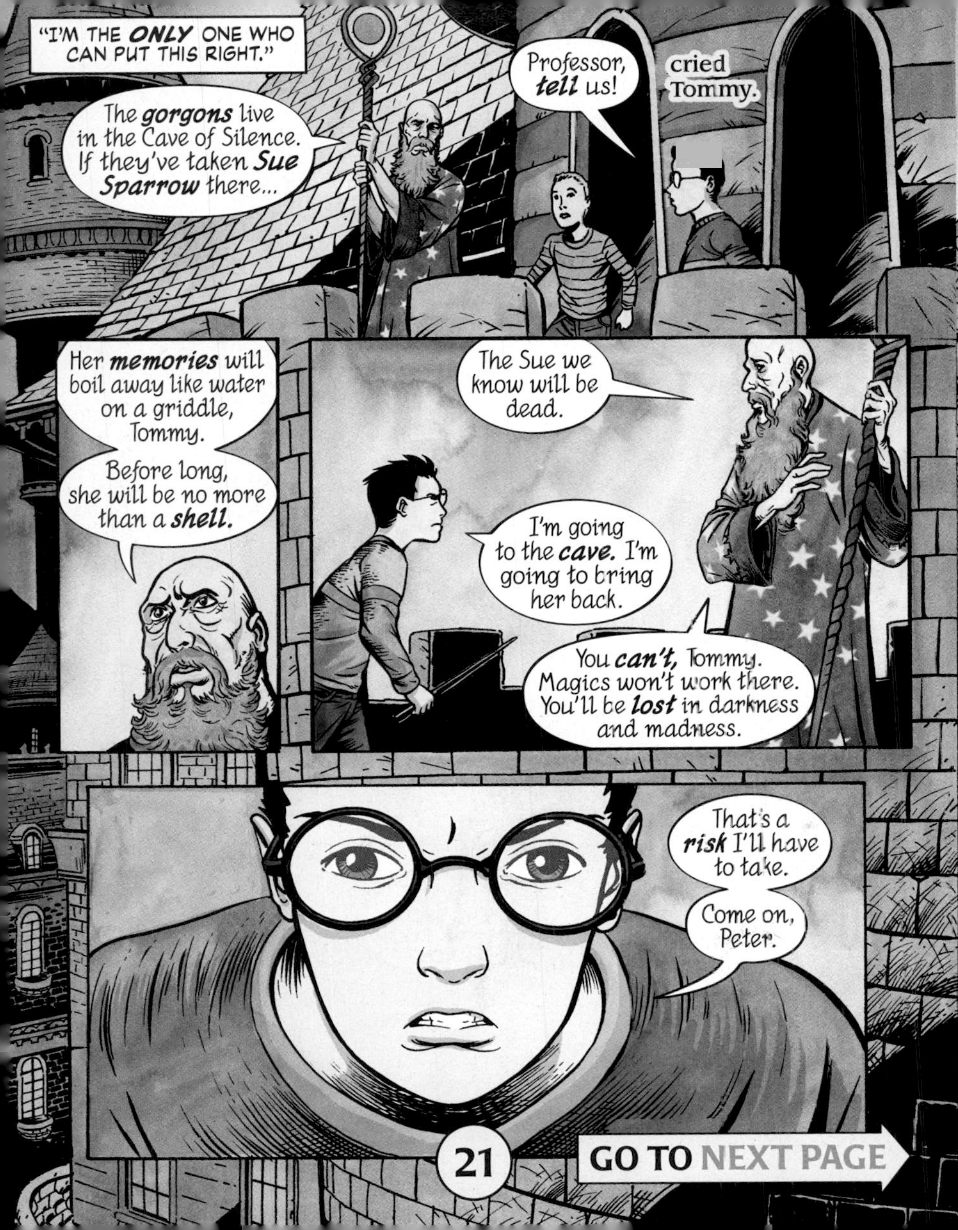
"I'M THE ONLY ONE WHO CAN PUT THIS RIGHT."
The gorgons live in the Cave of Silence. If they've taken Sue Sparrow there...
Professor, tell us!
cried Tommy.
Her memories will boil away like water on a griddle, Tommy.
Before long, she will be no more than a shell.
The Sue we know will be dead.
I'm going to the cave. I'm going to bring her back.
You can't, Tommy. Magics won't work there. You'll be lost in darkness and madness.
That's a risk I'll have to take.
Come on, Peter.

GO TO NEXT PAGE

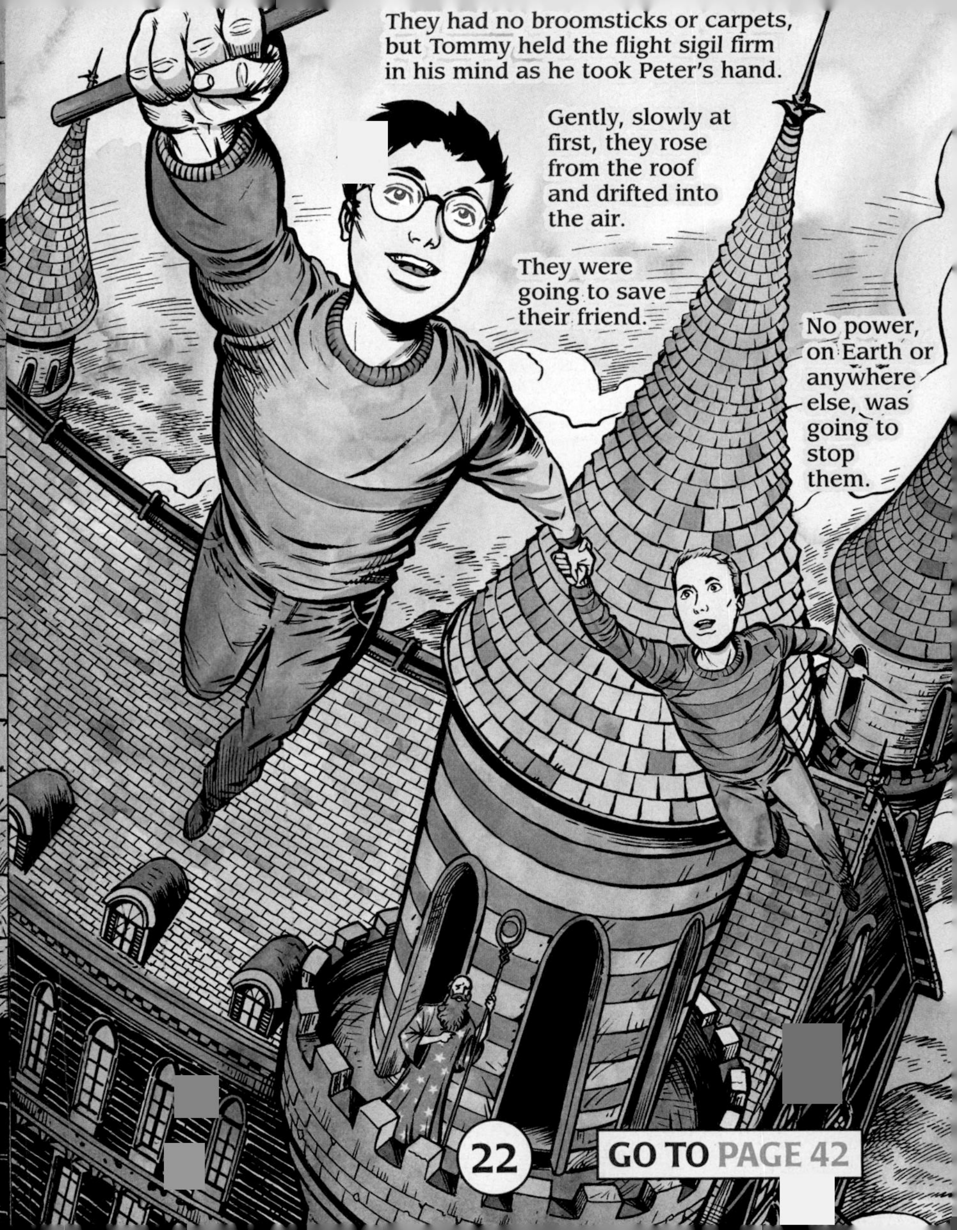
They had no broomsticks or carpets, but Tommy held the flight sigil firm in his mind as he took Peter's hand.
Gently, slowly at first, they rose from the roof and drifted into the air.
They were going to save their friend.
No power, on Earth or anywhere else, was going to stop them.

GO TO PAGE 42

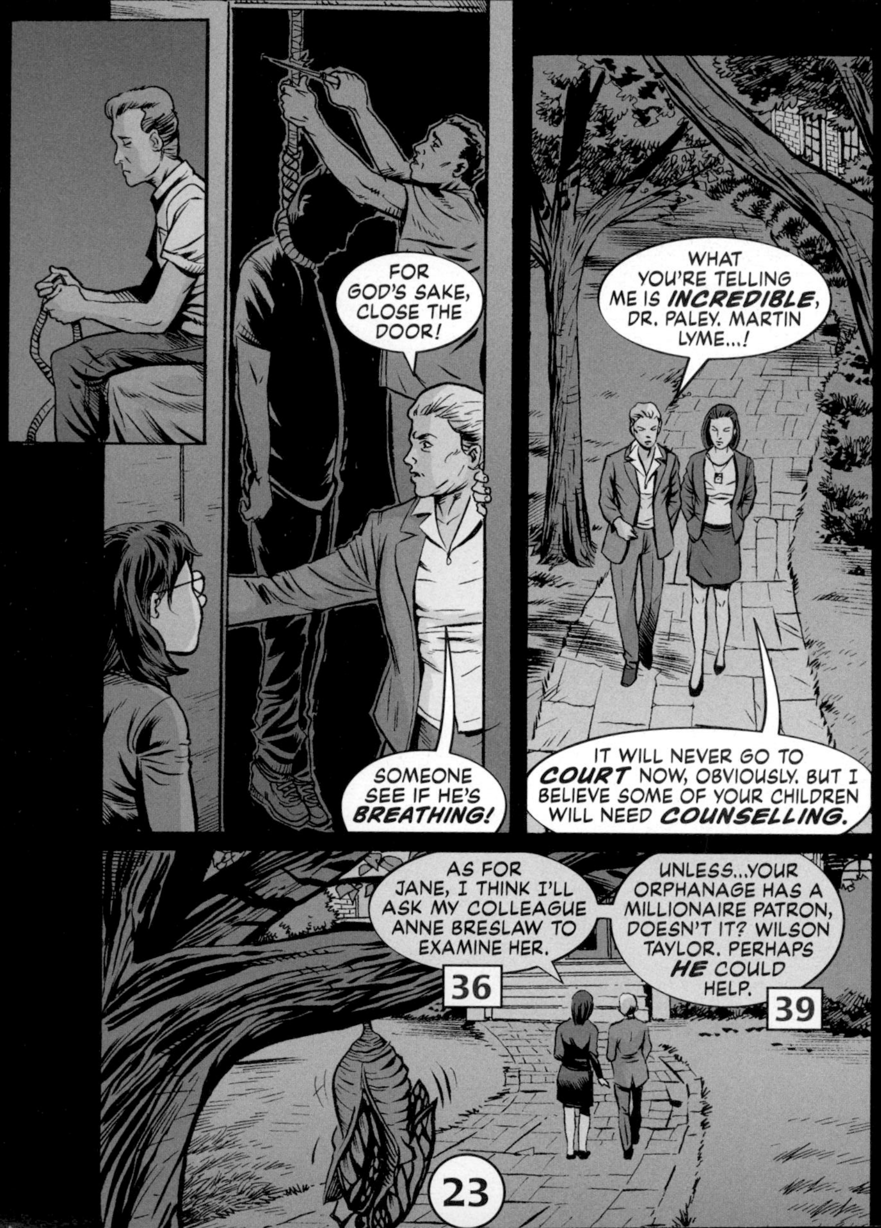
FOR GOD'S SAKE, CLOSE THE DOOR!
SOMEONE SEE IF HE'S BREATHING!
WHAT YOU'RE TELLING ME IS INCREDIBLE, DR. PALEY. MARTIN LYME...!
IT WILL NEVER GO TO COURT NOW, OBVIOUSLY. BUT I BELIEVE SOME OF YOUR CHILDREN WILL NEED COUNSELLING.
AS FOR JANE, I THINK I'LL ASK MY COLLEAGUE ANNE BRESLAW TO EXAMINE HER.
36
UNLESS...YOUR ORPHANAGE HAS A MILLIONAIRE PATRON, DOESN'T IT? WILSON TAYLOR. PERHAPS HE COULD HELP.
39
23

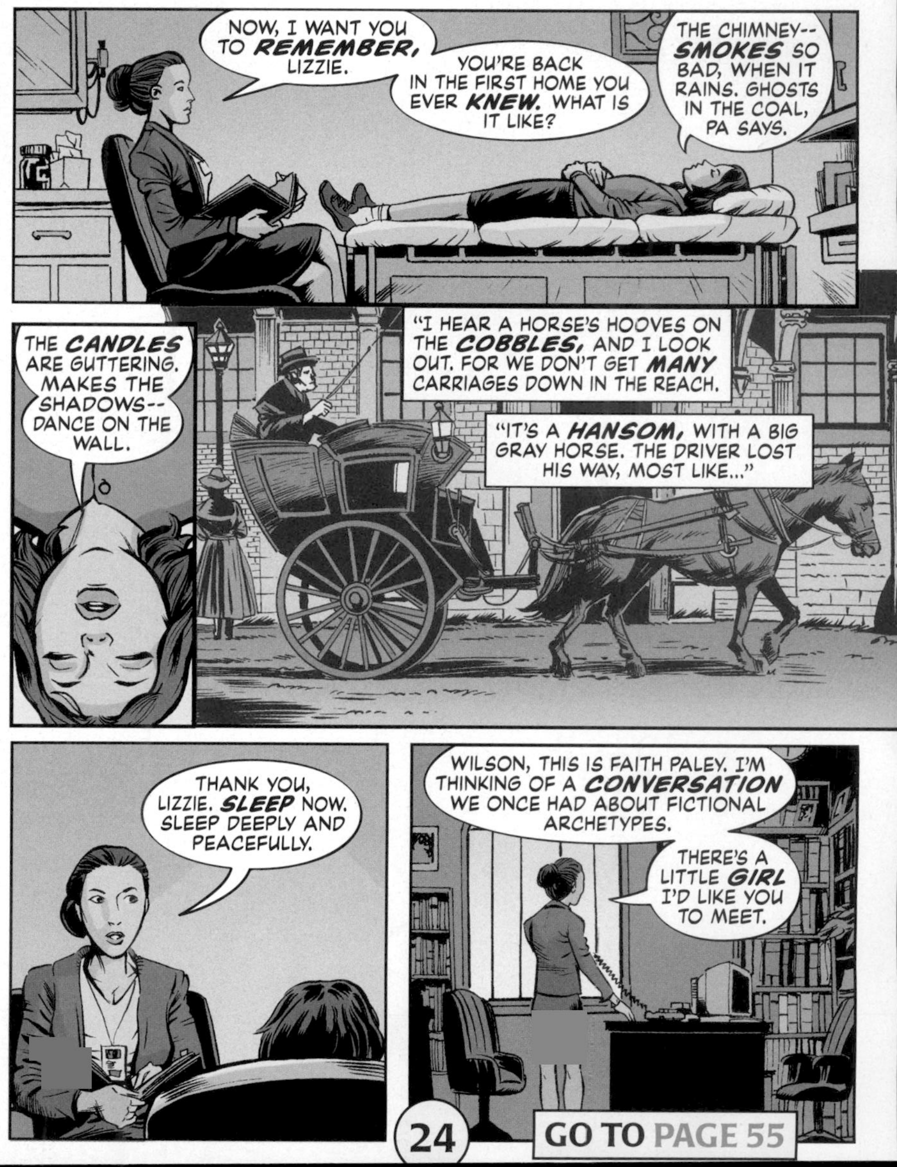
NOW, I WANT YOU TO REMEMBER, LIZZIE.
YOU'RE BACK IN THE FIRST HOME YOU EVER KNEW. WHAT IS IT LIKE?
THE CHIMNEY-- SMOKES SO BAD, WHEN IT RAINS. GHOSTS IN THE COAL, PA SAYS.
THE CANDLES ARE GUTTERING. MAKES THE SHADOWS-- DANCE ON THE WALL.
"I HEAR A HORSE'S HOOVES ON THE COBBLES, AND I LOOK OUT. FOR WE DON'T GET MANY CARRIAGES DOWN IN THE REACH.
"IT'S A HANSOM, WITH A BIG GRAY HORSE. THE DRIVER LOST HIS WAY, MOST LIKE..."
THANK YOU, LIZZIE. SLEEP NOW. SLEEP DEEPLY AND PEACEFULLY.
WILSON, THIS IS FAITH PALEY. I'M THINKING OF A CONVERSATION WE ONCE HAD ABOUT FICTIONAL ARCHETYPES.
THERE'S A LITTLE GIRL I'D LIKE YOU TO MEET.
24
GO TO PAGE 55

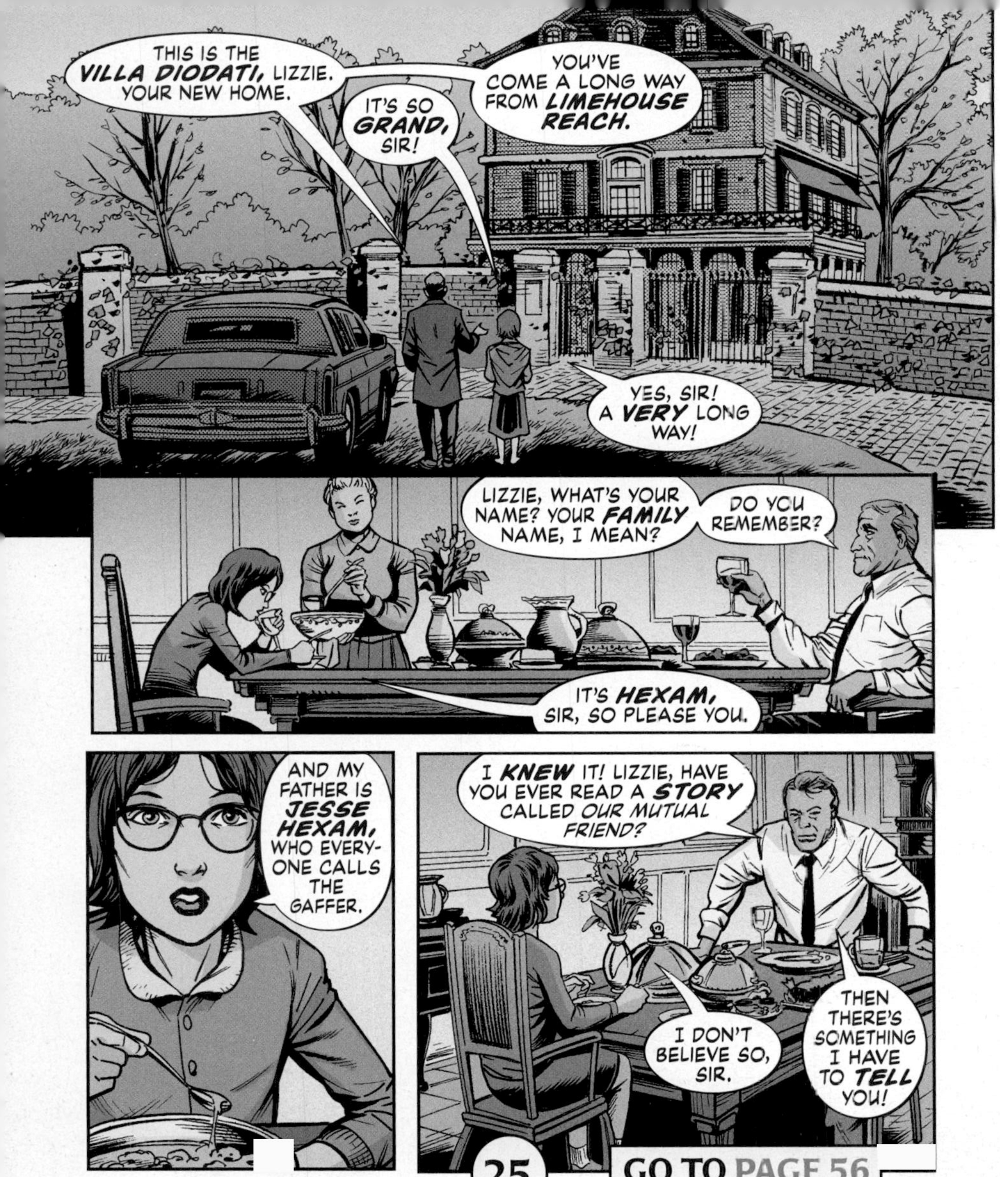
THIS IS THE VILLA DIODATI, LIZZIE. YOUR NEW HOME.
IT'S SO GRAND, SIR!
YOU'VE COME A LONG WAY FROM LIMEHOUSE REACH.
YES, SIR! A VERY LONG WAY!
LIZZIE, WHAT'S YOUR NAME? YOUR FAMILY NAME, I MEAN?
DO YOU REMEMBER?
IT'S HEXAM, SIR, SO PLEASE YOU.
AND MY FATHER IS JESSE HEXAM, WHO EVERY-ONE CALLS THE GAFFER.
I KNEW IT! LIZZIE, HAVE YOU EVER READ A STORY CALLED OUR MUTUAL FRIEND?
I DON'T BELIEVE SO, SIR.
THEN THERE'S SOMETHING I HAVE TO TELL YOU!
25
GO TO PAGE 56

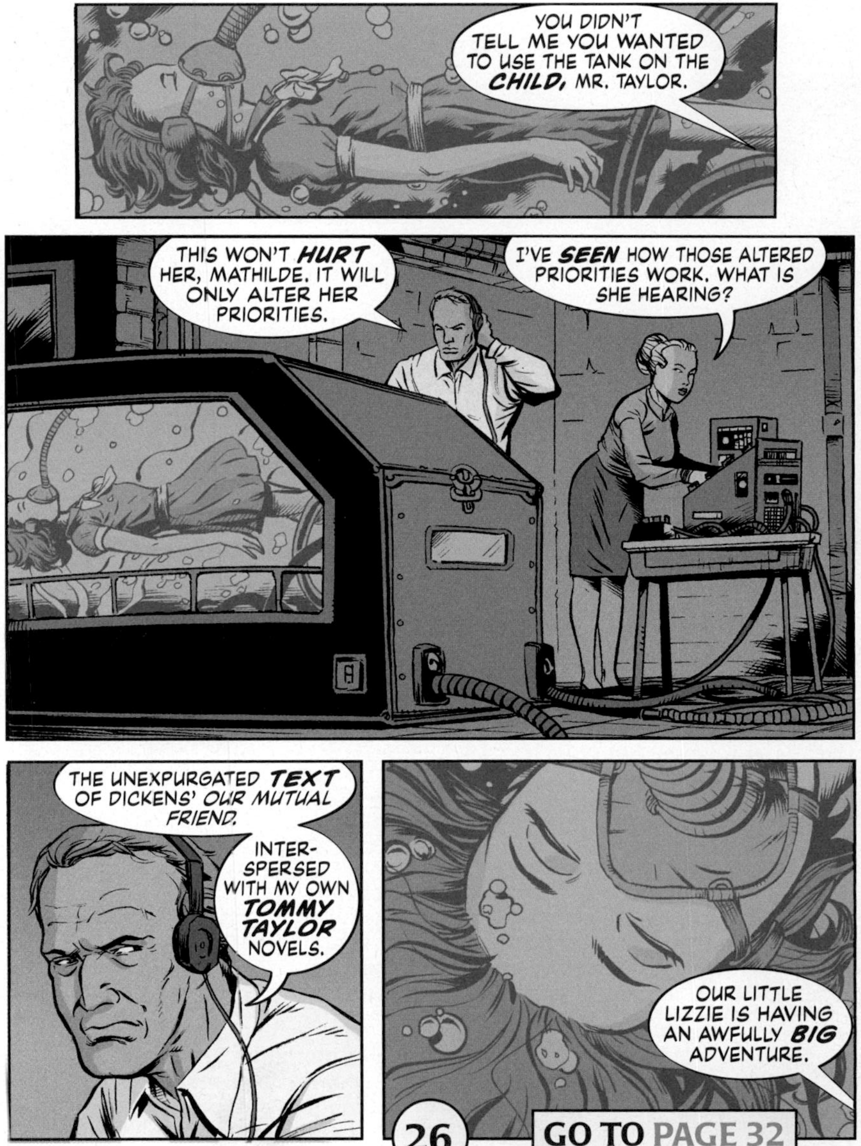
YOU DIDN'T TELL ME YOU WANTED TO USE THE TANK ON THE CHILD, MR. TAYLOR.
THIS WON'T HURT HER, MATHILDE. IT WILL ONLY ALTER HER PRIORITIES.
I'VE SEEN HOW THOSE ALTERED PRIORITIES WORK. WHAT IS SHE HEARING?
THE UNEXPURGATED TEXT OF DICKENS' OUR MUTUAL FRIEND.
INTER-SPERSED WITH MY OWN TOMMY TAYLOR NOVELS.
OUR LITTLE LIZZIE IS HAVING AN AWFULLY BIG ADVENTURE.
26
GO TO PAGE 32

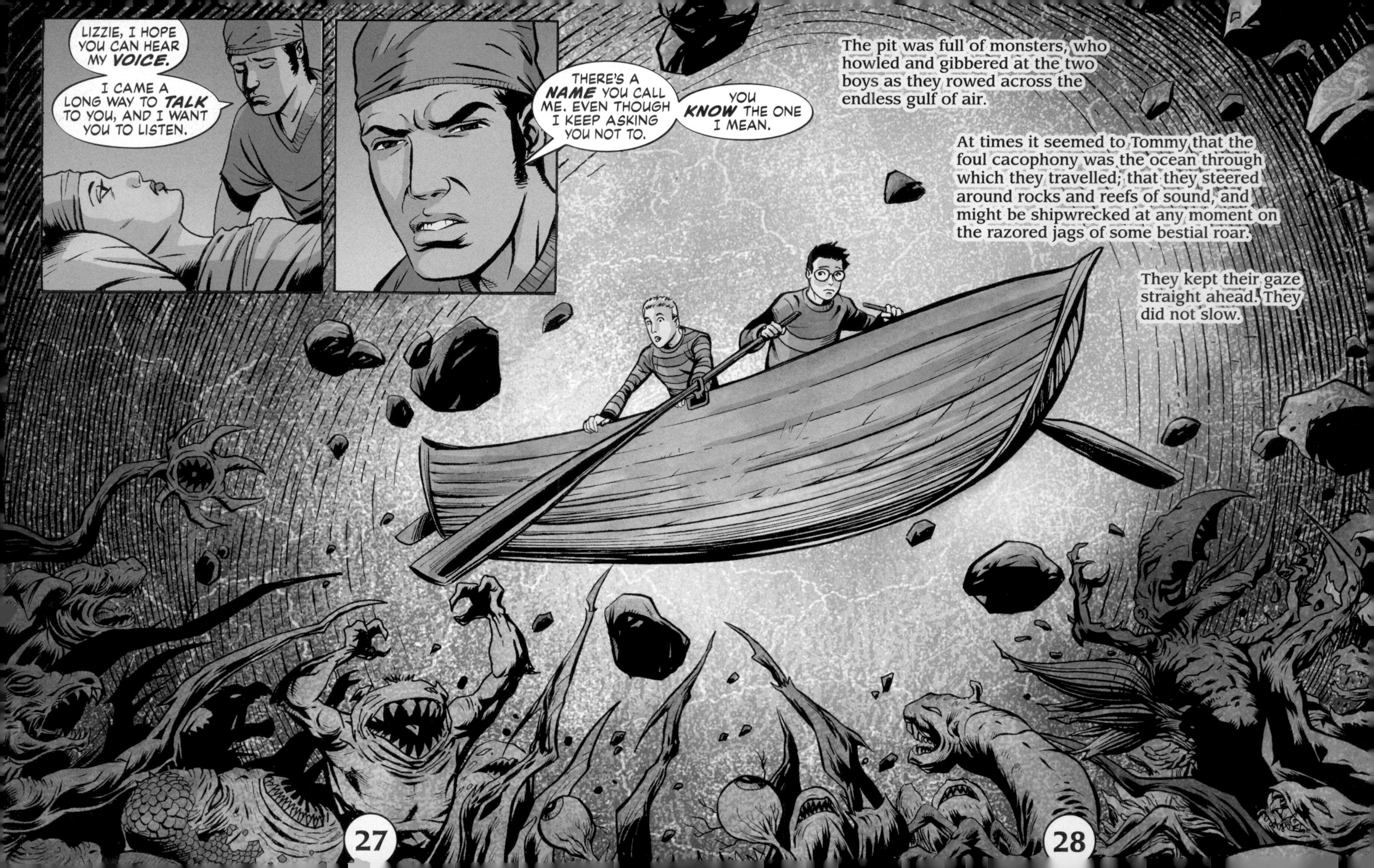
LIZZIE, I HOPE YOU CAN HEAR MY VOICE.
I CAME A LONG WAY TO TALK TO YOU, AND I WANT YOU TO LISTEN.
THERE'S A NAME YOU CALL ME. EVEN THOUGH I KEEP ASKING YOU NOT TO.
YOU KNOW THE ONE I MEAN.
The pit was full of monsters, who howled and gibbered at the two boys as they rowed across the endless gulf of air.
At times it seemed to Tommy that the foul cacophony was the ocean through which they travelled; that they steered around rocks and reefs of sound, and might be shipwrecked at any moment on the razored jags of some bestial roar.
They kept their gaze straight ahead. They did not slow.
27
28

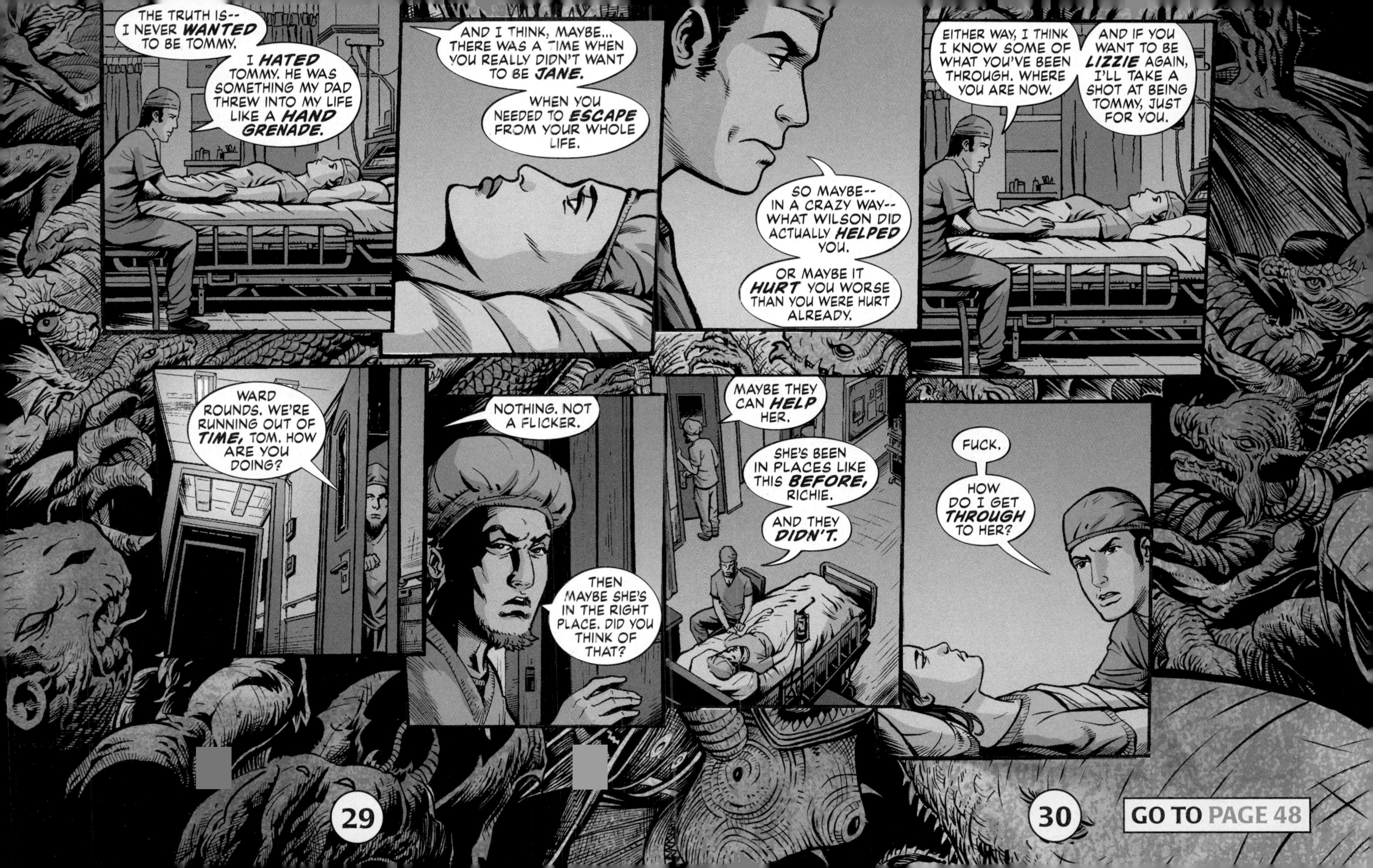
THE TRUTH IS-- I NEVER WANTED TO BE TOMMY.
I HATED TOMMY. HE WAS SOMETHING MY DAD THREW INTO MY LIFE LIKE A HAND GRENADE.
AND I THINK, MAYBE... THERE WAS A TIME WHEN YOU REALLY DIDN'T WANT TO BE JANE.
WHEN YOU NEEDED TO ESCAPE FROM YOUR WHOLE LIFE.
SO MAYBE-- IN A CRAZY WAY-- WHAT WILSON DID ACTUALLY HELPED YOU.
OR MAYBE IT HURT YOU WORSE THAN YOU WERE HURT ALREADY.
EITHER WAY, I THINK I KNOW SOME OF WHAT YOU'VE BEEN THROUGH. WHERE YOU ARE NOW.
AND IF YOU WANT TO BE LIZZIE AGAIN, I'LL TAKE A SHOT AT BEING TOMMY, JUST FOR YOU.
WARD ROUNDS. WE'RE RUNNING OUT OF TIME, TOM. HOW ARE YOU DOING?
NOTHING. NOT A FLICKER.
THEN MAYBE SHE'S IN THE RIGHT PLACE. DID YOU THINK OF THAT?
MAYBE THEY CAN HELP HER.
SHE'S BEEN IN PLACES LIKE THIS BEFORE, RICHIE.
AND THEY DIDN'T.
FUCK.
HOW DO I GET THROUGH TO HER?

GO TO PAGE 48

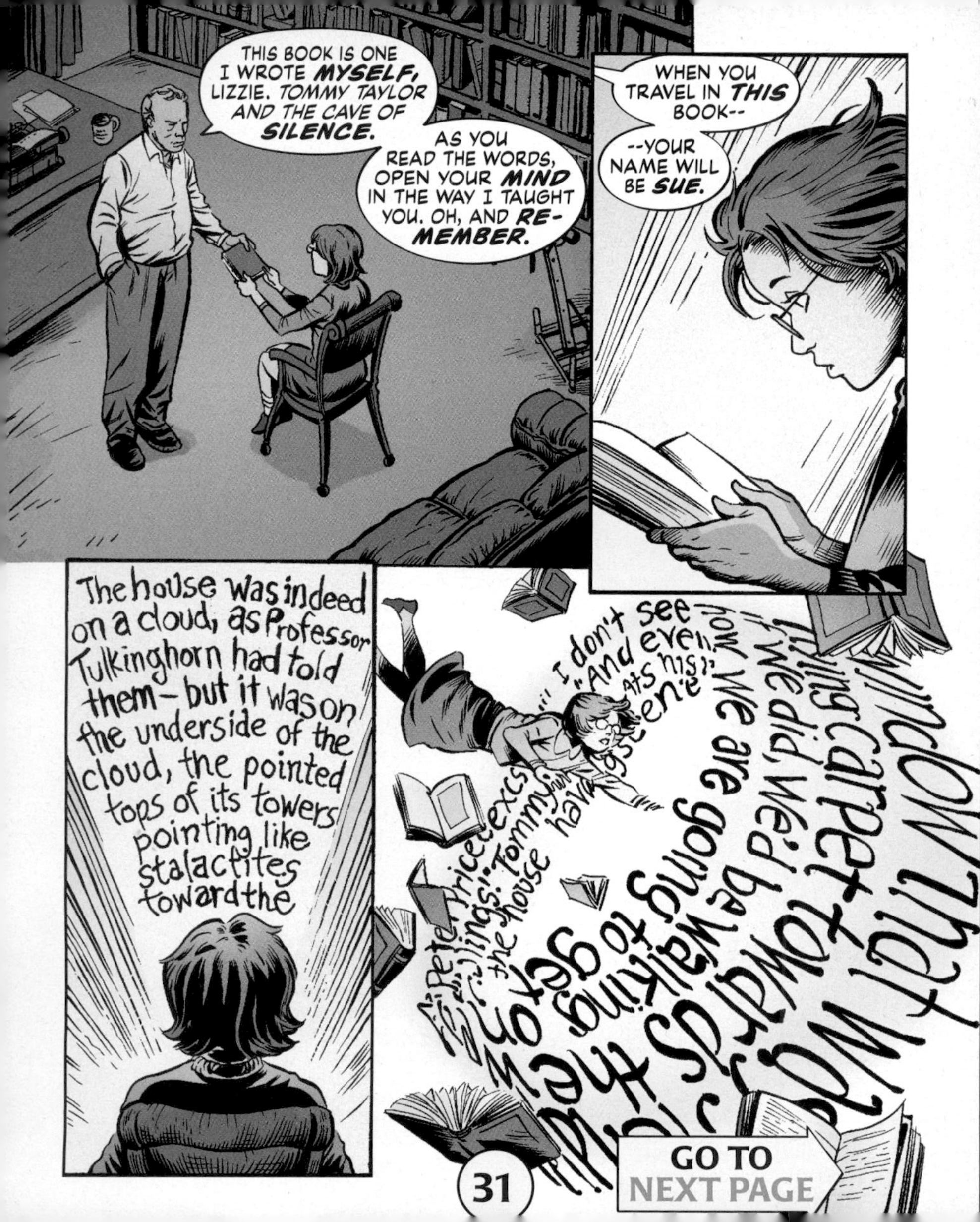
THIS BOOK IS ONE I WROTE MYSELF, LIZZIE. TOMMY TAYLOR AND THE CAVE OF SILENCE.
AS YOU READ THE WORDS, OPEN YOUR MIND IN THE WAY I TAUGHT YOU. OH, AND RE-MEMBER.
WHEN YOU TRAVEL IN THIS BOOK--
--YOUR NAME WILL BE SUE.
The house was indeed on a cloud, as Professor Tulkinghorn had told them—but it was on the underside of the cloud, the pointed tops of its towers pointing like stalactites toward the
window that was
flying carpet towards the
if we did, we'd be walking
how we are going to get on
I don't see
"And even

GO TO NEXT PAGE

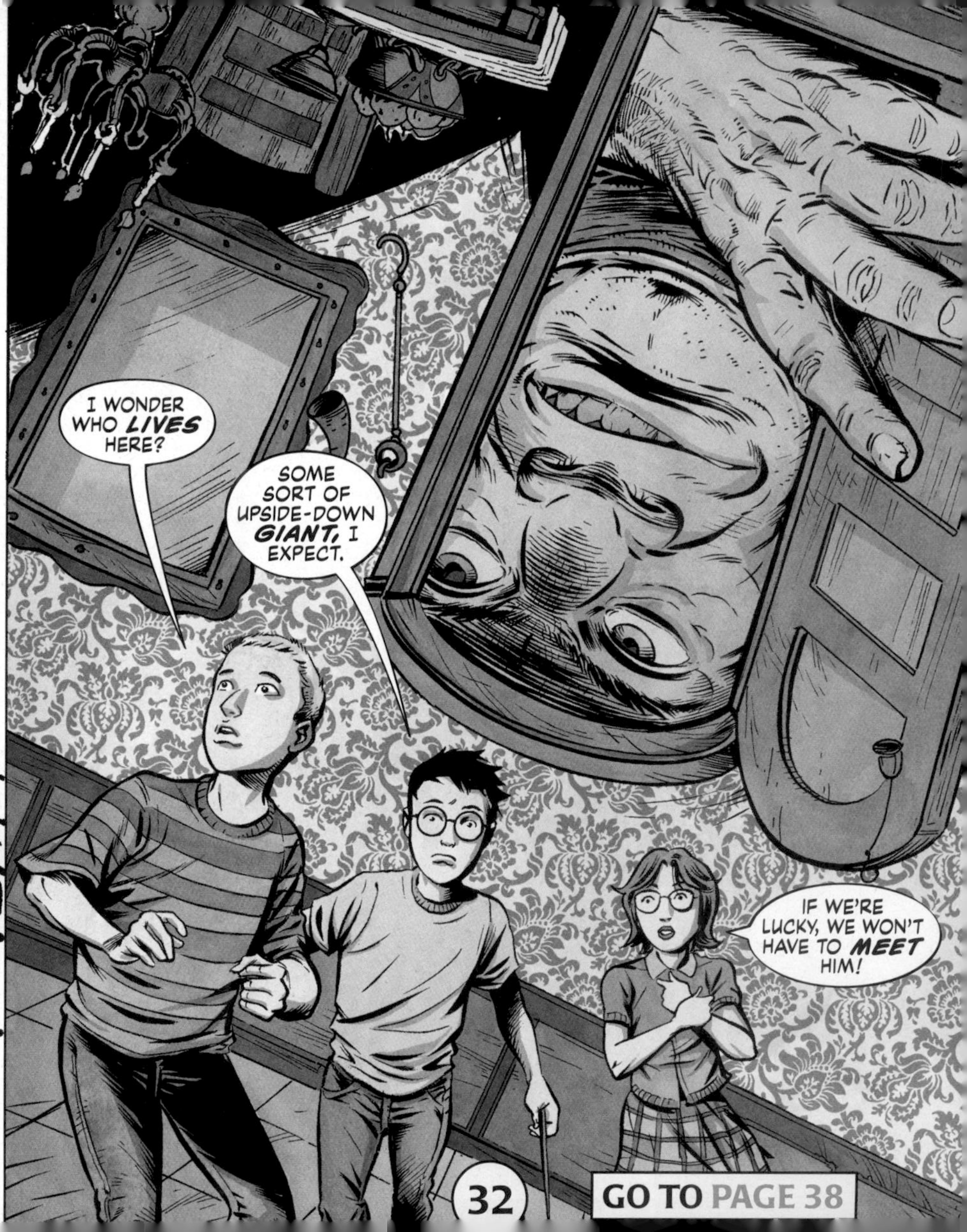
I WONDER WHO LIVES HERE?
SOME SORT OF UPSIDE-DOWN GIANT, I EXPECT.
IF WE'RE LUCKY, WE WON'T HAVE TO MEET HIM!

GO TO PAGE 38

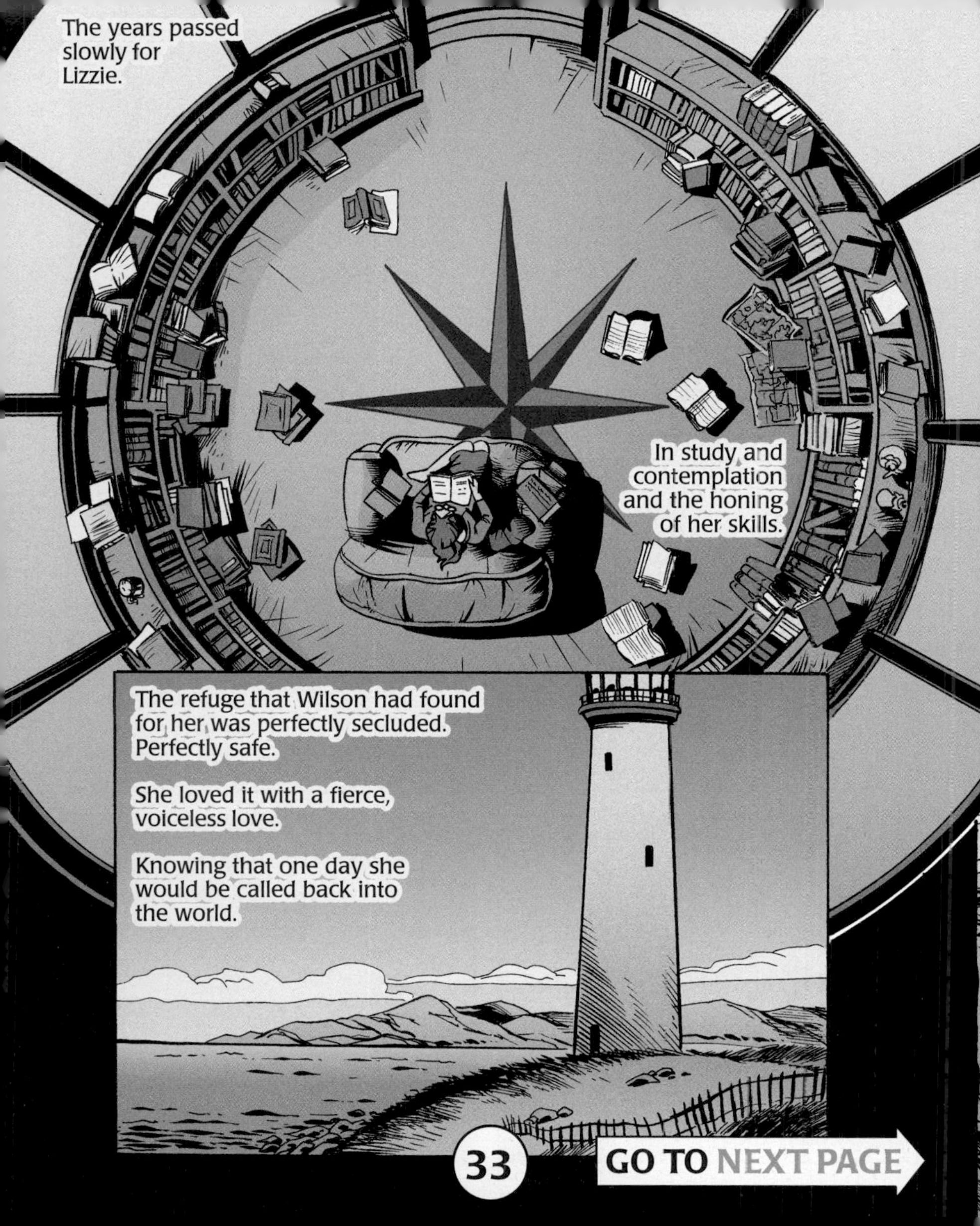
The years passed slowly for Lizzie.
In study and contemplation and the honing of her skills.
The refuge that Wilson had found for her was perfectly secluded. Perfectly safe.
She loved it with a fierce, voiceless love.
Knowing that one day she would be called back into the world.

GO TO NEXT PAGE

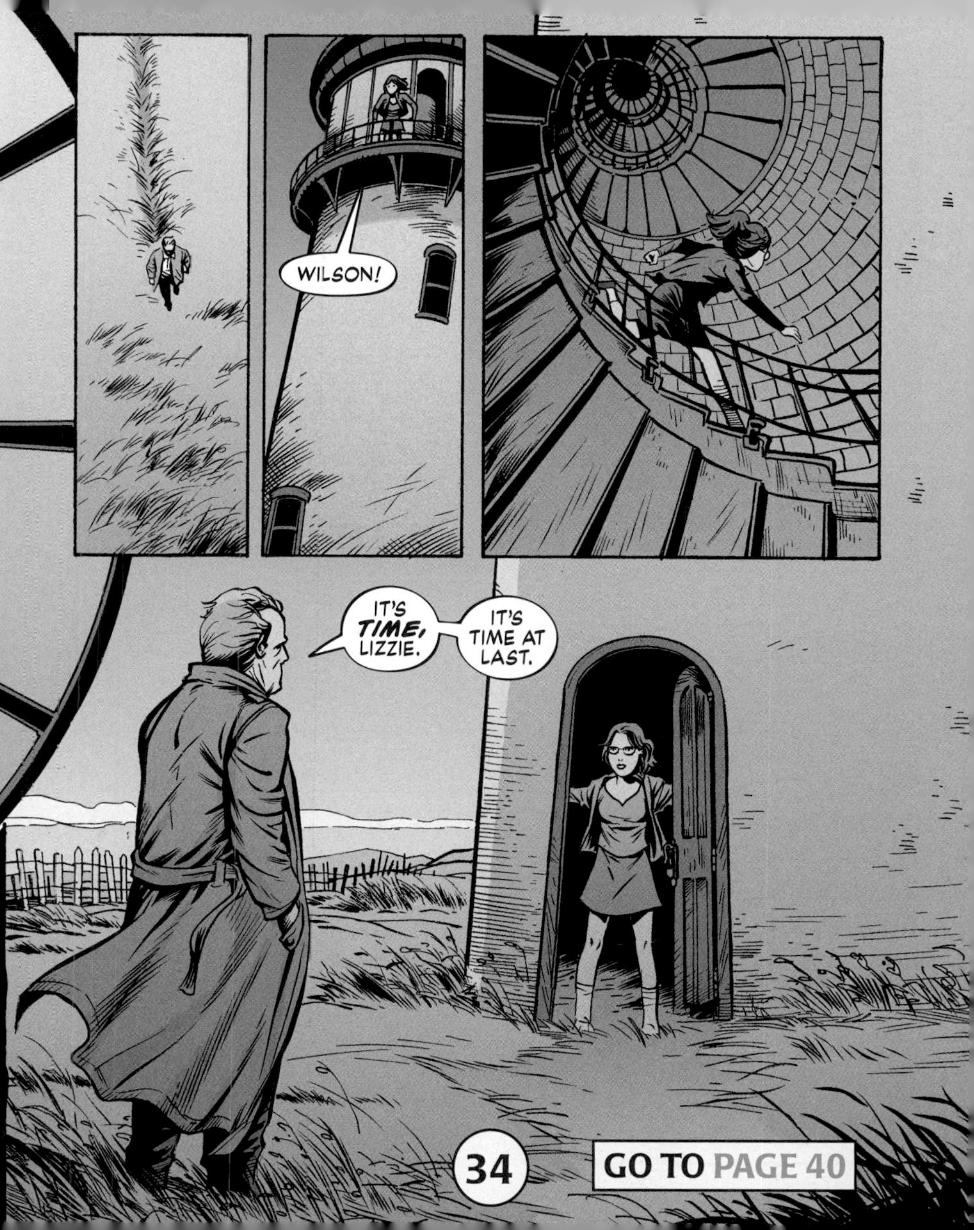
WILSON!
IT'S TIME, LIZZIE.
IT'S TIME AT LAST.

GO TO PAGE 40

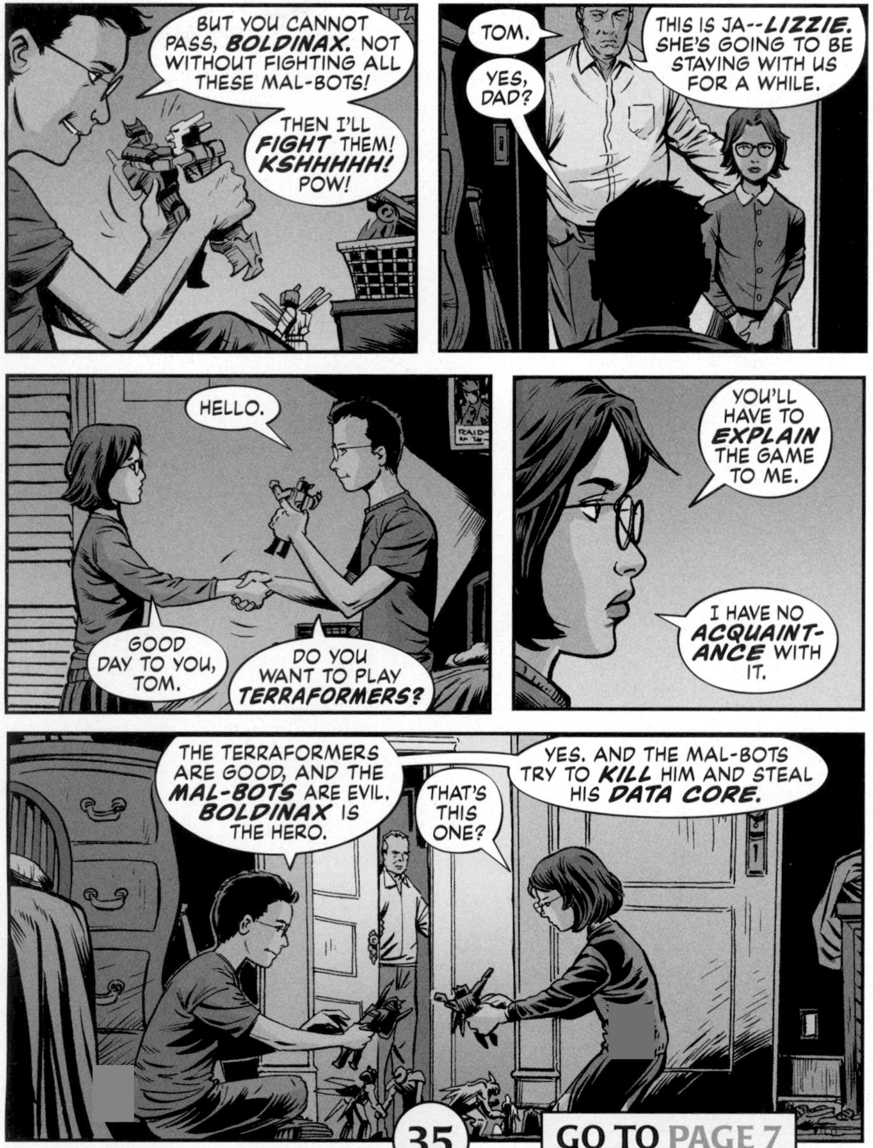
BUT YOU CANNOT PASS, BOLDINAX. NOT WITHOUT FIGHTING ALL THESE MAL-BOTS!
THEN I'LL FIGHT THEM! KSHHHHH! POW!
TOM.
YES, DAD?
THIS IS JA--LIZZIE. SHE'S GOING TO BE STAYING WITH US FOR A WHILE.
HELLO.
GOOD DAY TO YOU, TOM.
DO YOU WANT TO PLAY TERRAFORMERS?
YOU'LL HAVE TO EXPLAIN THE GAME TO ME.
I HAVE NO ACQUAINT-ANCE WITH IT.
THE TERRAFORMERS ARE GOOD, AND THE MAL-BOTS ARE EVIL. BOLDINAX IS THE HERO.
THAT'S THIS ONE?
YES. AND THE MAL-BOTS TRY TO KILL HIM AND STEAL HIS DATA CORE.

35

GO TO PAGE 7

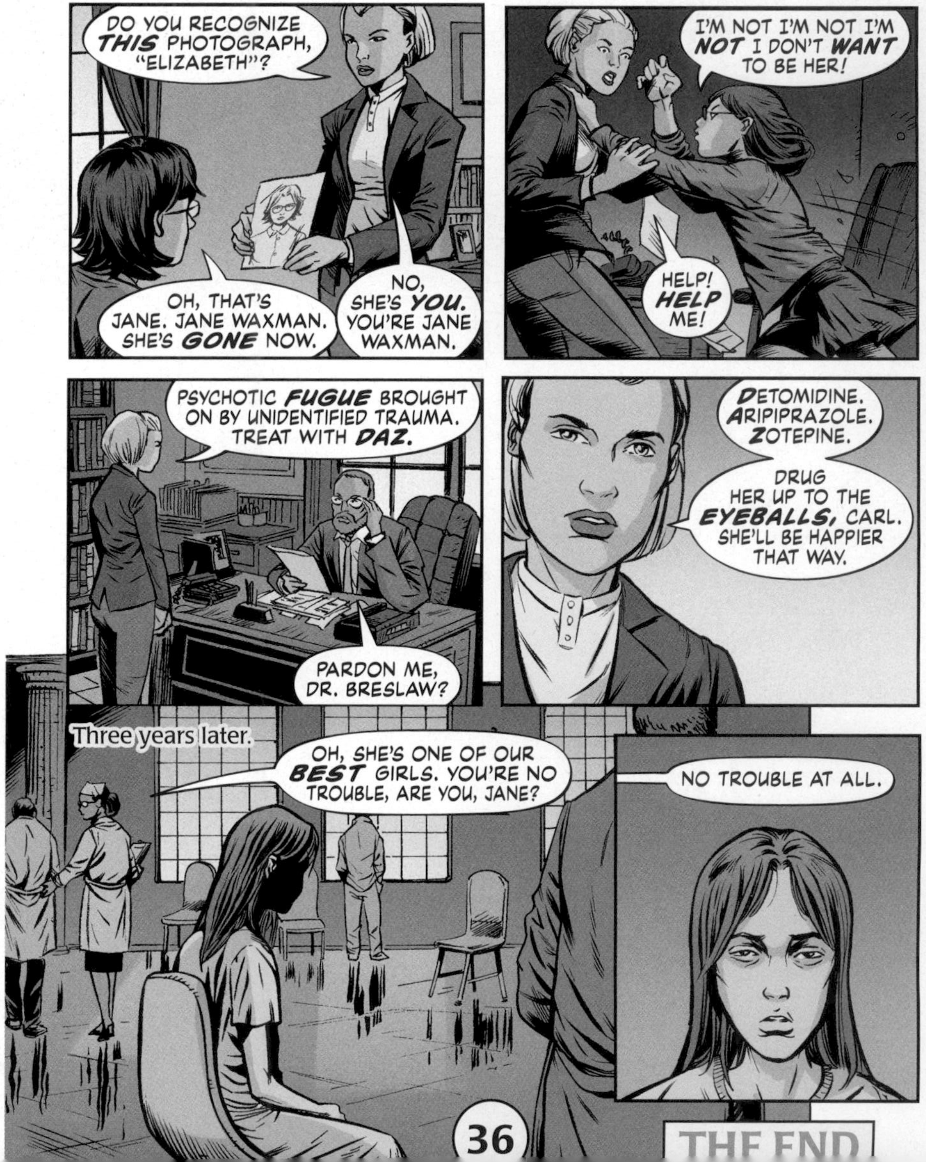
DO YOU RECOGNIZE THIS PHOTOGRAPH, "ELIZABETH"?
OH, THAT'S JANE. JANE WAXMAN. SHE'S GONE NOW.
NO, SHE'S YOU. YOU'RE JANE WAXMAN.
I'M NOT I'M NOT I'M NOT I DON'T WANT TO BE HER!
HELP! HELP ME!
PSYCHOTIC FUGUE BROUGHT ON BY UNIDENTIFIED TRAUMA. TREAT WITH DAZ.
PARDON ME, DR. BRESLAW?
DETOMIDINE. ARIPIPRAZOLE. ZOTEPINE.
DRUG HER UP TO THE EYEBALLS, CARL. SHE'LL BE HAPPIER THAT WAY.
Three years later.
OH, SHE'S ONE OF OUR BEST GIRLS. YOU'RE NO TROUBLE, ARE YOU, JANE?
NO TROUBLE AT ALL.

36

THE END

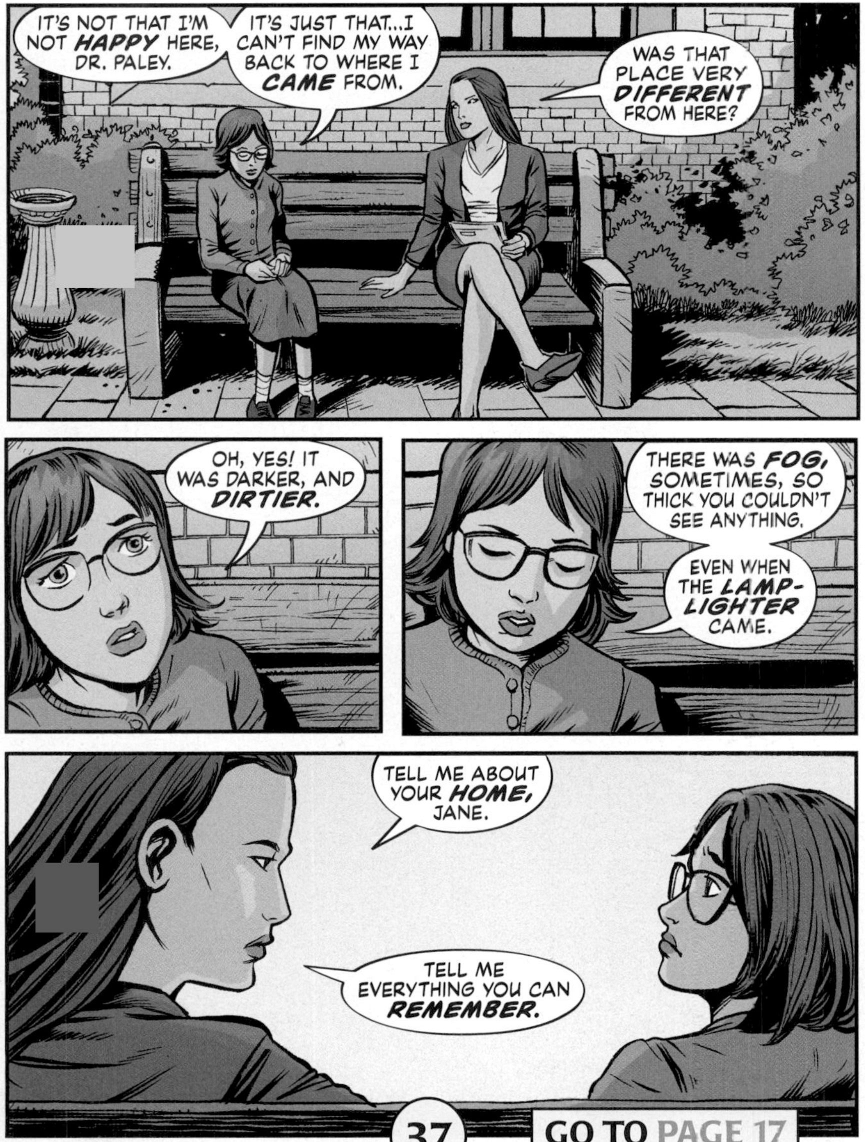

IT'S NOT THAT I'M NOT HAPPY HERE, DR. PALEY.
IT'S JUST THAT...I CAN'T FIND MY WAY BACK TO WHERE I CAME FROM.
WAS THAT PLACE VERY DIFFERENT FROM HERE?
OH, YES! IT WAS DARKER, AND DIRTIER.
THERE WAS FOG, SOMETIMES, SO THICK YOU COULDN'T SEE ANYTHING.
EVEN WHEN THE LAMP-LIGHTER CAME.
TELL ME ABOUT YOUR HOME, JANE.
TELL ME EVERYTHING YOU CAN REMEMBER.

GO TO PAGE 17

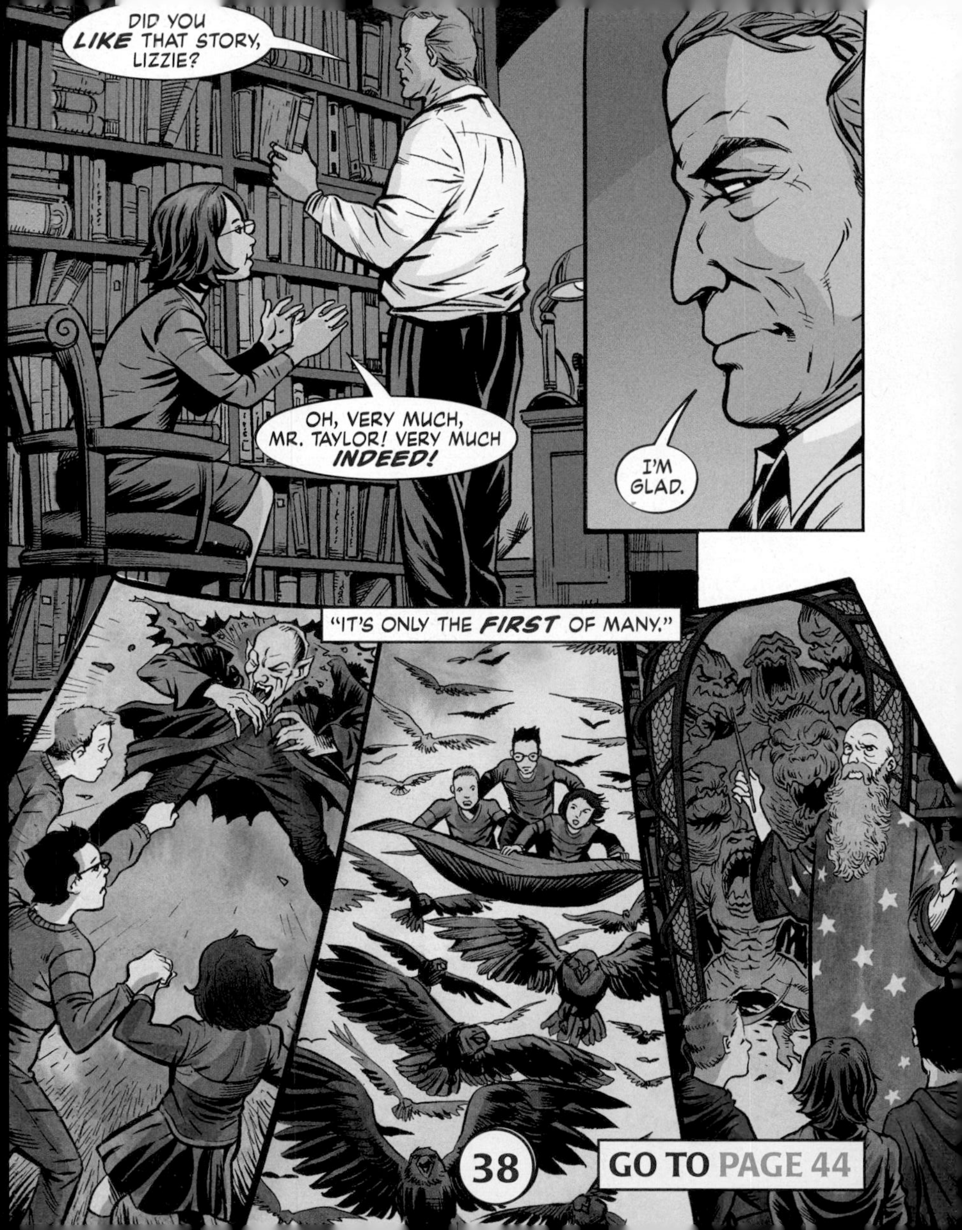

DID YOU LIKE THAT STORY, LIZZIE?
OH, VERY MUCH, MR. TAYLOR! VERY MUCH INDEED!
I'M GLAD.
"IT'S ONLY THE FIRST OF MANY."

GO TO PAGE 44

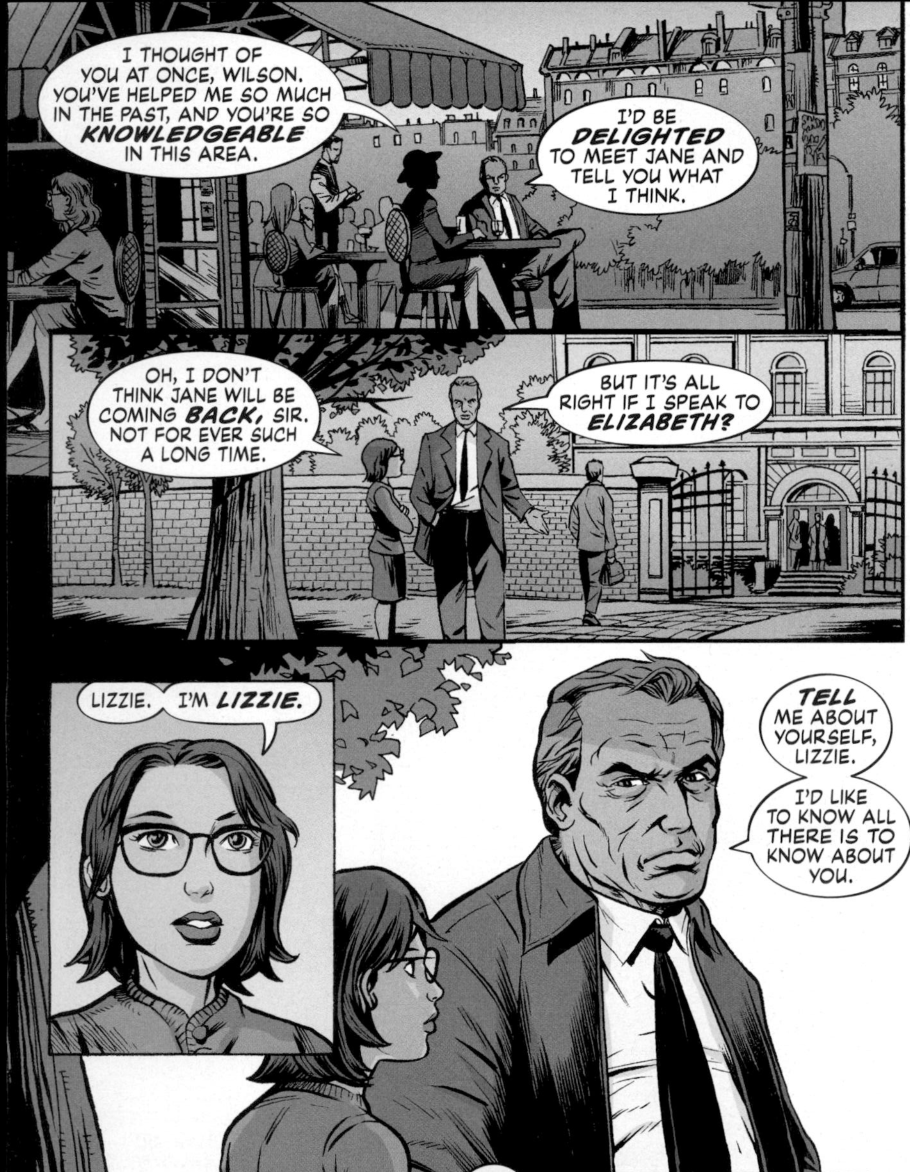
I THOUGHT OF YOU AT ONCE, WILSON. YOU'VE HELPED ME SO MUCH IN THE PAST, AND YOU'RE SO KNOWLEDGEABLE IN THIS AREA.
I'D BE DELIGHTED TO MEET JANE AND TELL YOU WHAT I THINK.
OH, I DON'T THINK JANE WILL BE COMING BACK, SIR. NOT FOR EVER SUCH A LONG TIME.
BUT IT'S ALL RIGHT IF I SPEAK TO ELIZABETH?
LIZZIE.
I'M LIZZIE.
TELL ME ABOUT YOURSELF, LIZZIE.
I'D LIKE TO KNOW ALL THERE IS TO KNOW ABOUT YOU.

GO TO PAGE 55

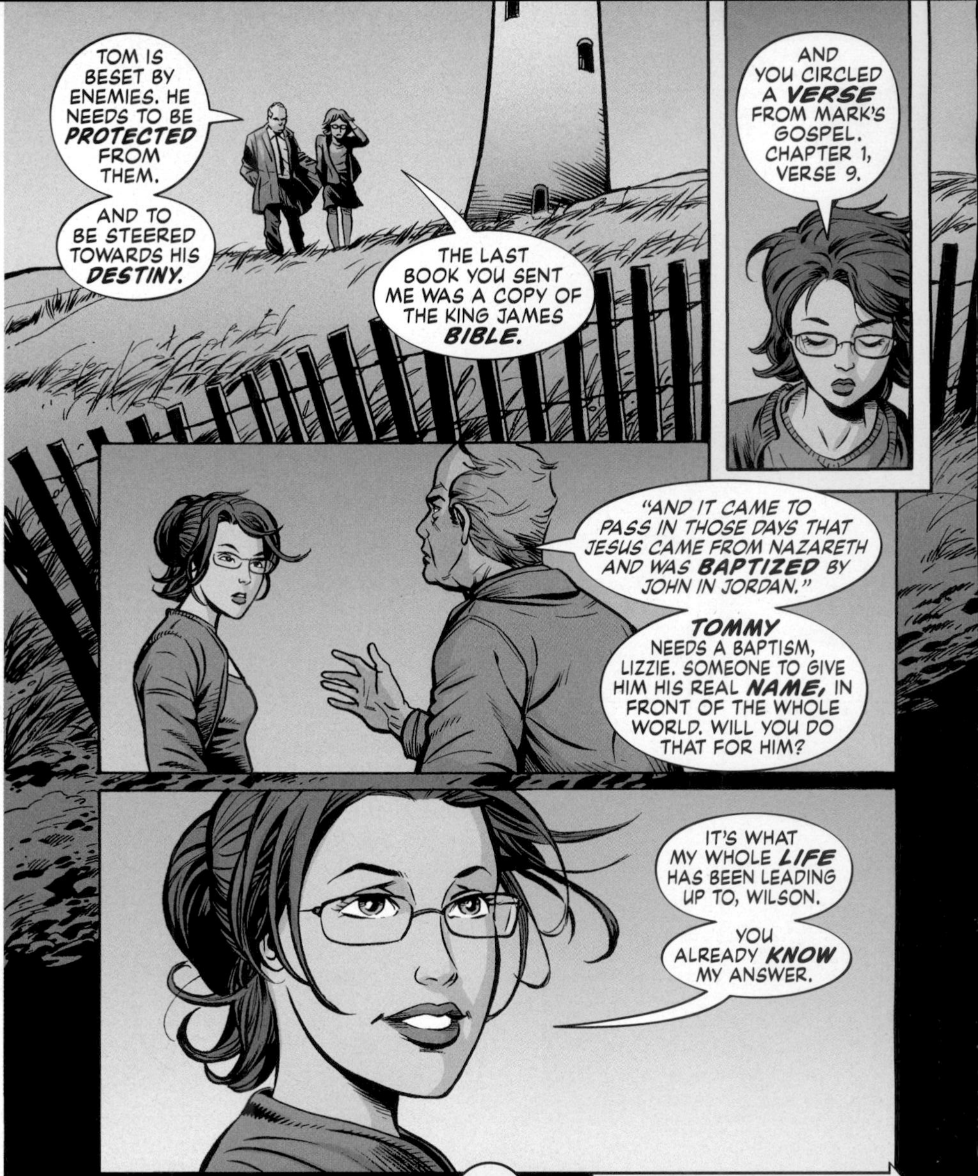
TOM IS BESET BY ENEMIES. HE NEEDS TO BE PROTECTED FROM THEM.
AND TO BE STEERED TOWARDS HIS DESTINY.
THE LAST BOOK YOU SENT ME WAS A COPY OF THE KING JAMES BIBLE.
AND YOU CIRCLED A VERSE FROM MARK'S GOSPEL. CHAPTER 1, VERSE 9.
"AND IT CAME TO PASS IN THOSE DAYS THAT JESUS CAME FROM NAZARETH AND WAS BAPTIZED BY JOHN IN JORDAN."
TOMMY NEEDS A BAPTISM, LIZZIE. SOMEONE TO GIVE HIM HIS REAL NAME, IN FRONT OF THE WHOLE WORLD. WILL YOU DO THAT FOR HIM?
IT'S WHAT MY WHOLE LIFE HAS BEEN LEADING UP TO, WILSON.
YOU ALREADY KNOW MY ANSWER.

GO TO NEXT PAGE

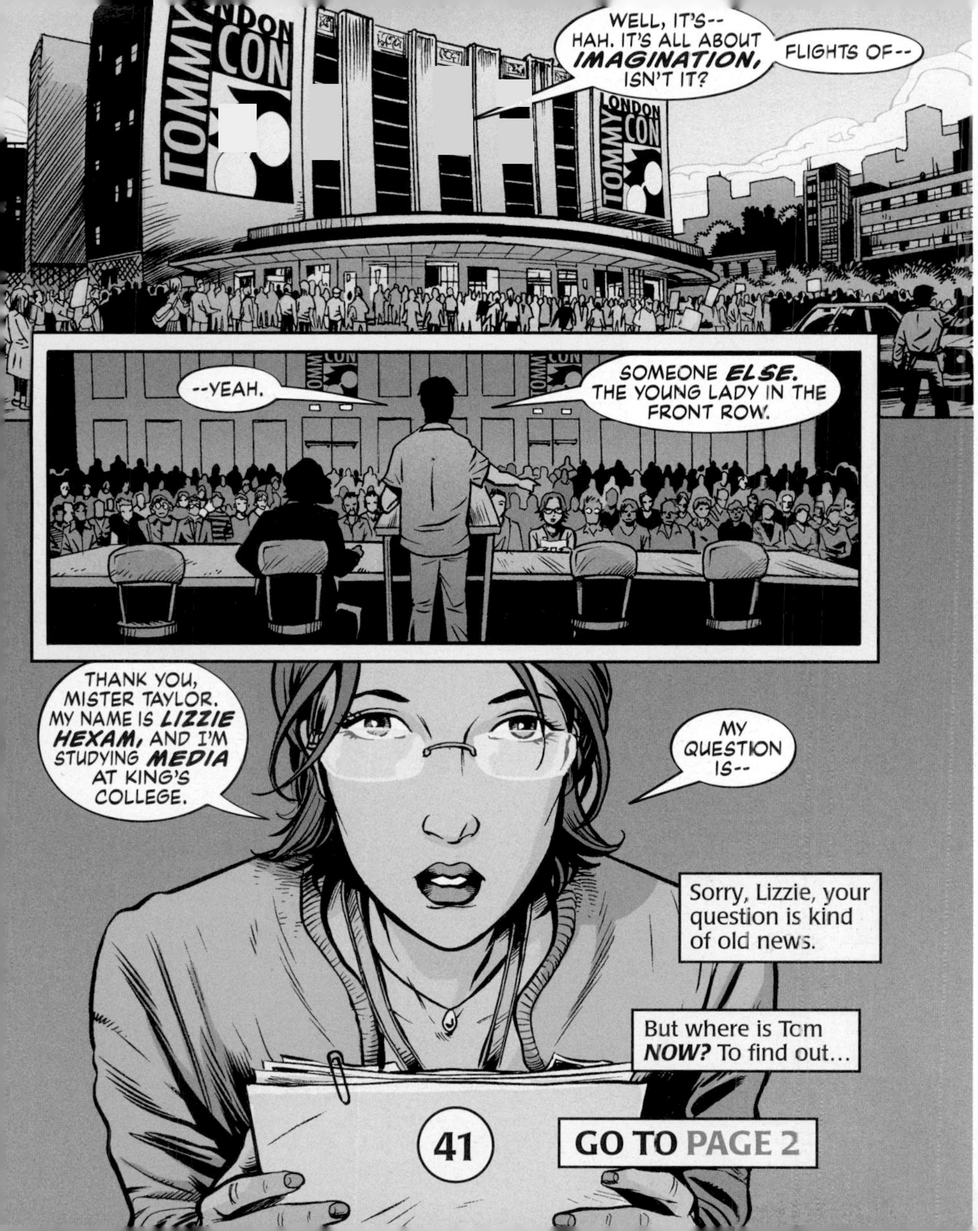

TOMMY LONDON CON
WELL, IT'S-- HAH. IT'S ALL ABOUT IMAGINATION, ISN'T IT?
FLIGHTS OF--
SOMEONE ELSE. THE YOUNG LADY IN THE FRONT ROW.
--YEAH.
THANK YOU, MISTER TAYLOR. MY NAME IS LIZZIE HEXAM, AND I'M STUDYING MEDIA AT KING'S COLLEGE.
MY QUESTION IS--
Sorry, Lizzie, your question is kind of old news.
But where is Tom NOW? To find out...

GO TO PAGE 2

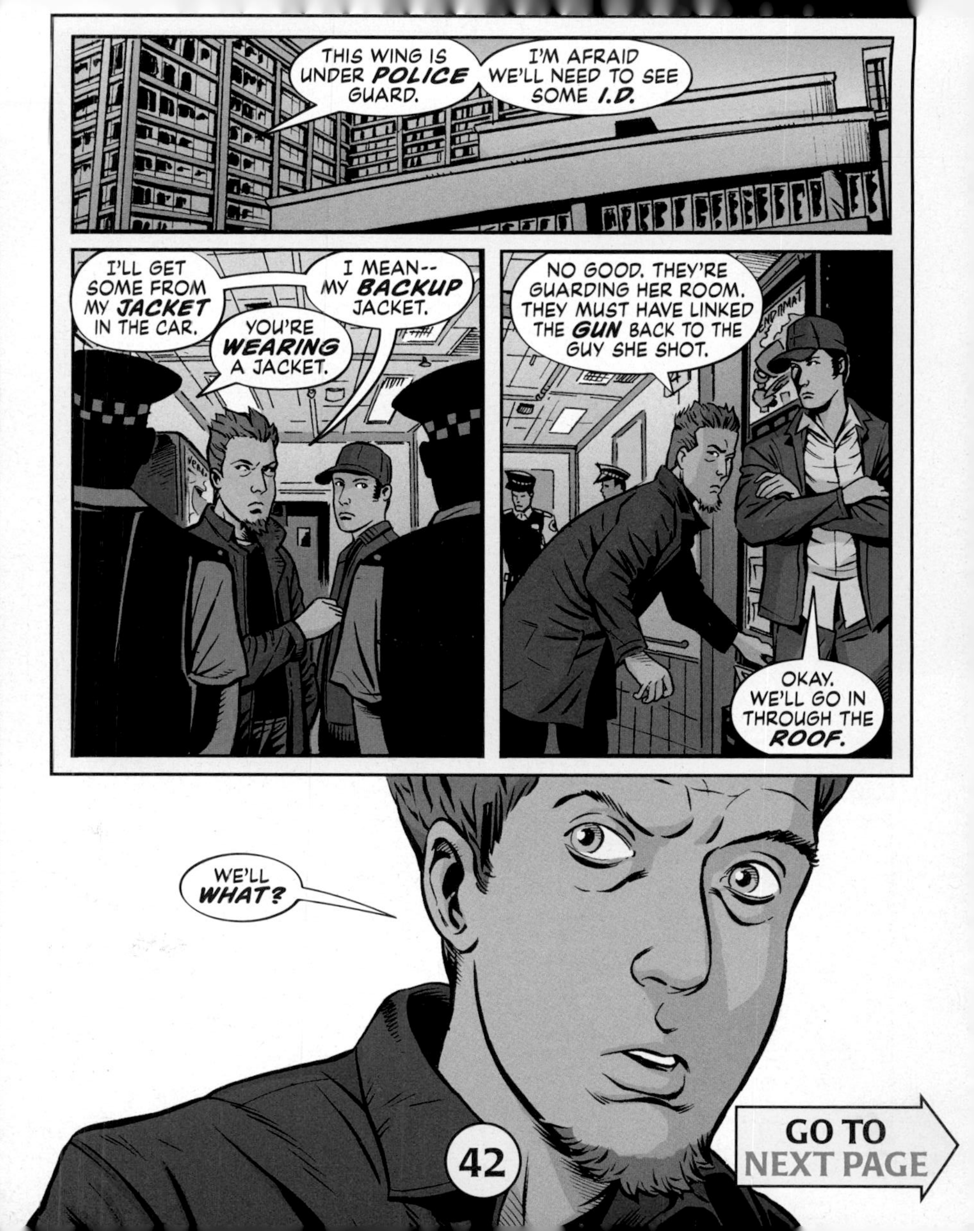

THIS WING IS UNDER POLICE GUARD.
I'M AFRAID WE'LL NEED TO SEE SOME I.D.
I'LL GET SOME FROM MY JACKET IN THE CAR.
YOU'RE WEARING A JACKET.
I MEAN-- MY BACKUP JACKET.
NO GOOD. THEY'RE GUARDING HER ROOM. THEY MUST HAVE LINKED THE GUN BACK TO THE GUY SHE SHOT.
OKAY. WE'LL GO IN THROUGH THE ROOF.
WE'LL WHAT?

GO TO NEXT PAGE

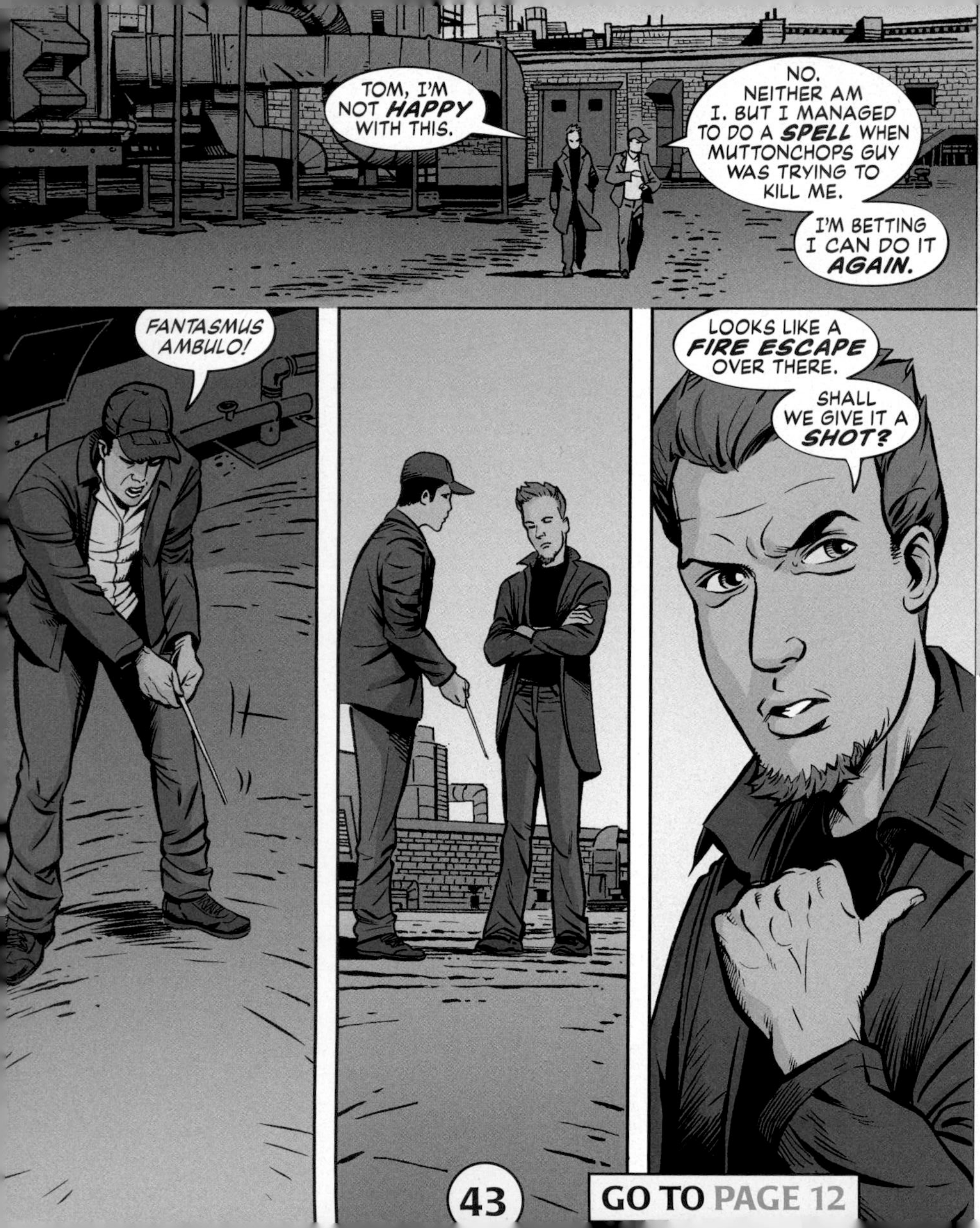
TOM, I'M NOT HAPPY WITH THIS.
NO. NEITHER AM I. BUT I MANAGED TO DO A SPELL WHEN MUTTONCHOPS GUY WAS TRYING TO KILL ME.
I'M BETTING I CAN DO IT AGAIN.
FANTASMUS AMBULO!
LOOKS LIKE A FIRE ESCAPE OVER THERE.
SHALL WE GIVE IT A SHOT?
43
GO TO PAGE 12

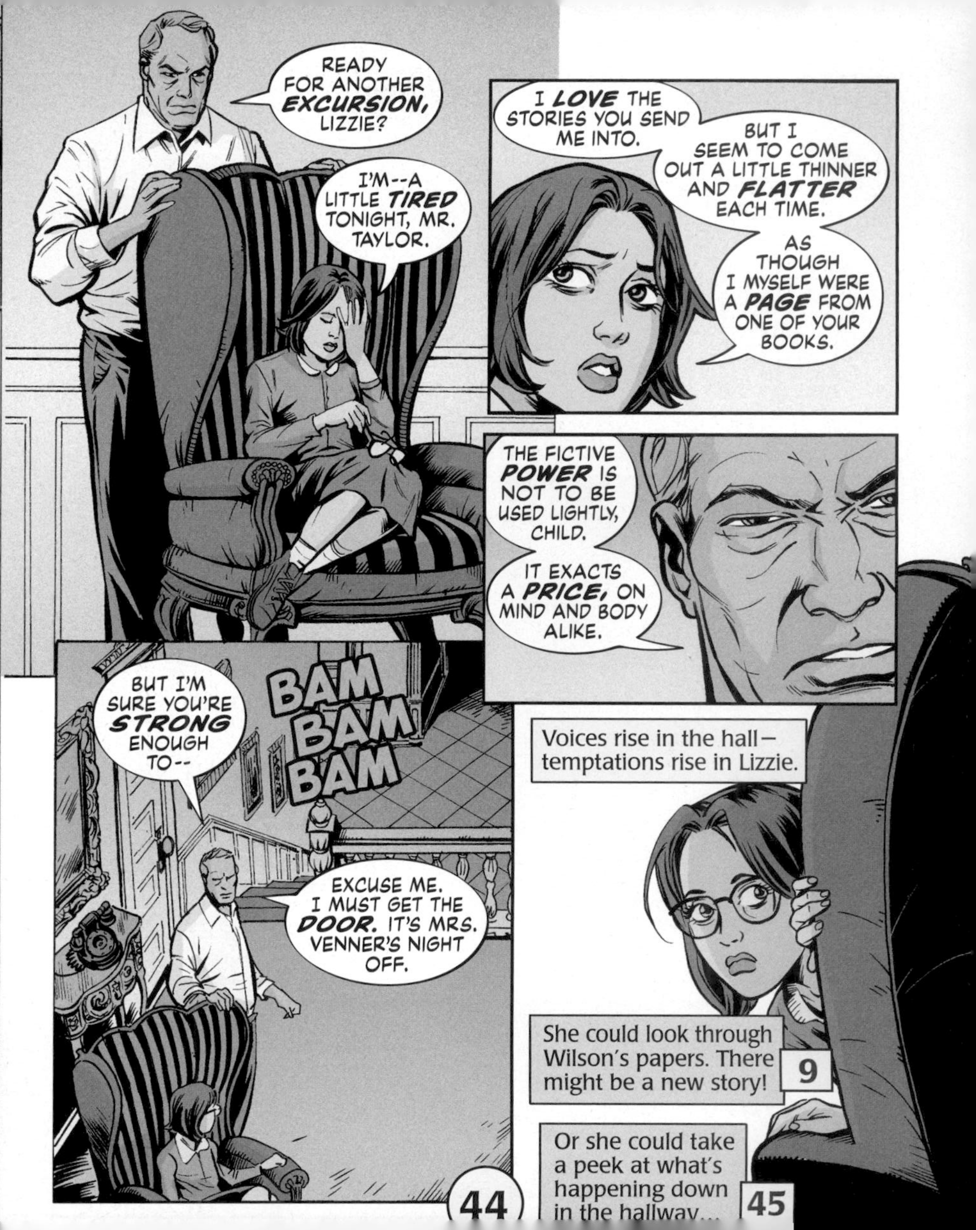
READY FOR ANOTHER EXCURSION, LIZZIE?
I'M--A LITTLE TIRED TONIGHT, MR. TAYLOR.
I LOVE THE STORIES YOU SEND ME INTO.
BUT I SEEM TO COME OUT A LITTLE THINNER AND FLATTER EACH TIME.
AS THOUGH I MYSELF WERE A PAGE FROM ONE OF YOUR BOOKS.
THE FICTIVE POWER IS NOT TO BE USED LIGHTLY, CHILD.
IT EXACTS A PRICE, ON MIND AND BODY ALIKE.
BUT I'M SURE YOU'RE STRONG ENOUGH TO--
BAM BAM BAM
EXCUSE ME. I MUST GET THE DOOR. IT'S MRS. VENNER'S NIGHT OFF.
Voices rise in the hall—temptations rise in Lizzie.
She could look through Wilson's papers. There might be a new story!
9
Or she could take a peek at what's happening down in the hallway...
45
44

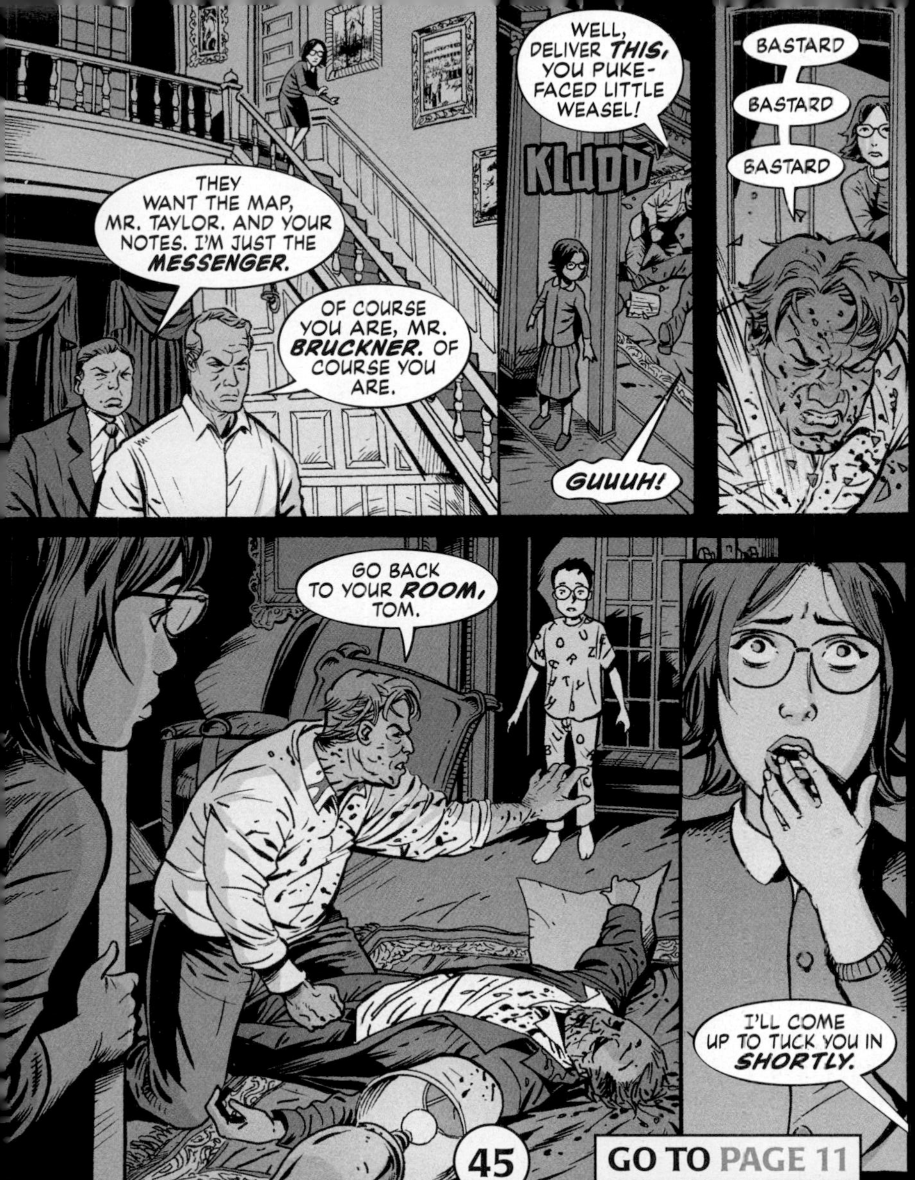
THEY WANT THE MAP, MR. TAYLOR. AND YOUR NOTES. I'M JUST THE MESSENGER.
OF COURSE YOU ARE, MR. BRUCKNER. OF COURSE YOU ARE.
WELL, DELIVER THIS, YOU PUKE-FACED LITTLE WEASEL!
KLUDD
GUUUH!
BASTARD
BASTARD
BASTARD
GO BACK TO YOUR ROOM, TOM.
I'LL COME UP TO TUCK YOU IN SHORTLY.

GO TO PAGE 11

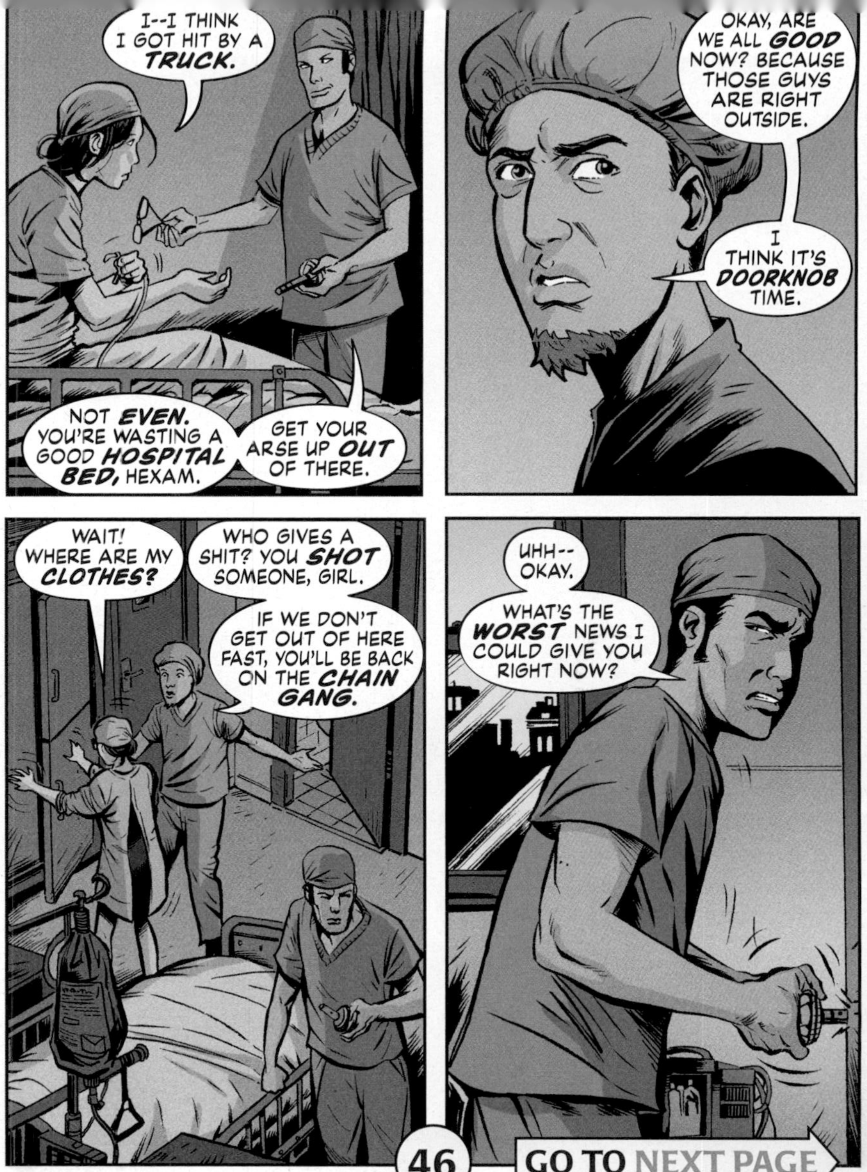
I--I THINK I GOT HIT BY A TRUCK.
NOT EVEN. YOU'RE WASTING A GOOD HOSPITAL BED, HEXAM.
GET YOUR ARSE UP OUT OF THERE.
OKAY, ARE WE ALL GOOD NOW? BECAUSE THOSE GUYS ARE RIGHT OUTSIDE.
I THINK IT'S DOORKNOB TIME.
WAIT! WHERE ARE MY CLOTHES?
WHO GIVES A SHIT? YOU SHOT SOMEONE, GIRL.
IF WE DON'T GET OUT OF HERE FAST, YOU'LL BE BACK ON THE CHAIN GANG.
UHH-- OKAY.
WHAT'S THE WORST NEWS I COULD GIVE YOU RIGHT NOW?

GO TO NEXT PAGE

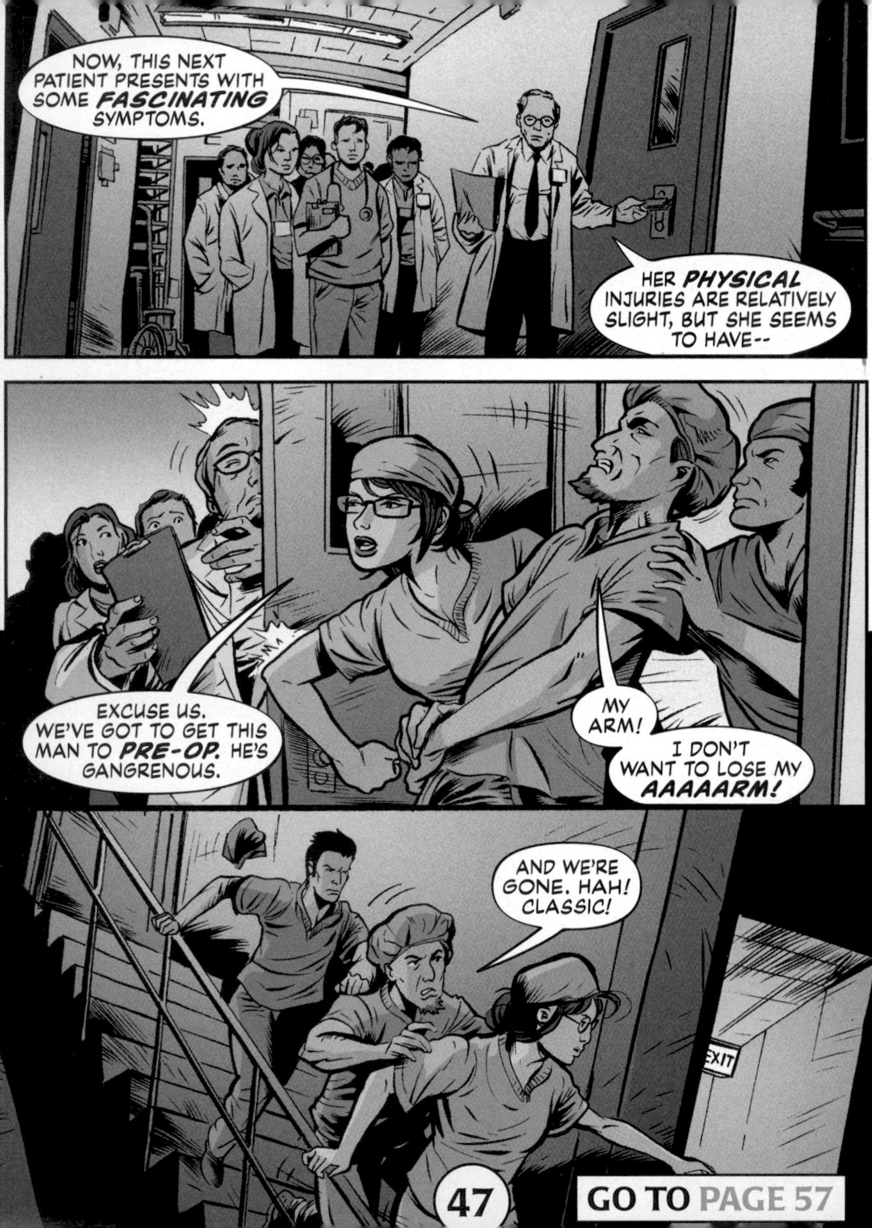
NOW, THIS NEXT PATIENT PRESENTS WITH SOME FASCINATING SYMPTOMS.
HER PHYSICAL INJURIES ARE RELATIVELY SLIGHT, BUT SHE SEEMS TO HAVE--
EXCUSE US. WE'VE GOT TO GET THIS MAN TO PRE-OP. HE'S GANGRENOUS.
MY ARM!
I DON'T WANT TO LOSE MY AAAAARM!
AND WE'RE GONE. HAH! CLASSIC!
EXIT

GO TO PAGE 57

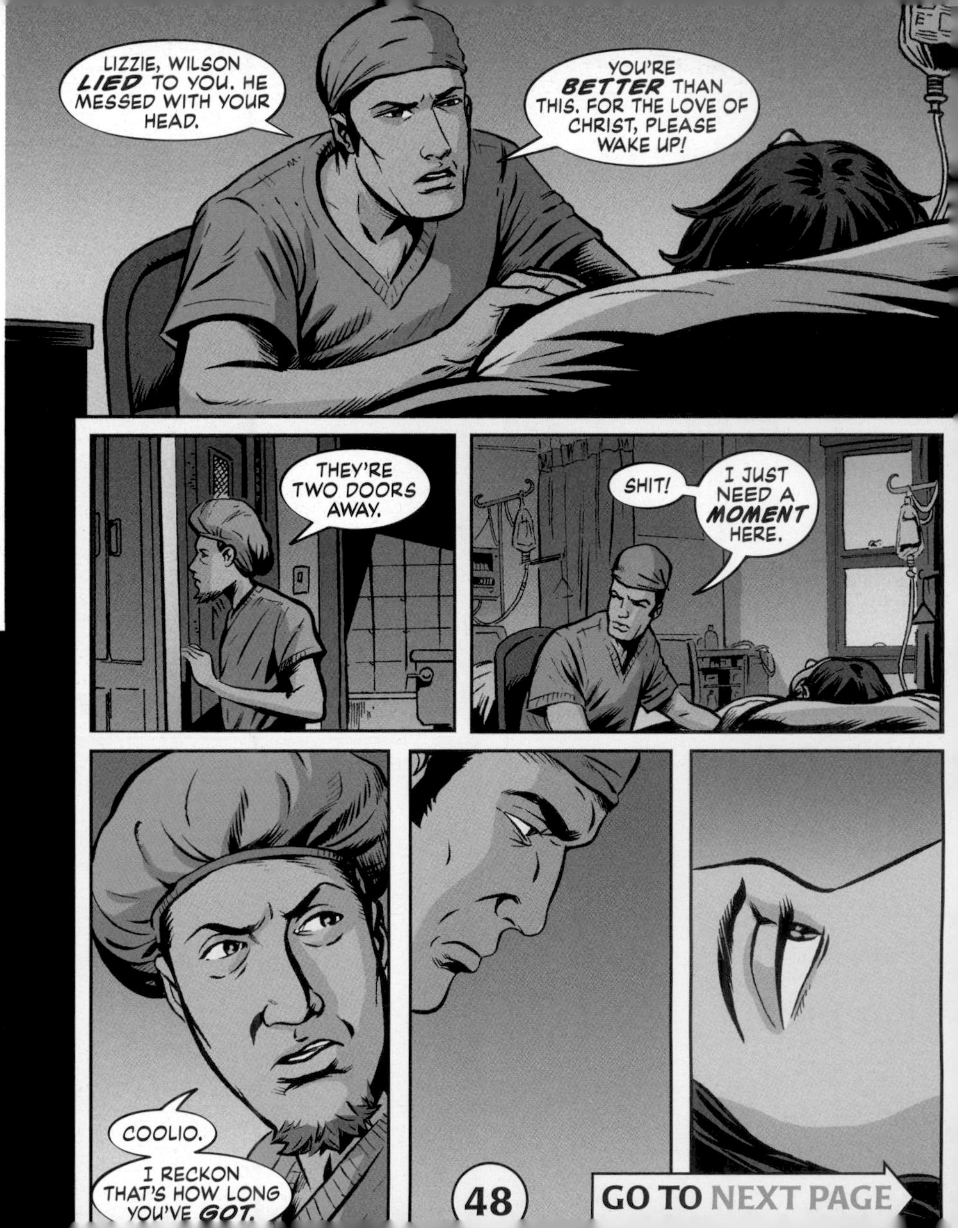
LIZZIE, WILSON LIED TO YOU. HE MESSED WITH YOUR HEAD.
YOU'RE BETTER THAN THIS. FOR THE LOVE OF CHRIST, PLEASE WAKE UP!
THEY'RE TWO DOORS AWAY.
SHIT!
I JUST NEED A MOMENT HERE.
COOLIO.
I RECKON THAT'S HOW LONG YOU'VE GOT.

GO TO NEXT PAGE

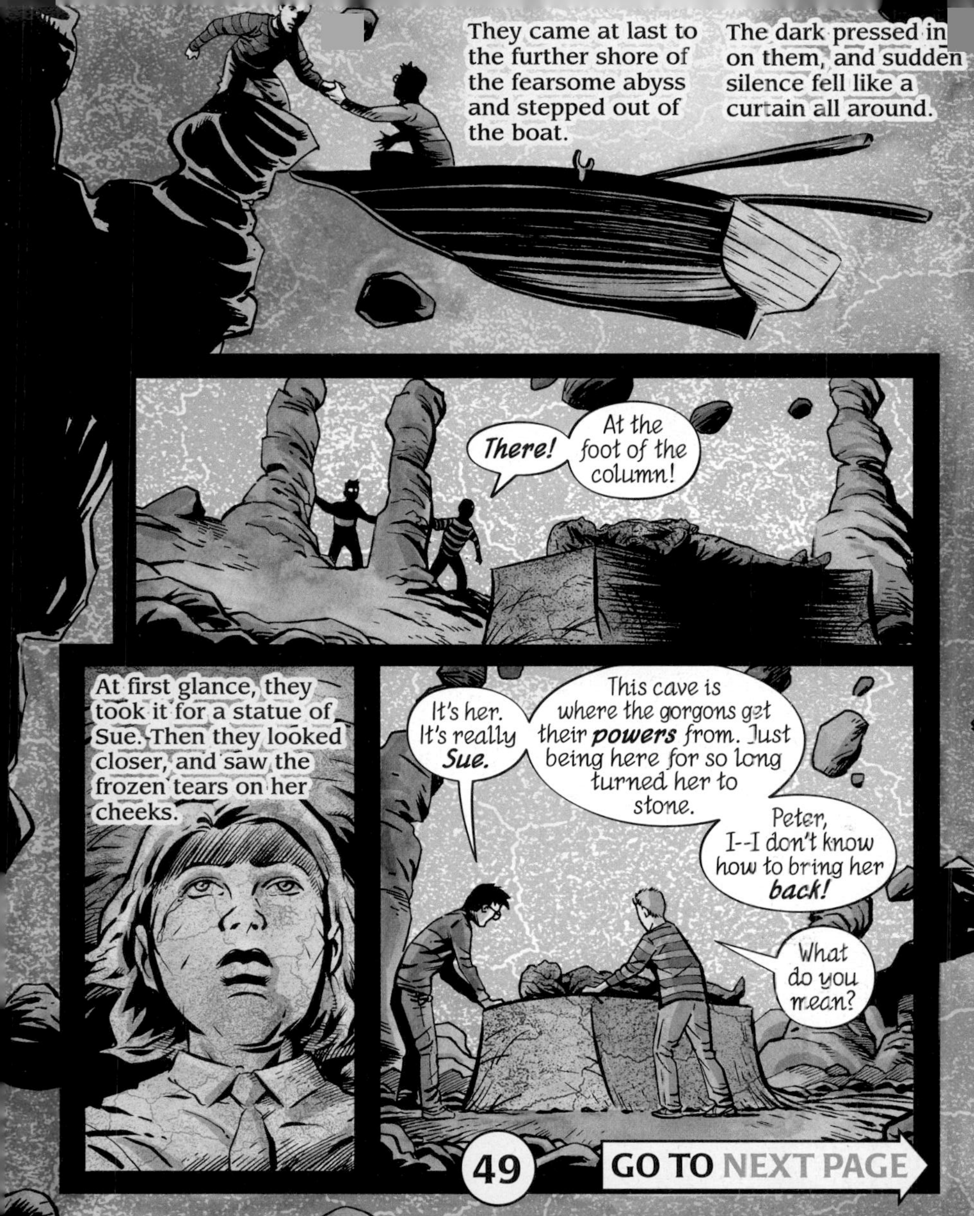
They came at last to the further shore of the fearsome abyss and stepped out of the boat.
The dark pressed in on them, and sudden silence fell like a curtain all around.
There!
At the foot of the column!
At first glance, they took it for a statue of Sue. Then they looked closer, and saw the frozen tears on her cheeks.
It's her. It's really Sue.
This cave is where the gorgons get their powers from. Just being here for so long turned her to stone.
Peter, I--I don't know how to bring her back!
What do you mean?
49
GO TO NEXT PAGE

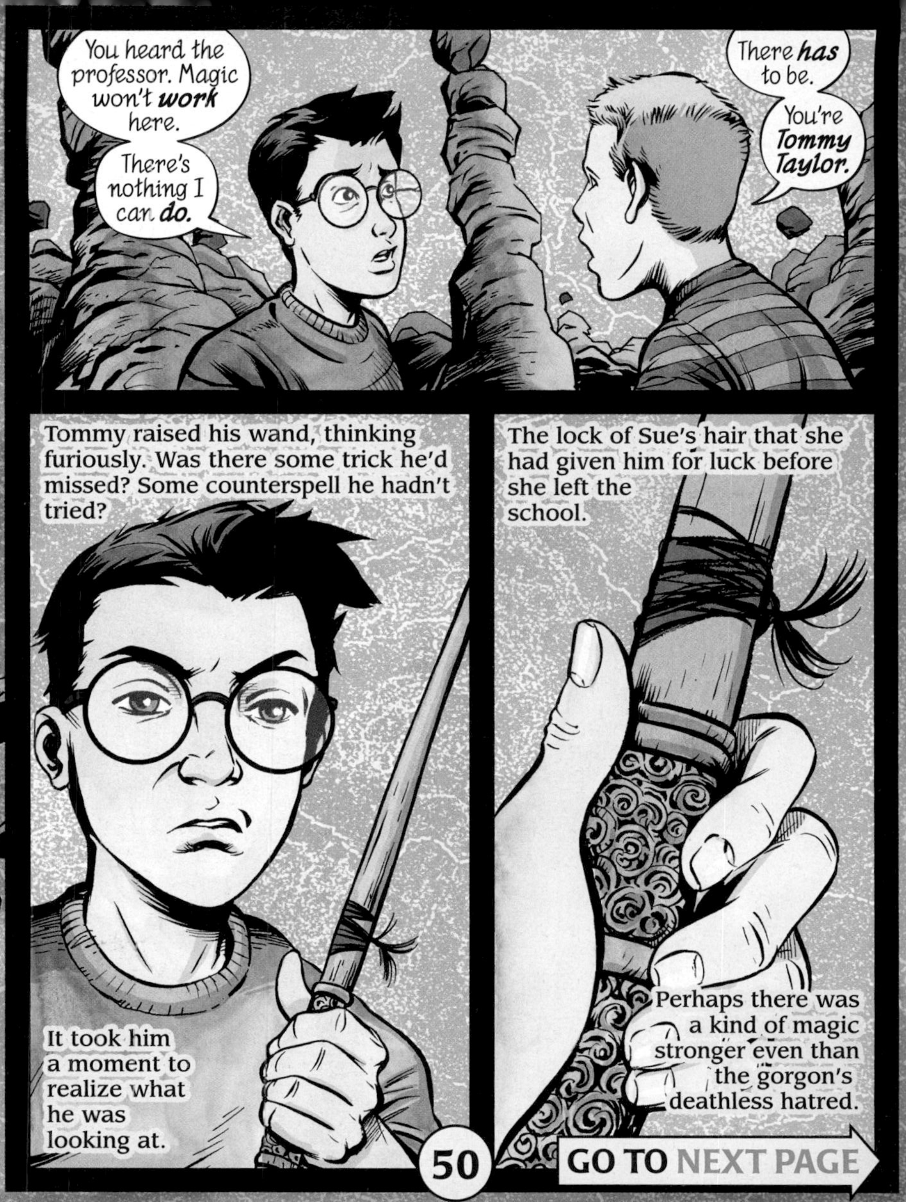
You heard the professor. Magic won't work here.
There's nothing I can do.
There has to be.
You're Tommy Taylor.
Tommy raised his wand, thinking furiously. Was there some trick he'd missed? Some counterspell he hadn't tried?
It took him a moment to realize what he was looking at.
The lock of Sue's hair that she had given him for luck before she left the school.
Perhaps there was a kind of magic stronger even than the gorgon's deathless hatred.
50
GO TO NEXT PAGE

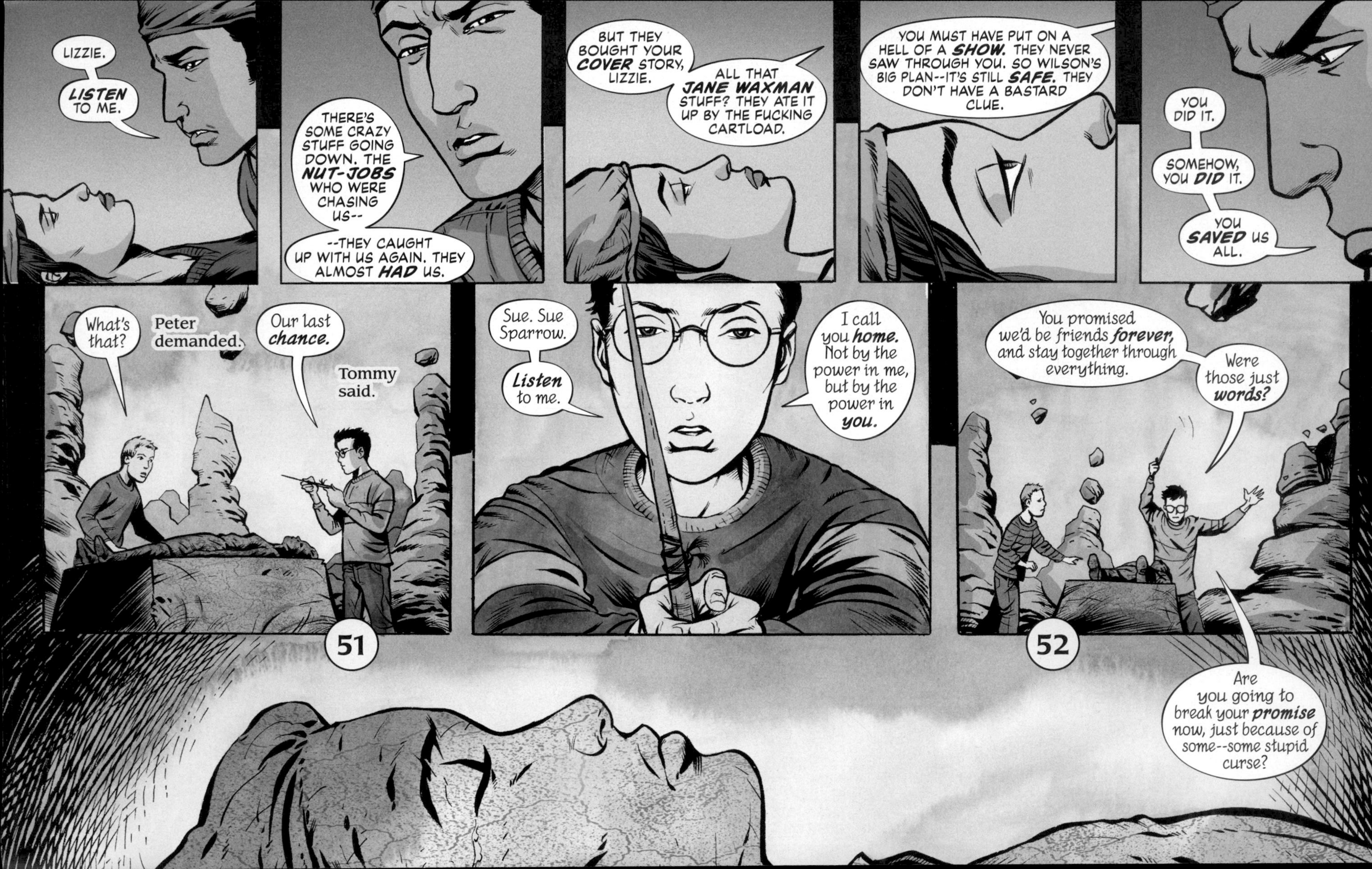
LIZZIE.
LISTEN TO ME.
THERE'S SOME CRAZY STUFF GOING DOWN. THE NUT-JOBS WHO WERE CHASING US--
--THEY CAUGHT UP WITH US AGAIN. THEY ALMOST HAD US.
BUT THEY BOUGHT YOUR COVER STORY, LIZZIE.
ALL THAT JANE WAXMAN STUFF? THEY ATE IT UP BY THE FUCKING CARTLOAD.
YOU MUST HAVE PUT ON A HELL OF A SHOW. THEY NEVER SAW THROUGH YOU. SO WILSON'S BIG PLAN--IT'S STILL SAFE. THEY DON'T HAVE A BASTARD CLUE.
YOU DID IT.
SOMEHOW, YOU DID IT.
YOU SAVED US ALL.
What's that?
Peter demanded.
Our last chance.
Tommy said.
Sue. Sue Sparrow.
Listen to me.
I call you home. Not by the power in me, but by the power in you.
You promised we'd be friends forever, and stay together through everything.
Were those just words?
Are you going to break your promise now, just because of some--some stupid curse?
51
52

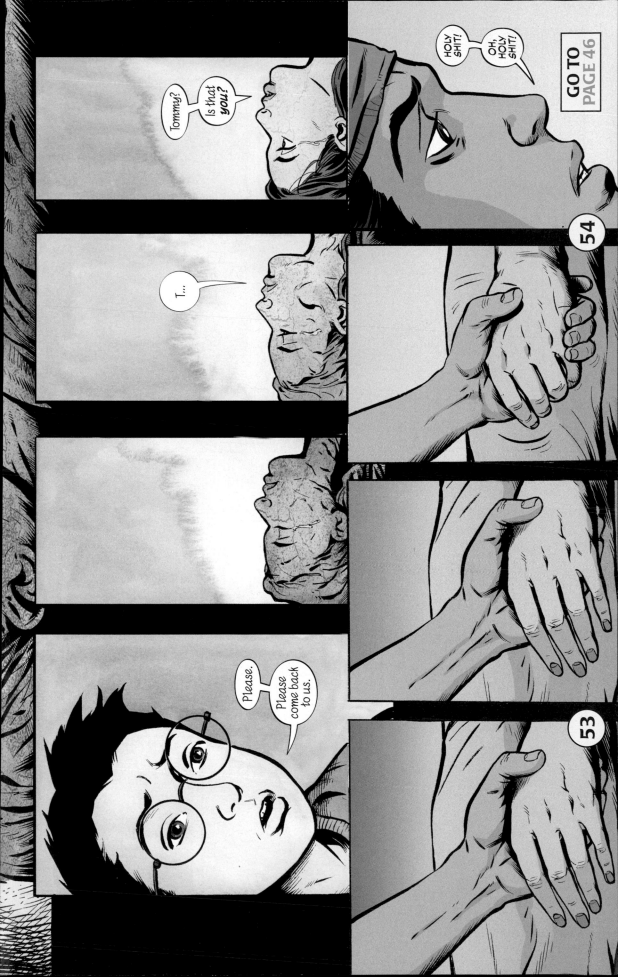

Tommy? Is that you?

T...

Please. Please come back to us.

HOLY SHIT! OH, HOLY SHIT!

GO TO PAGE 46

54

53

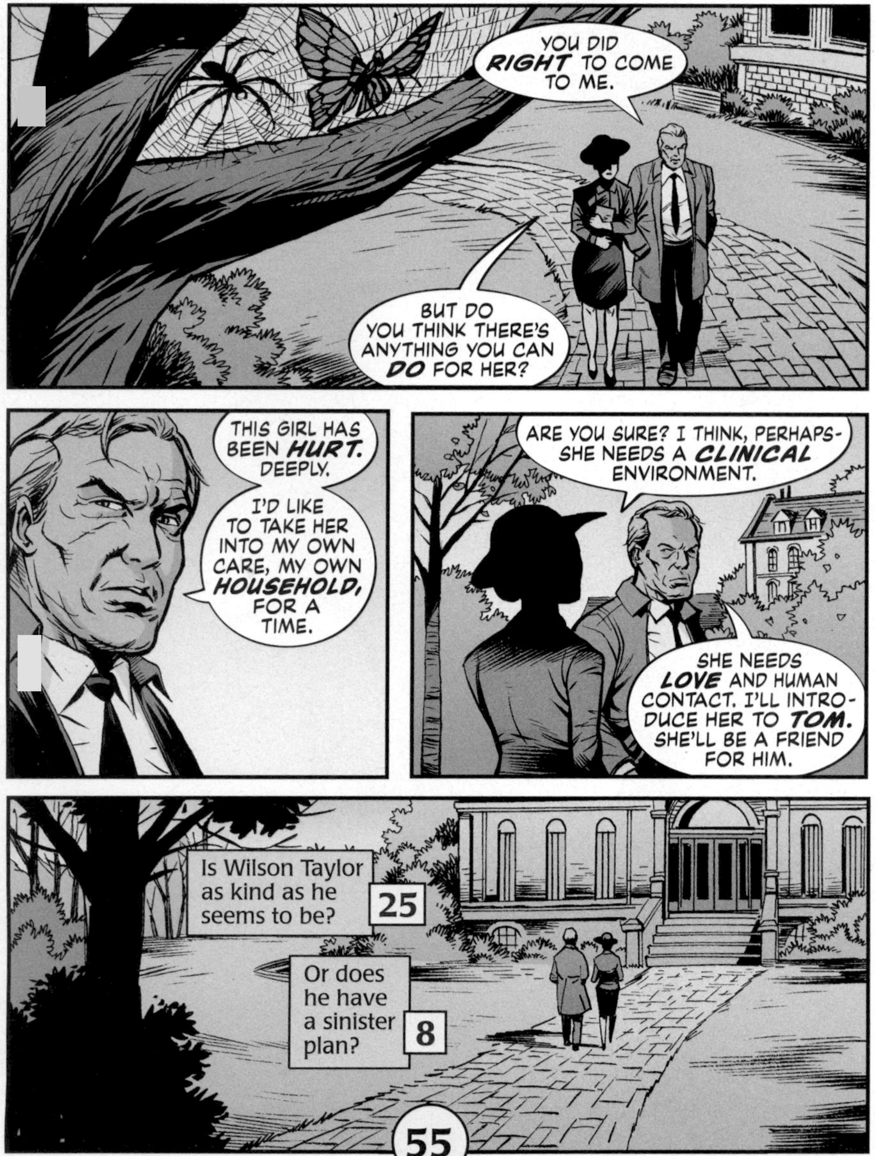

YOU DID RIGHT TO COME TO ME.
BUT DO YOU THINK THERE'S ANYTHING YOU CAN DO FOR HER?
THIS GIRL HAS BEEN HURT. DEEPLY.
I'D LIKE TO TAKE HER INTO MY OWN CARE, MY OWN HOUSEHOLD, FOR A TIME.
ARE YOU SURE? I THINK, PERHAPS- SHE NEEDS A CLINICAL ENVIRONMENT.
SHE NEEDS LOVE AND HUMAN CONTACT. I'LL INTRO-DUCE HER TO TOM. SHE'LL BE A FRIEND FOR HIM.
Is Wilson Taylor as kind as he seems to be? 25
Or does he have a sinister plan? 8

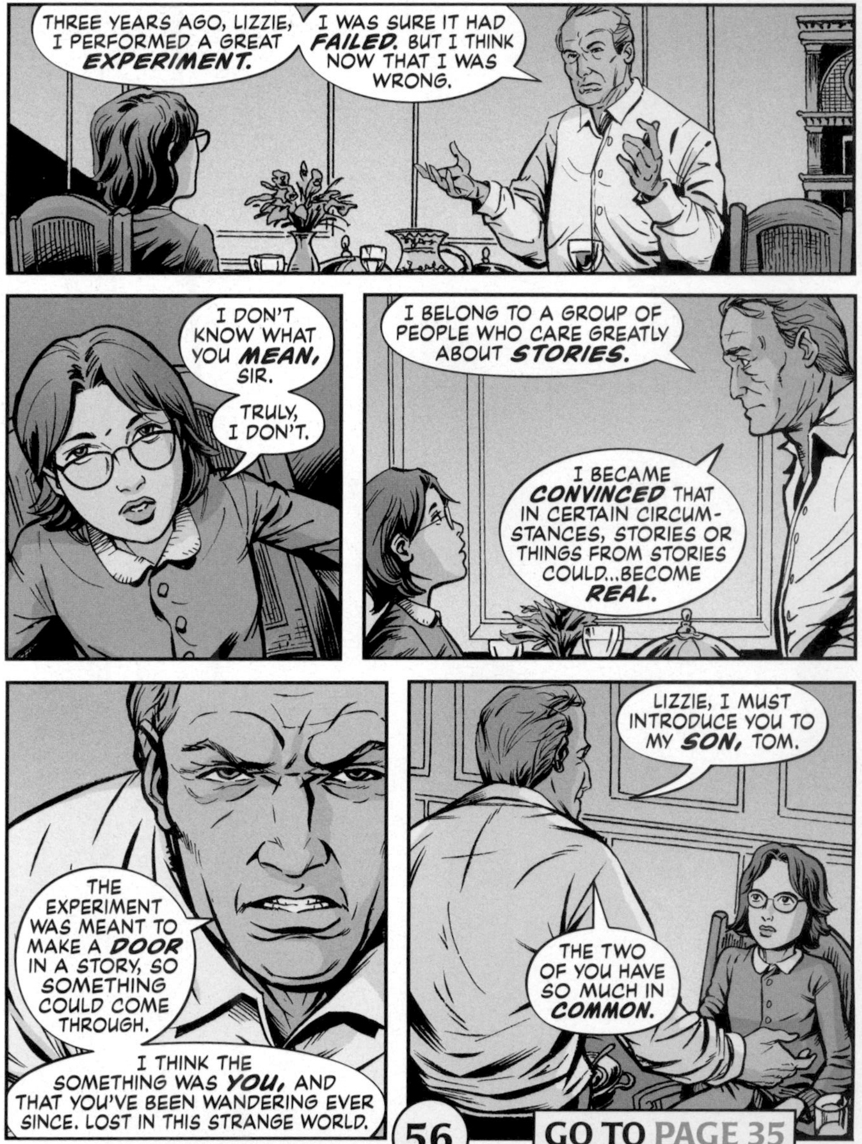

THREE YEARS AGO, LIZZIE, I PERFORMED A GREAT EXPERIMENT.
I WAS SURE IT HAD FAILED. BUT I THINK NOW THAT I WAS WRONG.
I DON'T KNOW WHAT YOU MEAN, SIR.
TRULY, I DON'T.
I BELONG TO A GROUP OF PEOPLE WHO CARE GREATLY ABOUT STORIES.
I BECAME CONVINCED THAT IN CERTAIN CIRCUM-STANCES, STORIES OR THINGS FROM STORIES COULD...BECOME REAL.
THE EXPERIMENT WAS MEANT TO MAKE A DOOR IN A STORY, SO SOMETHING COULD COME THROUGH.
I THINK THE SOMETHING WAS YOU, AND THAT YOU'VE BEEN WANDERING EVER SINCE. LOST IN THIS STRANGE WORLD.
LIZZIE, I MUST INTRODUCE YOU TO MY SON, TOM.
THE TWO OF YOU HAVE SO MUCH IN COMMON.

GO TO PAGE 35

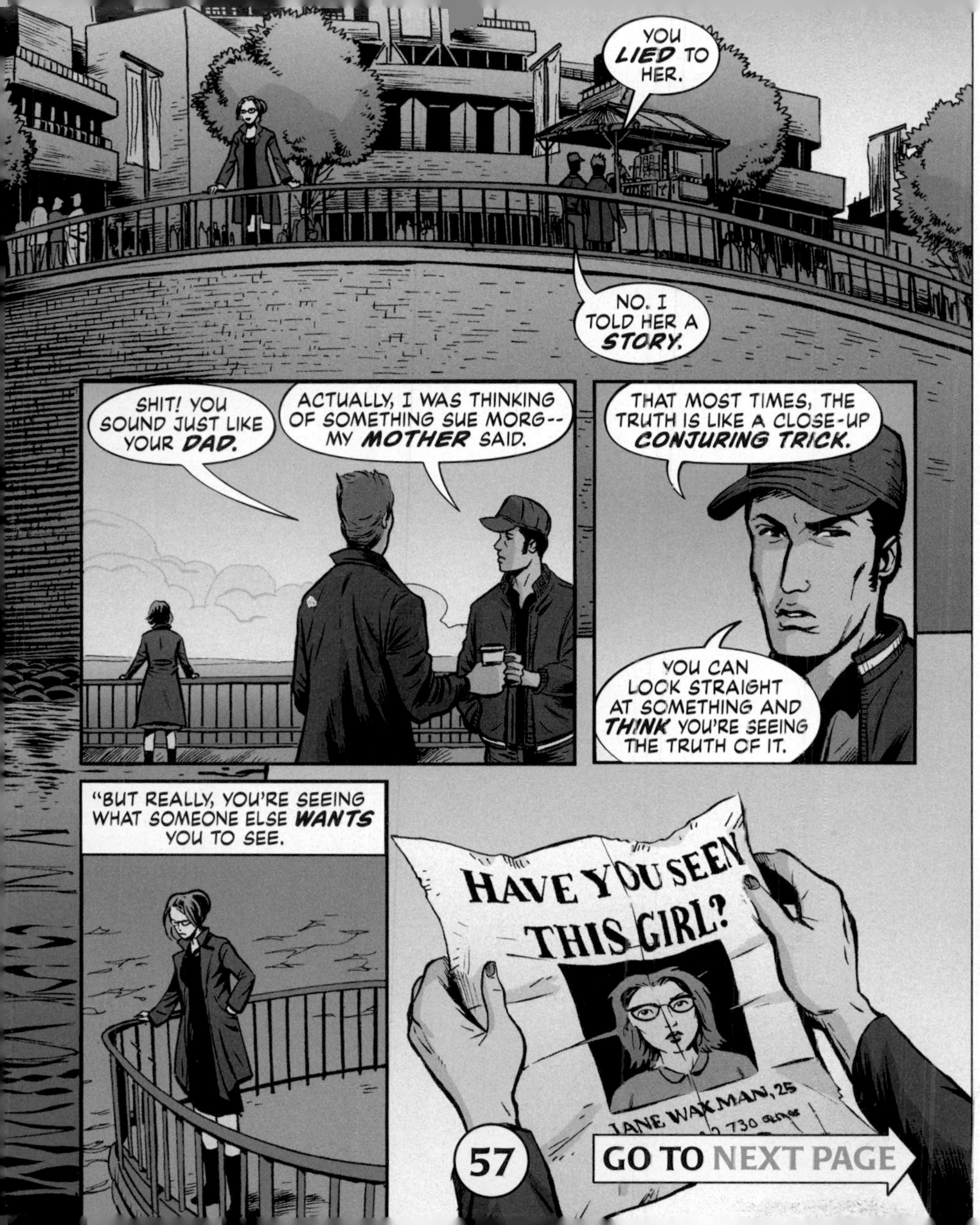
YOU LIED TO HER.
NO. I TOLD HER A STORY.
SHIT! YOU SOUND JUST LIKE YOUR DAD.
ACTUALLY, I WAS THINKING OF SOMETHING SUE MORG-- MY MOTHER SAID.
THAT MOST TIMES, THE TRUTH IS LIKE A CLOSE-UP CONJURING TRICK.
YOU CAN LOOK STRAIGHT AT SOMETHING AND THINK YOU'RE SEEING THE TRUTH OF IT.
"BUT REALLY, YOU'RE SEEING WHAT SOMEONE ELSE WANTS YOU TO SEE.
HAVE YOU SEEN THIS GIRL?
JANE WAKMAN, 25

GO TO NEXT PAGE

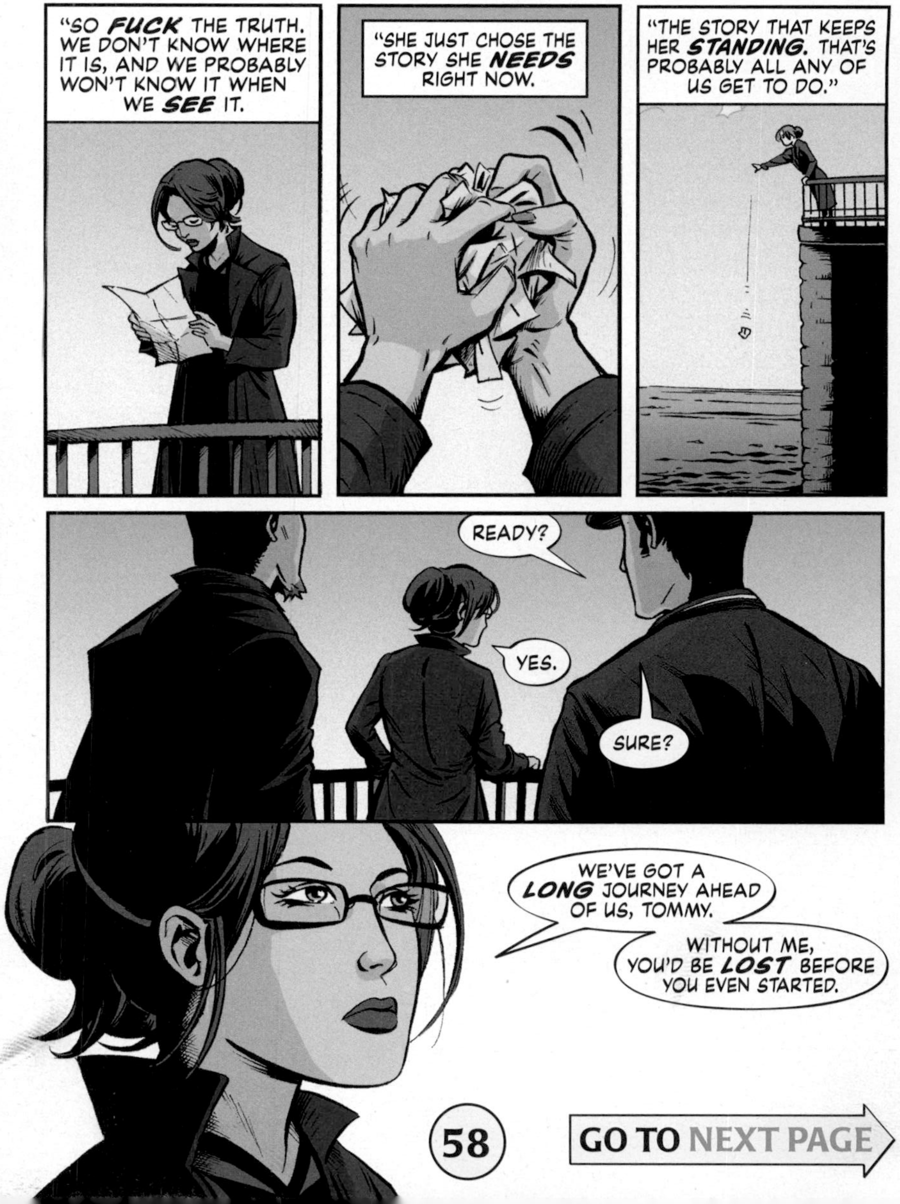
"SO FUCK THE TRUTH. WE DON'T KNOW WHERE IT IS, AND WE PROBABLY WON'T KNOW IT WHEN WE SEE IT.
"SHE JUST CHOSE THE STORY SHE NEEDS RIGHT NOW.
"THE STORY THAT KEEPS HER STANDING. THAT'S PROBABLY ALL ANY OF US GET TO DO."
READY?
YES.
SURE?
WE'VE GOT A LONG JOURNEY AHEAD OF US, TOMMY.
WITHOUT ME, YOU'D BE LOST BEFORE YOU EVEN STARTED.

GO TO NEXT PAGE

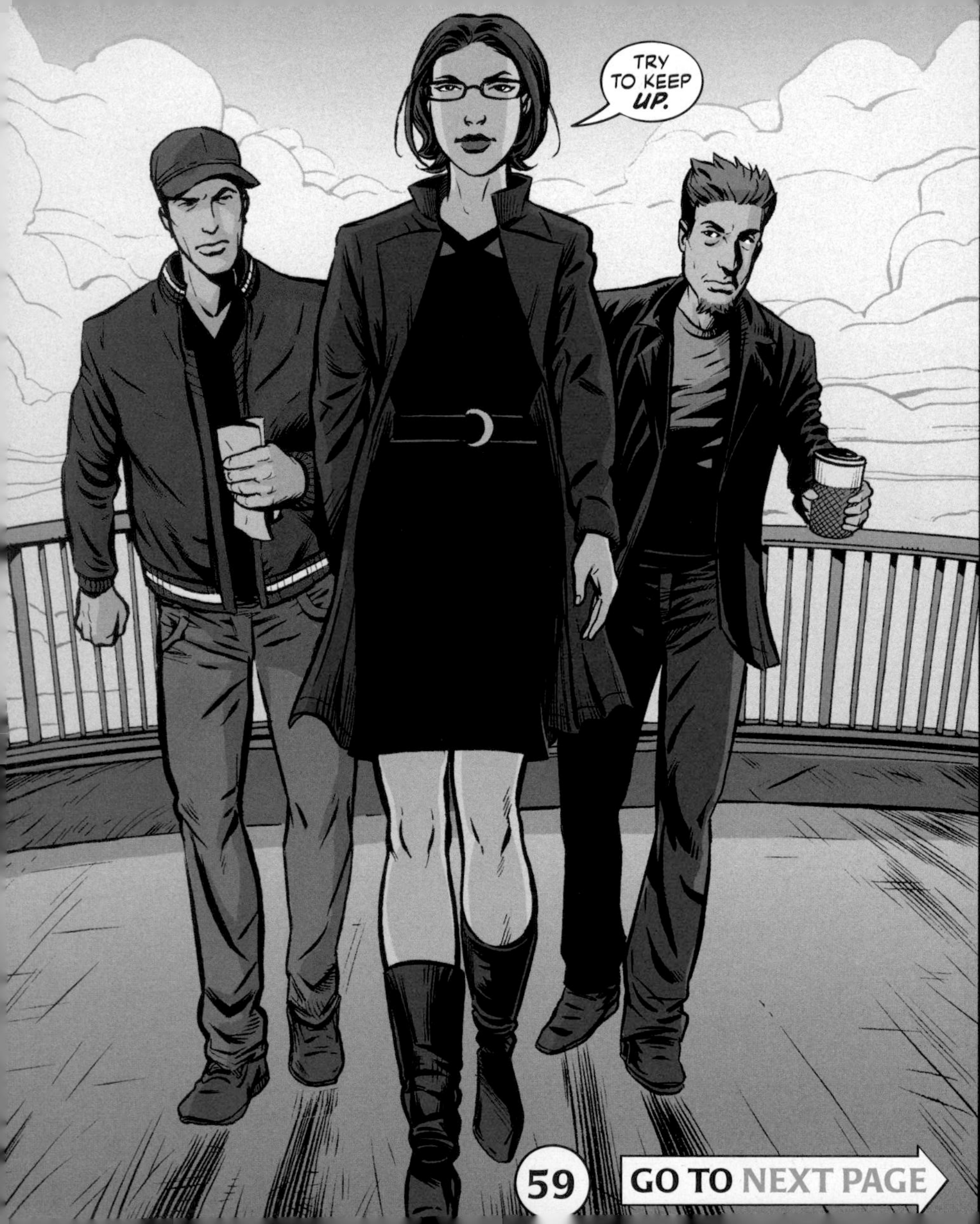
TRY TO KEEP UP.

GO TO NEXT PAGE

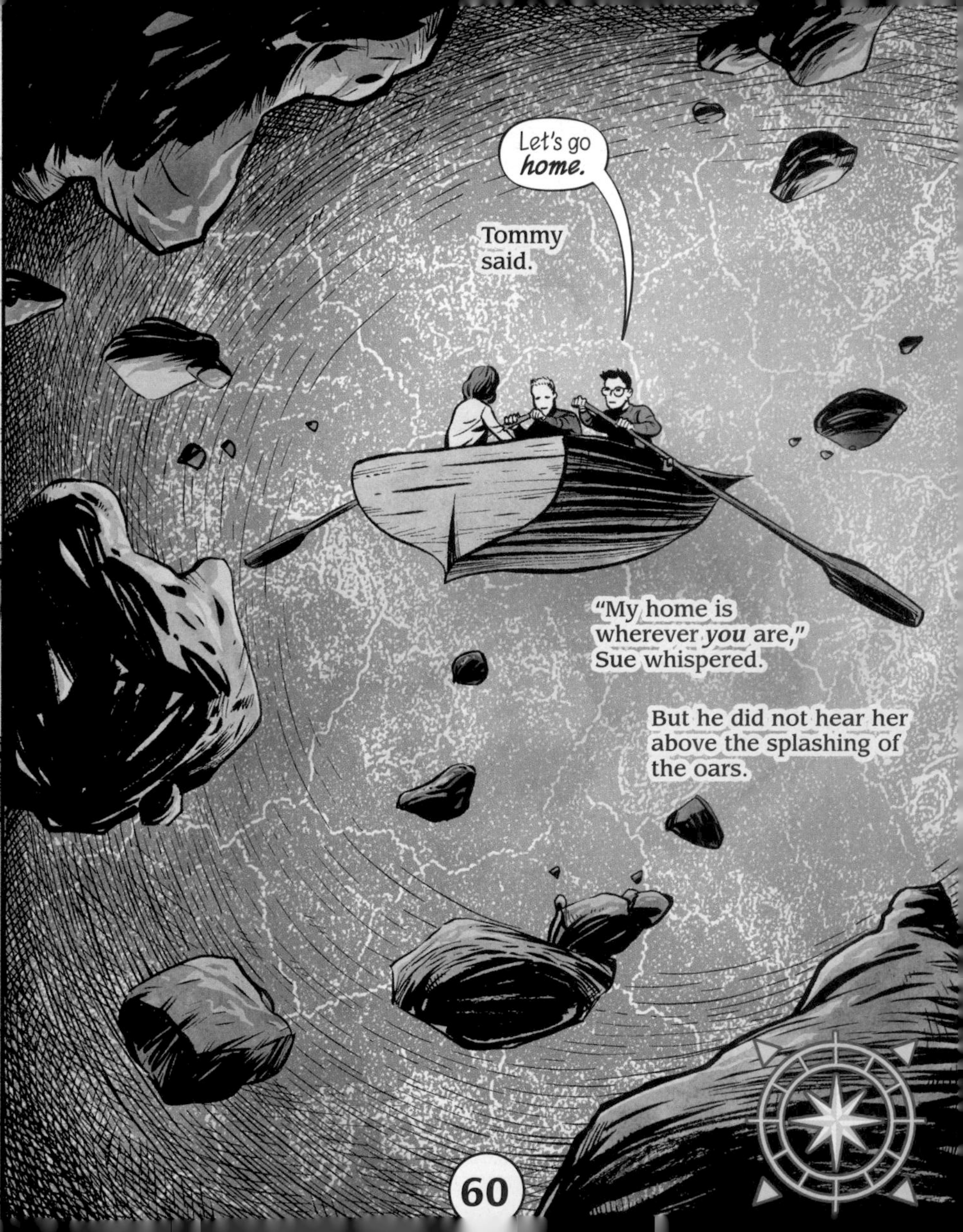
Let's go home.
Tommy said.
"My home is wherever you are," Sue whispered.
But he did not hear her above the splashing of the oars.

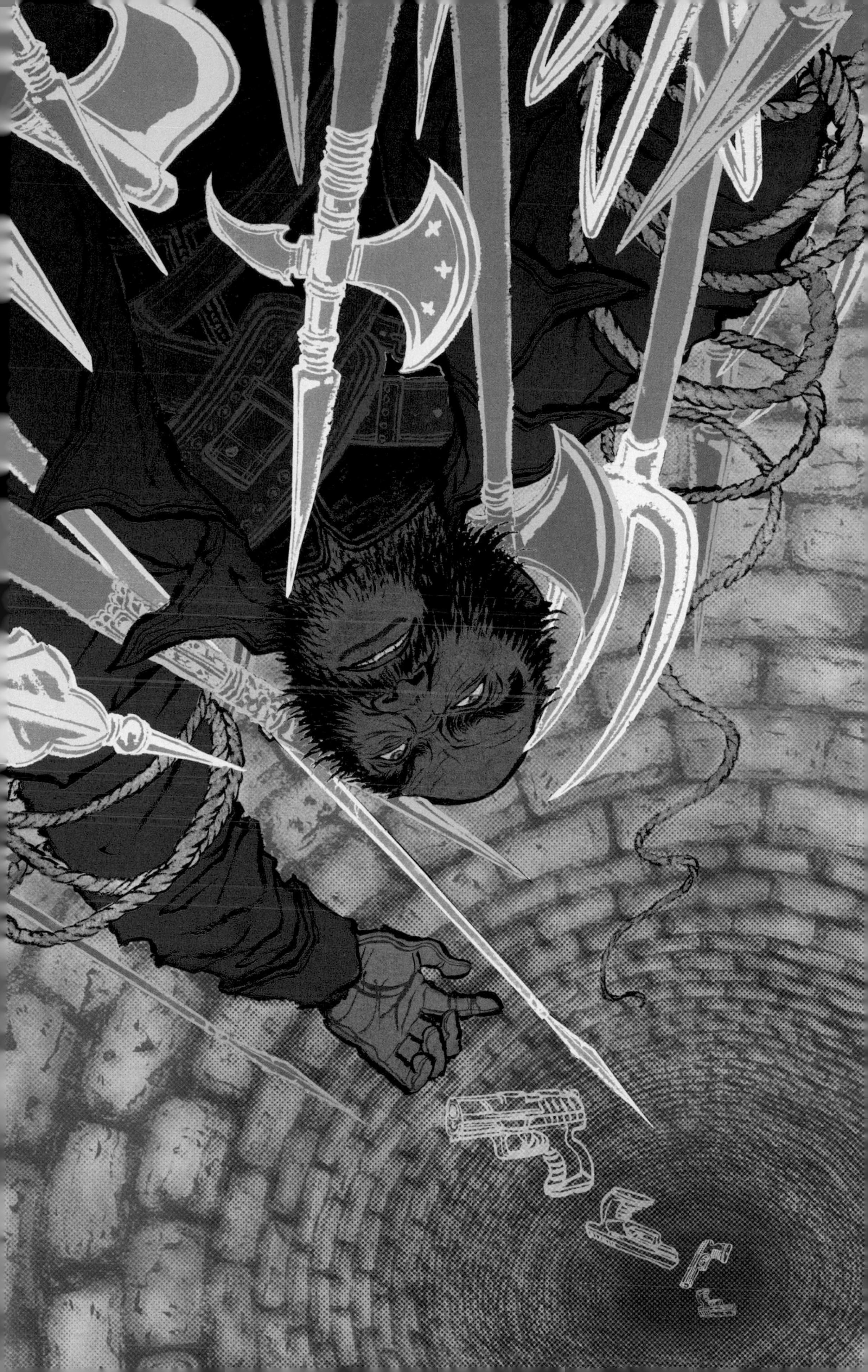

SO WE PRESENT THE UZBEK MASSACRES AS A *PERIODIC TRAGEDY.* INVOKE *FOLK MEMORIES* OF POGROMS, THE HOLOCAUST, SEBRENICE. WHAT ELSE?

RESURGENT TRADE UNIONISM IN SOUTH AMERICA. THAT WAS *FIRTH'S* BRIEF.

MR. FIRTH? WHAT DO YOU *HAVE* FOR US?

SHORT-TERM: WE STARTED A *RETRO* MOVEMENT BASED ON GAUCHO VIRTUES OF SELF-RELIANCE AND STOICAL ENDURANCE.

SEEDING FOR TEN YEARS OUT: THE SEVEN WRITERS WE CHOSE WILL LEAD A CHARGE TOWARDS DIFFICULT, *POST-MODERNIST* STRUCTURES.

THE THINKING IS TO CUT THE WORKERS OFF FROM THE *MAINSTREAM,* THEN BOLT THE DOORS.

THAT WORKS FOR ME. OVETTS, I THINK YOU HAD A *QUERY* ABOUT--

CALLENDAR, THIS IS *ABSURD.* WHAT ABOUT WILSON TAYLOR?

WHAT ABOUT THE *FOURTEENTH BOOK?*

WILSON TAYLOR IS *DEAD.* WITHOUT HIM, THE BOOK REPRESENTS NO THREAT.

I DON'T CONCUR.

ME NEITHER. WE'VE HEARD WHAT *PULLMAN* SAW. THIS GOES TO THE CORE OF OUR BUSINESS.

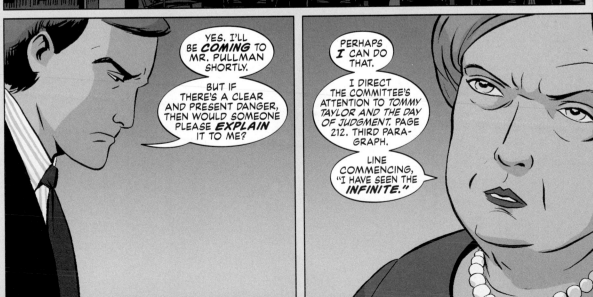

YES. I'LL BE *COMING* TO MR. PULLMAN SHORTLY.

BUT IF THERE'S A CLEAR AND PRESENT DANGER, THEN WOULD SOMEONE PLEASE *EXPLAIN* IT TO ME?

PERHAPS *I* CAN DO THAT.

I DIRECT THE COMMITTEE'S ATTENTION TO *TOMMY TAYLOR AND THE DAY OF JUDGMENT.* PAGE 212. THIRD PARA-GRAPH.

LINE COMMENCING, "I HAVE SEEN THE *INFINITE.*"

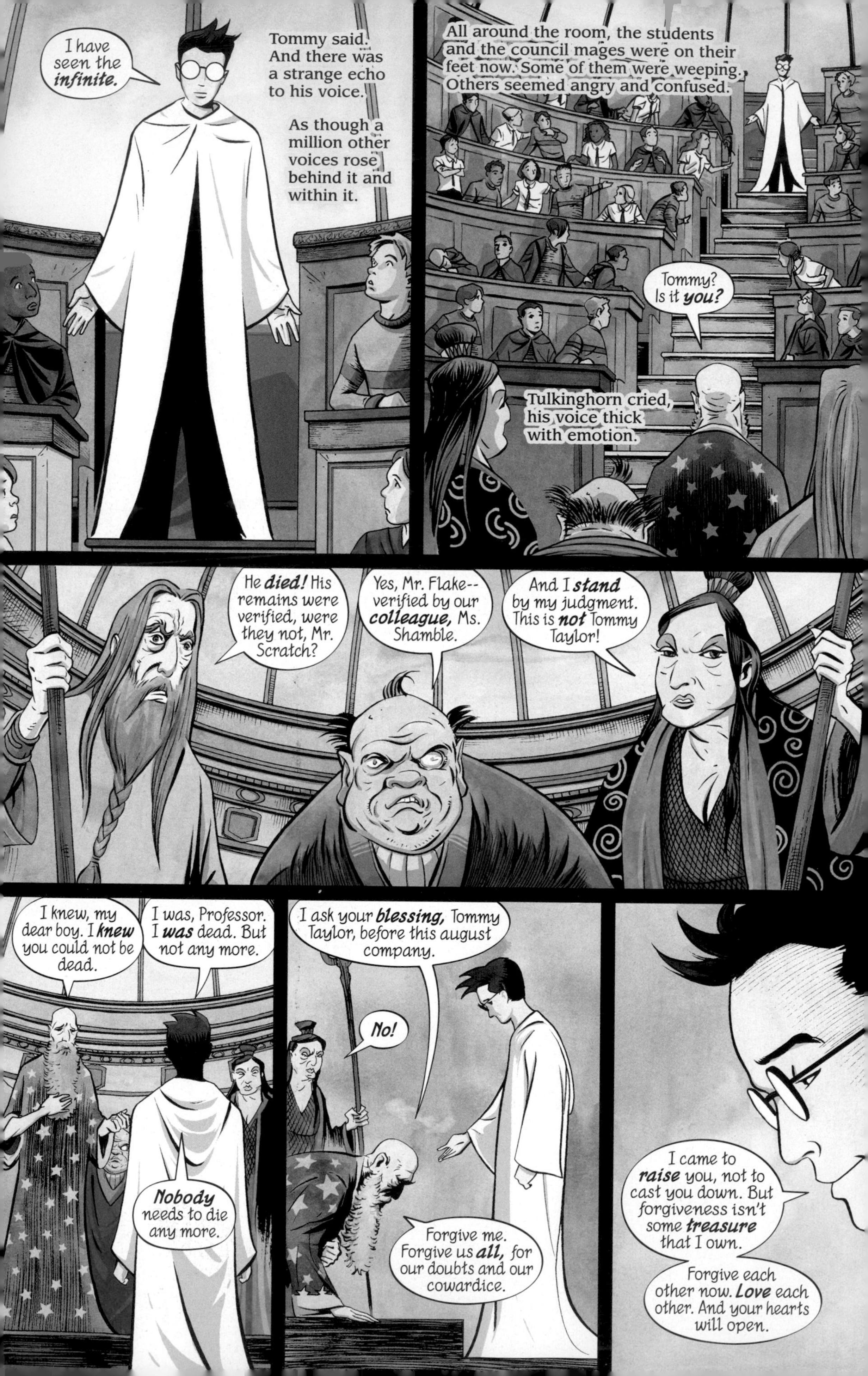
I have seen the *infinite.*
Tommy said. And there was a strange echo to his voice.
As though a million other voices rose behind it and within it.
All around the room, the students and the council mages were on their feet now. Some of them were weeping. Others seemed angry and confused.
Tommy? Is it *you?*
Tulkinghorn cried, his voice thick with emotion.
He *died!* His remains were verified, were they not, Mr. Scratch?
Yes, Mr. Flake-- verified by our *colleague,* Ms. Shamble.
And I *stand* by my judgment. This is *not* Tommy Taylor!
I knew, my dear boy. I *knew* you could not be dead.
I was, Professor. I *was* dead. But not any more.
Nobody needs to die any more.
I ask your *blessing,* Tommy Taylor, before this august company.
No!
Forgive me. Forgive us *all,* for our doubts and our cowardice.
I came to *raise* you, not to cast you down. But forgiveness isn't some *treasure* that I own.
Forgive each other now. *Love* each other. And your hearts will open.

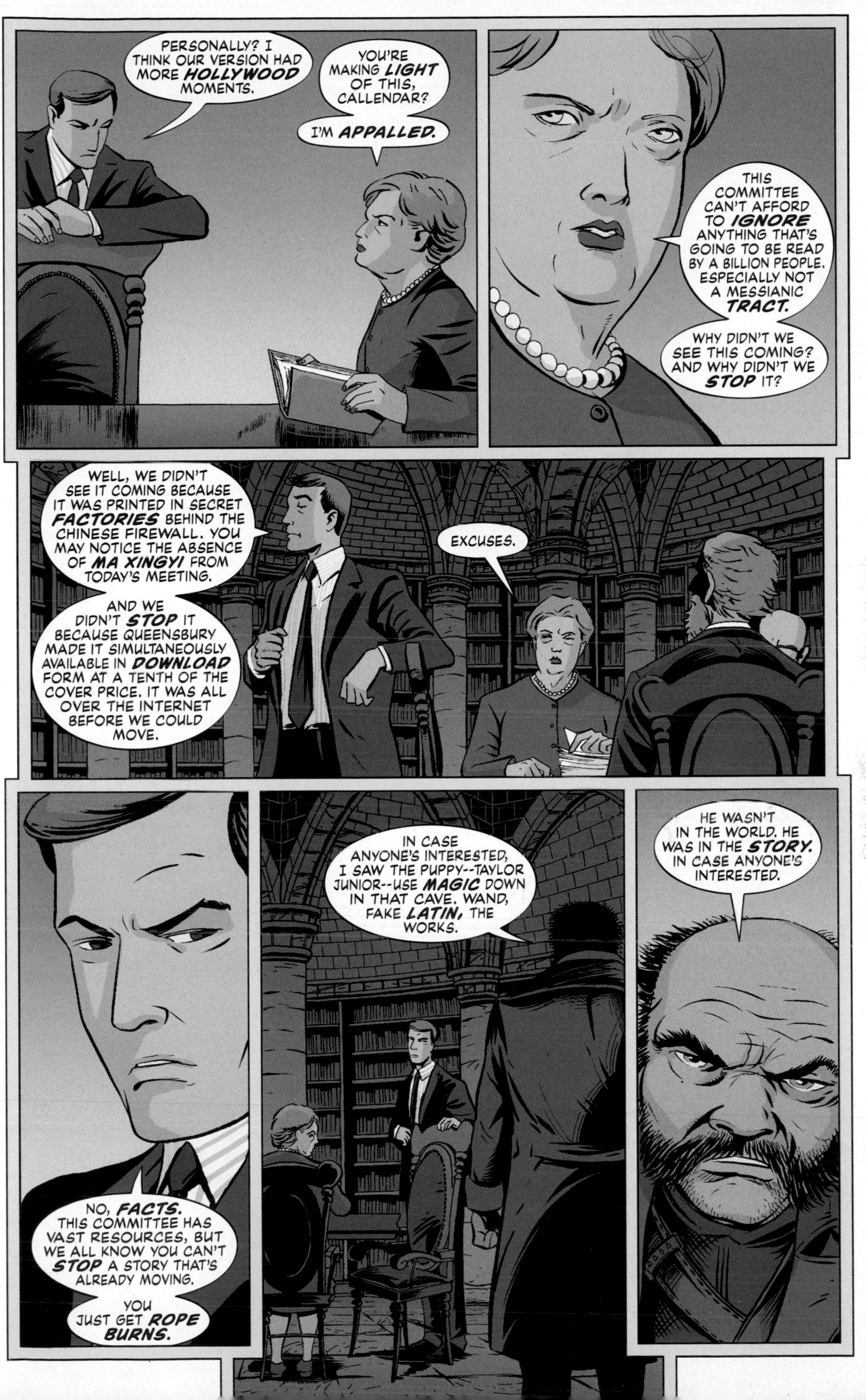
PERSONALLY? I THINK OUR VERSION HAD MORE HOLLYWOOD MOMENTS.
YOU'RE MAKING LIGHT OF THIS, CALLENDAR?
I'M APPALLED.
THIS COMMITTEE CAN'T AFFORD TO IGNORE ANYTHING THAT'S GOING TO BE READ BY A BILLION PEOPLE. ESPECIALLY NOT A MESSIANIC TRACT.
WHY DIDN'T WE SEE THIS COMING? AND WHY DIDN'T WE STOP IT?
WELL, WE DIDN'T SEE IT COMING BECAUSE IT WAS PRINTED IN SECRET FACTORIES BEHIND THE CHINESE FIREWALL. YOU MAY NOTICE THE ABSENCE OF MA XINGYI FROM TODAY'S MEETING.
AND WE DIDN'T STOP IT BECAUSE QUEENSBURY MADE IT SIMULTANEOUSLY AVAILABLE IN DOWNLOAD FORM AT A TENTH OF THE COVER PRICE. IT WAS ALL OVER THE INTERNET BEFORE WE COULD MOVE.
EXCUSES.
NO, FACTS. THIS COMMITTEE HAS VAST RESOURCES, BUT WE ALL KNOW YOU CAN'T STOP A STORY THAT'S ALREADY MOVING.
YOU JUST GET ROPE BURNS.
IN CASE ANYONE'S INTERESTED, I SAW THE PUPPY--TAYLOR JUNIOR--USE MAGIC DOWN IN THAT CAVE. WAND, FAKE LATIN, THE WORKS.
HE WASN'T IN THE WORLD. HE WAS IN THE STORY. IN CASE ANYONE'S INTERESTED.

BECAUSE OF WILSON. BECAUSE WILSON HAD SOME KIND OF **META-FOCUS** WORKING.

MAYBE WE COULD HAVE USED IT **OURSELVES**. BUT UNFORTUNATELY YOU **KILLED** HIM BEFORE WE COULD DEBRIEF HIM ABOUT IT.

THOSE WERE MY ORDERS. THE **WHOLE** OF MY ORDERS.

YOU **INTERPRET** THOSE ORDERS BASED ON THE SITUATION ON THE GROUND.

YOU'RE NOT A **BULLET** THAT WE FIRE. YOU'RE MEANT TO SHOW BASIC COMPETENCES.

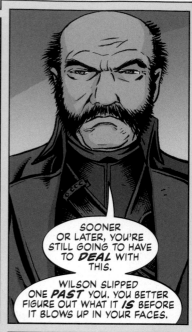

SOONER OR LATER, YOU'RE STILL GOING TO HAVE TO **DEAL** WITH THIS.

WILSON SLIPPED ONE **PAST** YOU. YOU BETTER FIGURE OUT WHAT IT **IS** BEFORE IT BLOWS UP IN YOUR FACES.

BUT **YOU** WERE THE FIELD MAN.

WORKING TO YOUR BRIEF. IF ANYONE **OWNS** THIS FUCK-UP, IT'S YOU.

YOU REALLY WANT TO WASTE YOUR TIME SHIFTING **BLAME** AROUND?

PULLMAN HAS **FAILED** IN HIS PRIMARY DUTY TO THIS COMMITTEE.

THIS IS BULLSHIT.

HE SHOULD FACE THE **SIBYL**. I CALL A VOTE.

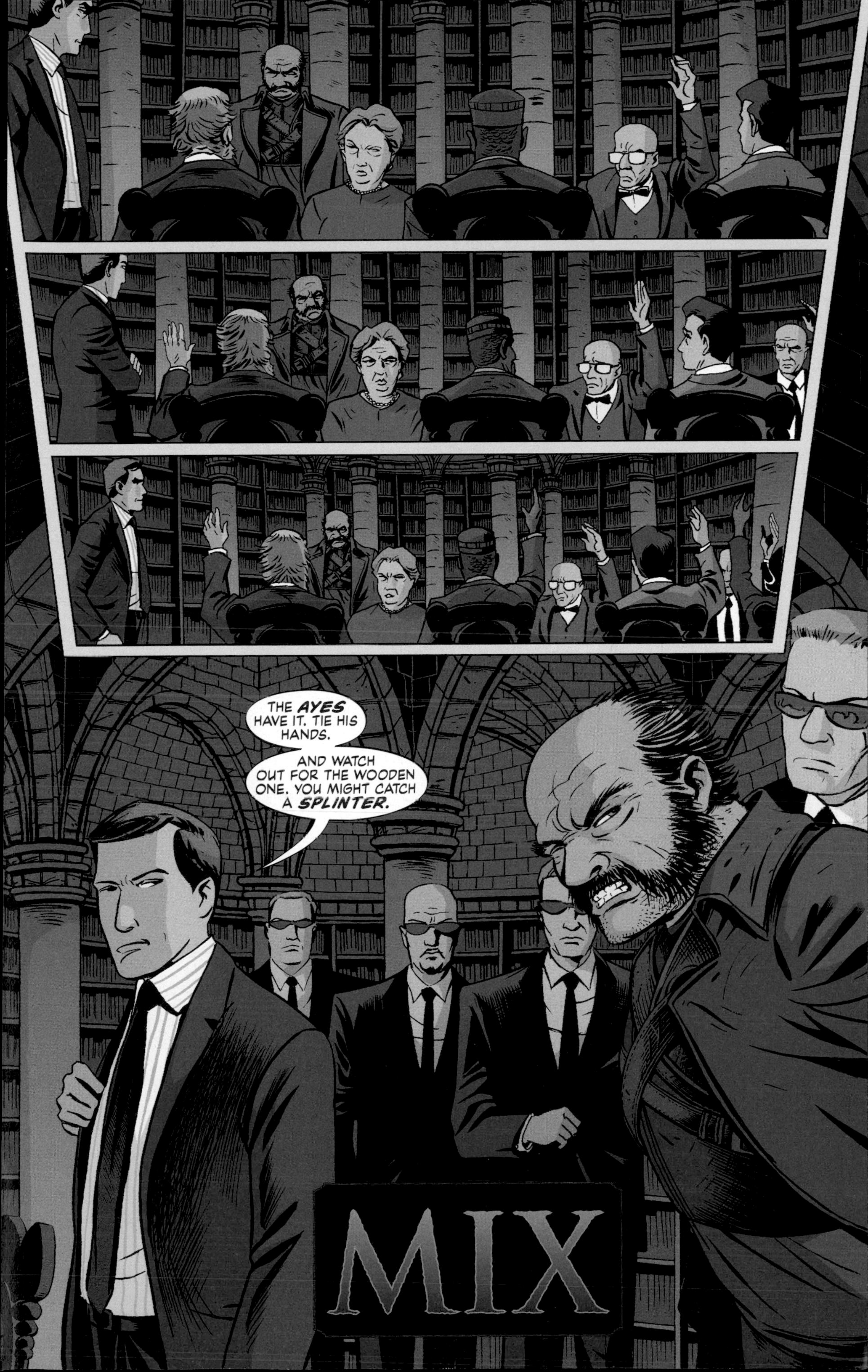
THE AYES HAVE IT. TIE HIS HANDS.
AND WATCH OUT FOR THE WOODEN ONE. YOU MIGHT CATCH A SPLINTER.
MIX

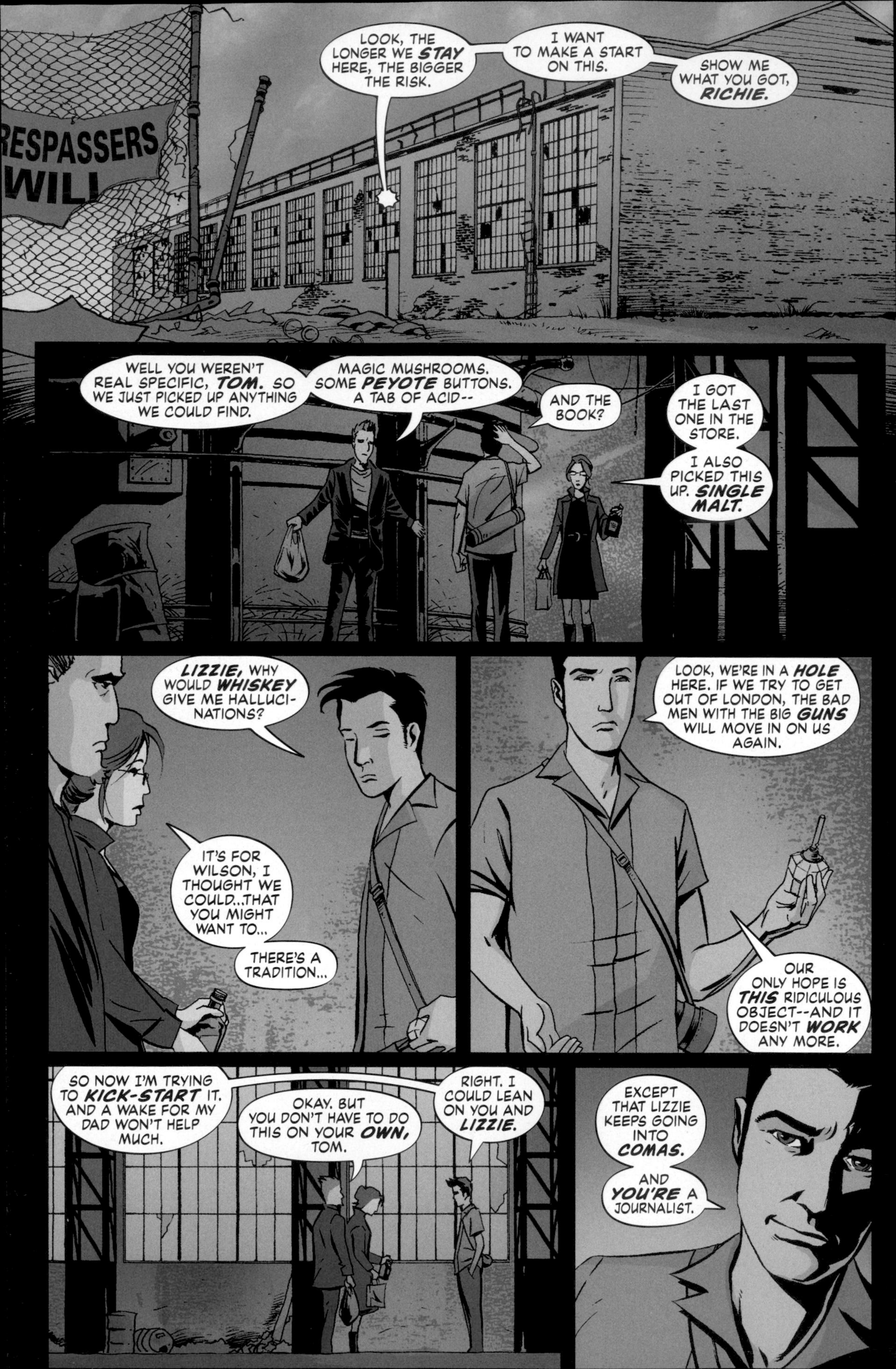

RESPASSERS
WILL
LOOK, THE LONGER WE STAY HERE, THE BIGGER THE RISK.
I WANT TO MAKE A START ON THIS.
SHOW ME WHAT YOU GOT, RICHIE.
WELL YOU WEREN'T REAL SPECIFIC, TOM. SO WE JUST PICKED UP ANYTHING WE COULD FIND.
MAGIC MUSHROOMS. SOME PEYOTE BUTTONS. A TAB OF ACID--
AND THE BOOK?
I GOT THE LAST ONE IN THE STORE.
I ALSO PICKED THIS UP. SINGLE MALT.
LIZZIE, WHY WOULD WHISKEY GIVE ME HALLUCI-NATIONS?
IT'S FOR WILSON, I THOUGHT WE COULD...THAT YOU MIGHT WANT TO...
THERE'S A TRADITION...
LOOK, WE'RE IN A HOLE HERE. IF WE TRY TO GET OUT OF LONDON, THE BAD MEN WITH THE BIG GUNS WILL MOVE IN ON US AGAIN.
OUR ONLY HOPE IS THIS RIDICULOUS OBJECT--AND IT DOESN'T WORK ANY MORE.
SO NOW I'M TRYING TO KICK-START IT. AND A WAKE FOR MY DAD WON'T HELP MUCH.
OKAY. BUT YOU DON'T HAVE TO DO THIS ON YOUR OWN, TOM.
RIGHT. I COULD LEAN ON YOU AND LIZZIE.
EXCEPT THAT LIZZIE KEEPS GOING INTO COMAS.
AND YOU'RE A JOURNALIST.

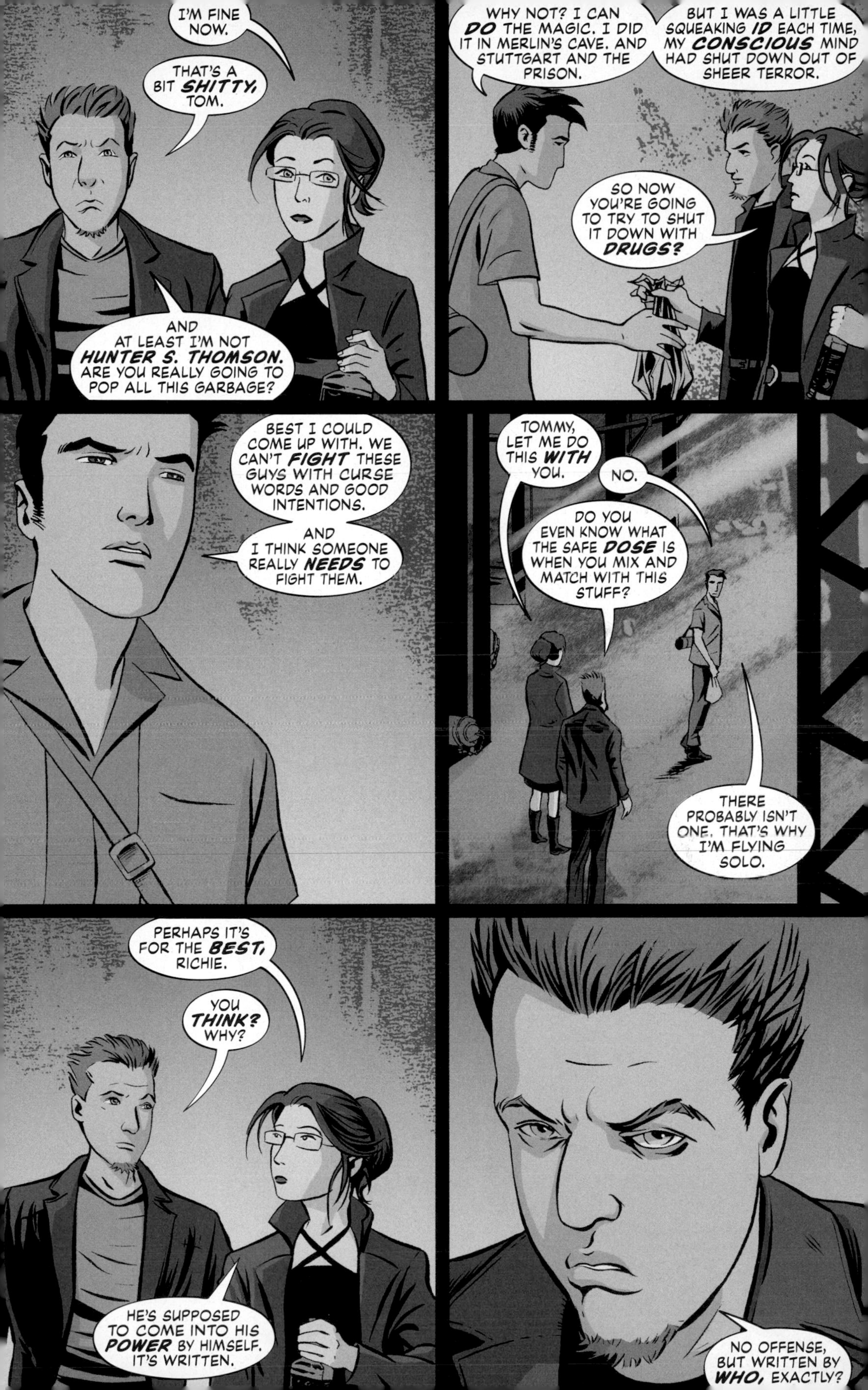
I'M FINE NOW.
THAT'S A BIT SHITTY, TOM.
AND AT LEAST I'M NOT HUNTER S. THOMSON. ARE YOU REALLY GOING TO POP ALL THIS GARBAGE?
WHY NOT? I CAN DO THE MAGIC. I DID IT IN MERLIN'S CAVE. AND STUTTGART AND THE PRISON.
BUT I WAS A LITTLE SQUEAKING ID EACH TIME, MY CONSCIOUS MIND HAD SHUT DOWN OUT OF SHEER TERROR.
SO NOW YOU'RE GOING TO TRY TO SHUT IT DOWN WITH DRUGS?
BEST I COULD COME UP WITH. WE CAN'T FIGHT THESE GUYS WITH CURSE WORDS AND GOOD INTENTIONS.
AND I THINK SOMEONE REALLY NEEDS TO FIGHT THEM.
TOMMY, LET ME DO THIS WITH YOU.
NO.
DO YOU EVEN KNOW WHAT THE SAFE DOSE IS WHEN YOU MIX AND MATCH WITH THIS STUFF?
THERE PROBABLY ISN'T ONE. THAT'S WHY I'M FLYING SOLO.
PERHAPS IT'S FOR THE BEST, RICHIE.
YOU THINK? WHY?
HE'S SUPPOSED TO COME INTO HIS POWER BY HIMSELF. IT'S WRITTEN.
NO OFFENSE, BUT WRITTEN BY WHO, EXACTLY?

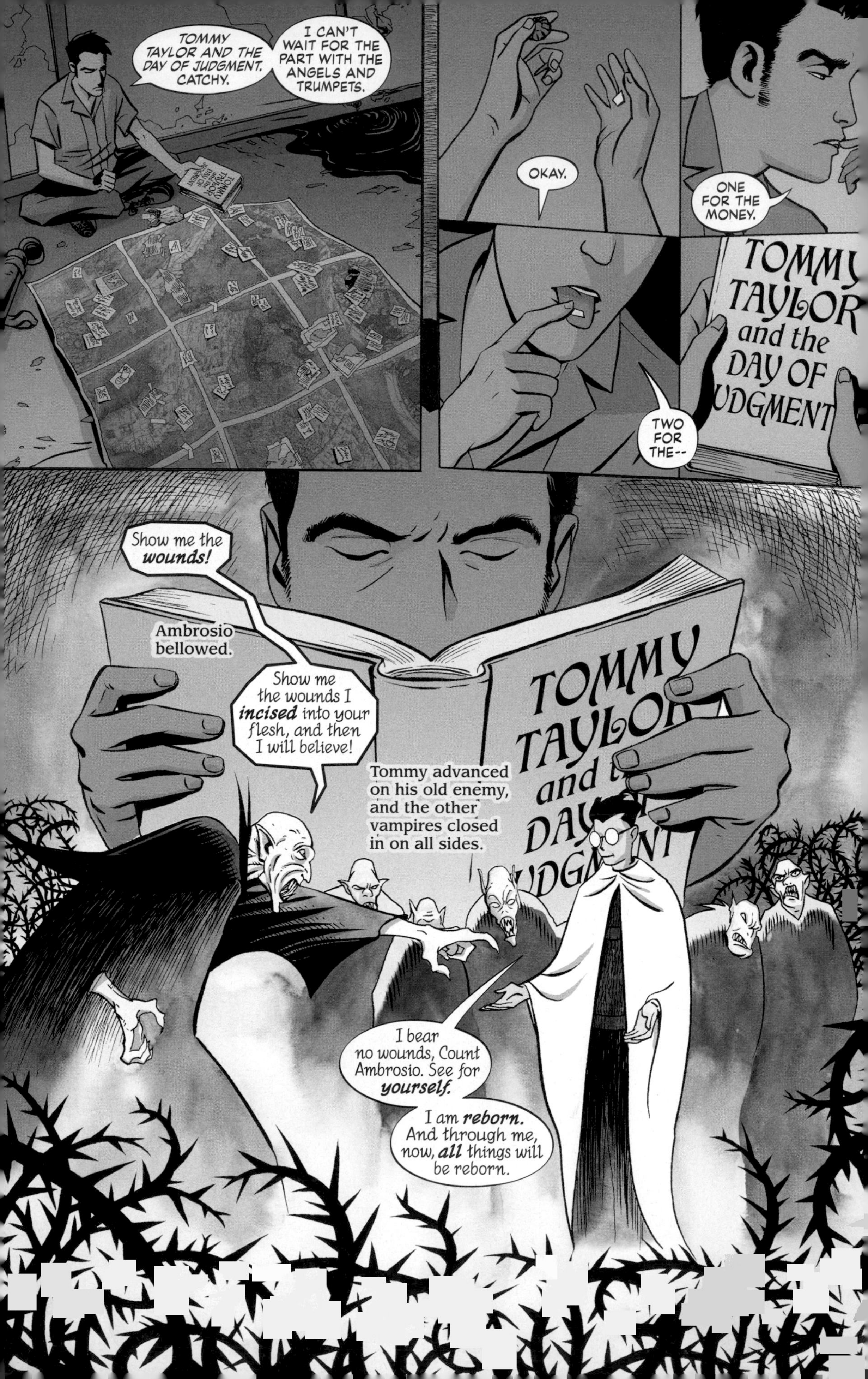
TOMMY TAYLOR AND THE DAY OF JUDGMENT. CATCHY.
I CAN'T WAIT FOR THE PART WITH THE ANGELS AND TRUMPETS.
TOMMY TAYLOR AND THE DAY OF JUDGMENT
OKAY.
ONE FOR THE MONEY.
TWO FOR THE--
TOMMY TAYLOR and the DAY OF JUDGMENT
Show me the **wounds!**
Ambrosio bellowed.
Show me the wounds I ***incised*** into your flesh, and then I will believe!
Tommy advanced on his old enemy, and the other vampires closed in on all sides.
I bear no wounds, Count Ambrosio. See for ***yourself.***
I am ***reborn.*** And through me, now, ***all*** things will be reborn.

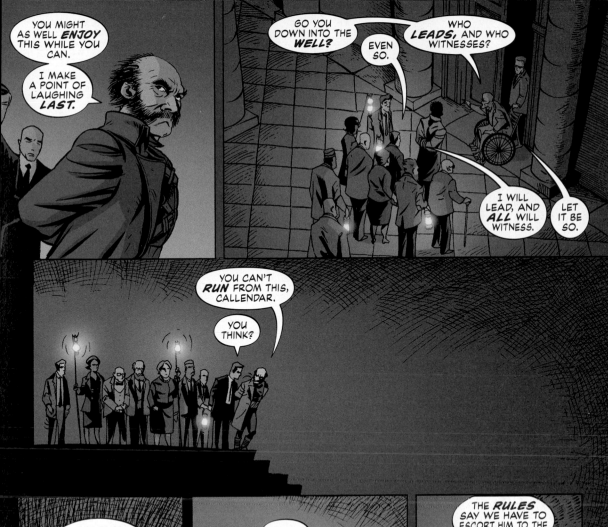

YOU MIGHT AS WELL **ENJOY** THIS WHILE YOU CAN.

I MAKE A POINT OF LAUGHING **LAST.**

GO YOU DOWN INTO THE **WELL?**

EVEN SO.

WHO **LEADS,** AND WHO WITNESSES?

I WILL LEAD, AND **ALL** WILL WITNESS.

LET IT BE SO.

YOU CAN'T **RUN** FROM THIS, CALLENDAR.

YOU THINK?

THE FAKE NOVEL WAS **YOUR** PLAN, NOT MINE. I MADE IT WORK THE BEST WAY I COULD, BUT I TOLD YOU--

OOPS.

GUUUH!

THE **RULES** SAY WE HAVE TO ESCORT HIM TO THE BOTTOM.

THEY DON'T SAY **HOW.**

THUD

THUMP

KRNCH

OKAY, WE'RE ASSEMBLED. FIRTH, YOU'LL HELP ME TO **OFFICIATE**.

I--I'VE NEVER **DONE** THIS BEFORE.

IT'S A SIMPLE ENOUGH CEREMONY. IN THIS, AS IN **ALL** THINGS, THE WELL KEEPS OUR SECRETS.

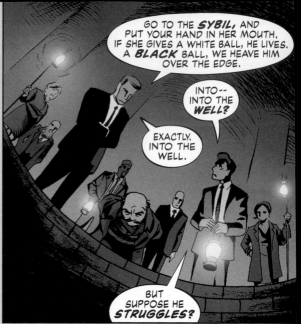

GO TO THE **SYBIL**, AND PUT YOUR HAND IN HER MOUTH. IF SHE GIVES A WHITE BALL, HE LIVES. A **BLACK** BALL, WE HEAVE HIM OVER THE EDGE.

INTO-- INTO THE **WELL**?

EXACTLY. INTO THE WELL.

BUT SUPPOSE HE **STRUGGLES**?

THEN WE PUT A **BULLET** IN HIS HEAD AND PITCH HIM IN DEAD. IT'S ALL THE SAME.

LAST CHANCE TO BACK **AWAY** FROM THIS, CALLENDAR.

WHY, PULLMAN. I DON'T THINK I'VE EVER KNOWN YOU TO **BLUFF** BEFORE.

THERE ARE THINGS THAT HAVE TO BE DONE. YOU'LL **NEED** ME.

NO. I REALLY DON'T THINK SO.

IF THERE WAS A SAFE WAY TO REMOVE YOUR **HAND**, I MIGHT TRY TO KEEP THAT.

BUT THERE ISN'T. AND REALLY, IN A LOT OF WAYS, I'LL FEEL **HAPPIER** KNOWING YOU'RE NOT AROUND.

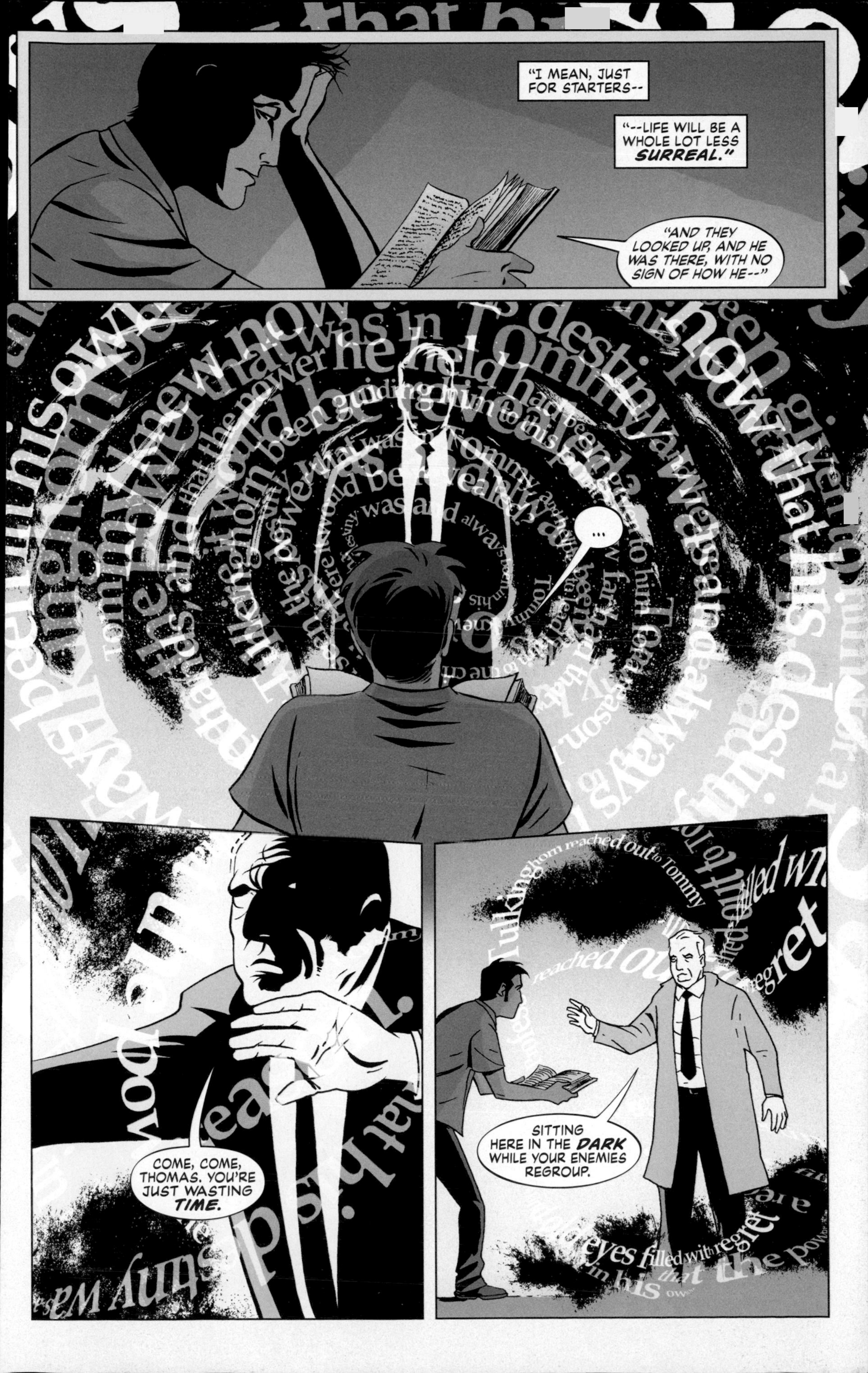
"I MEAN, JUST FOR STARTERS--
"--LIFE WILL BE A WHOLE LOT LESS SURREAL."
"AND THEY LOOKED UP, AND HE WAS THERE, WITH NO SIGN OF HOW HE--"
...
COME, COME, THOMAS. YOU'RE JUST WASTING TIME.
SITTING HERE IN THE DARK WHILE YOUR ENEMIES REGROUP.

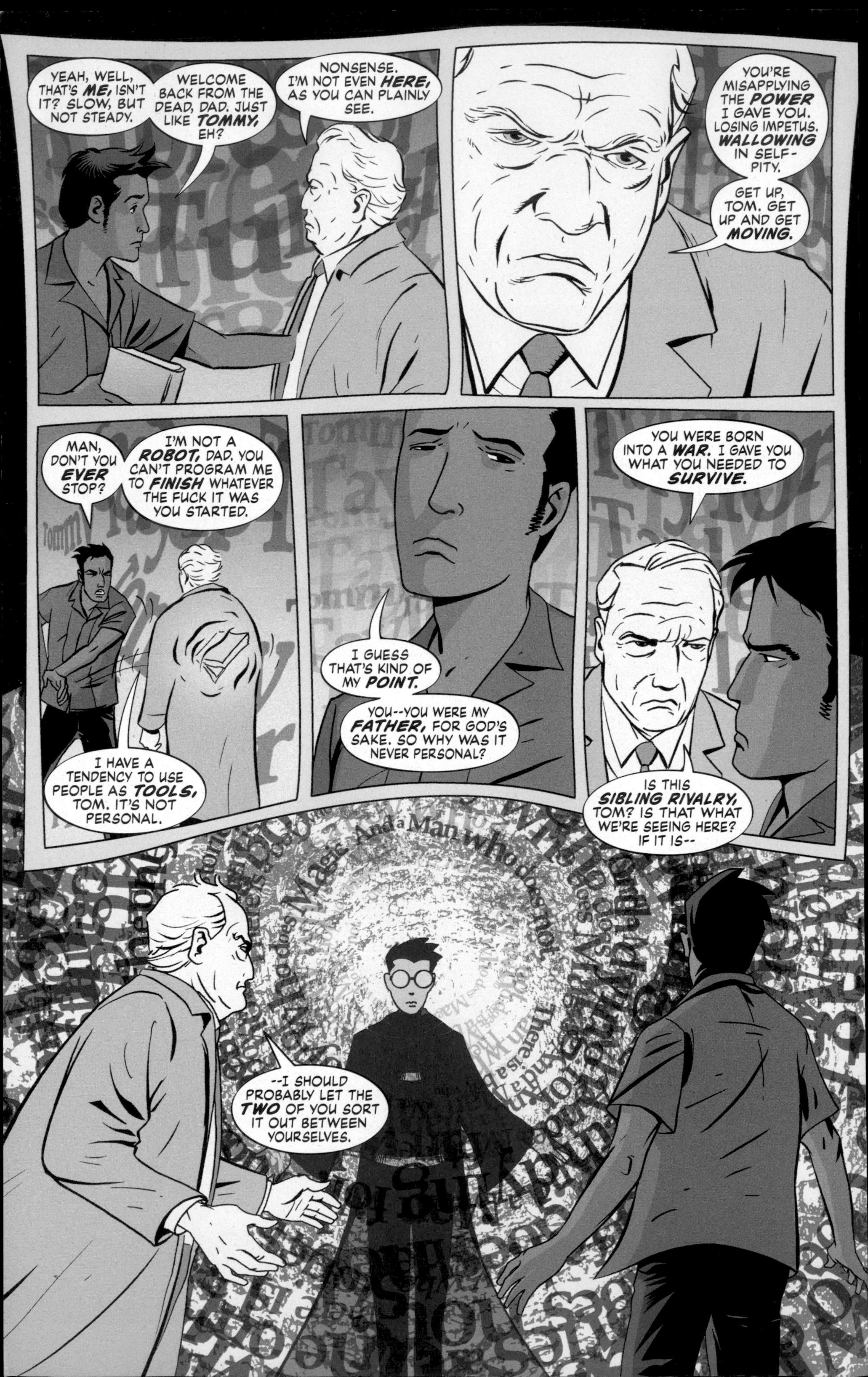
YEAH, WELL, THAT'S ME, ISN'T IT? SLOW, BUT NOT STEADY.
WELCOME BACK FROM THE DEAD, DAD. JUST LIKE TOMMY, EH?
NONSENSE. I'M NOT EVEN HERE, AS YOU CAN PLAINLY SEE.
YOU'RE MISAPPLYING THE POWER I GAVE YOU. LOSING IMPETUS. WALLOWING IN SELF-PITY.
GET UP, TOM. GET UP AND GET MOVING.
MAN, DON'T YOU EVER STOP?
I'M NOT A ROBOT, DAD. YOU CAN'T PROGRAM ME TO FINISH WHATEVER THE FUCK IT WAS YOU STARTED.
I HAVE A TENDENCY TO USE PEOPLE AS TOOLS, TOM. IT'S NOT PERSONAL.
I GUESS THAT'S KIND OF MY POINT.
YOU--YOU WERE MY FATHER, FOR GOD'S SAKE. SO WHY WAS IT NEVER PERSONAL?
YOU WERE BORN INTO A WAR. I GAVE YOU WHAT YOU NEEDED TO SURVIVE.
IS THIS SIBLING RIVALRY, TOM? IS THAT WHAT WE'RE SEEING HERE? IF IT IS--
--I SHOULD PROBABLY LET THE TWO OF YOU SORT IT OUT BETWEEN YOURSELVES.

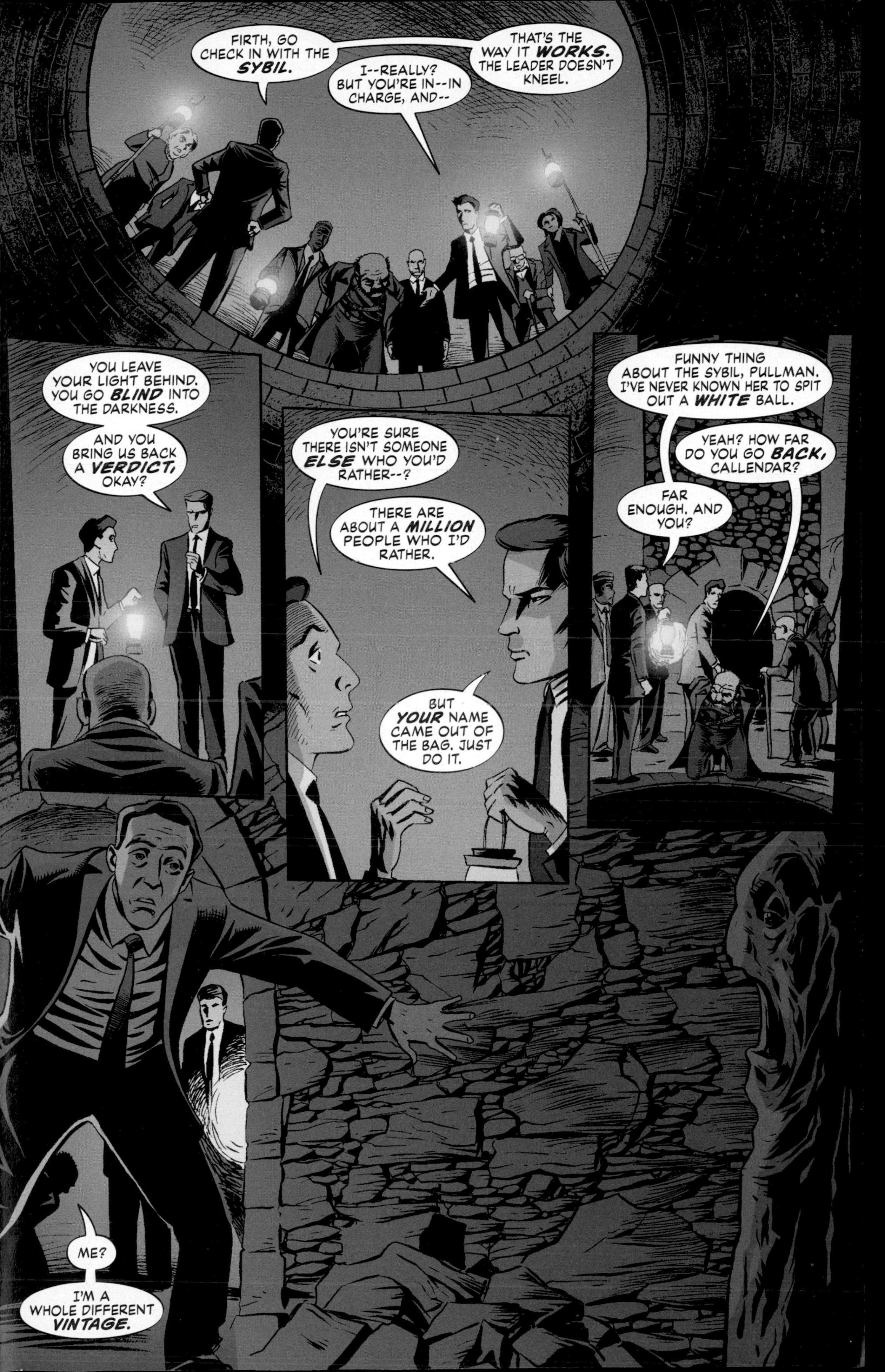
FIRTH, GO CHECK IN WITH THE SYBIL.
I--REALLY? BUT YOU'RE IN--IN CHARGE, AND--
THAT'S THE WAY IT WORKS. THE LEADER DOESN'T KNEEL.
YOU LEAVE YOUR LIGHT BEHIND. YOU GO BLIND INTO THE DARKNESS.
AND YOU BRING US BACK A VERDICT, OKAY?
YOU'RE SURE THERE ISN'T SOMEONE ELSE WHO YOU'D RATHER--?
THERE ARE ABOUT A MILLION PEOPLE WHO I'D RATHER.
BUT YOUR NAME CAME OUT OF THE BAG. JUST DO IT.
FUNNY THING ABOUT THE SYBIL, PULLMAN. I'VE NEVER KNOWN HER TO SPIT OUT A WHITE BALL.
YEAH? HOW FAR DO YOU GO BACK, CALLENDAR?
FAR ENOUGH. AND YOU?
ME?
I'M A WHOLE DIFFERENT VINTAGE.

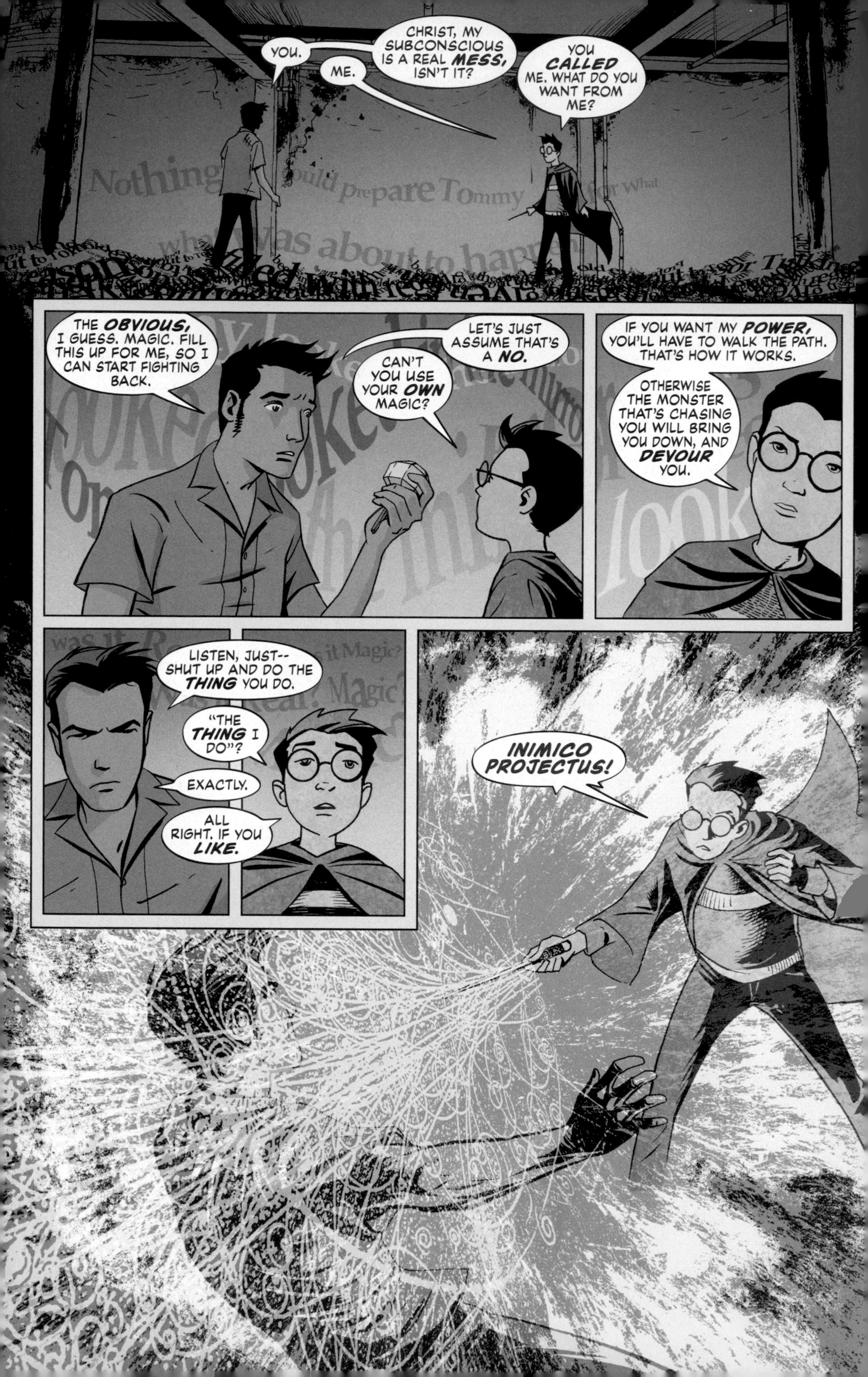

YOU.
ME.
CHRIST, MY SUBCONSCIOUS IS A REAL MESS, ISN'T IT?
YOU CALLED ME. WHAT DO YOU WANT FROM ME?
THE OBVIOUS, I GUESS. MAGIC. FILL THIS UP FOR ME, SO I CAN START FIGHTING BACK.
CAN'T YOU USE YOUR OWN MAGIC?
LET'S JUST ASSUME THAT'S A NO.
IF YOU WANT MY POWER, YOU'LL HAVE TO WALK THE PATH. THAT'S HOW IT WORKS.
OTHERWISE THE MONSTER THAT'S CHASING YOU WILL BRING YOU DOWN, AND DEVOUR YOU.
LISTEN, JUST-- SHUT UP AND DO THE THING YOU DO.
"THE THING I DO"?
EXACTLY.
ALL RIGHT. IF YOU LIKE.
INIMICO PROJECTUS!

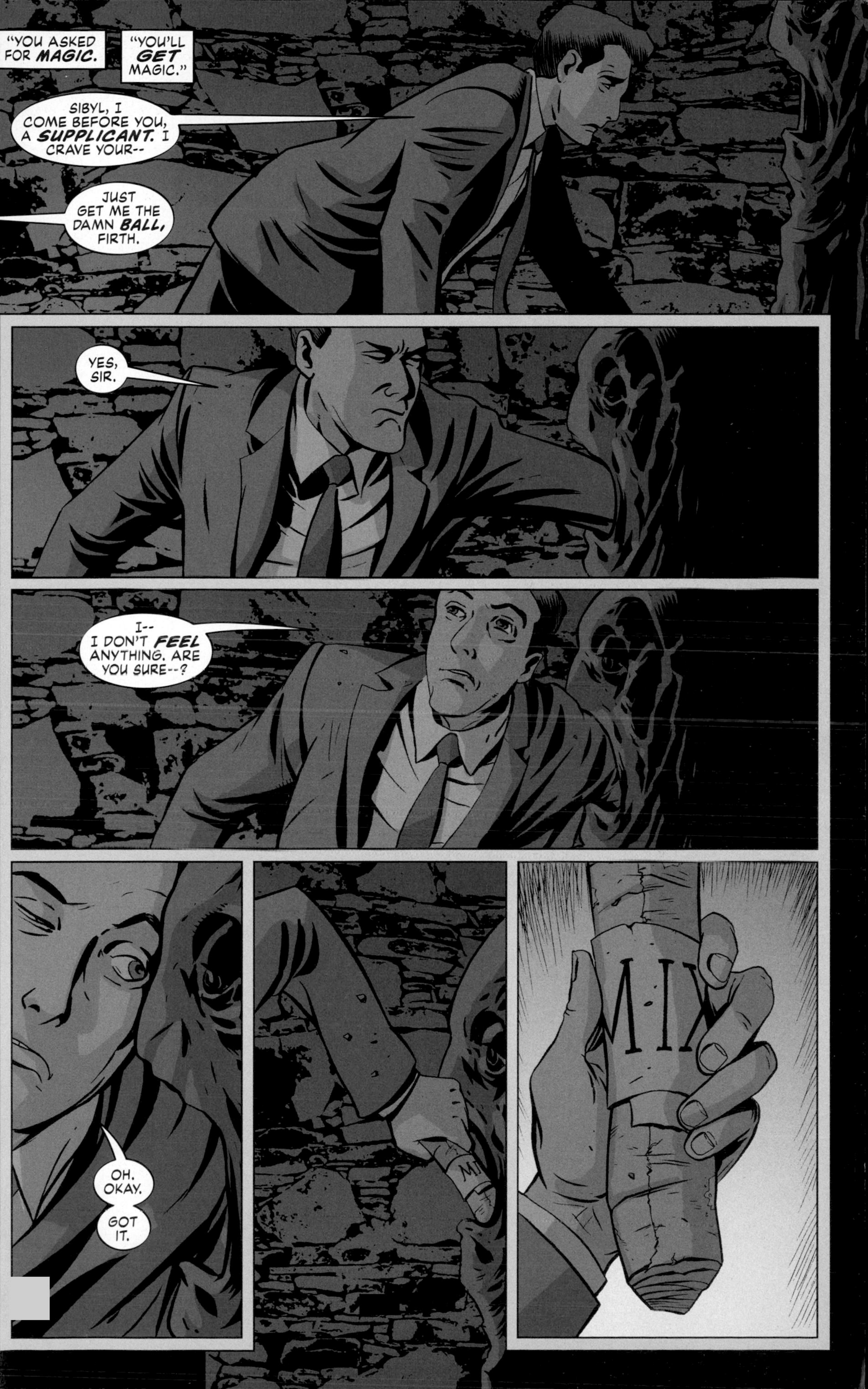
"YOU ASKED FOR MAGIC.
"YOU'LL GET MAGIC."
SIBYL, I COME BEFORE YOU, A SUPPLICANT. I CRAVE YOUR--
JUST GET ME THE DAMN BALL, FIRTH.
YES, SIR.
I-- I DON'T FEEL ANYTHING. ARE YOU SURE--?
OH. OKAY.
GOT IT.
MIX

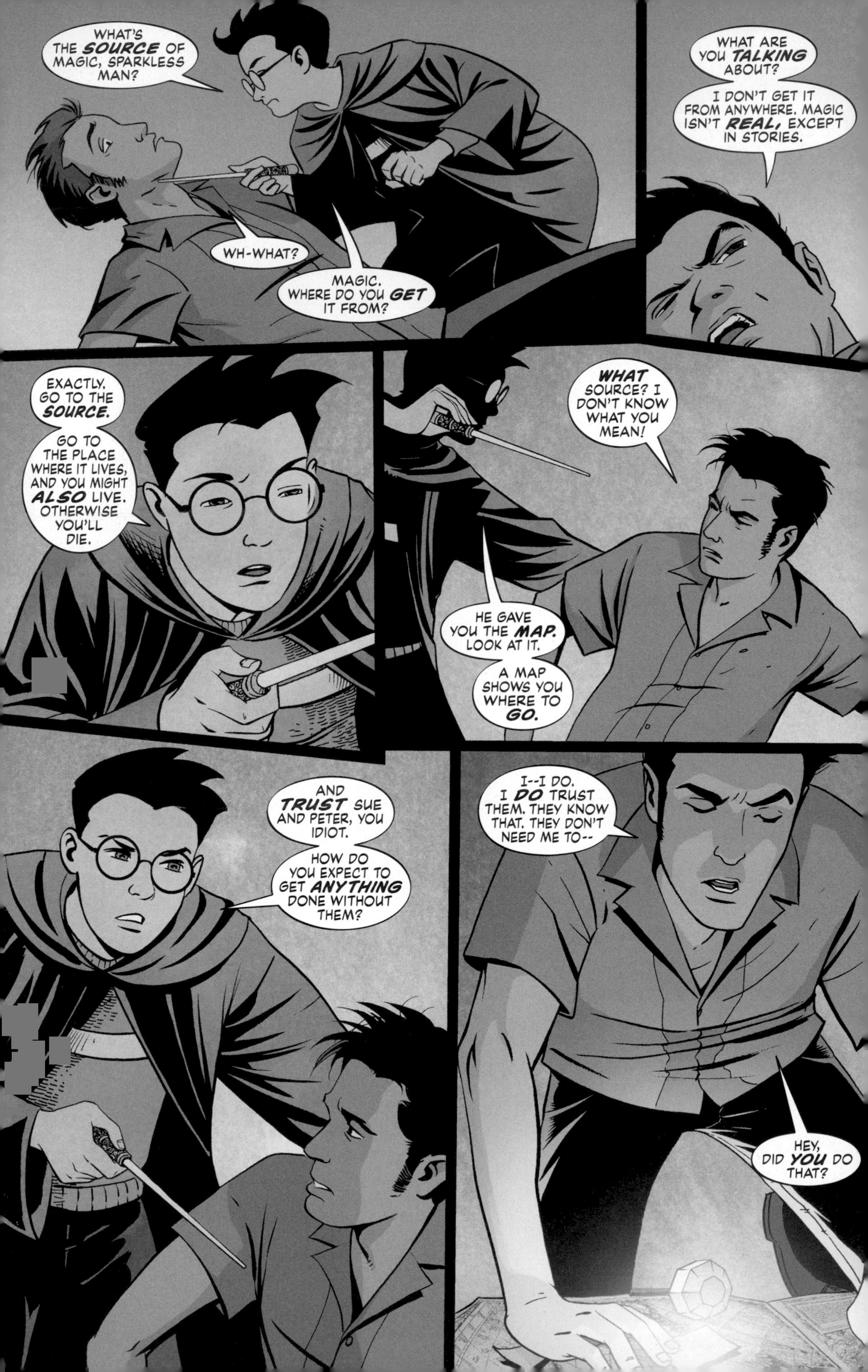
WHAT'S THE SOURCE OF MAGIC, SPARKLESS MAN?
WH-WHAT?
MAGIC. WHERE DO YOU GET IT FROM?
WHAT ARE YOU TALKING ABOUT?
I DON'T GET IT FROM ANYWHERE. MAGIC ISN'T REAL, EXCEPT IN STORIES.
EXACTLY. GO TO THE SOURCE.
GO TO THE PLACE WHERE IT LIVES, AND YOU MIGHT ALSO LIVE. OTHERWISE YOU'LL DIE.
WHAT SOURCE? I DON'T KNOW WHAT YOU MEAN!
HE GAVE YOU THE MAP. LOOK AT IT.
A MAP SHOWS YOU WHERE TO GO.
AND TRUST SUE AND PETER, YOU IDIOT.
HOW DO YOU EXPECT TO GET ANYTHING DONE WITHOUT THEM?
I--I DO. I DO TRUST THEM. THEY KNOW THAT. THEY DON'T NEED ME TO--
HEY, DID YOU DO THAT?

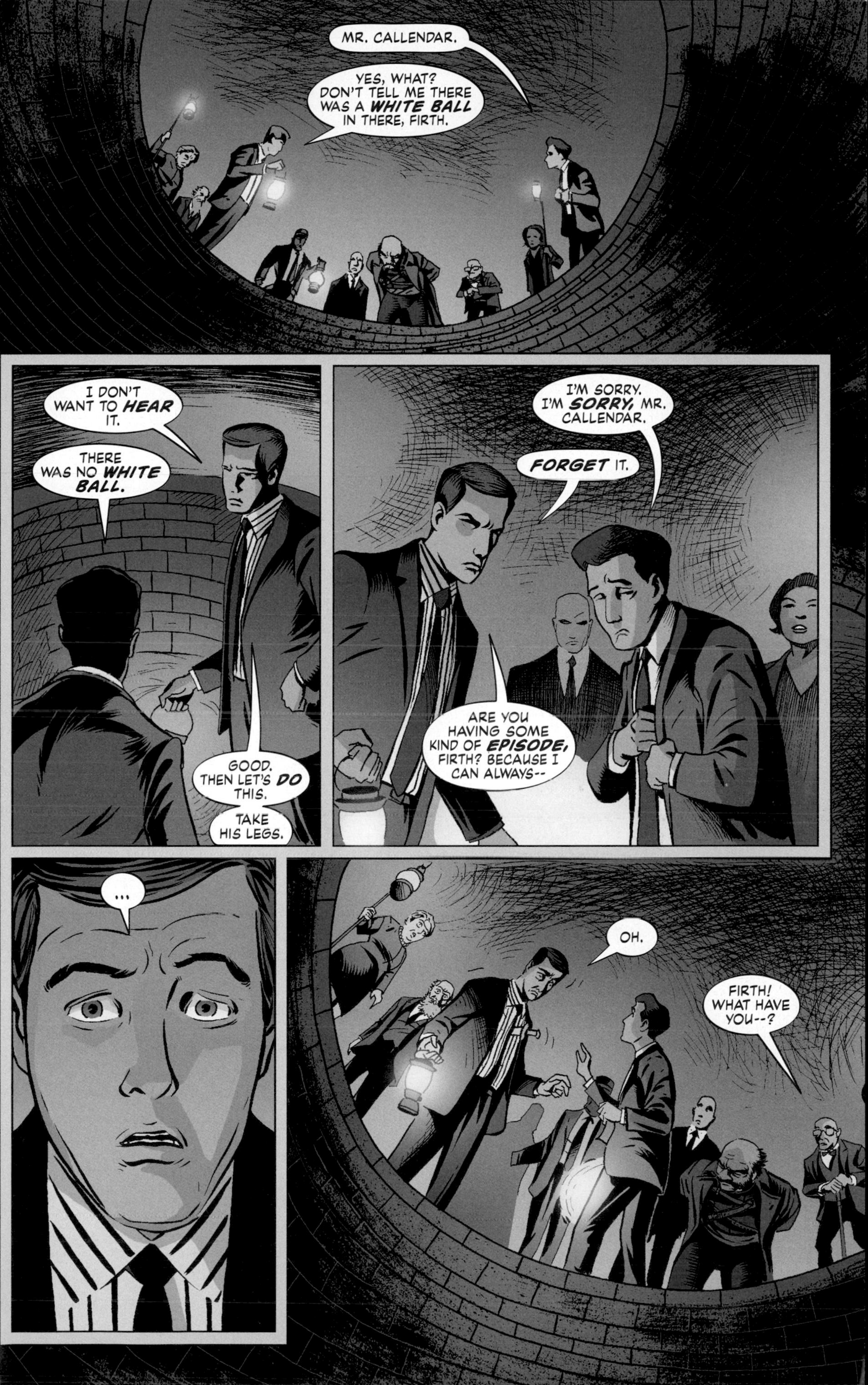
MR. CALLENDAR.
YES, WHAT? DON'T TELL ME THERE WAS A WHITE BALL IN THERE, FIRTH.
I DON'T WANT TO HEAR IT.
THERE WAS NO WHITE BALL.
GOOD. THEN LET'S DO THIS.
TAKE HIS LEGS.
I'M SORRY. I'M SORRY, MR. CALLENDAR.
FORGET IT.
ARE YOU HAVING SOME KIND OF EPISODE, FIRTH? BECAUSE I CAN ALWAYS--
...
OH.
FIRTH! WHAT HAVE YOU--?

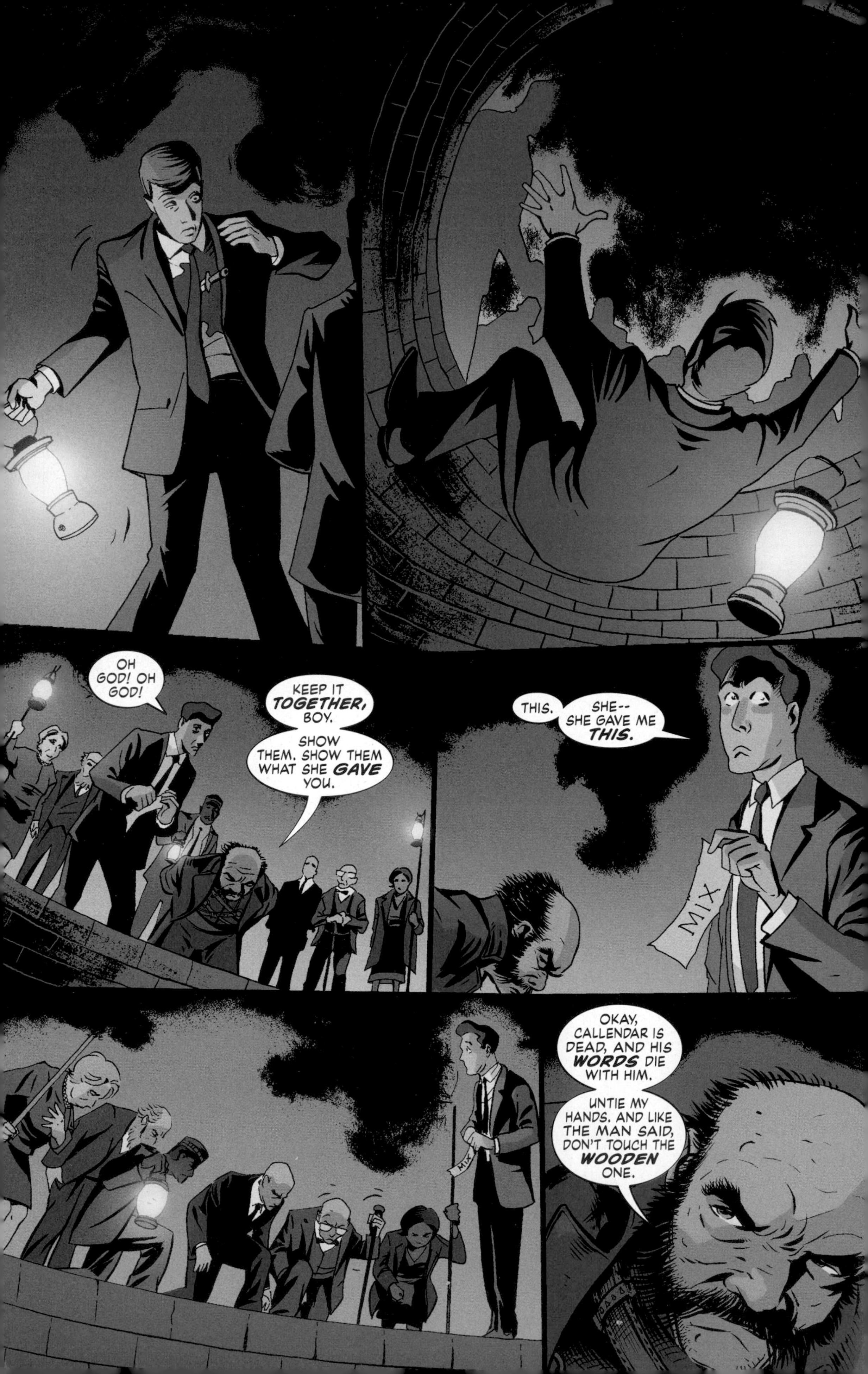
OH GOD! OH GOD!
KEEP IT TOGETHER, BOY.
SHOW THEM. SHOW THEM WHAT SHE GAVE YOU.
THIS.
SHE-- SHE GAVE ME THIS.
MIX
OKAY, CALLENDAR IS DEAD, AND HIS WORDS DIE WITH HIM.
UNTIE MY HANDS. AND LIKE THE MAN SAID, DON'T TOUCH THE WOODEN ONE.

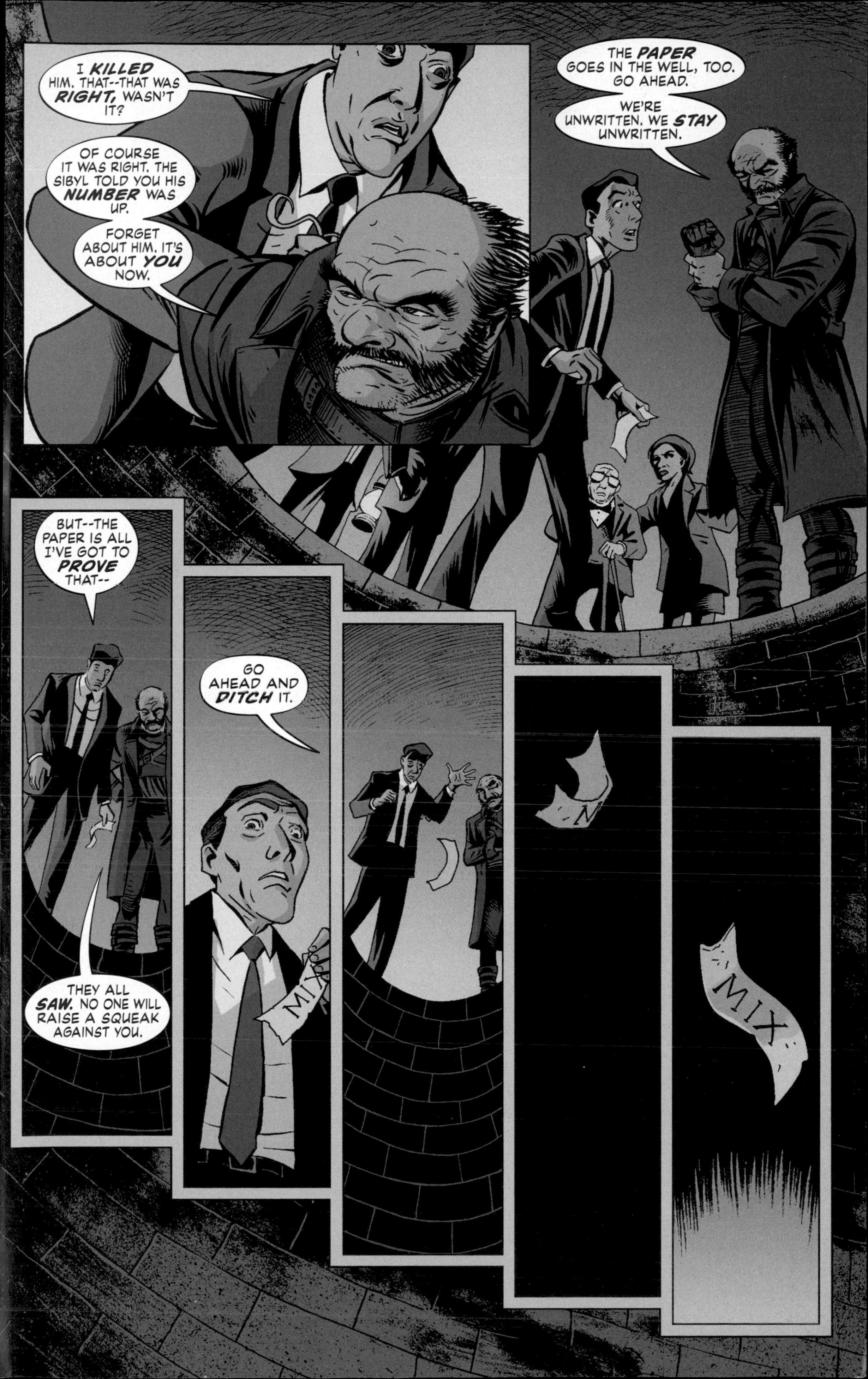
I KILLED HIM. THAT--THAT WAS RIGHT, WASN'T IT?
OF COURSE IT WAS RIGHT. THE SIBYL TOLD YOU HIS NUMBER WAS UP.
FORGET ABOUT HIM. IT'S ABOUT YOU NOW.
THE PAPER GOES IN THE WELL, TOO. GO AHEAD.
WE'RE UNWRITTEN. WE STAY UNWRITTEN.
BUT--THE PAPER IS ALL I'VE GOT TO PROVE THAT--
THEY ALL SAW. NO ONE WILL RAISE A SQUEAK AGAINST YOU.
GO AHEAD AND DITCH IT.
MIX
MIX

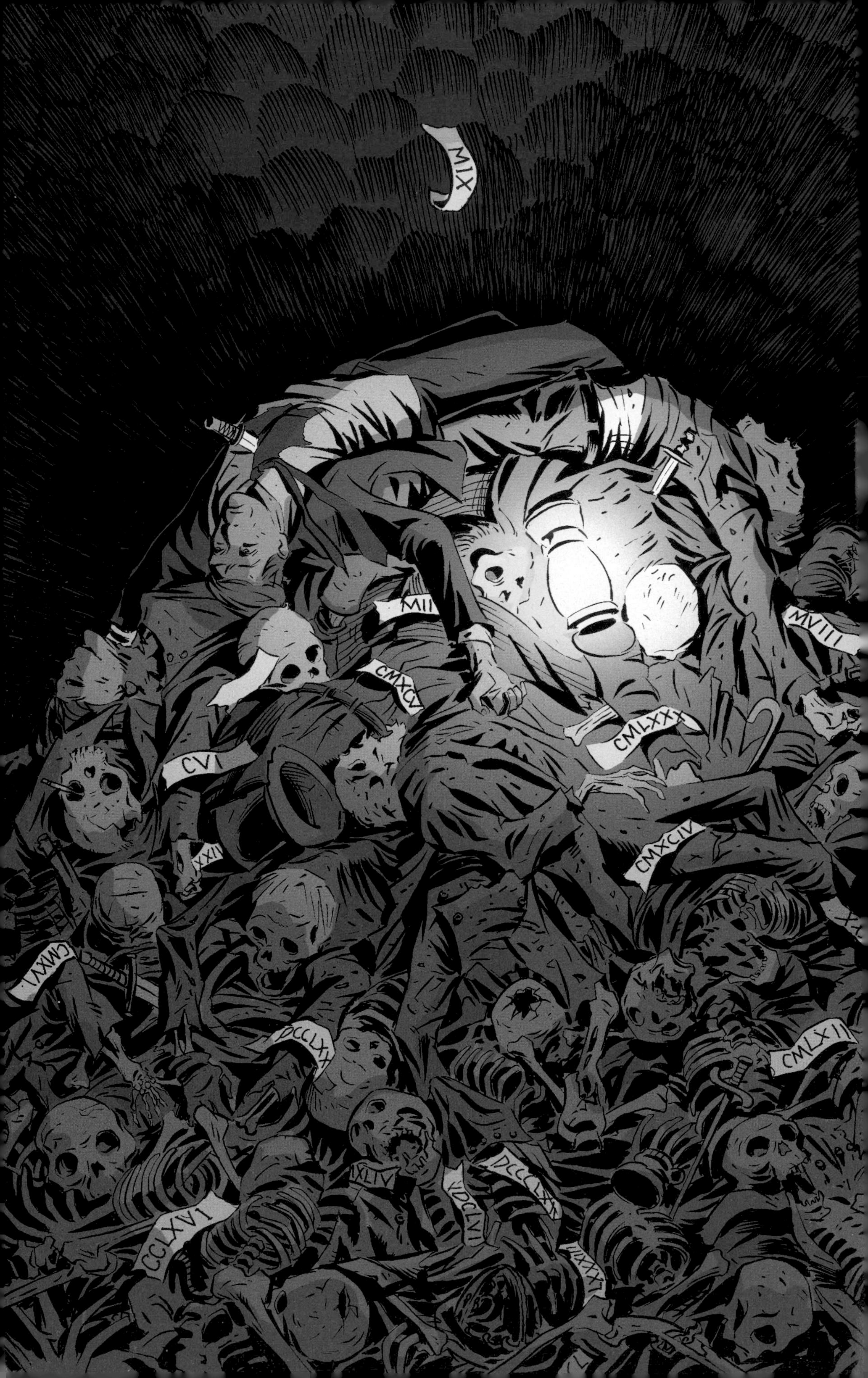
MIX
MVIII
CMXCV
CMLXXX
CVI
CMXCIV
CMLXII
CCLXVI

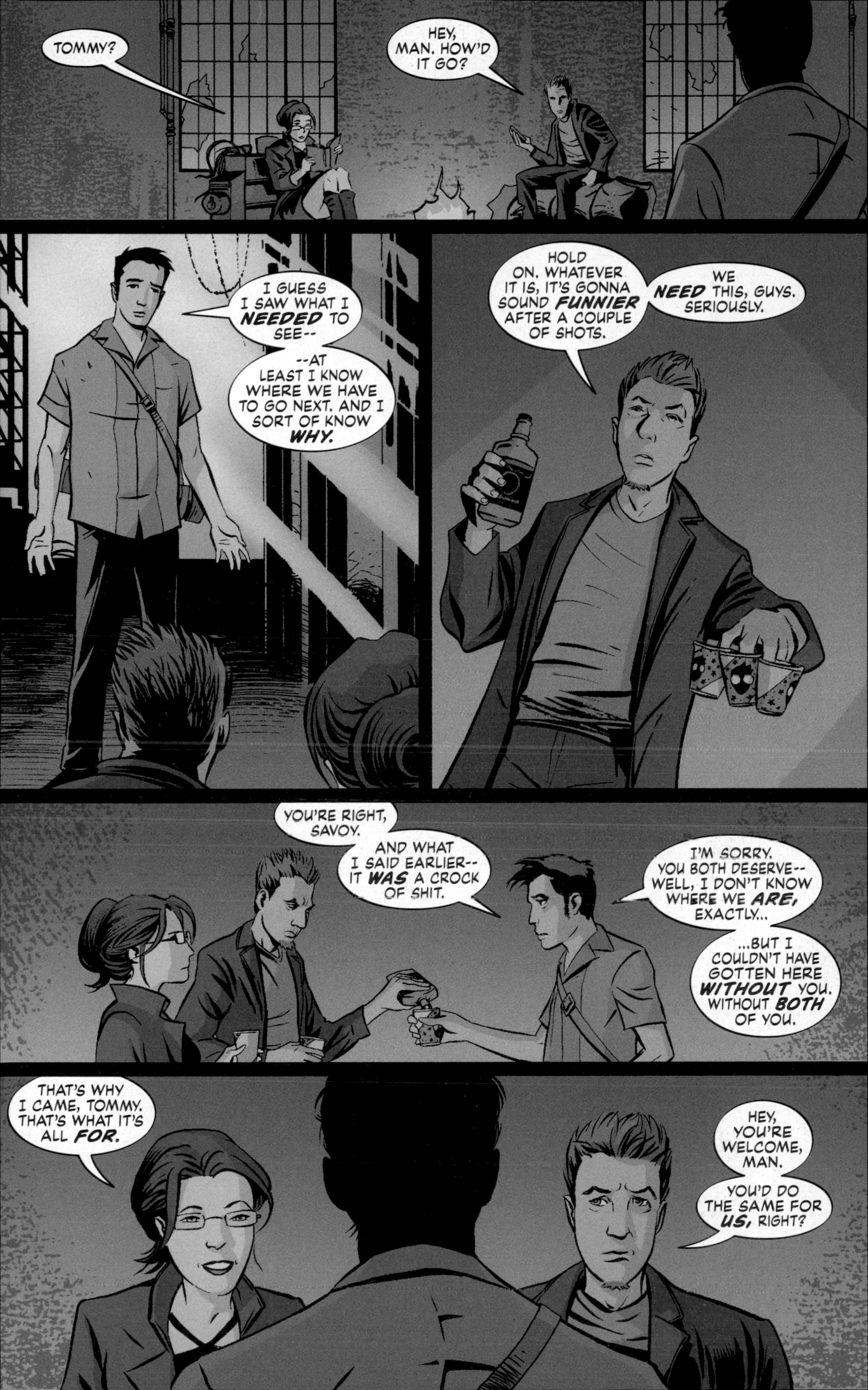
TOMMY?
HEY, MAN. HOW'D IT GO?
I GUESS I SAW WHAT I NEEDED TO SEE--
--AT LEAST I KNOW WHERE WE HAVE TO GO NEXT. AND I SORT OF KNOW WHY.
HOLD ON. WHATEVER IT IS, IT'S GONNA SOUND FUNNIER AFTER A COUPLE OF SHOTS.
WE NEED THIS, GUYS. SERIOUSLY.
YOU'RE RIGHT, SAVOY.
AND WHAT I SAID EARLIER-- IT WAS A CROCK OF SHIT.
I'M SORRY. YOU BOTH DESERVE-- WELL, I DON'T KNOW WHERE WE ARE, EXACTLY...
...BUT I COULDN'T HAVE GOTTEN HERE WITHOUT YOU. WITHOUT BOTH OF YOU.
THAT'S WHY I CAME, TOMMY. THAT'S WHAT IT'S ALL FOR.
HEY, YOU'RE WELCOME, MAN.
YOU'D DO THE SAME FOR US, RIGHT?

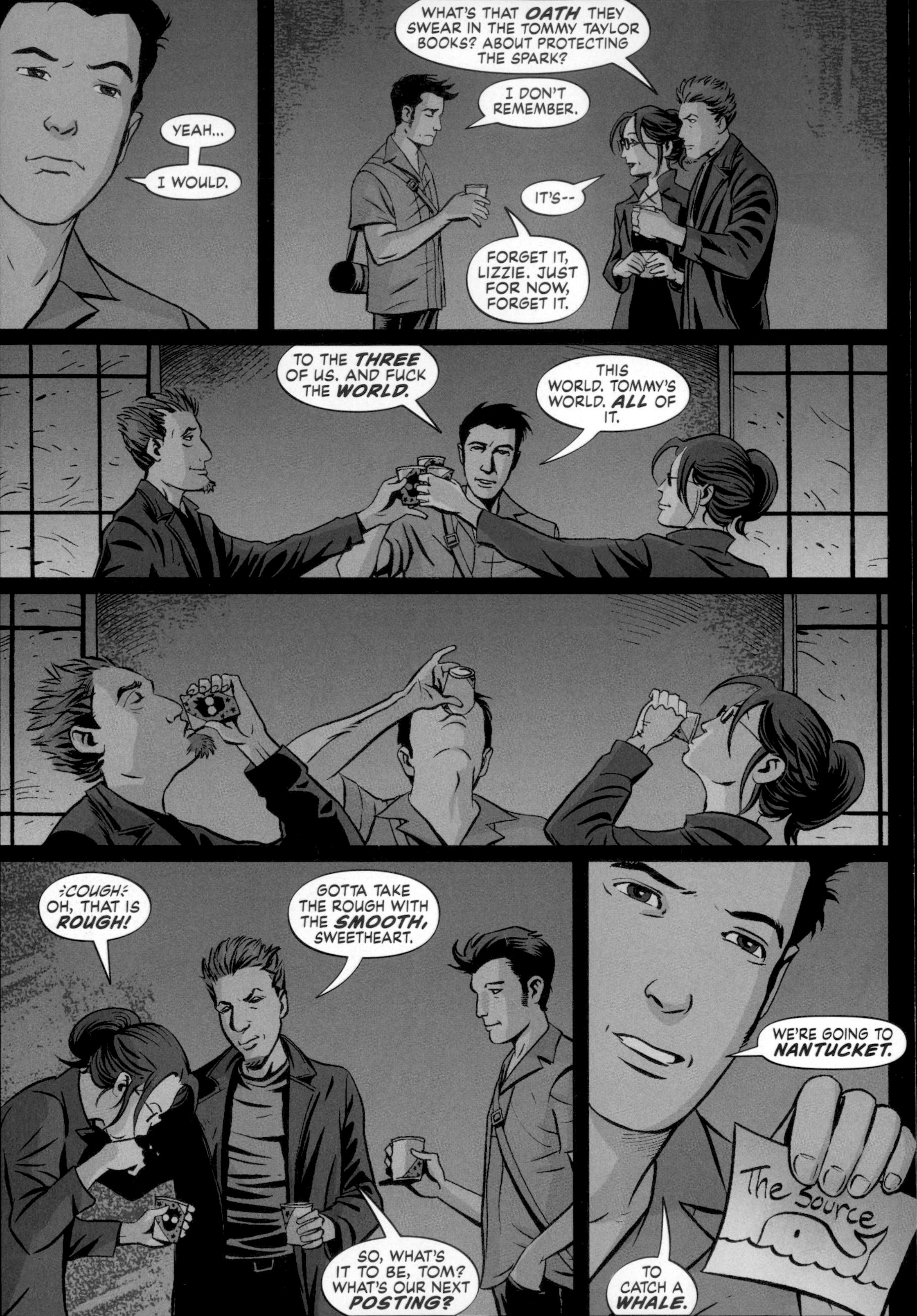
YEAH...
I WOULD.
WHAT'S THAT OATH THEY SWEAR IN THE TOMMY TAYLOR BOOKS? ABOUT PROTECTING THE SPARK?
I DON'T REMEMBER.
IT'S--
FORGET IT, LIZZIE. JUST FOR NOW, FORGET IT.
TO THE THREE OF US. AND FUCK THE WORLD.
THIS WORLD. TOMMY'S WORLD. ALL OF IT.
COUGH OH, THAT IS ROUGH!
GOTTA TAKE THE ROUGH WITH THE SMOOTH, SWEETHEART.
SO, WHAT'S IT TO BE, TOM? WHAT'S OUR NEXT POSTING?
WE'RE GOING TO NANTUCKET.
TO CATCH A WHALE.
The Source

VERTIGO
"FABLES is a must-read for any aficionado of fantasy in a contemporary setting."
— The Magazine of Fantasy and Science Fiction
"We hope this series lasts happily ever after."
— WIZARD
FABLES
LEGENDS IN EXILE
Willingham • Medina
Leialoha • Hamilton

WINNER OF TWO EISNER AWARDS
FABLES
STORYBOOK LOVE
Bill Willingham
Mark Buckingham
Steve Leialoha
VERTIGO

VERTIGO
WINNER OF FIVE EISNER AWARDS
FABLES
HOMELANDS
Bill Willingham
Mark Buckingham
David Hahn
Steve Leialoha

FABLES
1001 NIGHTS of SNOWFALL
AN ORIGINAL GRAPHIC NOVEL BY
BILL WILLINGHAM

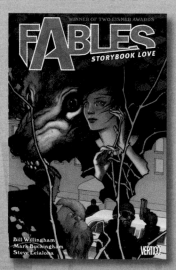